THE
COMPLETE
BOOK OF
Dreams

THE
COMPLETE
BOOK OF
Dreams

A practical guide to interpretation and dreaming creatively

Pamela Ball

ARCTURUS

ARCTURUS

This edition published in 2009 by Arcturus Publishing Limited
26/27 Bickels Yard, 151–153 Bermondsey Street,
London SE1 3HA

ISBN: 978-1-84837-377-8
AD001257EN

Printed in the UK

CONTENTS

INTRODUCTION

The least technical definition that can be found for creative dreaming is 'dreaming with awareness'. This encompasses a multitude of methods, a multitude of levels and a multitude of experiments. A creative dream, however, can also be called an altered state of consciousness. It may also be experienced only occasionally, or, conversely, on a regular basis. Indeed, whether such a phenomenon even exists, except on a subjective level, is debatable. For every person who believes implicitly in it, there is another who thinks such a belief is completely mad and the believer should be locked up! Scientists cannot agree, either, some saying that researching creative dreaming is a waste of time while others are prepared to devote most of their professional lives to the subject. Given this wide divergence of opinion, it is small wonder if the individual who initially takes an interest in creative dreaming becomes totally confused and decides that the subject is best left alone.

However, as with all things we do not understand, there is fascination and, because we find ourselves fascinating above anything else in life, we persevere. The starting point for an understanding of creative dreaming is acceptance that many layers of consciousness are available to us during sleep, layers of which we have previously chosen not to be aware. Once we have thrown off the straitjacket of previously held belief, we can begin to explore those levels for ourselves.

In this book we have attempted to combine the practical with the theoretical. If we look at creative dreaming in its historical perspective, we discover that people have used dreaming with awareness since time immemorial, to help themselves and their communities. Creative dreaming is not new, although it is only in the 20th century that a methodology has been developed for it by psychologists.

Creative dreaming offers many attractions and opportunities. It can help us to venture beyond the normal boundaries and restrictions which we tend to impose upon ourselves, and develop our ability to fulfil our fantasies. When we dream creatively we are, in principle, free to do, and be, whatever we want, restricted only by our ability to imagine and devise a scenario for ourselves. We are bound by no known laws, but can venture forth into our own universe where we can do and be anything and everything.

The experience of creative dreaming is different for each person, and only you will know whether your dream has been a creative one or not. This does not matter – even if you cannot definitely prove that your dream has been creative, if you have gained insight or released tension through it, then it has been of value. Despite the interest of scientists and the establishment of dream laboratories, many recorded experiences of creative dreaming have proved impossible to assess fully.

So why should you want to have creative dreams? What can you do with them? Apart from the pleasure of 'learning to fly', and the ability to ignore the physical boundaries that hamper us in everyday life, we can also reach areas of existence that are beyond us in waking reality. We can become a veritable Peter Pan (or even Tinkerbell!) during creative dreams. Many people have described their first creative dream as the most wonderful sensation of their lives. Others have discovered creative dreaming as a result of trying to control unpleasant dreams and at the same time have gained a measure of control over their ordinary, everyday lives.

It is also possible to develop creative responses to the symbols in your dreams and to learn how to express yourself in ways hitherto unimagined in your day-to-day life, through painting, words, sculpture or movement and dance. Creative dreaming may help you come to terms with the 'slings and arrows' of your workaday existence and to understand why certain circumstances have occurred. Finally, through creative dreaming, you may be able to enhance your ability to heal and be healed. All these things are possible once you have moved beyond the initial experimentation stage. Just as a child learns through play, so through creative dreaming you have the chance to learn the art of living fully, provided that you keep your feet firmly on the ground.

The aspect of living more fully is perhaps the most exciting of all. Not only can bad dreams be controlled through dreaming with awareness, but problems can also be solved in an intuitive and innovative way. Creative dreaming is also flexible in that it enables you to try out or reject different ways of working. It is possible to practise new ways of reacting or responding to others, such as overcoming shyness, becoming more extrovert in company, or changing the emotional tone within a certain situation. For instance, if a member of your family constantly makes you angry, you could ask your dreaming self for assistance in overcoming the problem so that you can control the anger.

As you begin to know yourself better, and gain mastery over your dreams, you will be able to practise new ideas and behaviour within the safe framework of the dream. You decide whether you have got it right. Since a creative dream will often fade when you start to question your actions, you can practise the art of waking up successfully and can give yourself the command to wake up in a good mood, or with enough motivation to complete a task.

When we are in the dreaming state, we have access to a great deal of information. Many dreamers become conscious of a kind of inner guidance through creative dreaming. Whether this guidance is accepted as the Higher Self, a guardian angel or a spiritual helper does not really matter. The consensus of opinion is that there is an integral part of us that seems to know better than our conscious self what is right for us. In putting ourselves in touch with this aspect, we are often able to crystallize the type of inner personality that will be most helpful to us as we move through life. The person who consistently uses meditation can manifest a being who becomes a helper, as Carl Jung did with his 'Wise Old Man', whom he named Philomen. Dreamers can also manifest an able inner mentor. When this mentor becomes available to us in both waking and sleeping hours, we are much more able to act with integrity and grace in everyday life. (Ways of calling upon this aspect are given in the Tips and Techniques chapter at the end of the book.)

The better able we are to control our dreams, the greater the access we will have to differing options of behaviour, which turn us away from extreme self-interest to care for others and the environment. In creative dreaming, we are able to make adjustments that would either not be possible in everyday life, or would take too long. We are able to experiment with changes which are ours alone. Because they do not take place in the waking world, these changes harm no one and yet allow us to perceive what life might be like were they to occur. It has been discovered that at certain stages in the development of control over creative dreaming some very bizarre distortions take place. This quality can be utilized to create an environment in a dream that pleases us and perhaps allows us to release our creativity. We are able to create – or uncreate – whatever we like.

The process of being creative within dreams can involve using their rich imagery to keep us emotionally balanced. We can put our creativity to good use by devising a project portfolio which helps us to remain grounded. How often has an aspect of a dream struck you as particularly weird or beautiful and worthy of note? Often objects in a dream scenario have a particular resonance and these can be preserved for contemplation later. In both the hypnagogic (semi-waking) state and in creative dreaming, flashes of colour and patterns have especial meaning. Too often, though, these are lost as everyday concerns take over. Maintaining focus is one of the biggest challenges for the creative dreamer. When we do become aware that we are using our dreams creatively, then the tendency is for us to wake and lose the clarity of dream perception. If you are able to preserve these colours or patterns, or can make a fair representation of them, you are truly putting yourself in touch with real creativity.

Each of us holds within basic archetypal patterns accessible through ordinary dreams. Creative dreams give us the added bonus of bringing them into conscious memory. If you keep a notebook with you at all times, you can make quick notes or drawings when something strikes you as particularly relevant to objects in your dreams. For example, you might find that in waking life your eye is caught by the formation of windows and arches because of a dream which featured these edifices.

You do not have to be a great artist, sculptor or writer to be creative. All you need are projects which please you. To give a personal example: through a dream in which there was a particular quality of light, a kind of glow, I was able to decorate my home in a way that created peace and tranquility. Conversely, I was not able to reproduce a certain shade of green of which I was conscious in another dream. In waking life, I have very little sense of colour or tone. The only way I can get such things right is to reproduce the feeling I have of them from the dream. While the inability to do this successfully can be frustrating, the sense of achievement when I do manage it is tremendous.

In our fast-moving world there is not always time to contemplate dreams in the way our ancestors may have done. There will be many who feel that, having assessed their dream for meaning and significance, they do not wish to explore it further. It is not suggested that all dreams should be subjected to every technique covered in this book – some dreams will lend themselves more naturally to one technique than to another. It is suggested that looking at dreams for inspiration and help in living is worthwhile.

One way of using dreams is to take them forward into some kind of resolution through your own creativity. You might try to capture what could happen next through the medium of words, poetry, music or art. Creative dreaming could even help to enhance your artistic ability in these areas. This actually sounds more difficult than it is in practice. You do not need to share with anyone the results of what you are doing, so once you have got over feeling rather stupid and totally frustrated because your pen/brush/body or whatever you are using will not do what you want it to, you can begin.

Initially the idea is to have fun with your dream and your aim is to be as creative as possible, so finding that you are expecting a character to act in a bizarre way does not really matter. Simply experiment and see what happens. There is a serious intent behind using your dreams in this way. You may find, for example, that an answer to a difficulty or problem pops up spontaneously. You may find your creative projects allowing you to get rid of negative thoughts or feelings. This can be helpful in effecting healing in some way.

Sometimes your dreams will seem to have no relevance at all to your everyday life, nor will their interpretation necessarily reveal great truths. However, using your dreams to initiate creative projects can start a process where blocked energies allow much more freedom of expression within your everyday life.

Another pleasing aspect of creative dreaming is the notion that in this state we are able to effect healing. Able creative dreamers are convinced that accelerated physical healing is possible. There is no reason to believe that healing of the emotions and of some spiritual ailments – such as the tendency to repeat mistakes without understanding why – could not also be helped through creative dreaming.

It is important here to sound a word of warning over the expectations you might have as regards creative dreaming and dreaming with awareness. A particular method may work for one person and not another. This does not mean the method is wrong *per se,* but wrong for the person for whom it did not work.

The art of creative dreaming puts me in mind of a scientific study conducted with monkeys. The scientists discovered that the habit of washing potatoes was transferred from one group to another without any apparent interaction between the groups. The basic behaviour was transmitted and learned in some non-specific way but without being understood. Creative dreaming is similar in that the skill seems to be transferable without necessarily understanding how it was learnt. Everyone has within them the ability to dream creatively, but how this ability develops is up to them. Those who have found their own way of working with their dreams do not have the right to say that their way is best. Equally, those who practise various methods with little success have no right to cast aspersions on the validity of the method simply because it has not worked for them. Keeping an open mind on all counts is a necessary development of your newfound skill and should be rigorously practised.

Open-mindedness is essential to reaching an understanding of the various altered states of consciousness, of how dreaming with awareness may be compared with out-of-the-body experiences and astral travel, and of the uses to which it may be put during states of transition – such as puberty, pregnancy and death – and in different types of healing.

The search for knowledge and deeper meaning through dreaming with awareness involves understanding the significance of various esoteric symbols, images and ideas. We look at the uses of archetypes, the tarot, myths, astrology and numbers to assist you in reaching your own personal truth. Understanding your personal creativity and enlightenment will bring you to a state beyond mere creative dreaming to an experience which is sometimes called 'witnessing'.

You will come across various practical exercises and techniques in creative dreaming and dreamwork throughout the book. In the Tips and Techniques section towards the end we have gathered them – and some others – together. These should enable you to apply what you have learnt and to recognize how these tools provide the means for you to be truly in charge of your own destiny.

It is but a short step from such an awareness to the belief that, through dreaming with awareness and using your creativity, you can build a world in which you can take a great deal of pride. Creative dreaming is a state between realities, those of the waking self and the dreaming self. When we are able to harness both realities, we are indeed within reach of a 'Brave New World' of our making.

SLEEPING AND DREAMING

In order to understand dreaming it is perhaps important to understand sleep. The cyclical nature of mankind means that periods of activity are interspersed with times of rest and relaxation. Sleep is a way of turning away from the external stimuli by which we are bombarded daily to an inner landscape which permits regeneration and rejuvenation. The human being needs sleep in order to function successfully, and sleep deprivation has a profound effect on efficiency and ability. Dreaming seems to be part of the process of regeneration. After periods of sleep deprivation, certain experiments show that the body seems to require additional dreaming time as though to make up for time lost. So one function of dreams seems to be to balance the psychological and physiological activity within us. It is also thought to be the mind's way of making sense of the various types of input with which it has had to cope. Mental and physical breakdown occurs very quickly without the alleviation of the dreaming process. Everyone dreams at some point during sleep without necessarily remembering the content of the dream.

ACTIVITY IN SLEEPING AND DREAMING

Sleep itself is passive, yet there is activity constantly occurring. Some kind of physical movement takes place at least once every fifteen minutes. This may be a discernible, almost deliberate movement of limbs and body which seems to take place at random. Initially, once we have found a comfortable position our physical body begins to relax. Learning a technique such as the one given on page 86 in the section entitled 'Relaxation, Meditation and Visualization' is of inestimable value, since it allows us to fall asleep more quickly and also permits deeper sleep. From a physical standpoint, when the muscles begin to relax from a state of extreme tension, there sometimes takes place an involuntary 'myoclonic jerk'. This is a physical muscular reaction when the muscles themselves involuntarily let go. As we drift into sleep this can be experienced as the feeling of falling – this can be quite frightening. It can waken us again, and the whole process of letting go must then begin all over again. Deep relaxation allows faster access to the hypnagogic state – that stage between waking and sleeping in which we can be at our most creative. Other involuntary reactions can occur during sleep such as a penile erection without apparent stimulus.

Dreams can be caused by certain physical stimuli from our sleep environment. Opinions vary as to whether, for instance, the sound of a doorbell or a dog barking will be translated into part of the content of our dreams. If we tie ourselves up in our sheets, will that cause us to feel trapped, or will the dream of being trapped cause us to tie ourselves up? Physical relaxation does enable us to get the best use out of sleep, and therefore to use dreaming as a tool for complete health. Opinions also vary as to whether eating certain foods and other physiological stimuli have an effect on dreaming.

Digestion does seem to have some part to play in dreaming, but probably more from the effect it has on our solar plexus. 'Solar plexus' actually means 'the gathering of the sun', and thus is an important centre for physical energy. In many people, any upset, whether physical or emotional, first registers in this area, so disturbing the equilibrium will have a profound effect on sleep patterns. (Some people will take refuge in the sleep state and therefore presumably in the activity of dreaming while others will find great difficulty in sleeping at all.)

During waking hours our emotional selves are continually aware of new stimuli and subtle changes which take place according to the situations in which we find ourselves. We can move remarkably quickly – particularly in today's fast changing environments – from circumstances where we have to remain calm and unflustered, to conditions where we can allow our emotions free rein. Conversely, we can find ourselves in stressful situations, with no way of discharging the excess of adrenalin which has been built up. All this has an effect on the subtle electrical impulses known as brain waves. As far back as the 1930s when the electroencephalograph (EEG) was invented, it was discovered that these tiny electromagnetic surges in the brain were measurable.

Over the years a much greater understanding has been gained of the links between sleeping and dreaming. Research into sleep rather than dreaming initially proved that the pattern of the brain waves changed as sleep occurred and certain common patterns were identified in brain activity during sleep. EEG patterns identify a kind of progression. In the waking state the wave activity is low, but the frequency is fast. As we relax the brain produces alpha waves, which in the first stage of sleep then sink into theta waves. In 1953 Aserinsky and Kleitman identified stages in sleep where rapid eye movement (REM) occurred. In 1957, Rapid Eye Movement was tied in with dreaming. It appeared that REM was some sort of scanning activity.

In the state of relaxation, electrical brain activity falls. Alpha brain waves range from eight or nine to eleven or twelve cycles per second, and are perceived as a feature of the state of deep meditation practised by trained practitioners of Yoga, Zen and Sufism, all exponents of the state of watchful awareness.

Beta wave activity happens when there is mental effort, concentration or watchfulness and the electrical activity of the brain is greatest. It is recorded at frequencies of thirteen cycles per second and above, up to about twenty-six per second. These frequencies can be evoked by anxiety and are also associated with poltergeists, thereby proving a link to human, rather than spiritual, energy.

Theta brain waves, slower than the waves associated with relaxation, are in the range of four to seven cycles per second. Oddly, they register during feelings of embarrassment and frustration, but are also linked with creativity and inspiration. Perhaps they are the interface between the physical and the spiritual realms.

Delta brain waves range from 0.5 to three cycles per second and are connected with deep sleep and a withdrawal from conscious activity. Irregular delta rhythms are very common in the months before and after birth, which is apparently associated with the release of the growth hormone. This ties in with the more esoteric belief that a baby 'dreams' himself into existence.

> Gamma brain waves have a frequency of twenty-seven cycles plus per second, and as yet are not fully investigated, nor generally accepted as being distinct from Beta.

Brain activity research continues. It has been discovered that a signal of 18,000 hertz fed into the brain induces mystical feelings, and may therefore eventually mean that dreams could be influenced by such external stimuli. Some researchers suggest that the brain is a filter whose purpose is to reduce the amount of data which would otherwise invade our consciousness and to eliminate what is superfluous. This filter is bypassed in certain states when information is 'paranormally' perceived.

REM sleep was at one time thought to be the only time during which dreams occurred, and it is these dreams which are normally categorized as being worthy of interpretation. They are usually active and realistic, though sometimes somewhat bizarre. We do dream during non-rapid eye movement (NREM) times, but the dream content is very different, less discernible, shadowy and more akin to thought forms. It seems that these latter are less easily reported.

The first period of dreaming REM sleep happens about an hour after we have first gone to sleep and into a state of deep relaxation. Unless we are woken immediately after this we are liable to lose or forget the dream. Oddly, however, we are less easily aroused at this point than at any other. We then travel back up the scale until it seems as though we are almost waking; REM and NREM sleep then alternate four or five times in the night. The longest period of REM sleep occurs just before waking in the morning and it is these dreams which are remembered most clearly and are available for interpretation.

Physiologically the brain seems to produce less of two substances called serotonin and noradrenaline during sleep. Both of these substances are involved in the transmission of nerve impulses and messages to the brain and may be involved in waking activity. We do not know whether sleep is affected by these two substances or vice-versa. Deep meditation seems to have the same effect on the body as sleep, though it does appear that psychologically we do need the escape of the sleep state.

There are several disorders that destroy the quality of the sleep and disturb the dreams we have. These are shown below.

SLEEP DISORDERS

Apnea

Apnea is Greek for 'want of breath' and the condition causes problems in both infants and adults. The symptoms include frequent bouts of difficulty in breathing – the sufferer ceasing to breathe for up to half a minute, and such periods are often accompanied by severe snoring akin to the sound of a road drill. Obstructive apnea is the most common, the muscles at the back of the throat relax to the point where they obstruct the upper airway. Central apnea occurs when the airway remains open, but the diaphragm and chest muscles stop working. This form is more dangerous because the sleeper must awaken several times during the night to resume breathing (snoring may not necessarily occur). Mixed apnea is a combination of the two, a brief period of central apnea, followed by a longer period of obstructive. This combination is common particularly in middle-aged men who are overweight.

The victim first becomes conscious that in many ways all is not right, perhaps not being fully aware of the severity of the problem. More often than not the first daytime indication of the problem may be a feeling of not having slept properly. Irritable and forgetful, also finding difficulty in concentrating, on waking, sufferers often have a fierce headache which lessens in an hour or so. Interest in sex may wane, not least because of the disturbance and distress experienced by the partner. All these symptoms can combine to cause depression.

Sufferers may suddenly fall asleep during the day and this may lead to the mistaken diagnosis of narcolepsy.

The causes are not fully understood but experts do agree that apnea is probably connected to a hormonal disorder, such as hypothyroidism (underactive thyroid gland) or occasionally acromegaly (excess bone growth due to oversecretion of growth hormone).

Marfan's syndrome, in which anatomical structures built of connective tissue are exceptionally weak, is an inherited disorder which may cause sleep apnea.

Solutions include taking a decongestant, avoiding sleeping on one's back, or surgery. The use of a special mask redirects air into blocked passages, giving some relief. Overweight sufferers whose condition is complicated by high blood pressure or heart problems will benefit from weight loss and improved diet.

Insomnia

Possibly the most well-known disorder, though the full name is rarely heard, is frank insomnia. Simply, it is a difficulty in sleeping, either getting off to sleep or staying asleep. Chronic insomnia is such difficulty extending for longer than a one month period. The causes can range from anxiety, depression, environmental factors such as a poor mattress or loud noises, general bad health, lack of adequate exercise and the use of drugs. Various complementary medicinal techniques such as acupressure, aromatherapy, herbalism, homeopathy and relaxation techniques (see page 86) are all helpful.

Narcolepsy

The principal characteristic of narcolepsy is completely overwhelming daytime sleepiness. The sufferer is likely to fall asleep or become drowsy at the most inappropriate times and in the most awkward places. Even an adequate night's sleep does not seem to prevent this.

There does not seem to be any known cause, although it is thought to arise from an abnormality in the central nervous system. Narcolepsy is as prevalent as Parkinson's disease or Multiple Sclerosis and it does seem as though there is a genetic link. It is often mistaken for attention deficit disorder, depression, epilepsy, laziness or the side effects of medication such as the use of steroids.

The four classic symptoms are:

1. Catalepsy (episodic loss of muscle function), which may be triggered by sudden emotional reactions such as laughter, anger or fear. There may be slight weakness or complete body collapse and the attacks may last from a few seconds to several minutes.

2. Daytime sleep attacks occur with or without warning repeatedly in a single day. Interestingly, night-time sleep may be considerably broken.

3. Hypnagogic hallucinations which are vivid, frightening experiences akin to the dream state while one is falling asleep or dozing.

4. Sleep paralysis – lasting a few seconds to minutes – is a temporary inability to talk or move when falling asleep.

The primary symptom is daytime sleepiness; the others often appear months or years later. Only about 20 per cent of sufferers experience all four. Indications first appear in teenagers and adults under the age of thirty.

The order and length of NREM and REM sleep periods is disturbed in narcolepsy, so it is a disorder where REM sleep and what happens during that time is abnormal (see page 15).

Restless Leg Syndrome

Restless Leg Syndrome seems to be a disorder of the circulation, which results in a number of unpleasant sensations when the sufferer sits or lies down for protracted periods. Principally occurring in the calf area, these sensations are noted as a creeping, crawling, tingling or pulling. Sometimes it can occur from the thigh to the ankle and one or both legs may be affected. There is an uncontrollable need to move the legs which often worsens during periods of relaxation. Symptoms can vary in severity over a period of time, often daily and sometimes with long pauses between attacks. These seem to be worse in the evening and at night, making it difficult for sufferers to relax and therefore sleep. There is another related sleep disorder called 'periodic limb movement in sleep', which appears to have some connection with the Myoclonic Jerk (see page 13).

By and large the cause is unknown but it does appear that the condition is more prevalent in some families; in other words, Restless Leg Syndrome seem to be inherited. Excessive consumption of caffeine seems to be connected, as do low levels of iron, and anaemia. Chronic diseases such as diabetes, kidney failure and rheumatoid arthritis may give rise to the condition. Women who experience it during pregnancy usually find that it disappears after having given birth. 'Growing pains' in young adults may also be connected with this condition.

Restless Leg Syndrome can be relieved by hot and cold baths, frequent bending of the knee, massage, stretching and walking.

Parasomnias

Parasomnias are disorders that intrude not only on the sleep of the victim but also on the quality of life of people round them. Some are:

Gastroesophageal Reflux

This is a type of heartburn which occurs during sleep, waking the victim and giving a sour taste, a burning discomfort or a pain in the chest. The condition can be helped by adjusting the height of the pillows.

Night Terrors

These begin in early childhood usually between the ages of three and five. Originally thought to only be a childhood disorder, such episodes continue into adulthood. They usually occur fifteen minutes to one hour after going to sleep and last for about a quarter of an hour; the person then goes back to sleep and is unable to remember anything in the morning. Why night terrors happen is not known, and perhaps the most startling thing about these attacks is that the patient is asleep throughout them. Such terrors mean that the subject wakes up gasping, crying and moaning, and often with a wide-eyed terror-filled stare. The heartbeat often rises to around 160 to 170, double the normal, and semi-conscious panic lasts for fifteen to twenty minutes after the event. The most effective way of dealing with the problem is through constant reassurance from loved ones and family members (who may well have experienced the same problem themselves).

REM Disorder

This occurs when the normal paralysis that happens during REM sleep is absent or incomplete. The victims recall vivid dreams which are often acted out. A condition more common in older men, it can result in injuries and violent behaviour.

Sleep Talking/Walking

Both of these afflictions tend to occur more often in younger people and both are associated with stress and illness. They, as with night terror, take place during the deeper stages of sleep and tend also to have a genetic link. Sleep talking is essentially harmless, though unfortunate for the partner, while walking when asleep has obvious dangers – people have been known to drive for many miles while still asleep.

Snoring

If we count snoring as a sleep disorder, it is more distressing for the relatives and associates of the sufferer. While snoring can occur in sleep apnea, the two conditions are not the same, and may need to be treated separately. There are various techniques which can be used to alleviate the condition. The well-known one of sewing a cork into the pyjama jacket works until the sleeper learns to sleep through the discomfort. An aromatherapy pillow (see page 30) also helps, as do therapeutic oils of eucalyptus, cajuput or sometimes pine, placed on the pillow. Sometimes an operation to eradicate nasal polyps may be called for, though this is obviously a last resort.

All of these conditions can be helped by good sleep hygiene – that is, learning how to sleep properly and well.

TIPS FOR BETTER SLEEP

Reduce stress as far as you can and relax. This means doing something which you find relaxing, which may mean an aromatherapy bath using essential oils, having a massage, going for a walk or whatever. Reducing stress can consist of, for instance, using a technique such as reviewing the day, deciding what has been done well, what could have been done better, and what was quite frankly not done well at all. There is no need to agonize over such things, but simply to note them and then let them go. This allows you to leave things behind, and means that the next day becomes easier to deal with, since it is not cluttered up with regrets and difficulties. Continued practice allows you to highlight those things which consistently give you difficulty, and therefore to learn new coping techniques.

Follow a regular routine so far as bed and waking times are concerned. A routine you keep to, without necessarily having to think about it, enables your body to slow down into a comfortable idling mode, and your mind gradually to relax before sleep. Following a set routine so far as waking up is concerned can also be helpful. For instance, do not allow yourself to be shocked out of sleep by a loud alarm, but use either soft music or a change in light levels to wake you gradually.

Avoid stimulating drinks such as caffeine, or alcohol. Alcohol may relax you initially, but tends to cause wakefulness later during the night, disturbing and decreasing REM sleep. Caffeine stimulates the system, making it more difficult to get to sleep initially, and again lowering the quality of the sleep itself.

Do not struggle to try to sleep. The frustration of lying in bed tossing and turning, for instance over health matters, can of itself prevent sleep and cause anxiety. Much better to try writing down your worries and perhaps prioritizing them. Then, having done something practical about them, you can put them to one side. Switching your brain into a different activity, such as reading a good book or watching a relatively mindless movie, can help to 'switch off' the brain.

When you do fall asleep, try to sleep only as much as you need. Your pattern will be totally different from anyone else's, and it is worth experimenting to find the best pattern for you. You may discover, for instance, that you are at your most creative early in the morning, and therefore prefer to preserve this time for yourself, without any interruptions.

Study your eating habits and use foods that are right for your system. Complex carbohydrates are often good, so the idea of a hot milky drink before retiring has some merit. A light meal containing some protein (such as milk, turkey and beans, containing l-tryptophan) not too late at night can be sleep-inducing: this is because that particular amino acid is converted into serotonin. Exercise in the late afternoon or early evening is also a good idea.

If none of the above reflects your circumstances, it might be that you are the victim of natural disturbers. These can range from the neighbour who uses the lift late at night, to the milk float with a bright light in the morning. Even pets which wake early in the morning can ruin sleep for their owners.

The use of any or all of these techniques can aid and improve sleep. One way to make up for lost sleep is take a short nap in the afternoon but limit the time to fifteen or twenty minutes. Anything more than that runs the risk of becoming deep sleep. Another way is to lie in one morning or go to bed early one night, but not both.

Herbs and Other Tools for Sleeping and Dreaming

*That the typical dreams induced by narcotics and
anodynes are due to the physical effects of the drugs
themselves is obvious to the modern dream analyst.
Impeded heart action, the effects of certain stimuli upon*

the various nerve centres and organs, the retina, the lungs,
the bladder etc., all these are translated by the dream
consciousness into terms of the individual temperament of
the dreamer. They may, however, be forced to give a
complete account of themselves as physical stimuli,
hence their physical value as dreams is of
little or no importance.

One of the difficulties any dream interpreter has is to sort out what can be accepted as 'real' dreaming, and which dreams are definitely caused by the use of drugs and herbs. In days of old, prophetic dreams, such as those experienced by the Delphic oracle, were most likely induced by the natural seepage of carbon monoxide and other noxious gases from fissures in the ground below the temples; the hierophantic class did not scorn the use of drugs and narcotics altogether. When the deadly fumes were lacking, other means were employed. Hypnotism, what later became known as mesmerism and other mysterious faculties were in the hands of the priestly orders, who guarded their secrets so successfully that they frequently lost them beyond recovery.

Incenses of various sorts are conducive to dreams and visions. The burning of sacrificial incense is one of the favourite themes of Egyptian frescoes, and Apollo's priestesses after eating the sacred Laurel inhaled its smoke before prophesying. Laurel is now known to be poisonous, as is ivy, used by the Bacchantes, but at this time people were not sure of the poisonous properties of various plants.

The poppy, from which the deadly narcotic opium is brewed, was known as the universal symbol of sleep and is the symbol of Demeter, Earth Mother and goddess of the harvest. Opium is probably the oldest of the narcotics, and De Quincey, who used powerful imagery, wrote some beautiful language to describe the use of opium. He says, 'Space swelled and was amplified to an extent of unutterable infinity'. He later admitted, however, that his 'dreams from being gorgeous phantasms of oriental imagery, gradually waxed heavy and oppressive, until at length they distorted to the menace of a nightmare'. It seemed at the time that the opium dreamer's images arose from oriental imagery and scenes. Whether this was because of the dreamer's subconscious association with the history of the drug, or whether, as may be more likely, they were accessing archetypal demonic images is open to question.

Morphine is, of course, a derivative of opium, and while it acts as a pain reliever also creates problems of hallucinations which become indistinguishable from dreams. Often as a terminally ill patient approaches death he or she can become very disturbed by the bizarre images which manifest themselves as two realities merge.

Ancient Dreaming Aids

There were many other herbs and plants and substances which were used to affect dreams in times gone by. We are certainly not recommending them for modern-day use.

Alcohol takes the dreamer beyond the first exhilarating stage of intoxication to cause dreams which are almost invariably unpleasant, often with a sensation of having being bitten or stung. This effect is due to the stimulation of nerve endings in the skin, because the skin is irritated by alcohol. After a while the dream is prolonged beyond the sleep state and manifests itself in a sort of over-the-top delirium. Flames and blood sometimes accompany the voices that occur in the alcoholic dream. It was alcohol which disassociated the subconscious from the conscious faculties, leading to the Bacchanalian and Dionysian excesses, which occurred in the religious rites of Greek and Roman times. The Mexicans also used a drink made from corn, called soma, which was heavily indulged in by the Incas, although it was forbidden to the common people.

Absinthe or wormwood was first brought to Europe from Algiers by French soldiers in the Middle Ages. It rouses weird unnatural dreams and hallucinations (wormwood is still used today in the treatment of round and pin worms).

Anise Seed was said by Pliny not only to impart a youthful look to the features, but to also have the power 'if attached to the pillow so as to be smelt by a person when asleep of preventing all disagreeable dreams'.

Pliny and other writers also make frequent allusion to briony or the poyemcy as a particular soporific (sleep aid), 'giving vivid dreams and causing somnambulism [sleep walking]. There are strange aspirations, and a longing for that which never existed even in the soul of the dreamer.'

Hemlock – an extreme poison – gave rise to hideous dreams overrun with superstitious horror and unease. It was a favourite remedy of the Middle Ages.

Gentle slumber was induced from the hop pillow, causing soothing dreams. Even today hops are used to induce sleep; see how to make a dream pillow on page 30.

Hypericum, or St John's Wort, was said to avert the evil eye, to reveal the presence of witches, and dipped in oil, to be a cure-all for every wound. Dew that falls on the plant on the 24th of June, St John's day, was carefully collected as a remedy for eye troubles. In *Materia Medica* Herring describes the dreams produced by St John's Wort as 'visions of spirits and spectres with the sensation of being lifted high in the air'. Increased intellectual power is furthermore attributed to the dreamer, and it is interesting to note that even today this plant is used to treat some of the symptoms of the menopause, such as forgetfulness.

Henbane (hyoscyamus), which has now proved to be toxic, causes double vision, presbyopia, and lights flashing before the eyes. Dreams under the use of henbane were often of people who lived at a distance, and it was almost as though one had summoned that person's spirit, for it seemed that the delusion of the presence of the absent one continued into the waking state. Visions of punishment and revenge meted out to others when there was jealousy and immoral behaviour made this drug dangerous.

Hyssop, Dittany and the male fern – the latter used today to deal with tapeworm infestation – were much used before the age of modern medicines. They did not necessarily bring about soothing, comforting dreams. Dittany and hyssop (used today as a mild sedative) were well known biblical remedies for inducing deep sleep. The nature of the dreams was specific to the dreamer's temperament, but they tended to include hideous images. It is possible that these herbs may well have been used by those who knew of their properties to manipulate the dreams of others.

Lobelia is still established in modern pharmacopoeia. It dates back to the days of the Crusades. Having an effect on the central nervous system, it brings restless sleep and many dreams. Overuse brought dreams of images of limbs that are amputated, or perhaps the sleeper would dream of a bullet passing through the head from one temple to another.

Pulque, or mescal was the chosen narcotic of the Mexicans. Distilled from the peyote cactus, it was said to rouse fiery dreams that devoured the innermost being of the dreamer.

Solanum, or belladonna (deadly nightshade), again now known to be highly toxic, held its remarkable, half-repulsive mystery through biblical lore and medieval magic to the stern, straight-laced Victorian era. The more recent name of solanum is derived from 'solamen' meaning solace or consolation, in that it induces sleep. Its visions were wild and fantastic.

Stramonium (Datura or thornapple) was, we are told, a favourite drug with the Druids, and historical descriptions of the dreams induced by this remedy corroborate the fact that the Druids were probably ostracized for tampering with the spirit realm and the alleged misuse of the black arts. Young wives of Portugal were said to have made use of stramonium seeds as a remedy for otherwise unruly husbands, thus lulling them into dreams of self-importance. Although the plant grows in abundance in the wild thickets and other neglected corners of North America, Native Americans know it as the 'white man's plant'. It was held in high regard by the doctors of the 17th century, who favoured its use more than laudanum.

Modern Sleeping and Dreaming Aids

In the present day there are many herbs which are of use in obtaining a good night's sleep and therefore making our dreams more accessible, rather than attempting to actually influence our dreams. These herbs are known as hypnotics or soporifics. Different herbs work for different people, so the order here is alphabetical, without any particular preference :

Hops provide a remedy for insomnia, having an effect on the central nervous system. Used as an infusion or tincture, the herb should not be used in cases of depression.

Jamaican Dogwood is a fish poison so should be treated with great care. Also used in cases of insomnia or broken sleep patterns, it is taken as a decoction or a tincture.

Mistletoe is a relaxing nervine which soothes and quietens the nervous system, and is used as an infusion or tincture. It is only the young leafy twigs which are used, and not the berries.

Passion flower acts without leaving any kind of a hangover effect, and makes it easy for those who suffer from insomnia on a regular basis to find restful sleep. It is best used internally as an infusion or tincture.

Skullcap has a sedative action *par excellence*. Working on the central nervous system it is particularly useful in cases of nervous exhaustion, and is taken as an infusion or tincture.

Valerian, included in many pharmacopoeias, as a sedative, is used to manage tension and sleeplessness caused by tension. It can be used as an infusion, tincture or in capsules.

Wild lettuce is invaluable where there is restlessness and excitability, and is both sedative and hypnotic – that is, relaxing and sleep-inducing. Usually taken as an infusion or tincture, it is particularly useful for children.

Nervines have a beneficial effect on the nervous system. Some which are relaxants include: Balm, Black Haw, Bugleweed, Camomile, Damiana, Lady's Slipper, Lavender, Oats, Pasque Flower, Peppermint and Vervain.

A Little Light Relief

There is a long tradition of using herbs both to aid sleep and to aid dreaming. Many spells and customs were devised to achieve certain ends, and below as a little light relief is a selection from various sources.

The following herbs are all by tradition those which may be used to enhance the dream state, often with the idea of revealing those things which at the moment remain hidden. This may be the face of your future lover or someone who has done you wrong.

The herbs given below are considered to have magical properties, although the author is not prepared to vouch for any of them! By tradition, each has been assigned a gender, an astrological body and an element.

Bracken

Gender:	Masculine
Planet:	Mercury
Element:	Air

Spell: Place under your pillow and it will solve any problem you have.

Buchu

Gender:	Feminine
Planet:	Moon
Element:	Water

Spell: Mix with Frankincense and burn just before you retire to produce prophetic dreams. It must be used sparingly and only in the bedroom.

Cinquefoil

Gender:	Masculine
Planet:	Jupiter
Element:	Fire

Spell: Find a sprig with seven leaflets and put under your pillow to dream of a future lover or mate.

Heliotrope

(Poison)

Gender:	Masculine
Planet:	Sun
Element:	Fire

Spell: Place under your pillow to induce prophetic dreams. If you have been robbed the face of the thief will be revealed in your dreams.

Jasmine

Gender:	Feminine
Planet:	Moon
Element:	Water

Spell: Burn in the bedroom for prophetic dreams.

Marigold

Gender:	Masculine
Planet:	Sun
Element:	Fire

Spell: Place under your pillow to make your dreams come true. It is also believed to reveal the face of someone who has robbed you.

Mimosa

Gender:	Feminine
Planet:	Moon
Element:	Water

Spell: Place under your pillow.

Mugwort

Gender:	Feminine
Planet:	Venus
Element:	Earth

Spell: Place under your pillow. It is burned with sandalwood or wormwood during scrying rituals. Drink an infusion before divination. Place it next to the bed to help with astral projection.

Onion

Gender:	Masculine
Planet:	Mars
Element:	Fire

Spell: Place under your pillow.

Rose

Gender:	Feminine
Planet:	Venus
Element:	Water

Spell: Drink rose tea before going to bed to induce prophetic dreams. It is said to be especially useful for women who want to see their future lover.

To make Swete Powder for Bagges
(A 17th-century recipe from *The Mystery and Lure of Perfume*)

This recipe is to make the bedroom a beautiful place. Take Damask rose leaves (petals), orris root, calaminth, benzoin gum and make into a powder and fill ye bagges.

A Pillow Full of Flowers
Place this under your pillow, and you will be lulled to sleep by the perfume of a country flower garden.

One cup of dried fragrant rose petals, one cup of other dried fragrant flower petals, one cup of dried lavender, one cup of dried lemon verbena, one cup of dried rosemary and six drops of essence of bergamot.

Mix the dried flowers and herbs. Add the essence of bergamot. Fill small muslin bags to put beneath your pillow.

St Agnes's Charm
This must only be used on 21st January – St Agnes's Day. You must prepare yourself by a 24-hour fast, drinking nothing but pure spring water, beginning at midnight on 20th to the same hour on the 21st. Go to bed and mind you sleep by yourself and do not tell what you are trying to do to anyone, or you will break the spell. Go to rest on your left side and repeat these lines.

St Agnes be a friend to me
in the gift I ask of thee
let this night my husband see.

You will then dream of your future spouse, if you see more than one in your dreams you will wed two or three times, if you sleep and dream not you will never marry.

The Myrtle Charm
A method of having your future husband revealed in a dream is by 'The Myrtle Charm' which is used on November 25th, St Catherine's Day.

Let a number of young women, not exceeding seven, assemble in a room where they will be safe from interlopers. As the clock strikes eleven at night, take from your bosom a spray of myrtle which you have worn all day, and fold it up in tissue paper. Light up a small chafing dish of charcoal and on it let each maiden throw nine hairs from her head and a pairing of her finger and toenails, then let each sprinkle a small quantity of myrrh and frankincense in the charcoal, and while the vapour rises fumigate your myrtle; the plant is sacred to Venus. Go to bed while the clock is striking twelve and you will dream of your future husband. Place the myrtle exactly under your head. Only virgins will find the charm effective. The myrtle hour must be passed in silence.

Mother Bridget's Wisdom

'The 1st of January – If a young maiden drink, on going to bed, a pint of cold spring water, in which is beat up an amulet, composed of the yolk of a pullet's egg, the legs of a spider, and the skin of an eel pounded, her future destiny will be revealed to her in a dream. This charm fails of its effect if tried any other day of the year.

'Valentine Day – Let a single woman go out of her own door very early in the morning, and if the first person she meets be a woman, she will not be married that year; if she meets a man she will be married within three months.

'Lady Day – The following charm may be tried this day with certain success; string thirty-one nuts on a string, composed of red worsted mixed with blue silk, and tie it round your neck on going to bed, repeating these lines:

> *Oh, I wish! Oh, I wish to see*
> *Who my true love is to be!*

Shortly after midnight, you will see your lover in a dream, and be informed at the same time of all the principal events of your future life.

'St. Swithin's Eve – Select three things you most wish to know; write them down with a new pen and red ink on a sheet of fine wove paper, from which you must previously cut off all the corners and burn them. Fold the paper into a true lover's knot and wrap round it three hairs from your head. Place the paper under your pillow for three successive nights and your curiosity to know the future will be satisfied.

'St. Mark's Eve. – Repair to the nearest churchyard as the clock strikes twelve, and take from a grave on the south side of the church three tufts of grass (the longer and ranker the better) and on going to bed place them under your pillow, repeating earnestly three several times:

> *The Eve of St. Mark by prediction is blest,*
> *Set therefore my hopes and my fears all to rest*
> *Let me know my fate, whether weal or woe*
> *Whether my rank's to be high or low*
> *Whether to live single, or be a bride*
> *And the destiny my star doth provide.*

Should you have no dream that night you will be single and miserable all your life. If you dream of thunder and lightning, your life will be one of great difficulty and sorrow.

'Candlemas Eve – On this night (which is the purification of the Virgin Mary), let three, five, seven or nine young maidens assemble together in a square chamber. Hang in each corner a bundle of sweet herbs, mixed with rue and rosemary. Then mix a cake of flour, olive-oil and white sugar; every maiden having an equal share in the making and the expense of it. Afterwards it must be cut into equal pieces, each one marking the piece as she cuts it with the initials of her name. It is then to be baked one hour before the fire, not a word being spoken the whole time, and the maidens sitting with their arms and knees across. Each piece of cake is then to be wrapped up in a sheet of paper, on which each maiden shall write the love part of Solomon's Song. If she put this under her pillow she will dream true. She will see her future husband and every one of her children, and will know besides whether her family will be poor or prosperous, a comfort to her or the contrary.

'Midsummer – Take three roses, smoke them with sulphur, and exactly at three in the day bury one of the roses under a yew-tree; the second in a newly-made grave and put the third under your pillow for three nights, and at the end of that period burn it in a fire of charcoal. Your dreams during that time will be prophetic of your future destiny, and what is still more curious and valuable, says Mother Bridget, the man whom you are to wed will enjoy no peace till he comes and visits you. Besides this you will perpetually haunt his dreams.

'St John's Eve – Make a new pincushion of the very best black velvet (no inferior quality will answer the purpose). And on one side stick your name at full length with the very smallest pins that can be bought (none others will do). On the other side make a cross with some very large pins and surround it with a circle. Put this into your stocking when you take it off at night, and hang it up at the foot of the bed. All your future life will pass before you in a dream.

'First New Moon of the Year – On the first new moon in the year take a pint of clear spring water, and infuse into it the white of an egg laid by a white hen, a glass of white wine, three almonds peeled white and a tablespoonful of white rose-water. Drink this on going to bed, not more nor less than three draughts of it; repeating the following verses several times in a clear distinct voice, but not so loud as to be overheard by anybody:

> *If I dream of water pure*
> *Before the coming morn,*
> *'Tis a sign I shall be poor*
> *And unto wealth not born,*
> *If I dream of tasting beer,*
> *Middling then will be my cheer-*
> *Chequer'd with the good and bad,*
> *Sometimes joyful, sometimes sad;*
> *But should I dream of drinking wine,*
> *Wealth and pleasure will be mine.*
> *The stronger the drink, the better the cheer-*
> *Dreams of my destiny, appear, appear!*

'Twenty-ninth of February – This day, as it only occurs once in four years, is peculiarly auspicious to those who desire to have a glance of futurity, especially to young maidens burning with anxiety to know the appearance and complexion of their future lords. The charm to be adopted is the following: Stick twenty-seven of the smallest pins that are made, three by three, into a tallow candle. Light it up at the wrong end, then place it in a candlestick made out of clay, which must be drawn from a virgin's grave. Place this on the chimney-place, in the left-hand corner, exactly as the clock strikes twelve, and go to bed immediately. When the candle is burnt out, take the pins and put them into your left shoe; and before nine nights have elapsed your fate will be revealed to you.'

Crystals

Crystals are an integral part of learning and understanding our inner self. The crystals mentioned below are all aids to sleeping and dreaming. Information on how to 'programme' (prepare) crystals to help with sleeping and dreaming is given in the Tips and Techniques section towards the end of the book.

Beta quartz is said to aid in decoding dreams.

Chinese writing rock is porphyric with patterns resembling Chinese script. It is a stone good for assisting you into the dream state and directing your dreams towards the intended subject.

Diaspor gives clarity of dream recall.

Green Sapphire encourages the remembering of dreams.

Jade is known as the dreamstone, and assists in dream solving and the release of emotions. Place under your pillow for successful dreaming.

Jasper (red) allows dream recall, as though you were watching a video and is good for the technique of carrying the dream forward.

Kyanite calms and clears and gives good recall and dream solving.

Lapis gives insights into one's own dreams. It makes possible a connection with the higher self.

Manganosite improves your dream state and helps your memory both during, and after, the dream.

Opal, the 'happy dream' stone, gives understanding of your potential.

Rhonite stimulates the vividness of dreams and allows you to 'hold on' to the dream while it is recorded.

Ruby protects against distressing dreams.

Star garnet helps you to remember your dreams, particularly those which clear the chaotic state.

Tunnellite stimulates beta waves (see page 15) and can promote creativity and the achievement of your dreams.

Having looked at various aspects of sleeping and dreaming, including some of what might be called 'the science bit', it is now time to turn our attention to the subject of dream interpretation itself.

DREAM INTERPRETATION

There are many different aspects to dream interpretation and this section covers the main areas of which you need to be aware. It looks at what dreams might be trying to tell us, the types of dreams we have and the different methods we can use to interpret our dreams. First we will look at what our dreams might be trying to tell us.

THE LANGUAGE OF DREAMS

The first thing to be looked at in dreamwork is the situation, or the environment in which we finds ourselves. This gives some indication of the overall feeling of the dream. For instance, to dream of being in a big building would indicate how we are relating to present circumstances. A dream of being lost in such a building might suggest that we are not fully aware of our own abilities, and if in addition it were an office building the solution might lie in the everyday work environment. We could then relate this to our present circumstances – this sets the scene for us to understand what our dreaming self is trying to make known.

After this the various images need deciphering and what is pertinent to us may be recognized as symbols of what is occurring at a very deep level of consciousness. Dreams often use symbolism so that the dreamer must work to uncover the meaning behind the dream rather than the dream itself. Just as a child learns that certain words represent certain objects, we begin to understand our own dream language.

The story played out in dreams often has no running sequence; the scenes jumping from one thing to another in apparently no particular order. If it is believed, however, that the mind gives emphasis subjectively to what must be brought to the dreamer's notice, then there is in fact some kind of order. The theme of the dream will be followed, rather than the sensible order. Once the theme of the dream is revealed, then the various aspects can be given definition and the symbols interpreted correctly for the individual.

It cannot be stressed too often that dream interpretation is a highly individualistic pastime. Through its uniqueness, for those with patience, it offers insight into the many-faceted personality. One insight can be into the types of dreams we have.

TYPES OF DREAMS

There are several types of dreams which are worth noting.

Recurring Dreams

Most people will remember having had recurring dreams of one sort or another. Often such dreams will recur in response to a particular set of circumstances in our waking life, when the scenario, the people or the actions will be the same or similar. In problems to do with my working life, for instance, a hospital theme is often apparent. This is partly because of my nursing background, partly because I am a healer, but probably most of all because the nursing experience was particularly stressful. Such a dream therefore suggests a stressful situation which needs to be resolved. Most recurring dreams are to do with some aspect of a dreamer's personality with which they have not yet come to terms. It is as though the record has got stuck, to be replayed until such times as the problem itself is understood.

Parts of dreams can also recur when there is a particularly difficult situation which has elements within it which we need to recognize. One such dream is that quoted on page 96 where the character known as the Nazi-type woman reappears quite frequently in dreams, although in different settings. In this case the dreamer is alerted to behaviour which is inappropriate and what action needs to be taken to avoid mistakes. The rest of the dream is in no way similar to any other dream, but the presence of this particular character adds a certain tone to the dream.

In popular belief, recurring dreams are those where the main elements are the same. More properly they may be considered as those dreams where the theme or themes are the same.

Anxiety dreams

Anxiety dreams are another type of dream needing consideration. Often remnants from childhood leave their traces within the psyche, and the dreamer must contend thereafter with the traces within dreams of the anxieties which perpetually rise to the surface. Anxiety dreams tend to be remembered more than most, purely and simply because the emotional content is more difficult to handle, and less well understood. Dreams often allow us to handle anxiety better than we do in the waking state, since the anxiety can be experienced in the dream, but also left within it. A friend dreamt of performing operatic songs without knowing the music – although he knew the words. This tied in with circumstances in his life at that particular time when he had no doubt about his abilities, but was unsure of what was expected of him. Anxiety dreams are often to do with some aspect of performance anyway, whether that is to do with our own ability to perform well or adequately, or whether we are presenting ourselves in a good light. They tend to stem from our need to 'fit in' to the world in which we live, and may well stem from our perception of ourselves at a very young age. If we do not feel that we have control of what is happening, then anxiety results.

Precognitive dreams

Precognitive dreams are another type of dream which causes people some concern. It is always difficult to prove that dreams are precognitive, since there are those who believe that strictly the dream should have been reported, preferably in writing, before the event. It is all too easy to claim knowledge after the occurrence, or to make the event fit the dream, so it is only recently that there has been a more scientific approach to such things. It is here that quantitative analysis can come into its own.

It is, however, possible that people will have single precognitive dreams, based on their knowledge of themselves and of people around them, which have not been classed as such. This is the type of dream where an action or behaviour is represented symbolically, but only the dreamer will understand the significance. A personal dream of this type is one where I myself dreamt of two friends who were to get married shortly. In the dream I saw them on an island which split down the middle, one part of which sank. This was borne out in later years, when the husband's business went bankrupt, and they parted. At the time there was little likelihood of this happening, and my interpretation was more to do with my own fears and doubts about our friendships. It was only with hindsight that this dream could be called precognitive. By keeping a journal, it is possible to build a record of the development of what might be called personal precognitive dreams, and to build a library of symbols which are recognizable. This may be a place, a feeling or a particular character within a dream.

Prophetic dreams

What might be called a sub-set of precognitive dreams are prophetic dreams, particularly those which forecast the fate of a baby. In ancient times the dream gift – that is, the ability to connect to the divine – was bestowed to the priesthood and to women. With their intuitive ability women appeared to be able to make that connection much more easily. The Druids of Gaul and Eire had ten prophetesses to every prophet.

It would appear that during pregnancy mothers seem to make a connection with the unborn baby and are able to receive information through dreams as to the future fate of the infant. It is recorded in the Mahabharata that in a dream Devali, the mother of Krishna, heard predictions of the priests and knew her baby would be divine.

Such dreams have occurred throughout history and it is perhaps a moot point whether the mother's dreams had an effect on the baby, ensuring the correct environment and education, or whether the baby was divine and informed the mother during pregnancy. Dagachi, the mother of Zoroaster, the founder of Zoroastrianism, the faith of Parsees of India and Persia) also dreamt her son would be divine.

The 'Gospel of Mary' is said to have been written by James, the son of Joseph, and shows that Mary, her mother Anne, and her cousin Elizabeth (mother of St John) were prophetesses and 'mystic dream women'. The dreams of Mary are said to have lacked the intensity of Oriental imagery, but nonetheless she was certain of the divinity of her son. This Gospel was accepted as genuine by the early Christians and indeed still is by Oriental churches, but by the early 14th century was believed to be apocryphal. The faith of the early Christians seems to have frequently manifested itself in mothers' dreams. Over the centuries all these mothers are recorded as having dreamt their sons would be great:

Rohes – Thomas à Becket.

Aethelwold of Winchester.

St Gudula.

St Euthymius.

Monica, mother of St Augustine.

Amina, mother of Mohammed.

Samson's mother dreamt her son would be the saviour of Israel.

Olympias, the mother of Alexander the Great, dreamt her son would be a great leader whose empire would rise and fall.

The mother of Nero dreamt he would be a monster.

Paganini's mother was asked by an angel in a dream what gift she wanted for her son and she said 'to be a great violinist'.

Even today it seems that during pregnancy women can receive information about their children on a subliminal level, and are not particularly surprised by what happens to them, or dream their future in a quite surprising way.

Nightmares

The negative side of dreaming can be encapsulated in nightmares. It seems that they arise from six main causes, many of which are based in childhood. Nightmares around loss and deprivation seem to be associated with the traumas and difficulties of the birth process. Those linked to a fear of being attacked may also centre around the same situation and anxiety about internal motivations, and are connected with a basic need for survival and the satisfaction of the need for food, warmth and shelter. The rage at being thwarted in the gratification of those needs that the child experiences may surface later as nightmares. Much research has been done lately on 'Post-Traumatic Stress Disorder' where it has been found that the distress experienced at the time of the original trauma can surface many years later. It seems that the brain has not been able to get rid of the shock enough for the sufferer to recover. It is this type of nightmare that may be suffered by those who were sexually abused as children. The motivation to survive can also surface in adults as fear of the future, change and growth – largely it is a fear of the unknown.

Many nightmares are centred around a sense of foreboding. It seems that the human being is capable of picking up information subliminally, which is then brought out in dreams. Many would say that these are pre-cognitive dreams. Serious illness with its fears and anxieties surrounding death can also cause nightmares; in this case help can be gained from therapy and counselling.

Sexual dreams

Sexual dreams often take place at times of life when formerly in primitive societies we would be taking part in various rites of passage. Modern-day people do not mark such times as puberty, birth and passage into old age with ceremony, and sexual dreams – that is, the integration of one part of the personality with another – often mark this process.

It is often helpful for the dreamer to be able to identify the type of dream he or she has had for further reference – this is where a journal is of use, particularly when dealing with a series of dreams. Many such series deal with the archetypes (basic pictures of ideals which each of us holds within); more details can be found beginning on page 132.

METHODS OF DREAM INTERPRETATION

Now that there are so many schools of thought about dream interpretation, it is worthwhile experimenting with more than one method to find out if the dream will yield all of its insights and intangible aspects. Here are a few methods to try:–

Anxiety, Fears and Doubts
It is worthwhile looking at your dreams in terms of the anxieties or negative feelings they cause you. We do tend to remember negative dreams more than positive ones, and if we can identify what is causing anxiety at a deep level in our lives then the dream can be interpreted much more clearly.

Association
This can be done with the whole dream, or with its component parts. Ask yourself what memories it makes you recall, and what comes first of all to mind. Some of the association will surprise you, some will be fairly obvious. The trick is to continue with the associations until there is nothing more left, or you become aware of a strong and certain knowledge that you have 'hit paydirt'. This is a process which can be done only by you as the dreamer, though the presence of someone else can facilitate the process. For example, you may have dreamed of filling a bucket with earth. The associations might be:
• Bucket and spade
• Sand
• Seaside

- Holiday
- Freedom
- Play
- Childhood
- Grandparents
- Ice cream
- Slippery
- Fall
- Pain
- Anger

It could be seen that the association could stop there or continue until the anger is thoroughly understood.

An extension of such free association is to write down all that you can think of in relation to one aspect of that process, but to do it in such a way that you can see the relevance of each link. You might try the process known as mind-mapping. Say, for instance, you choose one of the words in the above list. Let us choose 'Ice cream'.

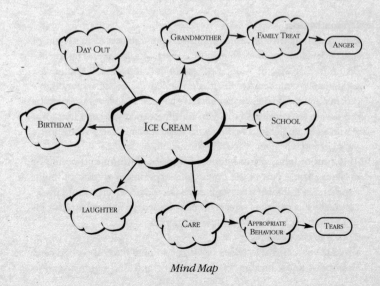

Mind Map

If you wished to take the process into even more detail you might take one of the further associations and perform the same exercise. Coming back to it days, or even weeks, later, you may have further insights into your own awareness.

Conversations

If we work on the theory that all parts of the dream are aspects of you, it is often worth while setting up a conversation between you and part of your dream. This you can do either in your head or by placing two chairs opposite one another and alternately being yourself, and the aspect of your dream.

Let us take the example of a bucket of earth. You might ask the bucket what it felt like to be filled up. As the bucket you might reply for instance 'Satisfying, thank you' or 'I wish they wouldn't throw this stuff at me'. It is what first comes up spontaneously without conscious monitoring that is important. You can also set up such a conversation between two parts of the dream, for instance, between the bucket and the earth. This method sounds very weird, but in fact can be most enlightening about our inner motivation, and indeed can often lead to further dreams of clarification.

Dramatization

Each dream that we have is a dramatic representation of some part of our understanding of the life we live, so acting it out and taking the dream further than its waking point can be interesting. If you have a group of like-minded friends it is possible to re-enact one another's dreams, and to find out what might have happened next. As an example, the dream scene might have you hurtling down the road in a lorry towards certain disaster. Act out what happened next; to you, the lorry, the road and whatever you did or did not hit.

A further extension of this technique is either to exaggerate or minimize some part of the dream and experiment with what might happen. For instance, what happens if the lorry is an articulated truck? Do you feel more or less safe? What happens if it is a little tiny toy model?

Traces of the day

Look at your dream in terms of what you may have absorbed on a subliminal level during the last 36 hours, and find out if a version appears in your dream. You probably need to ask yourself why the event has left an impression. Decide for yourself whether you need to explore your reaction further, and whether it gives you information of which you can make use.

Re-running the dream

It is possible to go over the dream in your mind as many times as you wish. Sometimes, it presents itself in the same way as you dreamt it, other times, there are additional images which surface either as a result of an insight which has occurred or as an explanation of something which you have not fully understood. You may also find that you have sensations, emotions and bodily feelings which you can explore.

Scene-setters

Certain parts of the dream may tell you a lot more than the various images, people and so on. Consider the environment of the dream (see The Dream Dictionary chapter), and what information it gives you.

Colours

Colours within a dream can give us many insights and therefore it is a vital part of symbolism. This is partly to do with the vibratory frequency which each individual colour has, and partly to do with tradition. Scientific experiments have now been carried out to ascertain what effect colour has, and have proved what occultists and healers have always known. In working with the colours of the rainbow, we discover that the warm lively colours – which give back light – are yellow, orange and red, whereas cold passive colours are blue, indigo and violet. Green is a synthesis of both warmth and cold. White light holds all colour in it.

By working with our own colour spectrum it is possible to maintain health. Some meanings given to colours are:

- **Black** This colour holds within it all colour in potential. It suggests materialization, pessimism and judgement.

- **Blue** It is the colour of the clear blue sky. This is the most effective healing colour. It suggests relaxation, sleep and tranquillity.

- **Brown** The colour of the earth, death and promise.

- **Green** This is the colour of equilibrium and compatibility. It is also the colour of nature and of plant life.

- **Grey** There is probably no true grey. It means dedication and service.

- **Magenta** This is in some ways a colour which links both the physical and the spiritual. It signifies surrender, altruism, perfection and meditative practice.

- **Orange** This is an essentially cheerful, uplifting colour. The qualities associated with it are satisfaction and autonomy.

- **Red** Vitality, strength, dynamism, life, sensuality and power are all connected with this colour. A beautiful clear mid-red is the correct one for these qualities, so if there is any other red in dreams the attributes may not be totally uncontaminated.

- **Turquoise** The colour is clear greeny-blue. This is thought, in some religions, to be the colour of the freed soul. It means rest and simplicity.

- **Violet** This colour, while found by some to be too strong, means grandeur, esteem, and hope. Its purpose is to uplift.

- **White** The colour containing within it all colours. It suggests innocence, spiritual purity and wisdom.

- **Yellow** This colour is the one which is closest to daylight. Connected with the emotional self, the attributes are reasoning, sometimes listlessness and judgement.

Colour confirms for us the existence of light. In spiritual terms, red is the colour of self-image and sexuality, orange is relationships – both with self and others. Yellow is the emotional self, green is self-awareness and blue is self-expression and wisdom. Indigo is the colour of creativity, while violet depicts cosmic responsibility. Emotions and feelings in dreams are worth studying since we may often express, in dreams, things that we feel might not be appropriate in everyday life, yet, we still experience them. Sometimes, also, it is worthwhile turning the dream around and expressing it with the opposite emotion to the one we actually experienced.

Position

The position of objects may be important. When a particular position is highlighted in a dream it usually signifies our moral standpoint, or our position in life. It can also give an indication of how we are handling situations in our lives. For instance, something in the wrong position means we are going about things in the wrong way.

Anything higher, or above us, represents spirit or an aspect of the higher self, the intellectual side and the ideals we hold. This applies also when dreaming of the upper part of anything (of a building or body, for example). Anything underneath, below, or downstairs signifies the anarchic or immoral side of our being; the sexual impulses can also be characterised in this way. Something appearing upside down emphasizes the potential for chaos and difficulty. Our personality has a need to balance the heights and depths of its experience, and if this does not happen a warning will usually appear in dream form.

Back/Front Rejection and acceptance can be shown in a dream as seeing the back and front of something.

Backward/Forward A backward and/or forward movement is usually indicating the possibility of adopting a retrograde, backward-looking disposition. There is a need or a tendency to retire into the past, rather than tackling fears and moving ahead.

Centre To be aware of the centre of any aspect of a dream is to be conscious of a particular objective, or perhaps our real Self. There is possibly a need to be the centre of attention whatever the circumstances.

Far/Near In dreams, space and time can become interchangeable. Dreaming of something which is far away may indicate that it is far away in time. This may be future or past, depending on other aspects of the dream. A long way in front would be future, a long way behind would be past. Near or close would mean recently, or in the here and now.

Horizontal This usually symbolizes the material everyday world.

Left The left side suggests the less controlling, more receptive side. Often it is taken to represent all that is dark, sinister and instinctive, and those parts of our personality which we do our best to curb. It is connected with what is experienced as good inside and with personal behaviour, without attention to any code of conduct. It is sympathetic in expression, and understanding by nature, so anything appearing on the left side in dreams can be accepted as evidence of support. Any pain experienced on the left side is interpreted in terms of sensitivity. Often, the left represents the past. It also expresses the more feminine attributes. Feelings of being left behind suggest a sense of inferiority, and of having to leave the past behind. Indecision over left or right suggests an inability to decide whether to rely on force or intuition.

Low In dreams, 'feeling low' can suggest a sense of inadequacy, reserve or depression. There may be submissive behaviour, which puts us in a lower position than others. Occasionally, to be below something or someone shows a need to explore the depths or negativity of a relationship or situation.

Opposite Anything in a dream which is opposite may suggest a dilemma in reconciling a paradox (good/bad, male/female, up/down, etc.). This may or may not suggest antagonism. One thing deliberately put opposite another suggests that there is a deliberate attempt to introduce discord. Changing the position from opposite suggests that differences may be reconciled.

Right/Left The conflict between right and left is usually between logic and intuition.

Right The right side signifies the more controlling logical and confident side, which perceives the exterior world in an impersonal fashion. It is to do with 'rightness' - propriety, morality and social behaviour. Anything on the right side is usually significant as the dreamer progresses. Pain experienced on the right side can be interpreted in terms of motivation. It also expresses the more masculine attributes. Movement to the right indicates that something is coming into conscious awareness.

Straight Straight suggests a more direct approach, the shortest way between two objects or places.

Top To be at the top is to have succeeded in our objective, usually after effort. To be on top is to have accepted leadership. Trying to reach the top suggests greater exertion is needed.

Up/Upper We have the proficiency to be able to achieve much. We are capable of getting the 'upper hand' (gaining supremacy) in whatever situation the dream refers to. We can move away from the mundane, ordinary, everyday world, and learn to win.

Under/Underneath Being underneath something signifies taking shelter or submitting to someone else's handling of a situation. It may also represent the part of us that we conceal, or the part that is less capable, and more vulnerable.

Vertical The vertical in dreams tends to represent the spiritual realm. The points of the compass appearing in dreams can give some indication of where we are spiritually: **The North** signifies the Unknown, and hence sometimes darkness. It is spirituality within the world. **The East** traditionally suggests birth and mystic religions. It also represents becoming 'conscious'. **The South** is representative of earthly passion and sensuality. **The West** can symbolize death, but more properly the state after death when there is increased spiritual awareness. Traditionally, it can also represent our more logical side.

Numbers
The geometry and the use of shape in dreams can be fascinating, arising from a subliminal awareness of numbers' significance. Many shapes can manifest, which we recognize on a dream level without consciously knowing what they mean. The significance of numbers is as follows:

Summary of qualities represented by primary numbers:

One *Independence, self-respect, resolve, singleness of purpose. Intolerance, conceit, narrow-mindedness, degradation, stubbornness.*

Two *Placidity, integrity, unselfishness, gregariousness, harmony. Indecision, indifference, lack of responsibility, bloody-mindedness.*

Three *Freedom, bravery, fun, enthusiasm, brilliance. Listlessness, over-confidence, impatience, lackadaisical behaviour.*

Four *Loyalty, stolidity, practicality, honesty. Clumsiness, dullness, conservatism, unadaptibility.*

Five *Adventurousness, vivaciousness, courage, health, susceptibility, sympathy. Rashness, irresponsibility, inconstancy, unreliability, thoughtlessness.*

Six *Idealism, selflessness, honesty, charitableness, faithfulness, responsibility, superiority, softness, unpracticality, submission.*

Seven *Wisdom, discernment, philosophy, fortitude, depth, contemplation. Morbidness, hypercriticism, lack of action, unsociability.*

Eight *Practicality, power, business ability, decision, control, constancy. Unimaginativeness, bluntness, self-sufficiency, domination.*

Nine *Intelligence, discretion, artistry, understanding, brilliance, lofty moral sense, genius. Dreaminess, lethargy, lack of concentration, aimlessness.*

The more esoteric interpretations are:

One *Oneself, the beginning; the first; unity.*

Two *Duality; indecision; balance; male v. female; two sides to an argument; opposites.*

Three *The triangle; freedom.*

Four *The square, strength, stability, practicality; the earth; reality; the four sides of human nature – sensation, feeling, thought, intuition; earth, air, fire and water.*

Five *The human body; human consciousness in the body; the five senses.*

Six *Harmony or balance.*

Seven *Cycles of life, magical, spiritual meaning; human wholeness.*

Eight *Death and resurrection, infinity.*

Nine *Pregnancy; the end of the cycle and the start of something new; spiritual awareness.*

Ten *A new beginning; the male and female together.*

Eleven *Eleventh hour; the master number.*

Twelve *Time; a full cycle or wholeness.*

Zero *The feminine; the Great Mother; the unconscious; the absolute or hidden completeness.*

Managing
Your Dreams

OUR DREAMING SELVES

It has been ascertained that dreaming plays a part in the development of the young human being. It is the most helpless of all animals at birth and needs physical parental protection for at least as long again as the period of nine months in the womb – conventionally, of course, much longer. Sleep is a natural way of ensuring that the baby is kept in one place and that growth, learning and the development process continues apace within a secure environment. Rapid Eye Movement (REM) – an indication of a specific type of activity within the brain – has been detected in babies in the womb, and certainly occurs in the sleep patterns of a young child.

The theory then developed that a baby dreams itself into existence. In slightly more technical terms, there is an internal source of excitation during REM sleep which enhances the growth of the child's nervous system. According to one eminent sleep researcher, this allows for the testing and practising of genetically inherited patterns of behaviour without there being any conscious movement. This theory is interesting in that it could account for certain tendencies towards various types of illness – both mental and physical, hitherto thought to be genetically inherited – in families. Examples are heart disease, breast cancer, alcoholism, depression and even what is now called 'the addictive personality'. It can also be seen that this testing and practising is very close to the conscious use of creative dreaming. It has still not been clarified whether we sleep in order to dream or whether dreaming developed as a function of sleep, but we do have some clues in the development of children's waking perceptions of dreams.

Any parent is well aware of the way in which a child can be terrified by his or her own dreams. This is principally because initially a child believes that a dream occurs outside himself – in other words, his dream is actually happening to him – and therefore he has no control over what goes on.

The second stage, the development of the ability to differentiate between an inner reality and one which is external, occurs fairly predictably as the child begins to grow. He realizes that he can exercise a degree of control over circumstances around him, and therefore dreams become partially an external event and partially internal. The child realizes that it is *his* dream and that it will go away if he wakes up.

A third stage of awareness can occur when a child recognizes that the dream is something inside himself and has no reality within the everyday world, while still being very real to him. He can then accept that it is his mind which is producing the images. There is an acceptance that it is 'only a dream'. The inner world is separate from the outer world. Many children develop the ability to recognize within the dream that they are dreaming; this, of course, is the precursor to creative dreaming.

During dreams, the majority of both children and adults tend to remain within the first stage of awareness (i.e. that the dream is an external event). In terms of childhood development, these various realizations take place at relatively predictable stages of growth. An adult dreamer will accept that the second stage is a transition process often recognized by hindsight. The realization that the dream world has a reality of its own, separate from the material world, is a conscious act and many will not wish to take their knowledge any further than that. The next stage of development occurs only when that recognition is incorporated into the dream scenario itself and then we begin the process of creative dreaming. We have to learn, or rather train ourselves, to lucid dream.

Creative Dream Development
We can assume that creative dreaming is an extension of the art of dreaming. Taking into account that children often develop the ability to creative dream spontaneously, we can see that, equally, the art can easily be forgotten. Therefore, if we are to ensure that everyone can make use of the rich source of information available to us, we first need to relearn how to achieve the altered state of consciousness known as creative dreaming. We then need to ensure that the knowledge and practice are passed on in such a way that they become part of our natural inheritance. Grotesque or strange dreams will no longer seem quite so strange and creative dreaming will become one of the ways of educating ourselves and ensuring the survival of the most able. Sleep then

becomes a natural tool rather than simply a means of regeneration – either physical or mental.

Dreaming sleep is seen as having a distinct advantage over other types of sleep in that there is some merit in there being a mechanism which allows us to have a kind of reprogramming function. This prevents our lives from being contaminated by incoming material. Indeed, the brain seems to work in a sort of compare-and-contrast mode. This means that before a piece of knowledge is assimilated, the waking brain runs through its database of material in order to find the closest match it can to the information presented. Only if there is an insufficiently good match does the brain accept the need for an update. It seems that women may be better equipped to assimilate new material, though this may be because they are more able to feel the information through their emotions. A real case of 'feeling it in their waters'!

Dream Function

Dreams also seem to have a part to play in reducing the excitability of the brain. REM sleep – and therefore, presumably, dreaming through the restoration of various neurochemicals – helps us to adjust on an internal level to the environments we have created. It has an effect on mood, memory and other cognitive functions. We have probably all at one time or another been aware of information overload – too much information to take in at one go.

As well as being connected with learning and memory, dreams seem also to play a part in the processing of other material dealt with by the nervous system. This includes handling traumatic experiences and necessary emotional adjustment to various stresses. It is probably for this reason that in Post-Traumatic Stress Disorder, handling the nightmares that ensue is a valid part of the healing process.

This ties in with the premise that in dreams we have the opportunity to experience – in manageable fashion – those dramas we play out that reflect our true psychological state and the changes that are occurring spontaneously. Dreams are therefore a kind of experimental forum where we can try out changes in our inner psyche before manifesting them in waking life. This clearly aids psychological change and transformation.

Accepting that dreams are a tool for psychological change means that while dreams that we remember are important and of use to us, those that we 'forget' will be equally valid. It would be better to call these dreams 'those we do not retain' rather than 'those we forget', since because dreams are a subjective experience – they happen inside us – we have no proof that we *have* forgotten them except that obtained through scientific exploration. Put simply, dream researchers have discovered that when there is REM activity, the subject is usually dreaming, so the assumption is that when there is REM activity a dream is occurring. (When awakened during this time, the subjects will more often than not remember their dreams.) Under normal sleep conditions, we do not know we have been dreaming unless we remember the dreams.

As we develop language we have a tool which enables us to vocalize our concerns, yet at some level there may be no need for us to remember or interpret the dreams we have. The question arises whether, without language, we would need to differentiate between the inner reality of the dream world and the physical external world. It could be argued that a dream will be remembered only when the sleeping self cannot properly process the material presented. This may be why we consistently forget our dreams on waking up.

'Unlearning' our Dreams

However, researchers have argued that there is a process which goes on during dreaming that might be called 'reverse learning' or the opposite of learning. They also stress that it is not the same as forgetting, but is a way of ensuring that the cortex of the brain functions to its maximum efficiency. It is postulated that certain forms of neuronal activity exist which may be monitored and suppressed by a particular activity which is operated only during REM sleep. This gives a scientific twist to Freud's theory of suppression.

According to this theory, any dream is designed to have the individual actively 'unlearning' (clearing the decks of) what is no longer needed. When we do remember our dreams we are retaining exactly what we were trying to unlearn. In theory, remembering several dreams a night would bring about negative responses and reactions and thus lead to the potential for illusions, fantasies and obsessional behaviour. In fact, neither remembering dreams nor deprivation of REM sleep seems to lead to such difficulties. Creative dreaming, where the pattern of REM sleep may be disturbed – and other altered states of consciousness such as meditation – may well lead to changes in perception, but seldom to breakdown.

To reiterate, dreaming may well be an activity developed by some process of natural selection to repair and to test the brain circuits. This occurs according to a particular pattern in order to regulate behaviour and recognition. It has also been proposed that the function of sleep which leads to dreaming is in order to get rid of certain interchanges between networks of cells in the cerebral cortex. In the next section, we will look more closely at the various theories and experiments on the actual activity which takes place within the brain and body during sleeping and dreaming.

WAYS OF CONTROLLING DREAMS

Whenever we look at creative dreaming, the first thing that strikes us is that there is a degree of control needed over both dreaming and the waking up process. Without this, it is unlikely that we shall have the ability to recall and remember what we have dreamt.

To be able to control dreams, we first have to define what 'control' actually means on an individual level. You may decide that you wish to stop having bad dreams – indeed, later in the book, we devote space to such control. You may wish to use dreams to make something happen in ordinary everyday life; again, this book gives you techniques to help this happen.

For the purposes of this section of the book, the definition of control is simply 'the potential to be able to influence, either voluntarily or involuntarily, what happens'. The suggestion is first of all that you can influence your dreams through dreaming lucidly and by asking for the dream that you want. The second suggestion is that you can have an influence on your everyday life through using your dreams. Your actions will have an effect on what occurs. You do at the same time need to differentiate between voluntary and involuntary control. Voluntary control means that you decide you want something in particular to happen and take steps to cause it – involuntary control refers to unintended consequences of your actions. An example of voluntary control in a dream is to confront a figure within a nightmare and to bring it into submission. Involuntary control is to wake up from the nightmare, not dealing with the issue in hand.

Choosing a topic

It is possible to begin to control dreams even before you enter into the dream state. The simplest way to learn control is to try to choose the topic of the dream. This is a type of dream incubation in which a person works to induce a dream to answer a question or resolve a conflict. It does not necessarily require great creativity. It is, however, a creative use of dreaming.

Often, attempts to choose a topic are initially woefully abortive and it seems that the subject of the dream has little relevance to the chosen topic. With practice, however, you will begin to see that it is what the unconscious has understood of the topic that has been processed. Supposing you have set the topic as 'the way forward'. In your dream, you become aware that you may have the image of playing a ball game with a dictionary instead of a ball. The dreaming self has interpreted forward as 'for word'.

When, after some practice, you are confident of your ability to dream creatively, you can either accept the image for what it is or, by choice, change it into something more appropriate. For instance, you may decide that the way forward is a game of words and that you need to use your knowledge of words to help you. Then again, by recognizing that you are dreaming and deciding that you are subconsciously using the wrong technique, a need to change becomes obvious. In a creative dream, you will tell yourself that you are dreaming and change the image of the dictionary into a ball.

Influencing the setting

Another aspect of dream control is to try to influence the setting of the dream. Normally such attempts have had little success – it is almost as though the dreaming self needs to choose its own scenario to put its message across. It is actually a complete mystery as to what determines the original setting and situation where we finds ourselves in a dream, unless it is the search for information and psychological balance. Some dream enthusiasts contend that dream control can only occur within the framework of the original dream setting – any actions within the dream are only appropriate within that original setting. That is, any inappropriate action we may attempt to force is blocked within that particular framework.

This line of thought does not allow for the inexplicable and sudden changes which may occur in the ordinary dream scenario. Often these spontaneous changes alert us to the fact that we are dreaming and open up the possibility of dream manipulation. We do have the ability to exercise what has been called concurrent control – the ability to decide on, or change, the course of a dream as it happens. We can choose to change a dream setting at will and exactly how to do this is dealt with more fully in the section on nightmares.

As we become more proficient at becoming – and staying – creative, it becomes easier to change small details and then more important aspects of the dream scenario. This type of control is not exercised only in creative dreams, however. Whenever we make a choice or act in a dream we are exercising an element of control. Trained creative dreamers are simply able to make coherent choices and actions in the knowledge that they are dreaming, and are therefore able to observe their effects on the dream scenario. The ability to control a dream setting comes from the manipulation of something which is formed from our own inner reality. When we are able to accept that that construct can be adjusted, we are able to manipulate the various parts of our dreams.

Being successful in creating a dream scenario does not necessarily mean that we have the ability to control the developing story of events in a dream. It is only with fairly comprehensive training that we are able to make adjustments to more than one component of a dream. It is the observer part of the dreamer – the self-awareness – which experiences and assesses the events happening in a dream. There is some evidence that highly motivated people can consciously choose to dream about their chosen subjects. Post-hypnotic suggestions have also been used to bring about particular dream goals.

In controlling dreams there are inevitably questions which arise:

- Do we have more control over our experiences in dreaming than in waking?

- Can we programme or control our dreams?

- Does controlling dreams affect our waking life?

The answer to the first question is 'No, not consciously.' It is only when we choose to work consciously with our dreams and to impose an element of control on them, that we can allow ourselves to make comparisons between our waking and sleeping selves. In the waking state we are often consciously imposing controls and inhibitions, which means that we make decisions in the light of what we 'know' to be real; in the dreaming state, the subconscious rationalizes its decisions only in the light of the unfolding events of the dream story.

To the question of programming, the answer is 'Yes, with practice and belief in the ability.' As shown above, it is possible to choose, in our waking state, the topic of the dream although not necessarily the course of dream events or the actual dream scenario. Because dreams are entirely created by the inner self, it should be possible to experience anything imaginable. However, it may be that we fail because we are not able to summon up enough creativity. We may not have enough emotional investment in the process to enable us to create suitable images or energy patterns. Some dream workers also argue that there are physiological limitations on the ability to control dream imagery.

We would suggest that in answer to the third question there is an interrelationship between the dream state and waking life. There is, in fact, a two-way traffic. Just as our waking life affects our dream time (day's residue), so also we can use the information and images that we receive from dreams in various creative ways. Imposing control on our dreams allows us to move with purpose in a particular direction on a voyage of discovery. We are able to 'explore' the huge creative database of what has been, what is, and what is to come – sometimes known as the Akashic Records. From a spiritual point of view, we are able to put ourselves in touch with the part we might call the Higher Self and make use of its ability to guide and monitor our behaviour. How well we can influence dreams will depend on our perception of our own abilities.

If perhaps we subscribe to the Buddhist belief that all life is illusion, then we will believe that we can manipulate each and every aspect of the dreaming process. We will believe that anything is possible and that without losing consciousness we can pass from one state of reality to the next without any difficulty and without harm. The ultimate aim is to achieve union with the Absolute, whether we do this through dreams or through death. It is through manipulation and passing through the various states of illusion that we finally reach a state of bliss. Dreams are just one stage of this unreality, and creative dreams are a realization of that state of illusion.

To control or not?

Masters of Tibetan dream yoga have perfected the art of passing in and out of sleep without losing consciousness. The Tibetan Buddhists, creators of the dream yoga, teach that it is possible to control every aspect of dream imagery. They use dream control as a method of understanding the illusory nature of all experience. They have as their goal the transcending of the relative state and the embracing of the Absolute. In the 'Doctrine of the Dream State' from *Tibetan Yoga and Secret Doctrines,* we find the following instructions:

> At the outset, in the process of realizing [the dream] to be *maya,* abandon all feeling of fear;
>
> And, if the dream be of fire, transform the fire into water, the antidote of fire.
>
> And if the dream be of minute objects, transform them into large objects;
>
> Or if the dream be of large objects, transform them into small objects:
>
> Thereby one comprehendeth the nature of dimensions.
>
> And if the dream be of a single thing, transform it into many things;
>
> Or if the dream be of many things, transform them into a single thing.

There are, of course, many dream workers and researchers who disagree with the principle that dreams should be controlled in any way whatsoever. However, because you as dreamer are not in a laboratory setting, you may want to experiment and to try out various ways of controlling aspects of your dreams. It is worth remembering that even now opinions vary as to why we dream, so it is more than probable that your own beliefs will play a significant part in how much control, or what sort of control, you will impose. If you believe that dreaming helps to balance your psychological makeup in some way, you will not wish to impose too much control on the dreaming process. If, however, you believe that the awareness reached in dreams can help you gain a measure of peace and tranquillity and eventually bliss, then you may choose to experiment with more control. Equally, if you believe that the dreaming self holds within itself answers which are not consciously available, then you will wish to access this material through dreams.

Dream experiments

Many people would find it extremely difficult to produce creative dreams under laboratory conditions. We are fortunate that people such as Alan Worsley have been able to give us the benefit of both their own personal research and that done in co-operation with others. Worsley found that ordinary dreams use a number of principles that can be utilized in the art of creative dreaming. It is more than possible to deliberately search for information on a chosen subject by 'selecting' the correct material, for instance from a particular book. The selection in ordinary dreaming is more random. Some actions are easier than others in creative dreams – reading is hard but is one of the best ways of testing whether a dream is creative or not. Reading single words or short phrases is relatively easy, but reading long sentences is more difficult.

Apparently, Worsley was never able suddenly to turn on a light in a dark room, although he was able to do so easily in a light room. This brings us to some interesting experimentation carried out by Dr Stephen LaBerge and associates into the ability to manipulate light and mirror images within a creative dream.

In this experiment, dreamers were asked, while dreaming of an indoor scenario, to find a light switch. They were then asked to try to turn it on and see what happened, then to turn it off and again see what went on. They were then additionally asked to turn the lights on and off by willing it to happen and then to observe the results. In the actual experiment these two tasks were varied, so that some people tried the act of will first and some second. One interesting finding was that people found it easier to 'use' a dimmer switch to alter the intensity of the light rather than a conventional on/off switch.

The instructions for this particular experiment asked the individuals to practise the task while they were awake before attempting it in the creative state, so that they would know exactly what they were doing. Then they were asked to attempt each action at least once in a creative dream, using the state of awareness as often as necessary. As soon as they woke up, they were to report what had happened.

A second part of this experiment entailed working with mirror images. The dreamers were asked to find a mirror in their dreams. Then the instruction was to observe their reflection in the mirror and, watching the image carefully, move their hand to their face. They were to note how the image behaved, finally trying to pass through the mirror into a different scenario on the other side. You may like to experiment with these tasks yourself in order to find out exactly how much control can be imposed, since it varies considerably from individual to individual.

The success of such experiments does depend on both practice and belief. This 'mirror' task is very similar to the experiments which can be done when first attempting to learn out-of-the-body techniques and astral travel by passing through barriers. Worsley found that flying close to the ground was easy, progressively getting harder the higher he rose. Ullman and Zimmerman in their own study also found that a complete change of scene would be difficult to achieve.

Creative dreams are also closely related to the act of meditation. Studies at the Maharishi International University (MIU) by Suzi Gackenbach and her colleagues discovered that trained meditators consistently reported more creative dreams than did control subjects. Traditional Tibetan Buddhist monks believe in accordance with their teaching that meditation – and therefore creative dreams – should be virtuous and not self-promoting in nature. Tibetan thought also says you should use a form of reality-testing by trying, when you are awake, to convince yourself that you are dreaming; that is, thinking to yourself, 'This is a dream'. As mentioned elsewhere, it is advisable to be careful how you differentiate between fantasy and reality. This method helps you enhance perceptual awareness and therefore increase the frequency of creative dreams. Physical form – size and shape – can become subject to the will when the mental powers have been properly developed by the use of yoga.

It would seem that such practices teach the practitioner of yoga to appreciate the part that his own mental powers play in the manipulation of matter. The practitioner learns by his own experience and experimentation that he can alter the character of his dreams through the use of his own will. In the dream state he learns to manipulate the images and proves they are constructs of the mind and therefore unstable. It is but a short step to the point where he realizes that form and perception are closely linked to one another in the 'real' world as much as in the world of dream and fantasy – he has discovered the power to create. Modern exponents of creative dreaming have developed a technique, based in part on ancient belief, to help them towards efficient creative, or lucid, dreaming.

The MILD Technique

The MILD (Mnemonic Induction of Lucid Dreams) technique was developed by Dr Stephen LaBerge and his colleagues during their investigations into creative dreaming. Most people who are interested in any type of dreamwork will have developed their own version of the technique, since the recall of dreams is a tremendous aid to personal growth. The steps as they were set up are as follows:

1. Set up dream recall
Learn to wake up from dreams and to recall them. Initially, you may need to use an alarm clock, soft music or diffused light. Eventually you will be able to wake up at will by giving yourself the instruction to do so. When you do wake from a dream, try to recall it as fully as possible and, if necessary, write it down.

2. Focus your intent
As you go back to sleep, concentrate intensely on the fact that you intend to remember to recognize that you are dreaming. Use an expression to fix this idea in your mind such as: 'Next time I'm dreaming, I intend to remember I'm dreaming.' Keep focused on this idea alone and don't allow yourself to be distracted by stray thoughts.

3. See yourself become creative
Perceive through your imagination that you are back in a dream you have had, whether it is the last one or another one that you clearly remember. Tell yourself you recognize it as a dream. Look for something odd or out of place that demonstrates plainly that it is a dream. Tell yourself 'I'm dreaming' and, knowing what it feels like to be dreaming, continue to remember your chosen dream.

Then imagine what your next creative dream will feel like. See yourself carrying out your chosen plan. For example, note when you would 'realize' you are dreaming. See yourself carrying out a dream action such as flying or spinning around.

4. Repeat until your intention is fixed

Repeat steps 2 and 3 until your intention is fixed; then drift off into sleep. Sometimes while falling asleep your mind may wander. If so, repeat the steps so that the last thing in your mind before falling asleep is the thought that you will remember to appreciate the next time you are dreaming.

This technique is a method or process designed to allow a dreamer to induce creative dreams at will at any stage during a night's sleep. Many people find that waking early and then dozing for another hour or so induces the best types of creative dreaming, while others find that deliberately taking a nap at other times of the day has the maximum effect. The condition of the brain and body at the time of day when naps are to be taken needs to be just right to bring about lucidity – relaxed and aware. It has been established that probably the best time for creative dreaming is during the final period of sleep. In a full night's sleep it seems that creative dreams tend to be grouped towards the end of the night – or rather the early morning – and become more likely with each REM period of the night.

Short naps versus long sleeps

Experiments and dream diaries show that creative dreams are not evenly distributed throughout the night. It seems that a period of wakefulness just before an attempt to become aware might help to focus the dreamer's attention on the matter in hand. Thus the *intention* to dream creatively also plays a part in the process.

In a study to discover whether short naps were better than full nights for creative dreaming, those who took part agreed to maintain the same number of total hours of sleep. They agreed to change their pattern of sleep to waking up for two hours before going back to sleep for two, or waking for four and going back to sleep again for two. This meant that the brain would have got back into its waking rhythm before being deliberately switched off again and presupposed that all the participants could easily fall asleep again.

During this study, which admittedly was very small and therefore inconclusive, there was some indication that the nap delayed by two hours was better for creative dreaming than one delayed for four hours. Lucid dreams seemed to happen more often in the nap periods than in the nights and the number of dreams per hour in the nap periods was also higher.

When we look objectively at such findings it is easy to see that creative dreams are more easily incubated in the nap periods, presumably because the hypnopompic and hypnagogic states – explained a little later in this section – are more easily accessible. The dreamer is in a relaxed state, having already slept, and is of a mind to pay more attention to his dreams and to deciding whether he is dreaming or not. It may be that dreams being more common in the later hours of sleep are more accessible and easily remembered after short naps in the morning. The results did show that such short periods of sleep were worth considering as a potentially very powerful creative dream-induction technique.

In a second study – which also unfortunately did not have many participants and therefore should probably not be considered statistically viable – the time at which people took the last one and a half hours' sleep of their night's sleep was experimented with. This was compared with what happened when people simply stayed in bed for an extra 90 minutes. The three variables considered were:

- To get up 90 minutes early, stay awake for an hour and a half, then doze for 90 minutes.

- To have the usual amount of sleep but wake up one and a half hours early and practise MILD for five minutes before completing the last 90 minute period of sleep.

- To sleep as normal, then wake up to do MILD for five minutes before sleeping an extra hour and a half.

When the data from prolonged sleep periods were studied it became obvious that simply staying in bed for an extra hour and a half did not cause creativity by itself. Deliberate techniques had to be used as well for any significant awareness to be present. An analysis of the number of creative dream incidents occurring in each dream recalled showed that the 'delayed nap' creative dream frequency was six times higher. It appears that this delay does contribute in quite a major way to success with creative dreaming. There does not seem to be a 'best' time to take a nap. It would depend a great deal on the dreamer's own routines and how they managed their own sleep patterns.

In a further study, participants were asked to note the times they woke up during the night and whether they had just awakened from an ordinary dream or a creative one. This was an attempt to find out what the relationship between creative dreaming and the cycles of the biological clock was, if any.

It is not clear whether the 64 subjects who took part expected to have creative dreams or not. If they were practising the MILD technique, one would assume that they were. In 79 per cent of the recorded awakenings, people had just had a dream; 7.6 per cent of those were creative dreams.

In this study, creative dreams occurred later in the night on average than non-creative dreams. When people awoke during the night without having recalled a dream, non-creative dreams then tended to happen later on during the sleep period. Most creative dreams in this study occurred after four hours of sleep, and about half after 6.5 hours of sleep. It would appear from this study that going to sleep with the express intention of being aware of what happens during the night is enough stimulus to promote awareness for a number of people. It would be interesting to discover whether creative dreams occur according to the rhythms of the principles of the regeneration of *chi* (essential energy). Chinese medicine dictates that organs and cellular structure are regenerated or rested according to quite stringent rules of rhythmic activity dependent on the time of day.

Yet another study attempted to find out whether creative dreaming could be stimulated by brief periods of intense focusing. Creative dream-induction techniques do require us to remember to attend to the task in hand. This particular study aimed to find out whether fifteen minutes of intense focusing had any validity. Again, quantifiable results were very thin on the ground. This meant that, once again, the results could not be said to be statistically significant. However, periods of focusing for fifteen minutes at night time (rather than in the morning) did seem to have more of an effect on an individual's chances of becoming lucid the following night.

Such experiments are very useful in the study of creative dreams, but it is worth remembering that it is such an individual pursuit that many people may not wish to become part of an experiment for fear of losing their hard won ability.

DREAM INCUBATION

When we learn how to ask for guidance and help through dreams to make decisions which may well be life-changing, we are truly becoming creative. This ties in with the belief that somewhere within there is a part of us which truly knows what is the best or ideal course of action. This part is called by some the Higher Self. Often we are not consciously aware of this part, but giving ourselves permission to access it through dreams can have a profound effect on the way we manage our lives. Obviously it can be extremely effectively used for problem solving, and for clarifying feelings with which we are having difficulty coming to terms. However, more importantly, dream hypothesizing can give us ways of dealing with negative tendencies we may have. It can also encourage positive ones and enhance our natural abilities and talents. There is the potential to obtain results in what often seems to be a magical way.

Asking for the Dreams You Want

This technique is of most use when there is a strong, passionate, deeply-felt association with the question or request. It works most effectively for those who have already learnt how to recall and record their dreams, because they have already established the lines of communication, but it also works well for those who have learnt to meditate, or for those who use other kinds of self-management tools such as creative visualisation or chanting. The technique is a very easy one, particularly if you have learned through work or other experience to remain focused on issues at hand. It is a little like being able to consult a management guru who has at his or her disposal a wealth of information.

Using that analogy means that the steps are very easy to remember. You can simply remember to use as a memory jogger a very simple word – that being '**CARDS**'.

- **C**larify the issue
- **A**sk the question
- **R**epeat it
- **D**ream and document it
- **S**tudy the dream

C means that you spend some time in *clarifying* exactly what the issue really is. By identifying the basic aspects of what seems to be blocking your progress or where you are stuck you can gain some insight into your own mental processes. You have thus dug over the ground. Try to state the issue as positively as you can: for example, 'Promotion eludes me' rather than 'I am not getting promotion'. This is because the subconscious tends to latch on to negative statements in preference to positive, so by stating the problem negatively you are already giving weight to pessimistic aspects of the situation. There is no need to try to resolve the situation at that point.

A suggests that you *ask* the question with as much relevance as you possibly can. Using an old journalistic technique, ask the questions 'who? what? where? when? why?' and then sort out in your own mind exactly what the relevant question is. For instance, in our example, you might ask:

Who can best help in my search for promotion?

What must I do to be in line for promotion?

Where do the best opportunities lie for me?

When will I be able to use my greater experience?

Why is my expertise not being recognized?

It should be recognized that all of these questions are open questions, and are not necessarily time-specific. If you ask a confused question you may well have a confusing answer, so try to get as close to the heart of the matter as you can. Conversely, by asking inappropriate or vague questions you may notch up answers you do not wish to have.

Repeat the question. By *repeating* the question over and over, you are fixing it in the subconscious. Blocks of three repetitions often work very well, so repeating three sets of three means that it should have reached every part of your being.

Dream command means informing your inner self that you will have a dream which will help. As you compose yourself for sleep and use your various relaxation techniques, tell yourself that you will have a dream which will give you an answer.

A word of warning for you though. The dreaming self can be quite capricious, so to begin with you may not receive an answer on the night you request it. You may only receive part of an answer, or perhaps nothing for several nights, and then a series of dreams in quick succession which tell you what you need to know. It is a highly individual process, and no one can tell you how it should be. With time you will recognize your own pattern, but be prepared to be patient with yourself.

Dream it. When you do *dream*, document it briefly as soon as you can in your dream journal, this time noting down only the main theme. There is an explanation of dream themes in the previous section. Information on how to keep a dream journal for all your dreams is given on page 93.

Study the dream in more detail when you have time enough to do so. Look carefully at the imagery within the dream, which will probably be fairly clear-cut and straightforward. Look for details, clues and hidden meanings, and see whether you can apply any of them to situations in your normal everyday life. Sometimes the answer to your question can come from applying your knowledge to a different sector of your life, before tackling the question you have asked.

As you become more proficient at dealing with the blockages you may find the nature of your questions changing. For instance, you may find yourself asking, 'How can I make so and so happen?' or 'What if I did?' This is true creativity and is a manifestation of the inner you appearing in your external life. It is an exciting process, which is much enhanced by using the awarenesses of the so-called 'hypno' states.

THE HYPNAGOGIC AND HYPNOPOMPIC STATES

The hypnagogic and hypnopompic states can be thought of as the entrances to the 'bridge' between waking and sleeping. At one time it was thought that hypnagogic activity was more common in women and subjects of lower social class – yet at the same time others thought that those who were able to achieve an imagery closer to proper dream symbolism were more creative and less conformist in their attitude. It does seem that the more an individual's creativity is recognized and developed, the more potential there is both for hypnagogic images and later for creative dreaming. While there may be distinct differences between the hypnagogic state and what some call lucid dreaming, many researchers feel that the boundaries between the two states are blurred.

The rich imagery which is available to us in dreams, both creative and otherwise, means that we must learn to make use of two states of awareness. These are of prime importance in the management and understanding of dreams. Many people feel that the states of alertness which occur just before (hypnagogic) and just after (hypnopompic) sleep are akin to – or may even be – creative dreaming.

To some extent this is true, in that they are both times in which the material available to the dreaming self is presented for review. In the state of passive observation, you are aware that you are dreaming, while in the hypnagogic state you are aware that you are not. Some dream interpreters feel that the hypnagogic state particularly is very similar to the creative dreaming one; it is certainly worthwhile comparing them.

In the hustle and bustle of everyday life, it is very easy to lose the images which manifest in dreams. The hypnopompic state occurs between going to sleep and waking up and is one in which we are often able to retain the images of the dream state, to remember the 'great' dreams or anything which we consider to be important. In this state, the images are not necessarily connected with one another but pop up at random, and very quickly disappear. Only if we train ourselves to remember and work with the images do we make use of this state. It is often in this condition that we hear our name being called – the voice is often accepted as that of a relative who has passed over, or by some as that of the Spirit Guide or the Higher Self. When people cannot accept that this is feasible, they will often disregard this highly creative time and lose a great deal of information. With practice, it can be a time when wishes and desires can be given substance and brought into reality.

The hypnagogic state is one which occurs between being awake and going to sleep. As the untrained dreamer settles into the sleep state, images occur apparently without any particular order. Such images might be of tranquil scenes or beautiful landscapes. Archetypal images representing such things as the four elements, shamanistic animals and spirit faces – familiar or otherwise – can also occur. This is akin to the random scanning which goes on when a graphic artist selects pictures to illustrate a particular theme. It is doubtful if a dreamer necessarily knows or recognizes any of the images.

As a dreamer begins to accept more responsibility for their dreams, perhaps incubating particularly creative ones, the images become more pertinent. The more a dreamer becomes 'open' to such images, the quicker the mind responds to the inner images which are 'the stuff of which dreams are made'. The images become more meaningful and detailed, tending to appear more rapidly when their validity is accepted by the dreamer. When the dreamer accepts the images as part of the subconscious, clarity becomes more attainable.

It is sometimes worthwhile to use straightforward dream symbolism to make sense of the figures and shapes which can appear in the hypnagogic state. During the semi-dream state and the fluctuation of awareness of the hypnagogic period, images may be transient but nevertheless offer food for thought and a way of getting rid of the remaining traces of everyday existence (known as the day's residue – you can find an exercise in analyzing such dreams in the Tips and Techniques chapter). This leaves the mind free to deal with the more meaningful images which can then be released through either creative or conventional dreaming. It seems that the mind is more receptive to 'programming' for more explicit dreaming in both the hypnagogic and hypnopompic states.

This idea of the mind needing to be programmed gives a great deal of validity to the techniques used in creative dreaming to confirm creativity, such as affirmations and reality-testing. During the dream itself, spinning and flying and expectations of success can be enhanced by work in the hypnagogic state, because the usual filters which operate within the conscious mind are no longer operative.

The faculties of clairvoyance, clairaudience and precognition can all begin to become apparent during the hypnagogic period. During this time images often become very well-defined, auditory fragments are heard and we 'know' something which was previously unknown. This awareness becomes the basis for true understanding in dreams and the dreamer learns to look for what have been called 'dream signs'.

EXTRA SENSORY PERCEPTION (ESP)

Most people think of ESP as being the sighting of ghosts, premonitions and other such psychic phenomena. More correctly, it should be defined as the above mentioned faculties of clairvoyance (clarity of perception), clairaudience (the hearing of auditory fragments), precognition (knowledge of a future event) and psycho-kinesis (movement of physical objects). Mediumship, channelling, and awareness of the spirit realm might also be included in ESP. All of these states of awareness are seen as apparently paranormal. Telepathy is sometimes included in the consideration of ESP, but is more a meeting of two minds and the sharing of impressions.

All of these happenings require conscious awareness, but their initial appearance usually occurs spontaneously - often in the 'hypno' states. How many times have we stated 'I knew that was going happen', or 'I've heard this before' without quite knowing where this knowledge has come from? Indeed we have known all this, because we have accessed the information on the bridge between waking and sleeping.

By their very nature, flashes of ESP are symbolic and indistinct. When they occur spontaneously in the 'hypno' states they are more readily accepted as valid, and capable of interpretation in the same way as dream images, from which they are sometimes not easily distinguished. By becoming more practised at working in that state, we become more able to use the psychic senses if we so wish. We are able to make use of a far more creative input than our 'normal' awareness.

PROLONGING DREAMS

One of the problems which occurs as we learn to have creative dreams is that we tend to wake up within a very short interval of realizing that we have become aware. This problem does disappear the more adept we become, but it takes time and patience to overcome the initial hurdle. Most people develop their own methods of holding on to the awareness of creativity, but there are also some tried and tested techniques which will work.

It was Harold von Moers-Messmer who, in 1938, first described a technique for stabilizing creative dreams. He proposed the technique of looking at the ground in order to stabilize the dream image and stay aware at the same time. Such methods of focusing on an aspect of a dream, in order to stop oneself from waking up, have also been tried by several other researchers.

As with mediumship and psychic channelling, our own body offers the easiest way of checking reality in dreams. When there is a change of consciousness, our perception of the body changes and as we leave that state and becomes more aware of the everyday world, the body can seem larger or smaller, heavier or lighter, more twisted or straighter than is usual. By looking at your hands or feet, becoming aware of them and recognizing whether they feel 'right', you can assess whether you are in the everyday world or not, and can return to normal.

This is the case in assessing whether you are awake or dreaming or indeed in a state of awareness. If the hands or feet seem anything other than normal, then you are probably dreaming. It seems to be the act of concentration which stabilizes the surroundings; the more you make use of such techniques the easier it becomes to remain aware or even to deepen the conscious awareness of other dimensions. Being conscious of your extremities, and whether they are the way they should be, allows you a measure of control over your own process.

However, one of the biggest problems in using vision to stabilize a creative dream, particularly for the novice, is that the visual sense tends to destabilize and disperse first when a dream comes to an end. Other senses can also diminish, touch usually being the last to go. Often the first sign that a creative dream is about to come to an end is the loss of colour and clarity. It therefore becomes necessary to find some way of prolonging the state of changed consciousness in order to experience further lucidity. One of the methods favoured by experienced creative dreamers is a technique called Dream Spinning. This technique was first put on record by Dr Stephen LaBerge after his own experiments in December 1978. In common with other methods of working with changes of consciousness, this procedure requires, for the Western mind, a certain degree of suspension of disbelief.

While the yogis and dervishes of Eastern religions had long been aware that sound and movement could influence the mind, they knew it was also an inner state of being. This concept is less acceptable to Westerners. Anyone with an interest in the inner personality does need to experiment with ways of controlling the mind with its varying states of consciousness. LaBerge correctly identified – as did others who were experimenting at the time – that it was the sensation of movement within the body rather than relaxation which allowed creativity to be maintained, thus preventing the dreamer from properly awakening. Initially it seemed as though less muscle tension – and therefore greater relaxation – might hold the key to not waking up.

In fact for LaBerge himself it seemed that this simply led to what he termed a 'false awakening'. Further experimentation suggested that both falling backward and spinning were effective in producing creative dreams of awakening and therefore deepening the dream state. Once he had perfected the technique, he discovered he could spin himself successfully into new dream scenarios most of the time. Lucid consciousness was present in the majority of these new scenarios. His results suggest that spinning could be utilized to produce transitions to match any expectations the dreamer might have. Some of the methods used both by LaBerge and others are outlined below.

Spinning

This method could be used when you have recognized that you are in the middle of a creative dream. As the dream begins to fade, but before you become properly awake, try spinning on the spot. You should do this as rapidly as possible and begin from an upright position. This should happen while you are still aware that the 'essential you' is still in the dream body. Sometimes it will work with your arms outstretched and sometimes with your arms folded or crossed on your chest. Do experiment until you find what is best for you. Try not to have too many expectations to begin with; these techniques do take time, patience and practice. One of two things should happen next:

1. You may wake up, in which case for your own records you should first of all note the time, then lie as still as possible and finally compose yourself for sleep again. It is possible that you may go back into the same dream.

2. You may find that you have spun yourself into another vivid dream scenario, in which case, remembering that you are dreaming, continue with that particular dream.

While spinning, keep repeating to yourself that the next scene will be a dream. (It is important that you experience a strong sense of movement in this.) Experienced dreamers may also wish to instruct themselves that the dream will be a meaningful one.

During the day, if you wish, you may actually practise spinning. Try to imagine that you are in a creative dream and that it is fading. Then actually spin around as you would in the dream. Allow yourself to reorientate within the physical world before going about your normal duties. With a little practice, you may be able to induce the feeling of spinning without actually spinning. Do treat this exercise with caution if you have, or think you have, a health condition which may make it difficult for you.

Going with the flow
A second way of prolonging creative dreams is to use the technique of 'going with the flow'. In this method, when you find yourself in the middle of a creative dream and it is beginning to fade, the idea is that you carry on with what you were doing in the dream, but ignore the fact that the dream is losing clarity. Some people find this process somewhat difficult. Initially, this method was devised as a control experiment rather than an actual technique. Again, if it works for you then it is worth using. As you continue with whatever activity you were doing, repeat constantly to yourself, 'The next scene will be a dream'.

As a variation on both the ideas of spinning and flying, going with the flow can consist of the sensation of riding a large wave, much as one would at sea. When you become aware of instability, switch to riding the wave; the dream will either stabilize or you will find yourself in a different scenario. The up and down motion seems to have the same effect as spinning, probably because it has an effect on the very delicate structure of the inner ear which monitors balance within the body.

On a personal level, I find this method preferable. I discovered this some years ago without the benefit of other people's experience when experimenting with creative dreams. In actual fact, in waking life I detest such a movement, which is usually found on fairground rides.

Once again, it is perfectly permissible to practise during the day for these dream activities. In the first case, imagine you are in a particularly interesting dream and that it is beginning to lose colour or becoming unstable. Then continue to do what you were already doing while remaining aware that you would be dreaming. In the second case, experience the feeling of riding the wave for a few moments, not forgetting to reorientate yourself in the everyday world when you have done so.

Rubbing your hands together

A third method of prolonging creative dreams is to rub your (dream) hands together. For some people, this may take a little more practice, but in some ways it is an extension of the method given above of concentrating on your extremities. When you are aware that you are dreaming and that dream begins to fade, try rubbing your hands together very hard. You do need to experience the movement and friction, because your physical body then reacts as though it was really happening. Continue to rub your hands either until you wake up or move into a different dream scenario. Keep repeating to yourself a phrase which reminds you to remain in the dream, such as 'I am continuing to dream'.

Again, take the time to practise during the waking day. Perceive yourself as being in a creative dream that is fading. Rub your hands briskly together, as you will in the dream, so that you can replicate that feeling within your dream.

Flying

Flying is not strictly a way of prolonging dreams, but it has so much in common with spinning that it is worthwhile including it among techniques to be used. It is fun to do, and once you learn how to do it, is worth doing for the sheer joy and escapism that the sense of movement and freedom gives. You can fly in just about any way you please, inhibited only by your imagination. Some people may fly with arms extended in front of them, to be aerodynamically correct. Others may find themselves with arms held by their sides. Yet others may find themselves using a kind of swimming movement, or using a paddling movement of their hands. There will also be others who quite logically grow wings in their dreams.

Trying to fly is often a good way to do a reality check. If you are flying without assistance, then you can assume that you are dreaming. The technique for dream-flying is very easy. First, push off against some kind of resistance and see if you are capable of floating in the air. Next, concentrate and see if you can move through the air towards a dream object. Lastly, see if you can pass through a barrier in your dream without rationality superimposing itself. Remind yourself that you are dreaming, but stay focused on the act of flying. You might continue the experience by repeating an affirmation which reinforces the feeling. You might, for instance, say 'If I am flying I am dreaming'. Initially, you may find that you are waking up but gradually you will find that you can hold the state of flying.

Sensory manipulation

We have already mentioned that the visual sense is often the first to fade, followed closely by the other senses. One way of prolonging your dream is to use the senses to help you to stay with the dream. Some people have used the hearing sense, by listening to voices, music, or their own breathing. Others have used the faculty of speech, by initiating or continuing a dream conversation with their dream characters. Touch also can play a part in anchoring a creative dream, such as by rubbing or opening your eyes in the dream; touching your dream hands and face; touching objects or being touched.

It is fascinating to discover that apparently your senses continue to operate in dreams as they do in real life. Within the dream scenario, all of the senses tend to be enhanced when we finally achieve the art of creative dreaming. Everything seems brighter, more colourful and in greater detail than before. Those who have used mind-enhancing substances comment that creative dreams can be similar in effect to hallucinogenic drugs.

There can be great pleasure in achieving such intensity within the dream state without any other assistance. It is worthwhile experimenting and playing with these effects to find out just exactly what your own limitations are. We tend, in waking life, to block out a great deal of both sensory input and output. In creative dreaming, we are able to concentrate on what is happening with the 'inner' being and to achieve a kind of personal pleasure that is not possible in any other way. So when you have the time and the inclination, try playing in dreams with each sense in turn, to your own satisfaction. Gradually you should find that it is almost as though someone has turned on a light switch in your workaday life. The intensity spreads to ordinary everyday occurrences, allowing you to use each of the senses with more of the pure joy which is inherent in everything.

These techniques allow you to prolong most of your truly creative dreams. You will find that as you experiment with other people's favourite methods, you will develop your own unique versions. Part of developing your own system does mean that you have to have some control over the process of waking up, and for that we must go back to basics. This requires a real understanding of the hypnopompic and hypnagogic states, as well as of the principle of dream signs.

DREAM SIGNS

Dream signs help a dreamer to recognize that they are in the middle of a creative dream. Not all of them occur at one time and sometimes only one triggers the awareness of the beginning of awareness. These differences can be:

1. In the dream ego state.

2. In the characters within a dream.

3. In objects.

4. In the setting.

The ego state
In the ego state, the perception of our Self is changed. These changes are perceived mainly in the following ways:

Action
The actions taken by us are unlikely or impossible in waking life. The most extreme example of this is 'flying', although such an act seems very simple in the dream state.

Body Sense

In this state, we become conscious of an unusual sensation or sensations on or in his or her physical body. For instance, it may feel as though the skin of the body is too tight or too loose.

Emotion

During the dream, we experience unusually intense emotions. As an example there may be extreme terror, or the recognition of being in love with one of our own dream characters.

Form

When there are changes in form, we become aware that the physique is distorted or that we are in a body that is somehow different from the way it should be (e.g. a limb may seem to be larger or smaller than it actually is in waking life).

Out of Body

Here, we become aware of sensations as if we were out of our body. This seems like an altered state of consciousness within the dream state.

Paralysis

In this state, we find ourselves totally unable to move, often feeling completely trapped. This awareness is recognized by meditators and spiritualists as part of changes in consciousness.

Role

Here, we are is playing a role completely different from that of our normal waking self – perhaps one that in waking circumstances would be odd or strange (e.g. being a parent when in waking life we are childless).

Senses

The senses may be considerably sharper or duller within the dream and we are able to see, hear or feel things differently. Colours, for instance, may have a different tone or hue from normal.

Sexual

In this state, we may feel sexually aroused or become aware of different sensations in the erogenous area. This may occur as a result of the dream, or other sensations may be translated as being primarily sexual.

Thought

We become aware within the dream that we are actually thinking, or recognize that they have altered the dream through power of thought. An example of this is changing the ending of a bad dream for a better outcome.

Characters

The characters in dreams can also show changes which can alert us to the fact that we are dreaming. As with the ego state, these are more particularly:

Action

A dream character takes an action which is either unlikely or impossible in waking life (e.g. walking through a wall).

Form

A character in a dream is in some way different from what could be expected. For instance, oddly formed or dressed inappropriately.

Place

The background of the dream seems inappropriate for a dream character and not what we would expect.

Role

The role that a dream character plays is totally different from the one known by us.

Bizarre objects

Another way in which we can become aware that we are in fact dreaming is when objects seem bizarre or inappropriate. This tends to happen in three ways:

Action

An object in a dream moves or acts in a way that would normally be impossible in waking life. For instance, a live fish moving on dry land.

Form

We become conscious that something is constructed in a very strange way or doesn't even exist in waking life (e.g. a composite animal which is neither one thing nor the other, perhaps with the head of a horse and the body of a cow).

Place

An object in a dream is positioned where it is not likely to be in waking life – the combination may be somewhat bizarre – for example, a penguin on a tropical island.

Setting

Finally, we may be alerted to the fact that we are not in the real world but are dreaming because the setting or environment is weird or strange. Again, this can be recognized in three ways:

Form

It may be that the environment of the dream is out of place, wrongly built or impossible. An example of this might be the dream taking place under water.

Place

Here the dream happens in a place where we are not likely to be or want to be in waking life (e.g. being in a brothel when it is highly unlikely and indeed would seem improper).

Time

Often dreams happen where we recognize that they are either in the past or in some future place of which they have no knowledge. This is sufficient to alert them to other bizarre elements in the dream.

As you begin to record your dreams, it is worthwhile noting anything which you think may constitute a dream sign, since it is then possible to build up a personal 'file' of occurrences which will alert you to the beginnings of a state of awareness.

These occurrences also alert you to the need for the development of ways in which to control your dreams and other altered states of consciousness.

ALTERED STATES OF CONSCIOUSNESS

Dreams and altered states of consciousness seem to open up channels of communication with the supernatural. Hallowell, working specifically with the Saulteaux tribe, has shown that their dreams enhance everyday life, confirming or verifying the belief system by which they live. This helps them to make various adjustments to their day-to-day experiences.

Where altered states of consciousness are accepted as normal (generally initially in so-called 'primitive' cultures), dreams and creative dreams form an integral part of the development of the individual. Bourguignon, Hallowell and Wallace in their various researches have discovered the point that creative dreams are used to expand experiences and enhance the development of the self. By studying primitive cultures and their use of dreams and/or drugs, we gain fresh insight into the workings of our own subconscious. This is backed up by research into hallucinogenic drugs by people such as Timothy Leary in the late 1960s.

There has developed a cultural patterning within the community of modern-day drug takers which offers well set out shared expectations and a degree of social support for the individual both during and after the experience. The development of 'positive' ritualization, such as the communal use of drug-taking equipment – whether right or wrong – approaches very closely that which is seen in primitive cultures. Such rituals seem to provide comfort, support and security in the introduction to altered states of consciousness achieved through the use of drugs.

Creative dreams, hallucinations and spirit visitation represent only three aspects of a whole series of altered states of consciousness where certain steps and changes can be acknowledged. In most human societies, the handling of these three aspects has been culturally accepted. It is only in 'sophisticated' Western society that widespread acceptance of the requirements of the inner self has not been manifested. Ways of understanding these altered states can develop as follows:

1. Perception and cognition

The way different people manage altered states of consciousness and the expectations they have can make a contribution to the building of behavioural patterns and rituals. Such patterns can provide outlets for the various belief systems to function properly, religious or otherwise.

2. The psychobiological

The actual inductions of the varying states of consciousness do have similarities – they often depend on the usual environment and the learnt experiences of the individual. For instance, someone who has learnt to induce awareness through yogic practices will naturally find it easier to stay with those techniques than to use dream techniques.

3. Interpersonal and 'other-worldly' aspects

Alterations in personal perception and contact with the spirit world can dramatically change individual behaviour when they are permitted to do so. Also, there can occur some modifying of group action, through the use of altered states of consciousness, whether through the individual or group leadership. The growth in cult activity in the lead-up to the new millennium is one such example.

4. Social structure

Just as the individual can have an effect on group behaviour, so a group with common aims and ambitions can affect the society of which it is part. The setting up of women's consciousness groups in the 1960s (of which dreams and expectations of the future played a major part) has gradually led to women believing that they can not only survive in a hitherto mainly male environment, such as the business world, but also maximize their own potential.

As a means of influencing society in a wider sense, altered states of consciousness such as meditation, creative dreaming or a combination of both have a profound effect.

MEDITATION

Meditation is, and always has been, a tool for entering an altered state of consciousness during which it is possible to experience other realities and different states of being. It requires the development of several sorts of discipline.

- Firstly, there is the physical discipline which teaches the participant to be able to sit or lie still without difficulty.

- Secondly, there is the ability to quiet one's mind and empty it of all distractions, both internal and external.

- Thirdly, there is the ability to accept the imagery and symbolism that such a mind produces when left to 'idle' and scan the databanks of all awareness.

- Fourthly, the state of perfect peace which is the final aim of all meditative practices.

One of the instructions most often given to the creative dreamer is designed to have them remain as still as they can and maintain their position once they realize and appreciate that they are dreaming. This is to enable them mentally to hold onto the images which appear, and not to wake up, thus driving the dream away. Looking at physical control, it is possible to see that to enhance creative dreaming, the ability to control and relax the physical body is an important attribute. Those techniques such as *hatha* yoga, *qi gung, t'ai chi* and so on which are often considered to be moving – or, more correctly, standing – forms of meditation, enable us to remain in contact with our inner being without undue strain on the physical. The natural changes that occur in diet and exercise as you become more proficient in such techniques also make the achievement of creative dreams more probable, since you are less likely to be clogged up by toxins and 'dis-ease'.

In the normal run of things when we put oneselves in a learning situation, the mind takes over and seems to create, of its own volition, all kinds of distractions which take our attention away from the matter in hand. Meditation is a tool which can be used to help to focus the mind and prevent the intrusion of unwanted thoughts. Many of the exercises, such as concentration, contemplation and creative visualization, which form the basis of meditation, can be applied to the art of creative dreaming. Concentration on an external object initially, then on an internal image, trains the mind not to be distracted by external sounds or stray ideas – that is, not to go off on some wild-goose chase, but keep the mind on the matter in hand.

Contemplation enhances this ability, but also gives the ability to remain within your own space, continually observing what appears to be going on without any particular input from you and without trying to affect the outcome. It gives the ability to choose consciously a particular thought or idea for consideration. Visualization, on the other hand, helps to train you to accept that you can call images to mind or 'make things happen' on an inner level. Having this ability increases the potential for a state of aware.

As we progress further in learning about and understanding meditation, much of the symbolism and imagery which develops is similar to dream imagery. Creative dreams are, it is thought by some, a development of hypnagogic imagery. Meditation helps to stabilize the fleeting images which first appear as we begin to explore the edges of the mind. It is these images which appear as the facility of creative dreaming develops. There is a shorthand form of symbolism, as well as a fund of archetypal images, which can be harnessed in meditation and then cross-referenced into creative dreams.

Relaxation, Meditation and Visualization

As aids to sleep, the techniques of relaxation, meditation and visualization are all excellent tools. The more proficient we become in these techniques the easier it is also to achieve creative dreaming. Some suggestions are included below:

Relaxation

An easy relaxation technique which can be performed whether or not you wish to meditate is as follows:

- Beginning with the toes, first tighten and relax all the muscles in your body, so that you are able to identify the difference between tight and relaxed.

- Then tighten each part of your body in turn.

- First tighten your toes and let go. Do this three times.

- Then tighten your ankles and release them. Again repeat three times.

- Tighten your calves and let go. Repeat three times.

- Tighten your thighs and let go. Repeat twice more.

- Finally for this part tighten the full length of your legs completely and release, again repeating three times. (This exercise is also good for restless leg syndrome.)

Now move on to the rest of your body:

- Repeating three times for each part, tighten in turn your buttocks, your stomach, your spine, your neck, your hands, your arms and your neck (again), your face and your scalp.

- Finally tighten every single muscle you have used, and let go completely. Repeat three times, and by now you should recognize the difference between the state of relaxation at the beginning of the exercise, and the one at the end.

In time, with practice you should be able to relax completely just by doing the last part of the exercise, but for now be content with taking yourself slowly through the process.

Meditation and Creative Visualization

A way of training ourselves to harness that part of the brain which roams inconsequentially and to begin to focus on a desired result is creative visualization. We learn to concentrate, to 'play' creatively and finally to make things happen to manifest our dreams in the real world.

Meditation and Creative Visualization Techniques

The aim in meditation is to keep your mind alert yet relaxed, and focused upon a single subject, rather than to listen to the 'chatterbox' in your head. A short period of meditation or creative visualization last thing at night gives us access to the full creative world of dreams, while a similar period in the morning allows us to work with, and understand, the dreams we have had.

Choose a place where you will not be disturbed and make sure that the telephone is disconnected. To begin with, five minutes' meditation is enough. Sit in an upright chair or cross-legged on the floor with your back supported if necessary; it is important to be as comfortable as possible, although probably not to lie down since you may fall asleep before the process of meditation is completed.

Partially close your eyes or close them completely. If you are an experienced meditator you may find it easier to focus your eyes on the bridge of your nose or the middle of your forehead.

Begin to breathe evenly and deeply; initially breathe in for a count of four and out for a count of four. Once this rhythm is established, breathe out slightly longer than is breathed in, but at a rate that is still comfortable for you. Rather than being conscious of your breathing, become more aware of the breath itself. As you breathe in, breathe in peace and tranquillity; as you breathe out, breathe out negativity. It should be possible to achieve a deep state of awareness which if so wished can allow you to move straight into the sleep state, or in the morning to concentrate on any dream you may have had. Any stray thoughts can be noted and dismissed.

At night, you may instruct yourself to remember any dreams which may follow, or consider any problem you may wish to solve. You may also use this period to visualize creatively something that you desire so that this may be carried over into dreams. Obviously in the morning the concentration may be focused on the solution to the problem or the realization of your desire.

As your practice improves so you will find the period of meditation tends to extend of its own free will to anything up to twenty minutes. When you finish the meditation, keep your mind in the same calm and tranquil state. It's best to go straight to bed. Keep your physical movements unhurried, as if they are flowing in harmony with your consciousness. When you settle to sleep, allow your awareness to rest gently in the same place as your meditation.

The Tower Meditation

Any building may be taken in dreams as a symbol of the 'self' or of the personality. Using this, visualization or meditation can give us access to information about ourselves which may allow us to use more creativity in our dreaming. Experience teaches that one of the best images to use is that of a tower. Sometimes the tower can appear spontaneously in a dream or after a meditation and it can be used to focus the mind ready for information which will help us to live our lives more fully. This meditation can either be done from memory or can be recorded on a tape recorder. The more experienced meditator will recognize within this practice the relevance of the seven spiritual centres (chakras).

Dream interpretation and meditation share many symbols, so the visualization allows the dreamer access to the language of creativity. The first image of the tower gives us an insight into how we present ourselves to the outside world: a round tower might suggest a more spiritual approach, while a square tower might indicate more practicality.

The meditation is as follows:

Visualize a tower, note its shape and structure but at this point do not spend too much time on the intricacies. Simply note how you approach the tower, including how the entrance appears. Does it open inwards or outwards? Is it strong or flimsy? Is it decorative or plain?

All of these things will, with a little thought, show how in everyday life we allow ourselves to be approached by others.

Now enter the tower and look around, taking note as to whether it is furnished or bare and attempt to find some stairs; these may lead either up or down. If they lead downwards you will first explore your subconscious self, if upwards, a more accessible side of your personality. Any obstacles on the stairs may be translated as difficulties which need to be overcome. Each level of the tower can then be explored in turn, noting colours, shapes and anything odd about each stage (often such things will form images in your dreams later).

When ready, progress to the top of the tower noting points of interest on the way up. These may require contemplation later on, or perhaps form images in dreams at a later date. When the top is reached spend some quiet moments contemplating what you have just achieved and then come back down to each level noting any changes which have spontaneously occurred. These changes may give you clues as to the types of changes which may be important to you in everyday life. When you get back to the ground floor take a last look round and come back out into the sunshine, closing the door behind you. Remember now that you can come back to this tower whenever you like either in meditation or the dream state and next time you may even discover secret rooms or passages which need further exploration. Walk away from your tower allowing the image to fade away and allow yourself to drift gently off to sleep.

WAKING-INDUCED LUCID DREAMING (WILD)

The close similarities between meditation and creative dreaming, particularly Waking-Induced Lucid Dreaming (WILD), have been noted by many. A variety of methods have been developed using and combining both techniques to achieve maximum lucidity.

These can be divided into three categories:

1. Meditating on your chosen subject and then using the altered state of consciousness to instruct yourself to become aware during a dream later on.

2. Meditating early in the morning, with the intention of going back to sleep afterwards. A brief period of meditation can be the equivalent of several hours' sleep; a period of meditation puts the mind into a state which is more conducive to creative dreaming.

3. Meditating and shifting consciousness into a state of waking awareness. That is, entering the creative dreaming state directly.

These categories obviously require a degree of experience and practice, but for the more experienced creative dreamer it is possible to enter directly into a creative dream straight from the waking state. Obviously this requires a high degree of control, both of the self and of the dreaming process. It also requires an understanding of the actual process of dreaming. We have already spoken of the hypnagogic state between waking and sleeping. What is now popularly called WILD actually begins when we enter directly into REM sleep and into dreaming from the waking state. This kind of dream has many similarities with out-of-body experiences – the main difference being that in the latter the individual does not believe that he or she is dreaming, but is truly experiencing something completely different.

The experience of weird vibrations, strange noises, electrical sensations, such as pins and needles, feelings of pressure on the chest, difficulty in breathing and floating – sometimes away from the body – are common to both states of awareness – out-of-body experiences and WILD. This may be put down to purely physiological factors as the body passes into the REM sleep state. In primitive cultures, though, these states may be the ones in which the individual faces his 'demons'.

What we are really concerned with is how to induce a WILD, and there are a couple of ways in which you can do this. The first method is counting yorself to sleep. Rather similar to the idea of counting sheep until you fall asleep, this method consists of recognizing that when you wake up, you repeat, 'One, I'm dreaming; two, I'm dreaming, etc.', until you fall asleep again. This helps you to be fully aware of your own state, and makes the transition from waking to sleeping considerably easier. The second method uses the technique of allowing your attention to focus on various points of the body in a particular order. Those familiar with acupressure points may like to use those as their reference points, while others may like to use more anatomical references. For instance, become aware of your hands and arms, feet and legs and so on. This ties in with the idea of doing a 'reality check', using your own body as a guide, and enables you to re-enter the REM state directly.

MANIPULATING THE DREAM STATE

There is another aspect of truly creative dreaming that needs to be considered. We have already defined a creative dream as one in which you become aware that you are dreaming and, with practice, maintain the ability to manipulate your dream and make desired changes. There are various states of awareness within this, just as there are various states of consciousness. Because there are so many layers of consciousness and because each person is so individual it is almost impossible to classify the various stages of consciousness and/or awareness which occur, and in many cases it is not until you have recorded many dreams and dream states that you yourself will be able to sense the differences.

We have spoken elsewhere of the hypnopompic and hypnagogic states as being the bridge between waking and sleeping. During those states, you can choose whether you are going to move into a state of awareness or into dreaming proper. A visual image might be that in your dream you have come through a doorway into a passageway. Close to the entrance, you can see two doors at the far end of the passage, through either of which you may choose to pass. One is labelled 'Dreams Proper' and the other 'Dreams Creative'. As you move closer, however, you see that they are both ajar and become confused as to which to go through. There is information coming from both and it depends where you stand as to how you pick up the information. On one side of the passage you are clearly dreaming, whilst on the other you are searching for enhanced perception. In the middle area there is some doubt as to whether he is either dreaming or lucid – chaotic or well-ordered. It is worth noting that if the dreamer is capable of asking the question 'Am I dreaming?' then he is probably in the perceptive state.

Dreams designed to help us create a different reality and dreams of such dreams actually feel very different – both need to be experienced to be clear which each individual dream is. Dreams of creative dreams are remembered as an activity of the dreaming self while perceptive dreams somehow seem more real – in the here and now. Thought processes after such dreams are stronger – it is easier to come back through the 'doorway' into a normal state of consciousness.

To try to get some perspective on the various layers we might perceive the progression as something like this: Wakefulness; Creative Visualization; Meditation; Dreams or Creative Dreaming; Dreaming of Creative Dreaming; the 'hypno' states; Awake and aware.

In order to sort out which dreams are which, it is necessary to keep a record of all your dreams – of whatever sort – and for this you need to learn how to keep a dream journal.

HOW TO KEEP A DREAM JOURNAL

Keeping a dream journal – i.e. documenting all of our remembered dreams – can provide a remarkable insight into our dreams. However, it can also be somewhat taxing. Over time, it can provide material for us to work on from hitherto hidden places. It may be that over a period of time most of our dreams appear to be connected with a specific subject. Having thought that we understand the sequence of dreams, we establish the theme and can shelve it and return to it later. The same theme may come about months or even years in the future, with greater vision and more dream material to work on. Keeping a dream journal enables us to observe and to map our improvement in learning about ourselves and comprehending everyday life.

Each dream has its own individual interpretation at the time of being dreamt, although it may need reassessing when recognized as being as part of a series. The dreaming brain is highly effective in that it will offer material for consideration in as many different ways as possible until such times as we understand. That same dreaming self can obscure the information in non-essential material which needs removing before the dream can be worked with. Even creative dreaming can lose clarity in this way, and what has started out as an easy process becomes cluttered and difficult. Creative dreaming particularly does not necessarily need interpretation through symbols in the same way as 'ordinary dreams'. Dreams have so many elements that they can be interpreted in many different ways and usually need multiple explanations.

Using a dream journal helps us to take note of both the material of our dreams and also the way in which our dreams are put together. The more we learn to remember our dreams, the better at dreaming we become. So many individuals who claim not to be very good at dreaming are amazed at both the quality and quantity of their dreams when they do start recording them.

People who are learning to experiment with creative dreaming will, by and large, have learnt how to keep a dream journal. For those who have not here are some brief instructions:

1. Any paper and writing implements can be used – whatever is most pleasing for you.

2. Always keep your recording implements at hand.

3. Write the account of the dream as soon as possible after waking.

4. Use as much detail as possible.

5. Note at which point in your dream you consider you 'went lucid'.

6. Be consistent in the way that you record your dreams.

One simple scheme is given below.

> *Name*
> *Age*
> *Gender*
> *Date of dream*
> *Where were you when you recalled the dream?*
> *State the content of your dream.*
> *Write down anything odd about the dream (e.g. animals, bizarre situations, dream signs, etc.).*
> *What were your feelings in/about the dream?*

Writing down the dream has a particular kind of satisfaction. However, just as many people now like to use a computer and any available software to make their records easier, there those who would rather use a recording device in order to secure the uninterrupted flow from sleep to the waking state. Using a tape recorder and 'speaking' the dream fixes it in your mind and requires less concentration than writing it down. You are therefore much more in touch with the feelings and emotions of the dream. Try clarifying the dream as though it is still happening to you. For instance, 'I am walking through a forest' rather than 'I was walking through a forest'. This allows you to get hold of what was happening to you as a participant as well as an observer.

When you make your preparations for sleep into a habit or ritual you will concentrate your mind on the activity of dreaming. This also includes the preparation of your journal, perhaps recording the date and time you went to bed, the subject you hope to dream about and so on. Using affirmations to achieve creative dreaming or to dream about a certain subject helps to train the subconscious to respond to your needs rather than introducing material at random. Impressing on your mind that you will have a dream to record in your journal is all part of that training.

Remember when you are recording dreams to make a note of times when you wake up during the night, or the approximate time into your dream that you think you have become aware. Initially you will find that this is quite difficult but gradually you will discover that you are fairly accurate at estimating the time – it is as though your body clock recognizes what is being attempted. You should then be able to highlight your most prolific dreaming period. Holistically, once we take care of the inner workings, we can dream more efficiently and be in touch with the physical body.

Those with a mathematical or scientific frame of mind will prefer to look at their dreams analytically and find instances of statistical relevance to make it easier to trace dreams with similar themes, energies and objects. These can also be recorded in your journal. Particularly when experimenting with creative dreaming it helps to carry your journal with you during the day. One reason is to note down instances of synchronicity – occasions when you see something which approximates to a dream image, whether bizarre or otherwise – and another is to note down possible subjects which might be worthwhile exploring further as subjects for creative dreaming.

In the beginning, don't try too hard to obtain results. Being laid back will enhance your chances of success rather than getting completely stressed out because the dreams are not appearing to order or are not what you thought they should be.

We have spoken elsewhere about the importance of not 'chasing away' the dream. Suffice to say that when you wake up, preferably gently, remember to lie still and recall your dream – whether creative or otherwise – before moving quietly and gently to record it in your chosen way. Your recall will be better and you may find more significance in the dream and your handling of it than if you have shocked yourself awake.

When experimenting with creative dreaming, you are not looking for meaning in the dream – you may wish to explore that later. You are instead looking to appreciate the sensations and feelings that your dream has given you and the insights that you might gain into your everyday life or your personality. It is just as important to record these latter aspects as it is to record the content of the dream itself. Note particularly if there are other aspects in the dream which might bear exploration from a creative standpoint. For instance, you might find that you are failing to land up in your chosen situation more often than is coincidental. You might then wish to experiment with becoming more focused and therefore more accurate in your targeting. Your journal will help you to become more aware of the whole of your own dreaming process and you will be able to experiment with whatever controls are important to you.

A Specimen Dream Journal Entry

I was going to have to live in a hostel with other women, most of whom were depressive types, and had boring jobs – not a type I liked at all, but the sort of person I could have become. To be accepted, there had to be some kind of inspection, at which it was discovered that I had head lice, particularly on the right side. This was a shock to me, and not something of which I was aware. This, incidentally, was after my hair had been washed with Derbac soap (a remedy for headlice) and combed with a small tooth comb.

The nurse/doctor was the 'Nazi-type' woman, who has been part of my dreams before – disapproving and totally judgmental. I had to accept that there was something desperately wrong, and went through to the dining-room. There, about half of the people took no notice, whereas others seemed to approve and accept, while others obviously hated the idea.

The Components of the Dream

Hostel
Women
Depression
Inspection
Headlice
Right side
Non-awareness
Old-fashioned remedy
Small tooth comb
Nurse/Doctor
Nazi-type
Acceptance

Something wrong
Dining-room
Notice taken or not

Sort Alphabetically

Acceptance: This sets the theme of the dream, which is about the acknowledgement of a group about which the dreamer is ambivalent.

Depression: The overall tone of the dream was depressive and 'grey'.

Dining-room: The dining-room was somewhat regimented and on the whole unwelcoming.

Head lice: This was an infestation from an exterior source, something the dreamer had caught.

Hostel: This emphasizes the idea of a group activity: living together.

Inspection: Having to pass some kind of test or judgement.

Nazi-type woman: Her appearance in dreams usually represents the restrictive side of a dreamer's personality.

Non-awareness: There is an element of surprise in the very idea of having caught an infestation.

Notice taken or not: In the dream it eventually did not matter whether the dreamer was accepted or not.

Nurse/Doctor: This represents the healer in the dreamer.

Old-fashioned remedy: Suggests outdated methods.

Right side: Is the masculine, logical side of our being.

Small tooth comb: Linked with removing nits, the source of re-infestation.

Something wrong: At this point there is a degree of additional negativity in the dreamer's life.

Women: Although in this dream negative, this is the dreamer's peer group, and perhaps needs to be looked at.

Theme

The theme in this dream is to do with acceptance within a wider group which obviously has fairly strict rules or codes of conduct. The group is female, and in the dreamer's view somewhat negative. The dreamer is put under scrutiny, which indicates that there is some kind of contamination (the head lice) on the intellectual side (right) which even after old-fashioned cleansing (the soap and comb) is still present.

The Nazi-type woman is a known quantity in that in previous dreams she has appeared as that part of the dreamer which is restrictive and does not approve of any behaviour which could be judged as over the top. Having been made to feel different, and negative about herself, the dreamer nevertheless realizes that if she wishes to be accepted then she must brave the opinions of the group, albeit in a nurturing environment (the dining-room). In fact, people would act as they saw fit. Thus this dream is more about how the dreamer experiences herself rather than about what other people think of her.

Further work might be done in working out what the head lice symbolize and in taking the dream forward to find out what happens after she has become a member of the group.

A more esoteric interpretation of the dream

Given that the group of women personified the feminine side of the dreamer's nature, it becomes obvious that she is experiencing negativity and anxiety within herself. Part of the personality is not able to be integrated into the total feminine due to the fact that there has been some kind of contamination or infection. (It is interesting to note that in waking life the dreamer was having to deal, emotionally, with the effects of dry-rot in her own home.) On some level she requires some kind of acceptance of her own inability to deal with ordinary mundane matters, and to make sensible decisions. She tends to judge herself too harshly, and should realise that in the event it is her own acceptance of herself which is important.

GAINING INSIGHT INTO DREAMS

There are several ways to gain insights through dreams, and this process is not necessarily the same as interpreting the dream. We can start off by defining the conventional meaning of something which comes up in a dream which will help us to understand our situation. Let us suppose that the dreamer is standing on a cliff top looking out to sea. The conventional explanation is that he or she is on the edge of something, perhaps a new experience (the cliff top). This experience may be to do with the emotions, since often water symbolizes emotions in dreams.

Insight comes when a dreamer applies conscious rationality to the dream scenario. Thinking about it allows the order and clarity to be perceived, rather than the randomness of the images. On this occasion the dreamer is aware of the vastness and depth of the sea, and therefore understands that his emotions are far deeper and more meaningful than previously realized. This is an insight into his personality. When the dreamer consciously applies this insight to his everyday life, the dream has been of use.

The dreamer is aware in his dream state that he cannot decide whether to jump off the cliff (take a risk) or move away from the cliff-top (refuse to face the situation or move away from danger). He discovers himself at the foot of the cliff. The interpretation is that he has achieved what he felt was right, the insight that it did not matter how. By keeping the interpretation simple, the insight may be more telling.

Given the basic meaning of the dream action or symbol, it is possible to extract the necessary information to understand the dream. Having the information offers an interpretation of the dream, and working with the interpretation gives insight. The dream vocabulary is both diverse and specific to each dreamer, and each person is so intricate that several simultaneous explanations are possible, all of which may be equally valid. It will depend on the person who has the dream which one has most validity.

Working at dream interpretation with other people, whether known to the dreamer or not, can be a highly illuminating experience. Taking the time to explore all facets of the dream – and bring into conscious memory all aspects of it – can deepen the insights that we obtain as we work with our dreams. Someone who knows us well may be able to see the relevance to the situation we are in of an image in a dream, whereas we are too close to the situation to be able to understand. Someone who does not know us well may have the degree of objectivity needed to round off an interpretation so that we can move forward. The support offered through the insights that friends gain in interpreting our dreams can make a tremendous difference to our lives and theirs. Sometimes, acting a dream through with friends and perhaps taking the dream into a consideration of what would happen next can be helpful and can clarify a course of action for us. This does not simply mean using the imagination. As a dreamer you have the opportunity to work interpretations through more fully using your own techniques. You may choose to use meditation, guided imagery, or other methods since these share much of the symbolism of dream imagery. Methods for doing this are given in the Tip and Techniques section at the end of the book.

WORKING CREATIVELY WITH DREAMS

When you have been recording your dreams for some time you may find it useful to turn one of them into a creative project. This could be a painting, sculpture or other artistic process; it could also be a short story perhaps taking the dream further forward, a play or even using nature creatively - it needs to be something which takes you beyond your normal everyday activities. By acknowledging the creative processes in dreams and making them tangible within the normal sphere of reality, you are opening yourself up to all sorts of possibilities and changes of consciousness.

One of the benefits is a different perception of events in the world around you. Colours may appear more vibrant, shapes sharper, and sounds clearer. These changes can be quite subtle, but usually bring more focus to your awareness and allow you to use creativity to its best advantage. Life begins to take on new meaning.

Dream symbols give fertile ground for meditation which can allow unconscious insights to come to the surface, thus giving rise to greater creativity. You may wish to meditate on the overall feeling or one particular aspect of the dream. When you find yourself dreaming about your chosen project you have come almost full circle – from an acorn to an oak tree and back to an acorn – a situation akin to rebirth.

It does not matter whether the project is good or bad; what is important is the enjoyment that you achieve from doing it. One of the most fulfilling aspects of such a process is the realization that you have entered a stream of consciousness which belongs to all of us, but which so few manage to tap into. This 'locking on' can give a strong physical sensation as much as an emotional or spiritual one. The counter-balance to this is the number of times that you will get stuck or come up against a brick wall in this part of the process, but perseverance does bring about a greater understanding of one's inner self.

For the purposes of self-development you may like to keep a separate journal or record of the processes and stages of awareness experienced during this strenuous activity – it is worthwhile spending a short while each day working with your project, and a journal allows you to see how far you have travelled in this journey of discovery. It can be fascinating to recognize, for instance, in looking back over your daybook how you have found it easier as time goes on to recognize when the fears and doubts arise, and how you have dealt with them.

It may be that your creative journal takes precedence over the dream one or vice versa. It is possible that with time you will recognize that your dreams change when you are in a more overtly creative phase. You may be able to unblock a creative hiatus by asking your dreams for an answer or by dreaming with awareness. You will gradually find that you will be able to intertwine the various states of awareness when necessary without losing the reality of each one. This is the true use of dream creativity.

ANALYZING DREAM STRUCTURE

Whether your dream is creative or otherwise, you will always need to analyze its structure. There are several ways in which you can do this. The more proficient you become, the more your dreams will begin to make sense. As time goes on, you will begin to see certain themes and ideas repeated over and over. These will begin to fall into place until you have internalized what you need to know. By keeping a dream journal, you will find that certain parts of one dream – and the way that they have been structured – may well relate to segments of another dream and the answer is hidden therein.

Firstly, write out a dream in your own words. The best way to analyze the structure of a dream is to split it into its component parts exactly as written it in your journal. You will need to decide how your dream may be split into segments – it is, after all, your dream. The way that you choose to divide it up may be very different from the way that someone else would. Try to look for natural breaks that divide it into two or three distinct parts – each with their own story. Take as an example the dream below, which we received via the Internet and have partially edited without changing any of the main components.

> *I was in a big building with a group of people and didn't know anyone. Somebody had been murdered by a member of the group I was with. We decided the murderer was the boy who was sat in the corner on his own. We had to kill him as he killed someone in the group. We all decided that he had to be stoned to death and all joined in. A large cat appeared that ate everyone one at a time, as slowly and 'curly' as possible. But he had taken a liking to me so he didn't kill me. Then I found out that the cat was really my best friend.*

Here the dream may be divided into four main parts:

1. Where the dreamer was and how she felt. 2. The action of the dream and her inclusion within the group. 3. What was happening to the group. 4. Her realizations.

1. I was in a big building with a group of people and didn't know anyone.

2. Somebody had been murdered by a member of the group I was with. We decided the murderer was the boy who was sat in the corner on his own. We had to kill him as he killed someone in the group. We all decided that he had to be stoned to death and all joined in.

3. A large cat appeared that ate everyone one at a time, as slowly and 'curly' as possible. But he had taken a liking to me so he didn't kill me.

4. Then I found out that the cat was really my best friend.

This dream can also be divided into only two acts or parts – the one dealing with the group and its actions and the one dealing with the cat:

1. I was in a big building with a group of people and didn't know anyone. Somebody had been murdered by a member of the group I was with. We decided the murderer was the boy who was sat in the corner on his own. We had to kill him as he killed someone in the group. We all decided that he had to be stoned to death and all joined in.

2. A large cat appeared that ate everyone one at a time, as slowly and 'curly' as possible. But he had taken a liking to me so he didn't kill me. Then I found out that the cat was really my best friend.

The next part of analyzing the dream structure is to find out which is the most important segment. Here, when we look at the first way of partitioning the dream, the part that is most important is the killing of the boy and the violence involved. We might give this part a title and call it 'Murder' or 'The Killing'. Giving each part a title helps to fix the section in your mind, and helps to give quicker recall. Also, should you wish at a later date to use this dream for creative work, it gives you a starting point from which to work.

Using the second method of dividing up the dream, both parts are equally important since they are both to do with death. It is the difference between the two ways of killing which is of note – the fact that the cat is discovered to be the dreamer's best friend is the resolution of the dream.

You should also name the other segments of the dream. Using the first method of dividing the dream up, section one could be called 'The Building' or 'Setting the Scene' – it is important that the name resonates with you. You might call the second section 'The Stoning' or 'An Eye for an Eye', depending on which aspect of the section has most meaning for you. Often, naming the part helps you to recall your reactions in the dream.

It is also necessary to discover within each section whether you, the dreamer, are active (taking action) or passive (inert). In the first section in our example, the dreamer is passive and is conscious of her lack of friends. In the second, she is aware of herself participating in the group decision-making but is also aware of the boy on his own. In the third, she becomes aware that she is somewhat passive since her survival is dependent on the cat, and she is again on her own. In the final section there is a partial resolution since she has her 'best friend' – the cat – and is neither active nor passive.

Looking closely at the dream in this way begins to uncover the similarities and differences between each segment. Each section, except the first and last, has an element of aloneness in it. In the first, the dreamer knows nobody; in the second, the boy is alone; finally, in the third, the dreamer is again set apart. There is also killing, violence and death in the main parts of the dream. Someone has been murdered and as a subplot the murderer must himself be violently killed by virtue of a group decision. At this point, however, the cat becomes an agent of death in that he (an individual) begins to eat (absorb) members of the group. The dreamer, also an individual, is saved by the fact that she realizes that the cat is actually her best friend. Thus, one theme of the dream is uncovered – that of needing to belong, contrasting with the need to be an individual.

The differences in the segments are also recognizable. In the first segment, the dreamer is alone, and knows no one. In the second, she is a member of a group, and in the third, she is watching a lone cat absorb the rest of the group. In the last segment, it is her relationship with the cat which is important. Thus another theme which is revealed is that of meaningful relationship.

A further similarity/difference comparison reveals that while each section is indeed to do with death, the methods by which death comes are different. In the section to do with murder, a particularly primitive method is chosen by the group: that of stoning. In the segment to do with the cat, the method is at one and the same time natural (a cat eats its prey) and also bizarre. The cat eats the members of the group in a slow and 'curly' way, one after the other. This would tend to suggest that the dreamer has to be conscious of her need to face some kind of ending – which may possibly be violent – in order to achieve a different standing with someone who has the potential to be destructive. The general theme therefore seems to be the need for change in the dreamer.

Once the dream has been worked on in this way the various themes can be listed and further work done on the symbols in each section which pick up these themes. As an example we have already seen that in the first section our dreamer is aware of not knowing anyone. She also does not seem to know the boy accused of murder, nor initially does she know either the cat or the fact that he seems to be her best friend. Some useful consideration might be given through dreamwork as to whether the dreamer is something of a loner and how she reacts to the world in which she lives.

There is an element of the absurd or bizarre in this dream, in that the dreamer unexpectedly recognizes that the cat is her best friend. It is at this point that she might have begun dreaming with awareness.

ABSURDITIES AND BIZARRE ELEMENTS

There is a fascinating aspect to creative dreaming, particularly as we first begin to learn how to handle the preliminaries. This is the presence of the absurd. Often it is the presence of the unusual which alerts us to the fact that we are in the middle of a creative dream. We still do not fully understand how the dreaming brain works, though we do know that dreaming is associated with REM.

There is a theory that the dreaming brain is less intelligent than the waking brain, although this would have to depend on the definition of intelligence. Certainly the sleeping brain works with a degree of irrationality which follows no known logic. In normal dreaming, REM signals tremendous variations in electrical activity and it is this activity which governs awareness and, apparently, irrationality. Cultivating the art of creative dreaming means that we have to discover how our dreams work and which boundaries are self-imposed and which not. Most bizarre episodes are errors of perception or errors of context.

Errors of perception occur when we 'forget' that anything is feasible in dreams and begin to impose the inhibitions and strictures that apply in everyday life. For instance, instead of accepting unquestioningly that we can pass through barriers or do quite naturally things which we would not do in ordinary life, we may become afraid of physical harm or impose a rational thought that something is dangerous. We then would not continue with the action. In ordinary dreams, we would complete the action without thinking about it; at the beginning of learning how to dream with awareness, we would find that we have stopped the action

– or have been stopped – while the practised creative dreamer will continue with the action anyway.

Being able to suspend disbelief is perhaps easier for people who have already practised out-of-body work, altering the perception of their personal boundaries or who have attempted astral travel.

By the time we have consciously decided to become creative dreamers, we will have picked up a number of inhibitions about our social behaviour. Just as in waking life we have to learn how to bypass those inhibitions, this must also be done in creative dreaming. When we dream of characters, we recognize these dream figures are our own *perception* of them and not necessarily how they really are. However, the way that we have understood their effect on us can have a direct influence on how we dream about them. We might, for instance, expect a mother to act in a nurturing way and become somewhat confused when she appears as a highly charged sexual being. Awareness dictates that rather than being shocked awake at this apparently bizarre behaviour, we are able to accept it and recognize that we are dreaming – the dream can then continue and unfold as we wish.

For creative dreaming to be successful, one further step needs to be taken. As children, before we have internalized social consequences, we are entirely innocent. It is to this innocent approach and purity that we must return if we are to understand the errors that the dreaming self can make. A dream can be so 'real' that objects and people seem to be truly present. It is as the level of awareness changes in a dream that it is possible to correct the error of thinking that a dream character is real. We realize that we are dreaming.

When we remember that there is an internal reality which exists, we can become aware that the dream character or object – however bizarre – has a valid existence within the dream. It is our perception which, for the purpose of the dream, is flawed. This gives rise to the necessity of accepting, with a degree of innocence, that creative dreaming helps us to differentiate between an inner and outer reality. The crossover between inner and outer reality is when we allow our dreams to help us to understand the way in which we unconsciously react to other people and to our environment. Irrational thought tends to follow patterns set up in childhood. There are those, however, who would still subscribe to the belief that, in the dream state, the brain is dysfunctional.

Researchers Hobson and McCarley have put forward an argument dealing with the bizarre elements and erroneous thought in the content of dreams. These aspects have been attributed to the suppression of unacceptable drives and urges, although they probably have a much simpler explanation when approached from a neurophysiological perspective. When a dreamer experiences oddities, such as the forming of dream symbols, inappropriate scene changes or two characters merging into one or becoming grotesque, these events may directly reflect the state of the dreaming brain. Hobson and McCarley have discovered that there is a strong possibility that the link between the brain stem and the fore brain may not be fully efficient: it is simply doing its best to create some kind of coherence.

Both arguments are well demonstrated in the mirror task mentioned previously given to dreamers being tested for creative dreaming in laboratories. Here, those who undertook the task discovered that there was a high degree of instability in the images of self as perceived in the dream mirror. There was also a tendency to not show normal images. This may be because the self-image is a very personal construct, heavily affected by experience. On the other hand, it may also be because in REM sleep the brain is in a particular state not conducive to tying the images down mentally in a logical way. The dreaming brain is apparently both capable of producing and of accepting the weird or bizarre.

Most of us are not fully familiar with the concept of creative dreaming, although we are aware that such a dream requires an element of control which is not apparent in 'ordinary' dreaming. Briefly, although we may be aware that we are dreaming while still apparently asleep, when something totally absurd happens in the middle of such a condition, we assume that we are not in control and therefore the dream is not lucid. This may not necessarily be so.

The apparently nonsensical may have a validity of its own which must be built into our understanding of the dream. Creative dreams show a pattern of abnormality that non-creative dreams don't. There is a belief in some circles that the presence of the apparently bizarre in creative dreams is associated with the pre-creative state. The absurd tends to vanish as beginners become better at creative dreaming, returning as the dreamer becomes even more adept. It would seem, therefore, that absurdity triggers dreaming with awareness.

There are several levels of awareness. The most elementary is the one that the majority of the uninitiated would accept – becoming aware of dreaming without understanding how dreaming is different from being awake. At the highest level, the dreamer is not only conscious of the fact that he or she is dreaming, but needs also to have total grasp of the ramifications of this knowledge, thus being able to make whatever adjustments are feasible and realistic within both the dream state and everyday life.

The absurd, irrational or bizarre in dreams, particularly in creative dreams, could be a result of not fully appreciating how dreams can, with practice, be manipulated. Perhaps the best analogy is that of aiming for a dartboard and just glancing off the outer rim as we throw our dart. We have hit something which is vaguely associated with our target, but which could deflect us from what we are trying to accomplish.

With practice we can either reject that part which does not belong within the framework of our dream, or 'store' it for further consideration. Technically, such cross currents may occur because of the different intensity of brainwave activity during REM sleep; this has been found to vary considerably at different times. It is possible that our inner perceptions and experiences change according to those brainwave rhythms. Only when we have patiently collected enough data about our own dreams are we able to test our individual dream reality. Hopefully this then gives us the courage to explore the anomaly we have thrown up, allowing us to use dreams creatively.

CONTROLLING DREAMS

The Marquis d'Hervey de Saint-Dennis in his book, *Dreams and the Means to Direct Them,* describes very clearly the development of the abilities needed to control dreaming:

- Increase dream recall

- Become aware you are dreaming

- Learn to wake at will

- Be able to direct dreams.

If we look at these four things in more detail, we have the framework necessary to be able to work towards a more coherent way of understanding – and using – our own dreams. Although there has been much research and experimentation done over the years and various methods have been developed to assist in this process of understanding, they are really all extensions of his very simple technique. Throughout the book, and particularly in the Tips and Techniques section, there are various suggestions and exercises to try, but to begin with it is vital that you do not try too hard to get results. Time spent now on the basics will give a good grounding when you find that suddenly and almost without effort you are dreaming creatively at will.

Increasing Dream Recall

Earlier in this section there are detailed instructions on how to keep a dream journal, but before actually doing that, you need to train yourself to remember your dreams. As a first step when you wake up in the morning, lie still and try to recall your dream. It does not matter if you can only catch hold of a small fragment. Ask yourself the question, 'What was I dreaming about?' Gradually, with practice, you will remember more and more of your dream. As a reality test, check that you really are awake – taking a note of the exact time for future reference.

Incidentally, the reason you should lie still is because movement seems to chase away the dream, whereas remaining still helps to 'set' it so that it is more easily recalled. Learning such a habit will also enable you to go back more easily into the dream state as you become more proficient at creative dreaming.

An extension of this technique will help to train you to remember more of your dreams. We now know that we dream more prolifically in those periods of REM which take place at approximately 90-minute periods after we have first fallen asleep. If you wish, you can train yourself to wake up at appropriate intervals, firstly by using your alarm clock or some such device, later by simply telling yourself that you will wake up. Use the same technique of lying quite still until you have recalled some aspect of a dream. Again, it does not matter if initially this process seems difficult – it does get easier with practice! Only when you have recalled as much as you can should you then move and use your dream journal to record as much of the detail as you can. Do remember that often the details of one dream can appear in another – nothing is too trivial to record. If you have remembered it, it has relevance. It is suggested, however, that you practise at weekends – or those days when you are not running to a tight schedule – at first.

Developing Awareness

Previously you have only been concerned with remembering the dreams that you have had. The next stage is to become aware that you are dreaming while still remaining asleep. Eventually this will give you a degree of control over the dreaming process; for now it is sufficient to be certain that you are actually dreaming. Various ways of testing reality are given elsewhere, but as a start, ask yourself a simple question such as, 'Am I dreaming?' or 'Is this a dream?' You will soon develop you own shorthand or dream signs which will tell you whether you are awake or asleep. These are explained more fully earlier in this section. There may, for instance, be some kind of distortion in what should be a perfectly ordinary object or perhaps an unexpected visual clue.

Learning to Wake at Will

In some ways, learning to wake at will is an extension of both dream recall and becoming aware that you are dreaming. The first step to learning to wake up at times predetermined by you will already have been mastered as you learn to recall your dreams. Recognizing that you are dreaming then gives you a choice as to whether to remain asleep and aware or not. Initially, as you come to an understanding that you are dreaming, you will wake up spontaneously, the dream will disappear and you will have had a frustratingly brief awareness of what awareness feels like. As time progresses the more bizarre elements of the dream can help you to anchor yourself in the dream reality, rather than in the waking self.

You can remind yourself that you are dreaming but aware – perhaps using an affirmation such as, 'This is bizarre or not the way it should be, therefore I know that I am dreaming' – and can allow yourself to 'hold onto' the dream. There are various techniques which have been developed by experienced creative dreamers for staying with the dream such as 'spinning' and 'going with the flow', as explained earlier, under 'Prolonging Dreams'. As a beginner, all you need to do is to establish some control over sleeping, waking, ordinary dreaming and creative dreaming. For many, the changes are so subtle that a dreamer can only quantify them himself. The transition between sleeping and waking is known as the hypnopompic state, which we explained earlier in this section.

Directing Dreams

It is now well known, since the RISC technique was developed as a therapeutic tool, that one can learn to direct dreams. Many people first begin to use creative dreams as a way of controlling bad ones – questioning and assessing your own state of consciousness is a proven technique in handling nightmares and night terrors. If you are prone to such disturbances, it is worthwhile pre-programming yourself several times during the day by repeating to yourself a phrase which will alert you to the fact that at those times you are not awake. You could use an affirmation such as, 'Next time I'm dreaming, I will remember I'm dreaming' or 'When I dream, I want to be aware that that is so'. Develop your own reminder that is a positive statement and has meaning for you. It will work for you because you really mean it. Keep your thoughts focused on this phrase for short intervals during the day. When you find your mind wandering, remind yourself once more that you will recognize when you are dreaming, then let it go and return to your everyday concerns.

The next stage is to direct the dream itself. After having pre-programmed yourself, you can incubate a dream, but the easiest part – once you have worked out how you do this – is to manipulate your own dream. Further instructions appear elsewhere in the book but, using the RISC technique below, which is, after all, very close to the Saint-Dennis way, it is possible to make small changes which can be very pleasing, simply by willing those changes to be so.

The RISC Technique

The assumption of dream therapy (using dreams as a therapeutic tool) is simple: if you have bad dreams which make you wake up in a bad mood, reframe your dreams. You can change the scripts. Improving the outcome makes everything seem better, and should lead to better moods. There are four steps that you can learn in the privacy of your own home.

Recognition When you are having a dream which you feel is a bad one, recognize that you do not need the feelings that it leaves you with, whether that is anger, fear, guilt or any other negative feeling.

Identification You need to be able to identify what it is about the dream that makes you feel bad. Look at the dream carefully and find out exactly what it is that disturbs you.

Stopping a bad dream You must always remember that you are in charge. You do not have to let a bad dream continue. You can either wake up or, recognizing that you are dreaming, become aware.

Changing the dream Each negativity in your dream can be changed for the positive. Initially, you may have to wake yourself up to work out a better conclusion, but eventually you will be able to do it while you are still asleep.

To begin with, you might try to make the changes you need on your own; it is amazing how quickly you will begin to feel the benefits even if you are not consciously aware of having made any changes. Working with a therapist sometimes facilitates the result, but it is not always necessary.

In using this method in a therapeutic setting, it is usually fairly easy for the dreamers to pinpoint for themselves the issues which need to be dealt with, though the therapist's experience may help. By starting with a change of attitude (to the dream itself), other such changes to deeper realizations which make themselves felt are made much easier. As a result, it becomes much simpler to change everyday behaviour. Using creative dreaming then allows us as individuals to practise different and more appropriate behaviour before actively making use of it.

One of the side-effects of using this particular method is that it enables the dreamer to handle difficult feelings or memories which surface from the past. By being gentle with yourself you are much more able to deal with traumatic events in a more objective way, building images which trigger feelings of strength and power and thus enabling you to decide how secure you feel in addressing the issues. Not only can you work through the interpretation of dreams, but also through dream manipulation to create more positive feelings about the past, cope with mechanisms in the present and lay the foundation for a more positive future.

BALANCING CREATIVE AND WAKING EXPERIENCES

It is extremely important when working with creative dreams to keep a strong hold on the reality of your present everyday world (the here and now). You must understand that while it is perfectly feasible to function in both realities, you do need to appreciate that the world of creative dreaming can be very seductive and can take you away from the true appreciation of the world you live in.

There is a danger in the initial stages of exploration of becoming obsessed with the idea of having a creative dream and allowing this to take over your waking life. We have talked of the various methods of altering your sleep patterns by napping and waking yourself from sleep in the search for awareness, and this is fine if you have a lifestyle which supports such activities. Questioning yourself periodically during the day as to whether you are awake or dreaming is also fine. The demands of everyday life can, however, conflict with the needs of the inner self and – as always when working with changes of consciousness and awareness – a sense of balance and discipline should be established early on.

There is also the possibility of getting caught up in the intricacies of the techniques themselves which are used to induce creative dreaming. It can be fun to learn to spin, fly and alter size and shape, but this is a little like having only a starter at an important meal, then leaving before the dessert. To appreciate a meal properly, one needs the whole experience, and so it is with lucidity – meaning 'of the light'. Many of today's spiritual traditions have, as an integral part of their beliefs, the experiencing of light, which ultimately suggests a perception of true reality. However, this light is initially an interior light and, when accessed through creative dreaming, should be treated with the dignity and respect it deserves.

From a practical point of view, the suggestion is that initially you attempt creative dreaming only when you know you have time the next day to process what has happened, quietly and sensibly. As part of your initial preparation, you will have already taught yourself how to incubate the dream you want (or need), to record your dreams and interpret them. Now a further stage is necessary to learn how to deal with the effects of creative dreaming. Almost inevitably your perceptions will change, but gradually, you will learn how to incorporate the higher vibration of lucidity into your everyday life. Then creative dreaming will become an integral part of your way of life. You will quite literally see and feel things more clearly. Indeed, as in the words of the song by The Waterboys, you will see 'the whole of the moon'.

Kelzer suggests 'the close tutelage of an experienced guide' when working with creativity or lucidity. As with meditation, talking through your experiences with someone more knowledgeable can help to deal with problems and put things into perspective. It has continually been stressed that each individual's experience is different but, as mentioned elsewhere, there are certain stages which are gone through quite naturally. It does help to obtain someone else's reaction to what is occurring.

A gentle warning

There is the danger for some people of an attack of the 'Messiahs'. In this, because the experience is so mind-blowing, it can seem as though one has been destined to 'save the world'. One wishes to share such an experience with anyone who will listen, and quite a few who do not. Those who have not been through any of the preparatory stages or have not achieved – either voluntarily or involuntarily – the same stage of lucidity, cannot have a full comprehension of the emotions associated with the event and may not enjoy being told that they are living inappropriate lives! This is truly a time to learn when to speak and when to remain silent.

Conversely, the experience can give such a sense of vastness and boundless energy that the individual is left feeling at the same time both humbled and vulnerable. A period of quiet contemplation and the careful management of everyday tasks can have a balancing and grounding effect, so that the dreamer has a better concept of living life in a mindful way – or of prayer through action.

There may be the distinct feeling that one should withdraw altogether from the world, and a strong sense of unworthiness. It is easy to begin to understand why monks and nuns of all denominations are required to undertake mundane and ordinary tasks as part of their discipline, as a way of belonging to the real world. A wise mentor will not allow the pupil to become unworldly in his explorations, and a healthy burst of normal activity such as cleaning or gardening can restore the mental balance. Such tasks undertaken with a degree of joy seem to be accomplished in half the time anyway.

Talking about your experiences with someone else often means that you are able to see and assess the quality and intensity of your own awareness. Just as there are various levels of perception, there are more and less intense experiences within the framework of creative dreaming. If every dream were of the same intensity we would become totally unbalanced, so it is right that we learn to use this new tool with circumspection and to learn from others what is possible and what is not. Your first experiences will tend to be spontaneous, containing a fair percentage of the 'wow' factor – a strong sense of awe and wonder.

New sensations and perceptions occur, possibly never to return with the same power, yet most creative dreamers have discovered that each new perception brings its own delights within the physical world. Accept each occasion on its own merits. It is said that comparisons are odious, so no one dream is better or of more use than another. If you have 'gone creative' or, rather, achieved awareness, it will be for a purpose often only understood after level-headed consideration.

One thing to be continually borne in mind is that it does not matter if you have not had a creative dream for some time even if you have diligently practised all the techniques, and set about to incubate such a dream. Creative dreaming is only one level of consciousness, and it is more than possible that your mind is benefiting from the practice in other ways. This apparently unproductive time may simply be a period where there is a great deal of internal adjustment going on. The more you gain mastery over your mind, the more focused your living becomes.

For this reason alone it is wise not to try to force awareness or creativity. As discussed throughout this book, each change of awareness occurs naturally and of its own accord. Trying to force it is like using a crowbar to open a box. Pandora's box ultimately contained Hope, but not before a great deal of sorrow was released into the world. You will wish to release your own inner joy and tranquillity, not things you cannot easily handle. Be gentle with yourself and work to achieve a sense of balance within.

In many ways, it is not until we achieve that sense of balance that we can begin to even think about manifesting our dreams and creating the world we want. This comes about by a deep appreciation of how well we understand ourselves.

CREATING
YOUR OWN
REALITY

In the next chapter we will be looking at the more spiritual and esoteric implications of creative dreaming through practising with Tarot, Archetypes, Myths and Numbers. However, in this section we will be considering a state of being, understood so well in Eastern philosophies. It is that of the Spiritual Self, and how this expanded state of awareness can affect your dreams and dreamwork.

It is not a completely passive state, but is one which allows you to recognize that you have maximum control over your total being and can create the world you want. It is as though, having reached the Ultimate, when you come back into everyday existence after experiencing this state, you will be able to appreciate everything around you in a new way.

Part of the joy of this state is recognizing that far from such knowledge leading to your isolation from the 'real' world, leaving you alone and without support, you now have access to what amounts to a universal family. This family consists of other people who, like yourself, have chosen to question their parameters and have moved 'beyond the ordinary'. Creative dreaming has been the tool you have used to reach this state and, along with the refinement of other altered states of consciousness, is what you will use to help you to move further towards the blissful states so beloved in Eastern religions.

Such states enable you to be *in* the world, but not *of* it. In other words, you are able to see the world in which you live for what it is – a state of illusion created by you and others like you. It is your responsibility to make it as 'real' as you possibly can. While talking about a state of awareness, the condition of blissfulness may seem totally unattainable and unreal. We can only suggest, at risk of being thought to be 'hippy-dippy', that you experiment for yourself.

WITNESSING

For many, creative dreaming is the epitome of how far they wish to go in understanding dreams and dreaming. However, there is a stage beyond creative dreaming which entails yet another change of consciousness. Known as 'witnessing', it is an aspect of consciousness which goes beyond the personal. Dream awareness may only be a forerunner of this state. It is one of the stages of self-contemplation which can occur in sleep. Just as we must learn to understand the pre-aware state and the manipulation of our dreams before we can rightly say that we have creative dreams, so also we must achieve awareness before we are able to reach a dispassionate observation of our dreaming selves. This state is close to that recognized in Eastern philosophies as *samadhi* or *satori*. We move along a continuum from taking part in the dream (acting within it) to observing the dream in a totally dispassionate and non-involved way.

Witnessing most often emerges spontaneously and seems to need you to go through five stages to achieve it sucessfully. The five stages of moving from 'the actor' to 'the observer' are outlined briefly below.

1. In the first stage, the focus is much more on active participation. At this stage, there is simply a recognition that the we are in the middle of a dream. The feeling is that the dream is external – beyond oneself – and that there is also an internal 'self'. You as an individual take part in the dream. There is a greater degree of wakefulness inside, but you are still tied into the figures and situations of your dream. Becoming more familiar with awareness means that you can make an attempt to manipulate the dream.

2. At some point, it may occur to you that what is apparently external to you is, in fact, 'inside' – it is occurring within the dream framework. This is the second stage. Two paths open up to you as the dreamer. You may either become fully involved in the dream episode, understanding that both the self and the dream ego are involved, or move your focus completely to the inside, allowing the dream environment to fade. While you are dreaming with awareness, you will still be aware of the dream even though caught up in its activity. It becomes easy during these initial phases to move

backwards and forwards between watching the dream in an uninvolved way and being actively aware. You can choose to manipulate the dream in some way, when the dream will continue, or you can move your attention away from the dream and become passive when it will fade or disappear.

3. Creative dreams in the third stage are usually brief. They consist of short periods of a spontaneous state of awareness that is similar to that in meditation where there is no need to interact with what is going on. Here you are learning simply to observe and to let go, without becoming involved. A meditation exercise is given the Tips and Techniques section which can help you to refine this process. The action of the dream is not particularly gripping or important, but recognizing that you are actually in this state of awareness of observing the various phenomena is. There is strictly no need to anticipate any outcome, to try to fulfil any desires, or to get caught up in any particular action.

4. In this fourth stage, an 'inner wakefulness' dominates, and there is no remembrance of having any dreams at all. All that is left is dreamless sleep. You should recognize that this is not the same as the dreamless sleep that occurs in non-REM states, however, but is a state of being where all imagery is completely eliminated and there is complete desirelessness. The Inner Self is still capable of perception, but is also aware that there is nothing separate from it to perceive. In other words, it is 'at one' with everything, but is also aware of nothing. It is a difficult thing to explain, but is a state wherein one is witnessing nothing but Self. It is the ability to remain in a state of total passivity, of beingness. There is a sense of having transcended the physical state and of suspension within a void or boundlessness.

5. Once the you have moved into this boundless state, where there is only pure consciousness, any images perceived take on the form of abstract shapes and conceptual symbols. They are almost entirely abstract and apparently without particular meaning, except that they are part of a whole. It is only their relationship with one another which gives them meaning, since there is no emotion or sensory

input associated with them. Witnessing these requires a non-judgmental appraisal of what is seen with no particular need to adjust the image. It is here that one has a real sense of what awareness is truly like, since the sense of expansiveness and light is truly all-pervading. You sense and appreciate the way that all things are interwoven. You are part of everything and everything is part of you. There is a sense of dynamic stillness – of motion and yet tranquility. Many people would not call this a dream state at all, but more a state of being, though such a feeling can only be appreciated from a state of total relaxation, coupled with a suspension of disbelief. This is truly the light of awareness.

There are really no words to describe these latter experiences. Just as the 'new' sciences of psychology and sociology had to find new words, meanings and shades of meaning to explain their findings, so these higher states of consciousness move away from mere words. They become aspects much more of feeling, sensing and 'being' in that order. Feeling can be taken as an internal state. Sensing is a slightly deeper awareness – akin to the subtle energy which, for instance, alerts an animal to danger or the human to pleasure. Being is a combination of both – an awareness of internal 'rightness' coupled with a subtle knowing that all is as it should be both inside and outside oneself.

There is only one word which describes such a state, and that is 'light'. In English, the word has two meanings – 'of little weight' and 'an appearance of brightness'; both of which are manifested in witnessing. Almost inevitably there is a sense of both weightlessness and clarity which comes with this experience. It is not something which is experienced visually, but with all the senses, and is indeed 'the light which passeth all understanding'. It is unique to each individual and yet belongs to all.

Our Inner Light

The Sufi believes that the inner light inherent in all of us is of differing strengths and only shows itself to those who wish to see it. It develops according to the understanding of the individual. Those who actively look for knowledge will have an inner light that shines more vividly. It can often be found more easily in the unconscious state, and colours the dreams of those who actively dedicate themselves to the search for knowledge. Our type of intelligence evolves from this light, not vice versa. When we have the courage to use the inner light to clarify the issues which intrigue us, we are better equipped to use the natural talents that we have.

Man is both spiritual and material, not one thing or the other. When his concerns are with more worldly matters he is more materially disposed and turned towards the more prosaic. He is more spiritual when he wants to escape the more mundane aspects of this mortal coil, and focuses on the wider issues. The difference is not a difference of type but of direction.

The dreams belonging to the two attitudes are different; materially-minded dreams are darker. If the dreamer becomes more spiritual, however, he will gradually see dreams containing more light in them and may eventually experience a vision of blinding light. This phenomenon is akin to the description of witnessing as given above.

The goal of the Sufi is to know his true self – the inner mind. To the Sufi the dream in itself is less important than becoming aware and conscious that we are dreaming. To experience the rich inner life that we have, we must dream, and those dreams come through different channels. The Sufis have named these as follows:

Kaybali is the Arabic word for dreams where the 'day's residue' is reproduced. This reproduction may happen very clearly or come across as totally confused and chaotic.

Kalbi means 'dreams of the heart'. They link fear and desire which, being closely related, tend to cloud reality. They are in fact the opposite of reality, being illusions created through the distorted mirror of fear and doubt. The distortion comes through emotion which confuses the picture of what is wanted and what is needed.

Nakshi denotes 'symbolic dreams only to be interpreted by the wise'. They show inner truths of which even the dreamer may not be aware on a conscious level. Interpretation will often lead to the True Self but can be painful and disturbing, particularly if the interpretation is coloured by someone other than us. Every detail is symbolic, being characterized by us ourselves, and deals with issues which cannot be dealt with in the conscious state. Caution is needed in the interpretation of these dreams because they may deal with parts of us that we do not want to – or indeed cannot – deal with and therefore could reveal hidden demons.

All these dreams deal with conflicts in our lives, male/female, right/wrong, inner self/outer self – or, put another way, the conflicts and choices that need to be met in both the waking and the sleeping state. Dreams use different standards to gauge what we should do compared to the waking state and can often provide a truer answer. This is because we are able to ask ourselves questions in the unconscious state that we are too afraid to confront in the conscious state. When the truer inner state senses that the conscious state has strayed wildly from the inner, there is physical difficulty and illness.

Prophetic dreams are called *ruhi* and are more comprehensive than *kalbi*. In this state, the dreamer senses rather more of the whole 'message' somewhat more objectively. *Ilhami* are divine messages shown to men where an angel or spiritual being can often be heard. Both *ruhi* and *ilhami* are more highly evolved dreams than most of us can imagine, and take on the nature of mystical experiences.

Before we are able to have such mystical experiences as a matter of course, we probably need to spend some time in developing the Spiritual Self.

DEVELOPING YOUR SPIRITUAL SELF

We have already seen how dreams can put you in touch with your inner selves, the part that is not easily revealed consciously in everyday life. Revealing this part will enrich and enhance your creativity and your ability to be the person you want to be. There is, however, a further step into the unknown which you can take if you are brave enough. It can completely alter your viewpoint, and ensure that your life will never be the same again – probably neither will the people with whom you come into contact. Through your dreams, you can develop a relationship with what some call Source, others the Ultimate, some the Centre, and yet others God.

This is the energy which has already been referred to above and is the Light of true understanding. This is not a journey which is undertaken lightly, since it requires discipline and commitment, but it is one which will delight and intrigue you. In essence, it means that you will come to accept that there is a force beyond yourself which permeates everything and allows you to be who you are – a Life Force, if you like. We have seen how creative dreaming can remove the obstacles to progress on many levels of awareness, and this final stage is about clearing away previously held concepts and beliefs which dictate that we are separate from this energy and do not have the right of access to it.

To be comfortable with this idea we must go through several stages:

• Create a new consciousness

• Develop insight from working with our dreams

• Use this to develop the Spiritual Self

• Use 'Great Dreams' to help with this process

• Develop a meaningful relationship with the Ultimate.

In the first stage there are several things that need to be accomplished in order to give us the security and stability to move to the next step. We need to use our dreamwork to clear the mind and develop an increased awareness of a source other than our own ego. In ordinary dreamwork or consideration of our dreams this means accepting the idea that beyond us there is a vast depository of information available to us – a library of all that is, was or ever shall be. This occasionally visits our dreaming self and makes some of that information available to us. The more we work with dreams, the more that information becomes available. Creative dreaming takes us one stage further in this process and allows us deliberately to seek information.

A simple technique to take us further is to use a statement of intent when preparing to have a creative dream, such as 'I wish to access the information I require'. Such a simple statement means that the knowledge then becomes available to you either through creative dreaming or in other ways – such as apparently by chance finding a book which tells you what you need to know, or perhaps overhearing a conversation. If you wish the information to come to you through creative dreaming, then your statement must reflect this: 'I wish to access the information I require through creative dreaming'. It is perhaps more satisfying to keep your parameters as wide as possible, however.

Manipulating your dream

As part and parcel of taking responsibility for your new consciousness, you probably need to look at some of your old attitudes and concepts and be prepared to let them go. This may include learning to manipulate your dreams. One of those manipulations may be to change the setting or scenario of your dream.

Many people do not feel that it is right to try to create new settings in their dreams. They feel that their minds already have the right information to create the correct scenario for whatever it is that they are trying to achieve. For them, trying to tamper with the basic components of a dream is tantamount to manipulating the very fabric of life. However, for those who are prepared to take responsibility for themselves you can use the technique of 'spinning' to change the dream scene.

When you first master the art of creative dreaming, you will have enough to do in remembering to prepare for creative dreaming, forming the intention and deciding on the subject. Once you become more proficient at doing these things, however, you can turn your attention to other aspects of the dream and begin to manipulate those. The questions you should ask yourself are:

Should I give myself permission to change the scenario?

Do I believe I *can* change it?

Expectations play such a huge part in this aspect of creative dreaming that, quite frankly, if the smallest part of you is apprehensive or anxious, the procedure will not work. It is that negativity that acts like a 'spanner in the works' and will not allow the scenes to change. You can deal with the negative thoughts by visualizing them as a dark cloud which can be absorbed into the light. Then you can operate your sense of integrity and allow yourself to become aware of the opportunities you have.

When you realize how easy it is to create an illusory scene, it will help you to be more creative in your other pursuits. You will then be able to set the scene to empower yourself to be in charge of your environment within your daily life.

Developing new attitudes

In creating a new consciousness, we can also use dreaming to develop new attitudes, as well as increasing our commitment and experience of manifesting our own connection with the Ultimate. The closer we get to our own understanding of this energy, the less the pettiness of everyday concerns will bother us. A warning has been given not to lose touch with the reality of the everyday, yet at the same time we do need to appreciate that we are able to create our own world. As we become more proficient at creative dreaming, we are more able to try out new ways of relating to others, new ways of making what we have learnt and experienced available and even new ways of being before we inflict these on others.

All too often, when we make changes, others do not understand, and we may be accused of madness, instability, wackiness and so on. Some might even accuse us of being mentally ill. Certainly as we venture further into this new way of being, we need to find a new inner stability, and again creative dreaming can assist in this process. The statement of intent needs to be as simple as possible. 'I wish to find my own inner core' or 'I wish to experience my own inner stability' will suffice.

In the next stage, it is possible to face in depth some of the key questions about ourselves and the world in which we live. From the question 'Who am I?' arises a number of thoughts. A start can now be made, however, by asking for clarity in your search, so rather than asking the straight question, you may find that it is easier to make a statement and a request. This might be, 'I wish to know who I am and therefore request clarity on this matter'. Put more simply, it might be, 'I wish to be clear on who I am'. Other philosophical questions, such as exploring Man's inhumanity to Man, could also be simplified to a statement of desire, prefacing any statement with the phrase, 'I wish to understand'. As always, a fair degree of patience with yourself (and with the universe) is required, since these are not concepts which can be absorbed in one sitting. Interestingly, meditation and creative dreaming will only give you as much information as you can handle at any one time, so you will learn to take your time anyway.

You are now in a position to be able to monitor your dreams for spiritual symbols, statements of wisdom, visitations from guiding figures and so on. Almost inevitably, to begin with, you will think you are imagining things because such appearances are fleeting and often scarcely noticeable.

As you become more proficient, however, you will find they appear more frequently. A little bit like learning to read, the 'words' become easier as you go on. With creative dreaming, you will be able to focus on such impressions and assimilate more and more information. Your affirmation of intent might be something along the lines of, 'I wish to make contact with the one who guides me' or 'I wish to deepen my understanding of the sacred meaning of numbers'.

Your Spiritual Journey

Now is also the time to experience and undertake your own spiritual journey. The shamanic journey has been practised for many years. The seeker on the spiritual path understands the need to enter a different dimension from our own in order to gain a deep understanding of the meaning of life. Spiritualists and practitioners of Eastern religions are well used to the idea of such a journey. You can now develop your own idea of your personal journey. An easy way of doing this is by a mixture of visualization and creative dreaming:

1. Visualize a path in front of you which stretches into the distance. As you see it it may be fairly straightforward, winding or perhaps not easily discernible from its surroundings. Remember that this is your construct, so how it presents itself to you will have meaning should you care to think about it. A winding path might, for instance, represent the fact that you generally choose not to accept straightforward solutions in your life. The path that is not easily seen may mean that you do not find it easy to make decisions. The interpretation is yours.

2. Now visualize yourself walking along the path and coming to a fork in the road. You must decide whether to go right or left – one way being relatively easy, the other more difficult; again it is your choice which way to go. At this point, you could choose to have a creative dream to help you to decide.

3. Remember to record and interpret your dream, this time looking for spiritual symbols and clues that can help you to conduct your life in a more spiritual way. Perhaps you will find that you wish to control your anger, monitor your behaviour towards others or perform better within the work situation. These are, of course, only examples and you will find that your own ideas make themselves felt.

4. The next step can be either a continuation of the process in the same night or at a later date. You continue to visualize yourself on the path – this time a little further along the way. Ahead of you the road goes straight forward but also has turnings to right and left where you must again choose your route. You might use either meditation or creative dreaming to progress further on your journey.

5. Repeat steps 3 and 4 as often as you feel comfortable.

6. During this time, you may like to attempt to gain some insight into yourself and the way you function. A question from the list below could be posed at each change in the road:

What am I hiding from myself or not facing?
What are my talents? What are those things I do well?
What are those things which have meaning for me?
What are my constraints? What takes me away from my comfort zone?
What are my expectations of life?
What are my desires in life?
What keeps me focused?

As you can see, you are now beginning to use dreams and dreamwork deliberately to develop your spiritual life. You may find that your dreams become more vivid and meaningful. At this point, we suggest that you step back and take stock how you wish to proceed. Hopefully the world around you is also becoming a nicer and brighter place, and you may wish to take time out to explore beautiful things such as fine art, sculpture, well written words or whatever takes your fancy. You will often be able to use creative dreaming to help you to understand the artist or author. This may give you an insight into your own creative process and the courage to experiment.

Further study

Another way in which you might wish to enhance your knowledge is by deliberately studying a religion or system of knowledge and finding out if it has meaning for you. Again, as well as reading and studying, you can use meditation and creative dreaming to round out your study. In that way, you will find that you develop a system which has personal meaning rather than following the crowd. The Archetypes, Myths and Tarot images covered in the next chapter are all good places to start. Remember to take things calmly and gently and not to experience frustration – unless this is part of your learning process!

Now you may find that you are developing the ability to experience what have been called Great Dreams. The principle of Great Dreams is well known to followers of Carl Jung, but less well known to others. Great Dreams are those which have a deeper meaning than ordinary dreams and which stay with us, requiring further interpretation and elucidation. In primitive cultures there were certain dreams which were meant to be shared with the community, and this is what Great Dreams are in essence. They are dreams which give us direction, reveal a truth or clarify an issue from a spiritual viewpoint – that is, from a wider perspective than just our own petty concerns. Through such dreams, we may gain a greater grasp of spiritual meaning. There does not seem to be any empirical evidence that creative dreaming enhances the occurrence of Great Dreams, though my personal experience would seem to show that it does.

Now it may be time to use dreamwork to transform your personality and life into a meaningful whole. Hopefully, you will now be relatively adept at making minor changes to your behaviour and the way that you relate to other people. Now you may choose to make further adjustments to take into account your new learning. This may be easy or difficult for you, but your practice in changing the scenarios in creative dreaming can help you to make small – rather than large – changes.

As you learn to follow philosophical arguments, you may find yourself spontaneously tuning in to a greater power and becoming aware of the many opportunities open to you both to change your life and the lives of those around you. Remember that you are a unique individual with your own abilities and talents, and can now make a commitment to the person you truly are and to that part of the life force which is singularly yours.

As you progress, each part of your life will take on new meaning and significance. It is more than likely that you will begin to feel that you are much more part of a greater whole. Coupled with this feeling is the realization that the aforementioned 'whole' is very large and that you are but a very small cog in the wheel. Life tends to take on greater meaning, however, and you will wish to perceive some spiritual significance in everything that you do and everything that you are. Creative dreaming is a way to help you to test your commitment to yourself as well as acclimatize yourself to the new feelings which are perfectly natural at this time.

Developing dreamwork

Another way in which you may choose to use the art of creative dreaming is to develop rituals and meditations from dreams and dreamwork. The ritual of setting out your dream journal and of preparing yourself for creative dreaming is a way of focusing your mind on the task in hand. Remembering and recording your dreams is a way of clearing your mind so that you can pay attention to the coming day.

You may like to use one of the symbols from your dreams to set the tone for your day in order to enjoy it to the full. This may give the ability to create circumstances around yourself which give rise to an advance in spiritual progress. It may be found that during the day you will recognize the need to make further adjustments in order to maximize your own potential. These can then be carried forward into lucid dreaming.

One of the best outcomes of working with dreams is that it enables us to link with a huge stream of healing energies which allows us to help ourselves and others. Those symbols and flashes of light which we saw at the beginning of our experiments with creative dreaming now take on a different meaning and can be recognized as indications of healing power. We can begin to use these symbols in everyday life to help us to focus within in order to help us to work with others. A circle, for instance, can be a symbol for wholeness, or indeed an arrow can suggest the correct direction. The more we work on our dreams, the greater we develop our own personal dictionary of symbols.

Dream symbols appear from the unconscious, so, having been brought into focus, they need to be assimilated in such a way that they become an integral part of our everyday life. They need to be contemplated perhaps with the help of creative dreaming from a state of dynamic awareness (a clear, functioning mind) and for this you need to be completely relaxed. Any relaxation techniques that work for you can be used and a simple one is given in the previous chapter.

There are three ways in which you can work with any symbol in your dreams.

1. The first is to allow it to come 'alive' for you, that is, to move from being simply an image in your dream to something that you give relevance to in your ordinary everyday life – the guide or 'wise old man' is one such figure.

2. The second way is to allow the symbol to develop further – to observe it and to watch what happens. Let us suppose that a violent storm has been experienced in the dream. Symbolically this can represent an upcoming problem, our own suppressed passion or even, for some people, the intensity of their spiritual belief. Only by being prepared to watch and wait can we be certain of its real meaning for us. Given the opportunity, the symbol will clarify exactly what is intended.

3. The third way is to allow the symbol to devolve – that is, to go back to basics. For those other than experienced meditators or creative dreamers this is a little more difficult to accomplish, although the technique of watching and waiting with your purpose in mind usually works. To dream of a pool of water, for instance, might by association take us to a contemplation of water, of rain, clouds and of the complexity of your own emotional makeup.

You have now come a long way in your exploration of creative dreaming and how it can affect your life. It is now perhaps time to take things a stage further and give you some suggestions which you can use as potent dream images to enhance your dreams even more.

ENHANCING YOUR DREAMS

There are many schools of thought to do with creative dreaming. Some hold that it is useless to start with an image, while others feel that it is easier to affect the dream if we have an image to start with. Simply let it be said that, as always, it is a matter of personal preference, and whichever way works for you is right. If both are equally good, then you are particularly fortunate.

Almost inevitably when working with images and dreams – and also in the field of self-development – we need to find and cultivate the tools that work best for us. In this section, I am putting forward some of my own particular favourites which have helped in my search for self-fulfilment and knowledge. Because the truths they articulate are so universal, these tools are widely used, albeit probably tailored to fit people's individual requirements. Any errors or biases you may suspect in this section are totally mine, so by all means do some research of your own and make your judgements accordingly.

At difficult periods in our lives, such tried and tested ways forward are both comforting and challenging. Having a positive frame of mind when trying to make progress inevitably helps. So, having left behind the difficult transition periods of life and come to an understanding of some of the traumas and vicissitudes that most of us face at one time or another, you may like to widen your own search to encompass some aspect of universal knowledge.

Please bear in mind that the techniques throughout this book are good not just for creative dreaming but also for developing the art of dreaming creatively. All of the suggested tools in this section – Archetypes, the balance between the masculine and feminine sides of ourselves, the Tarot, myths and astrology – are closely inter-connected. Over the years, they have been used by numerous individuals in many different ways to help in the understanding of the art of being human. They are offered here in the spirit of discovery in order to help you onwards on your own journey.

ARCHETYPES

In the Middle Ages, long before the advent of modern psychology, it was thought that every man carried a woman inside himself. Although it was Jung who first gave a name to the Anima (the feminine within) and to the various parts of the personality, and also recognized man's potential for developing symbols as a way of understanding himself and others, it had long been recognized that there was a duality in the way man thought. It is as though there was some kind of internal pendulum which eventually sorted out the opposing concepts into a unified whole. Nowadays we are aware that the unconscious mind appears to sort information by comparing and contrasting. When we are aware of disharmony within ourselves, whether this is between the inner and the outer selves, the masculine and feminine or whatever, we may dream in pairs (e.g. masculine/feminine, old/young, clever/stupid). Dreams have always been used to make sense of those things which are not understood in everyday terms, and it is perhaps sensible right at the beginning to define those parts of the character which have been accepted in the modern day to have a validity of their own.

There are three main aspects of the personality which continually manifest in dreams - the Shadow, the Animus or Anima and the Ego. Most of us become aware of these facets of personality when they can no longer be denied or suppressed, and much can be gained by working with the images which come up in dreams. Sometimes the images are of people we know, sometimes fictitious figures, or those from myths and fairy tales and sometimes images such as animals and birds.

The most forbidding aspect of the individual has been called the Shadow and is the characteristic of the most basic of our defects and shortcomings. Because of its shocking and unruly qualities it is the part that we instinctively subdue; it eventually manifests as the same gender as we are. Then there is the Anima in man and the Animus in woman – that component of the opposite sex inherent in the dreamer. In a man, it is all that is intuitive, feminine and perceptive. In a woman, it is her masculine properties of reason and impartiality. We look in detail at the Anima and Animus on page 138. Lastly, the True Self, the part which most often makes its appearance in dreams, is the most truly creative of all once it has been allowed the right to express itself.

Inner development happens as we grasp and harmonize each of

these aspects of our identity. Each part of the character has to develop on its own without confusing the purpose of the others. As each aspect expands, we are able to make use of more and more energy, but it is important to manage any initial disharmony which may arise. When this disharmony does make itself felt, there is no way that the individual should be harmed by the process, for while the effect may be distressing, it highlights an inner difficulty which, when handled, is ultimately beneficial. The communication and flow of energy between the various parts has the potential to increase and sharpen our makeup to the point where those aspects of the character first seen as separate entities can be blended into a harmonious and powerful whole.

The Ego

When in the dream state you become aware of what is happening the part that notices is the Ego. Our most conscious aspect, it tends to be more observant in dreams of the hostility it shows up with other aspects.

When the Ego has become divided from other aspects of the psyche, we do not appreciate the world in which we live in the best way possible. There is the danger of one becoming self-seeking and discouraging, having problems in connecting to others and often unable to tolerate anything other than one's own personal point of view. When this type of response goes too far, other attitudes come into effect and dreams make an attempt to redress the balance. If we are wise we will at that point use the skill of being able to dream with awareness to hasten the process.

The Ego is the aspect inside us that monitors our waking life and how we fit into the world, but often this can become grossly distorted and inaccurate. Being prepared to work with impartial self-criticism, taking note of the way in which we create fantasies and develop inner peace of mind can help us to control the wayward parts of the personality.

The correct self-control needed to balance the internal self and the one which deals with the external world is the delicate equilibrium between rationalism and emotion. This means that the Ego must be controlled, but can never be totally given up.

The Shadow (a figure of the same sex as the dreamer)

In the first instance this figure appears to be of the opposite sex and consequently becomes misconstrued as the Animus or Anima, depending on the gender of the dreamer. Only later do we acknowledge as the same sex as ourselves. It becomes visible in a dream as the character who we cannot identify and sometimes appears behind us. It is the disregarded part of us that we have failed to cultivate. Within it is hidden much that has been subdued and prevented from reaching maturity – as well as those aspects which, in truth, have never been understood.

Everybody has their personal Shadow and it is generally the most negative side of them that has deliberately not been recognized. Confronting the Shadow is distressing: it is the torment of viewing ourselves as we actually are at our lowest ebb. When we are capable of facing this gruesome entity with control, we are able to believe in ourselves, because from that recognition we acquire the ability to see the rest of existence genuinely. This leads to better consideration of others, and of new perceptions of the unconscious. When the nerve to confront the Shadow is acquired, admitting its reality and recognizing it for what it is, we are then adequately equipped to produce a genuine state of being rather than some tortuous fantasy. Those creative instincts that we have can then be resurrected – artistic aptitudes and potentials that have up till now consciously been repressed and buried along with the spiteful and damaging aspects of the self. This essential energy, when controlled and understood, becomes an impetus for progression rather than a dangerous foe. We are able to face our demons and prevail.

One way to consciously meet the Shadow is for you to ponder all the things you despise most about other people. Then add to that all that is found difficult to come to terms with in the human race's management of itself – this person is the representation of the Shadow. This will be a reasonably correct image of your own personal Shadow. Your first response is to be grateful that you are most definitely unlike that, but if you ask those close to you if those attributes are inherent in you, the reply is likely to be 'yes'. When we can genuinely highlight examples of the same type of behaviour within ourselves, the movement to totality is gathering pace! Often there will be an unforgettable disgust of a certain set of distinctive peculiarities which, if we are honest with ourselves, alarm us because they are simmering beneath the surface within us. Homophobic conduct is an example in many men, because many are troubled by their own sensitivity and artistic ability.

The Shadow frequently shows itself in dreams as someone we

unreservedly dislike, are scared of, or are jealous of and as someone we can't ignore. A true growth process is begun when we embrace a significant transformation in life that will give us a chance to bring the Shadow to the fore rather than hoping that it will disappear. When negative dream images are actively encouraged and dealt with, these harmful energies need not be projected onto others and thus can be utilized to diffuse defensive behaviour. Within the environment of creative dreaming, experimentation and 'playing' with different sets of behaviour can take place, learning to cope with the grotesqueness of the Shadow before finally gaining its help.

Without the creativity that comes with using the Shadow, we place ourselves in jeopardy of living in a world of delusion. Our lives lose substantial weight when we only centre on one type of perception – either internal or external. Different people look at things in opposite ways and often gain from a change in viewpoint. The introspective character benefits from encountering life changes from the 'outside' and vice versa for the extroverted. Experiencing creative dreaming allows us to practise new behaviour without harming anyone.

The Self
The Self is the archetype of the capabilities we possess. Always present, but hidden behind the prerequisite progress of the personality, the Self holds the secret of the integrated personality. The Shadow and Animus/Anima have almost always been neglected on purpose, whereas the Self is only gradually revealed. Because the latent possibilities beckon from the future, the first experience in dream form may be a figure encouraging us to move forward. Later it can develop into an icon of completeness with which we are capable of working in our waking lives to create a sustainable future.

There is within everyone an unknown, unknowable higher spiritual quality which becomes available to each of us as we make the effort to reach out further and further beyond ourselves to try to understand the world in which we live. Our own experience and the use we make of our awareness is unique but it is based on universal knowledge. It is an inner guidance which cries out to be understood, and gives access to unfathomable information which must, with practice, be applied to everyday life.

Often this aspect presents itself in dreams as a holy figure according to our perceived belief. Thus it may be recognized as Christ, Buddha, Krishna or some similar figure. As you become more efficient at dealing with – and understanding – the information you receive in your creative dreams, your perception of the energy of the manifestation changes and you are more likely to perceive it as light. You no longer have need of a personalized image on which to focus. This is akin to the perceptions present in the state of witnessing (see page 118), and is an awareness of the fact that we are all part of a multi-faceted totality. Each of us is at one and the same time an individual but also part of a greater interactive whole.

When images of this archetype, such as a guru, god, an animal with virtuous qualities, a cross, a mandala or other geometric shape begin to appear in dreams, you are ready to face the process of becoming whole. By becoming more aware of a greater spiritual reality, you are capable of moving beyond a self-centred approach to life. There is at this time the potential for a great deal of confusion, but if you have taught yourself creative dreaming you are able to separate reality from illusion and thus recognize the call of the material world contrasted with the requirements of the spiritual. By recognizing that you are dreaming, you are able to prioritize your responsibilities in such a way that you can achieve a conscious balance between the two. You can then use creative dreaming to work out the correct course of action to maintain that balance.

When negative or destructive images occur connected with this element of the personality, you need to be aware that you are neglecting the power of the Self. It is often at this point that you will make a decision to advance and to change for the better. Unfortunately if you do not, change will usually be forced upon you.

A Woman's Self

Each and every woman is the essence of feminine dynamism. Her prime concern is the intangible quality in life, her own instinct and perceptive abilities. Her skills manifest themselves through that capacity for perception, along with empathy, intelligence and intuition. She recognizes the processes of life, death and rebirth. While often perceiving her prime function as being that of procreation, she also understands herself to be ruthlessly destructive of anything she sees as being without perfection.

Each individual woman attempts to express each facet of her personality as fully as she can. She will often try to compensate for her perceived deficiencies by pursuing balance in her relationships with men. These relationships will only work if she understands that in doing this she is developing the less versatile side of her personality. Her partner must grow and change with her, lest his lack of understanding prevents her from developing her true potential.

The Great Mother/Mother Earth

This archetype is not the wholly matriarchal aspect of woman, but is a more enhanced ethereal inner sense of her Self. She is the true epitome of all the attitudes of the feminine, both positive and negative. This is the symbol of totality in a woman, and is the aptitude for using all aspects of her character.

In aiming for this excellence, a woman must use and promote all the separate functions of her being. She must attempt to use perception, opinion, intelligence and intuition as tools rather than weapons. Her domain is all life's rich pattern, including an innate perception of the way it works. Her attributes can be cultivated in as many ways as there are women.

Creative dreaming is a wonderful tool for helping us to work with these aspects of the personality in seclusion and safety.

A Man's Self

A man's self will express itself much more through intellect, logic and conscious awareness, although today's society can mean that he will deny the intuitive function. Each person again matures by developing the functions of thinking or intellect, sensation, emotion and intuition.

For a man in this day and age the process of separation from the mother is understood as a process of individuation and development, and the need to be separate from – and yet connected with – his unconscious self. If a man loses himself too much on an intellectual, logical level, his dreams will begin to depict the danger he is in. Provided he remembers not to try to counteract his inner self by developing the macho side of himself at the cost of everything else, he will reach a state of equilibrium which allows him to relate to the rest of the world on his own terms. He will achieve a coherence which allows him to operate properly as a human being. He will not seek to express his inadequacies through his relationships or need to do so through his dreams.

The Wise Old Man
Like the Great Mother, the Wise Old Man is the synthesized figure of all the masculine characteristics when they are both recognized for their power and integrated into the personality. When a person understands that the best guidance arises from deep within himself the Wise Old Man puts in an appearance in dreams, sometimes as an authority figure, sometimes as magical. Only when you have learnt to access the deeper recesses of your unconscious you become able to consult your own personalization of a mentor friend and source of inspiration. Sometimes this personalization appears in times of deep trouble, offering help and solace when all other forms of help have disappeared.

All of the functions of sensation, feeling, thinking and intuition appear in the Wise Old Man, who thus gives a suitable focus for creative dreaming.

Anima/Animus (a figure of the opposite sex to the dreamer)
There is a representation of wholeness belonging to yoga which expresses almost all that needs to be said about internal balance. This is known as the *pak wa,* below:

Each part, positive and negative, contains within it an element of the other. In Chinese philosophy the feminine is negative and passive, and the masculine is positive and active. It is now generally accepted that from a psychological point of view each person holds within themselves an idealized version of their opposite – the Animus or Anima represents that part of the Self which is the opposite sex. This is part of the inner self which must be revealed and understood if the personality is to achieve a proper comprehension of itself.

Through dreams we are able to grasp the idiosyncrasies and quirks of character which differentiate us from everybody else. There may often be disharmony between the inner and outer being; there is always a danger that we will project onto others that part of ourselves which is not easily found, or the disharmony that is not easily managed. In personal relationships this can cause misapprehension and difficulty in seeing your partner clearly. Once, however, some kind of balance is established, the whole character can become more integrated and, indeed, more of an entity.

No one person can quite approximate to the feminine side of any masculine personality or vice versa. If you can allow yourself to come to terms with the hidden masculine or feminine and accept them for what they are, they become the basis of your understanding of the opposite sex. They also help you to open up to your inner realms. These inner figures are known as the Anima and the Animus.

It is unfortunate that when the potential for balance between the masculine and feminine aspects of a personality is overlooked or mistreated, in due course the individual will probably not be able to appreciate significant aspects of the opposite sex. This is likely to affect their attitude and conduct within intimate relationships.

Anima
Dreams try to heal conscious attitudes which are not properly aligned. The Anima – that is, the emotional and intuitive side of man's nature – tends to appear in dreams as a completely unknown woman, aspects of women he has known, or as feminine deities when he is not paying sufficient attention to the feminine side of himself. When he ignores the attributes of tenderness, obedience and sensitivity which are available to him, he puts himself in jeopardy and runs the risk of moodiness and temper tantrums.

As he becomes more aware of the feminine principle, he will realize that principally his mother, but additionally all the women he has known, have helped to form his perception of the feminine, thus giving focus to all the feminine forces within himself. With understanding and the ability to work with them, particularly with creativity, his dreams will show him how to be more able to develop warmth and genuine feeling and to accept the feminine qualities of openness, sympathy and other such sensitive and adaptable characteristics. Should he not be able to harmonize these feminine qualities, he may well be viewed as inflexible, obstinate or indecisive.

Often, instead of recognizing the Anima as an aspect of his own self which should be an accomplice, a man will project it onto an unobtainable 'object', avoiding proper contact with the opposite sex. Alternatively, he will cast his own distorted image of the feminine onto any woman he encounters, not understanding when all women seem to have the same faults, that it is his projection. When that inner feminine is frustrated, the Anima turns into a completely negative, destructive illusion. The Anima becomes a guide to inner wisdom only when the man learns how to handle the energy he has available, and stops his projection.

Animus

The Animus usually appears in dreams when there is the necessity for a woman to recognize and develop the masculine side of herself. This does not mean becoming loud and aggressive but does mean understanding the rational, considered parts of her personality and being able to make use of them. Her masculine side is influenced primarily by early contact with masculine energy. If, for instance, the men in her immediate family have made no effort to develop an understanding of themselves, a woman's Animus will later show evidence of that lack of understanding, perhaps in her behaviour towards others, including men. While the Animus manifests completely differently for each woman, she will be capable of using it as an inner guide only when she has taken pains to appreciate that side of her personality.

There is a danger of a woman not having the courage of her own convictions sufficiently to question conventional belief, such as her perceived lack of success. She has accepted other people's viewpoints but does not develop her own judgement. This can be destructive for herself and others. When able to develop her own determination she can then use the masculine within to manage her life better.

Relationships will fail over and over again for the same reasons until a woman can accept that she continually projects her own misperceptions onto her partners. Continuously she will suffer disappointment and disillusionment from her man until she realizes that she is only trying to reflect her own masculine side – her Animus, in fact. When she is prepared to mature and grow, the relationships she has will do likewise.

When in dreams the Animus continues to make itself known, it is time for a woman to make use of creative dreaming so that she gives herself the opportunity to develop clarity of thought and a workable strategy for life, by deliberately making use of her intuition. If, however, the negative side of the Animus dictates her way of thinking and planning, she may become stubborn and self-opinionated, feeling that men and life owe her fulfilment.

Masculine/Feminine Archetypes

There are various aspects of being which correspond to the basic four functions of sensing, feeling, thinking and intuition. As an easy way of coming to an understanding of how you handle relationships, it is possible to build up a kind of map of the interaction which goes on between these functions and how you use them in everyday life.

Following Carl Jung's work to identify these functions, it has been accepted that we all hold within us, at a very deep level, a series of basic 'pictures' which symbolize each function. These functions will frequently present themselves in dreams in recognizable ways to enable us to work with the distortions which may have been forced upon us through experience, perception and socialization in our everyday waking lives.

Each of the masculine and feminine sides of the personality has these four functions. In addition each function has a 'greater' and 'lesser' quality which have been designated as 'positive' and 'negative'. This is not strictly correct, but does pick up on the idea that some types of personality are less appropriate and meaningful than others. Each of us would do well to explore our reactions to all of these aspects of our personality in an effort to achieve an inner balance, since there are 64 (8 x 8) interactions possible.

Some of these interactions you are less comfortable with than others, and these will give you most difficulty in everyday life. For instance, you may find that you are continually in situations in the work place where you make your boss angry. With understanding, you will be able to discover whether your view is the distorted one, and you have been relying too heavily on the competitive side of your personality, or whether his or her perception of you is at fault and their Ogre or Destructive Mother is coming to the fore (see below). In other words this clash of personalities is in fact a projection of an inner conflict in both of you. By learning to use creative dreaming properly to resolve the conflict, you will both learn to cope with your own distortion and not accept the other's projection of their difficulty.

Perfect balance would be achieved by using all aspects of the personality as shown below, but in order to do this it is first necessary to have a concept of the archetypes or basic pictures.

MALE	FEMALE	POSITIVE/ NEGATIVE	FUNCTION
KINDLY FATHER OGRE	KINDLY MOTHER DESTRUCTIVE MOTHER	+ -	SENSATION
YOUTH TRAMP	PRINCESS SIREN	+ -	FEELING
HERO VILLAIN	AMAZON COMPETITOR	+ -	THINKING
PRIEST SORCERER	PRIESTESS WITCH	+ -	INTUITION

Feminine Archetypes

The feminine archetypes, in more detail, are:

Kindly Mother: This is the conventional picture of the caring mother figure, forgiving transgression and always understanding. Because much has been made of this side of femininity, until recently it was very easy to overdevelop this aspect at the expense of other sides of the personality.

Destructive Mother: This woman may be the 'smother-mother' type or the frankly destructive, prohibitive mother – the mother who prevents the adequate growth of her children. Often, it is this aspect that either actively prevents or – because of its effect on the dreamer – causes difficulty in other one-to-one relationships.

Princess: The fun-loving, innocent, child-like aspect of femininity. She is totally spontaneous, but at the same time has a subjective approach to other people. When thwarted, she will often become petulant and difficult.

Siren: This type is the seductress, the sexually and sensually aware woman who still has a sense of her own importance and power. In dreams she often appears in historic, flowing garments as though to highlight the erotic image.

Amazon: The self-sufficient woman feels she does not need support or the male; she often becomes the career woman. She enjoys the cut and thrust of intellectual sparring, and is often known as the strategist.

Competitor: She is the woman who competes with all and sundry – both men and women – in an effort to prove that she is able to control her own life, and probably those of others around her.

Priestess: This is the highly intuitive woman who has learnt to control the flow of information and use it for the common good. She is totally at home within the inner intuitive world.

Witch: This intuitive woman uses her energy to attain her own perceived ends. She is somewhat subjective in her judgement and therefore tends to lose her discernment. Often seen as negative, she can nevertheless be a tremendous force for change.

Masculine Archetypes
The masculine archetypes, in detail, are:

Kindly Father: This side of the masculine is the conventional kindly father figure who is capable of looking after the child in us, but equally capable of being firm and fair.

Ogre: This represents the angry, overbearing, aggressive and frightening masculine figure. Often this image has arisen because of the original relationship the dreamer had with their father or father figure. The ogre particularly represents masculine anger used negatively.

Youth: The fun-loving, curious aspect of the masculine is both sensitive and creative. This is often the 'Peter Pan' figure who has never grown up. There is a sense of adventure about him.

Tramp: This is the real freedom-lover, the wanderer, the gypsy. He owes no allegiance to anyone and is interested only in what lies around the next corner. He owes loyalty to no one but himself and is often seen as the pleasure-seeker.

Hero: The hero is the man who has chosen to undertake his own journey of exploration. He is able to consider alternatives and to determine his next move with relative ease. Often he appears as the Messianic figure in dreams. He will rescue the damsel in distress, but only as part of his own growth process.

Villain: The villain is completely arrogant and self-involved, not caring who he tramples on in his own search for autonomy. He is often the aspect of masculinity a woman first meets in everyday relationships, so can remain in dream images as a threatening figure if she has not come to terms with his selfishness.

Priest: The intuitive man is the one who recognizes and understands the power of his own intuition, but who usually uses it in the service of his god or gods. He may appear in dreams as the shaman or pagan priest.

Sorcerer: This is the man who uses discernment in a totally dispassionate way for neither good nor evil, but simply because he enjoys the use of his inherent power. In his more negative aspect, he is the Trickster or Master of unexpected change.

Discover your attitude to relationships

Your way of relating will depend on many factors: your perceptions as a child, the way your family handle such matters, how you have expressed your own gender and even the way your astrological chart dictates your life. An additional area which can be considered is the masculine/feminine archetypes; it can be very useful for you, when trying to work out your interrelationships, to experiment with them.

The matrix overleaf sets out the masculine/feminine archetypes in an easy to understand format so you can ask some questions. What you ask yourself each time is 'Do I think that (Archetype) has a good/bad/indifferent relationship with (Archetype)?' Depending on whether you are masculine or feminine, you will score the chart slightly differently. You might find it easier to use two pens of different colours to score your results.

If you are a man, you will place the masculine archetype first and decide on the relationship with the feminine, thus 'Does Kindly Father have a good/bad or indifferent relationship with Kindly Mother, Destructive Mother?' etc. Then, 'Does Ogre have a good/bad or indifferent relationship with Kindly Mother, Destructive Mother?' etc. Do this for each masculine archetype.

The next step for a man is to score the chart from his feminine viewpoint. The question then becomes 'Does Kindly Mother have a good/bad/indifferent relationship with Kindly Father, Ogre, Youth?' etc. We suggest that you use a tick for a good relationship, a cross for a bad relationship and a dot for an indifferent one.

If you are a woman, scoring will be slightly different, in that you will place the feminine archetype first. 'Does Kindly Mother have a good/bad/indifferent relationship with Kindly Father, Ogre, Youth?' etc. Then, 'Does Destructive Mother have a good/bad/indifferent relationship with Kindly Father, Ogre, Youth?' etc. Then score the chart from a masculine viewpoint: 'Does Kindly Father have a good/bad/indifferent relationship with Kindly Mother, Destructive Mother?' etc.

There are 8 x 8 (64) relationships which occur within each of us led by our gender (sex), and 8 x 8 (64) which occur led by our Animus or Anima depending on our gender. There will be 128 marks of one sort or another on the matrix. There are no right or wrong answers, only your own beliefs. You are now ready to score your matrix.

YOUR ARCHETYPE MATRIX

	KINDLY FATHER	OGRE	YOUTH
KINDLY MOTHER			
DESTRUCTIVE MOTHER			
PRINCESS			
SIREN			
AMAZON			
COMPETITOR			
PRIESTESS			
WITCH			
Score			

TRAMP	HERO	VILLAIN	PRIEST	SORCERER	Score

- Add up the number of ticks in each column and row and enter the total in the appropriate box.

- Add up both crosses and dots and enter into the appropriate box. For the purposes of this part of the exercise, bad and indifferent relationships are considered together. When you have time, you may wish to consider the indifferent relationship score to discover whether you wish to work on such relationships and how they manifest in your life. The totals will always reach 16. Broadly, any score on the right hand which is eight or over needs consideration. Your score box for the bottom line will look something like this.

	KF	O	Y	T	H	V	P	S	Score
A									9/7
C									4/12
P									8/8
W									11/5
Score	10/6	5/11	12/4	10/6	8/8	7/9	14/2	3/13	

- Thus, if the scorer is male he is likely to have problems with his own anger, recognizes his potential to be a Hero but can be totally ruthless if necessary (Villain) and is not likely to like using his own inner powers or may use them badly (Sorcerer). In his relationships with women, he will have difficulty with those who try to compete with him, but will be able to handle women who are more altruistic than maternal (Priestess).

- If the scorer is female, she might have difficulty in handling masculine anger and be attracted to, but at the same time repelled by, the manipulative male (Villain/Sorcerer). Her response is likely to be to try to compete with someone showing these qualities. This would make for a very lively relationship.

Anyone looking at this exercise from a scientific viewpoint would recognize that our methods could be seen to be flawed. However, as a rough and ready guide to enable you to make changes in your life, it is an effective tool. Using the technique of creative dreaming, you might structure your dream to confront an archetype with which you have considerable difficulty. For instance, in the examples above, the male might wish to confront or get to know his Sorcerer in order to enhance his life. If he were very brave, he might incubate a dream by using the phrase 'I wish to understand competitive women'. Being aware that he is dreaming would allow him to have some control over the process and in the dream perhaps turn negative responses into positive ones.

THE TAROT

The Tarot (which means 'truth') is possibly one of the most fascinating triggers which can be used for creative dreaming. Recognized as a kind of universal record which has resonated for many centuries across numerous cultures, the representation of the meanings of the cards is usually very beautiful. Though at one time there was a conventional sequence in which the cards were designed for use, this no longer applies. It is often a matter of personal preference for the designer.

For the purposes of creative dreaming, we suggest using only the Major Arcana, which consists of 22 cards which traces Man's journey through life. Later you may progress to using the Minor Arcana – a further 56 cards – but only when you feel ready to explore your own psyche further.

There are many different packs you can choose from. To choose your own pack you should give yourself the opportunity of looking at and handling as many packs as possible. There are now so many available that it would be impossible to suggest which one might be suitable, but we would suggest that you choose a simple one to begin with. You will usually find yourself drawn to the right ones. Any New Age store or bookshop will usually have examples for consideration and will order the less easily obtainable for you. If you are going to use your cards solely as a tool for creative dreaming, then it is suggested that when you first buy them you spend a little time with them just appreciating them for what they are. Keep them with your dream journal, so that working with them becomes part of your nightly routine.

I. The Fool

This card shows a traveller on a journey without an agenda in the world. Like the joker in ordinary playing cards, the Fool travels light. Often shown with a bundle in his hand and with a dog at his feet, he is seen at the beginning of life's journey. As he sets out with great naïveté not realizing the pleasures and the difficulties which lie ahead, he has no concept that at the end of that journey he will have no qualms about flying when he steps forward into a new beginning.

II. The Magician

Man is distinct from the beast because he has both mind and spirit which, with training, he can use. The magician shows his duality by being part of heaven and earth; and is capable of untold potential. He is often pictured indicating both heaven and earth (as above, so below), sometimes wearing a hat that represents infinity. He is often perceived as Mercury, the messenger of the gods. By the time the traveller reaches this stage, the magician is able to offer the gifts of intuition; those inner resources must be used as a guide to the best way forward.

III. The High Priestess

The High Priestess, as she stands in front of the doorway to the unconscious, represents hidden or secret knowledge and the occult sciences. She is pictured as a young woman, often holding a pomegranate (suggesting the fullness of life). Seen by many as Persephone in her role as Queen of the Underworld, sometimes veiled, she depicts all the potential of our dreaming selves. As the first representative of the feminine in the Tarot, her image leads us deeper in to the unconscious and all the wisdom that it reveals.

IV. The Empress

Here we have woman and mother and also domestic happiness – the female life-giving force. She is the feminine ruler, counsellor, open to all, practical and decisive. Shown often as a pregnant woman, richly dressed, she epitomizes fertility. In her negative aspect, she may be destructive and vengeful but nevertheless holds out a promise of things to come. As the archetypal mother, she offers an understanding of the mothering function for male and female alike.

V. The Emperor

Crowned and seated, he represents man in his positive aspects: willpower, authority, strength and courage. Usually depicted facing towards the reader, he suggests the benevolent father figure, though sometimes in danger of abusing power and becoming tyrannical. He offers a concept of authority in worldly matters, coupled with intelligence and sensibility. Sometimes it is important to come to terms with our father or father figure before we can become adults in our own right.

VI. The Hierophant

The hierophant characterizes knowledge, enlightenment, asceticism and inspiration. In the quest for spiritual understanding, we need to build bridges and form bonds we would not necessarily otherwise make. Often depicted as a priest with power over temporal life, he gives the impression of understanding and knowing his own mind. While not connected with religion as such, it is often in meeting the hierophant that the traveller along the way clarifies his attitude to spiritual belief.

VII. The Lovers

Here the masculine and feminine unite together in harmony, each having learnt about themselves and each other. Usually portrayed as two young people hand in hand, there is often a third figure in between. This represents the dilemma caused when someone else must be considered. Also standing for youthful indecisiveness, uncertainty and instability, it can mark a new stage of existence.

VIII. The Chariot

Suggesting the successful balancing of alternatives and forward progression, this card represents the harnessing and control of forces. It is also conquest and advancement over physical nature through using the finer forces controlled by one's spiritual nature. Usually shown as a man controlling two horses – sometimes pulling in different directions –

the chariot is often canopied, suggesting protection of the highest order. This card can also indicate the choices that we must make in moving forward to a better future. Seen as Apollo riding daily across the sky, he promises better things to come.

IX. Justice
Depicted as a wise figure holding scales with which to weigh one's choices and a sword, this card is encountered when we need to establish equilibrium in our lives. Impartiality, balanced judgement, integrity and arbitration are all qualities associated with the card of Justice. Also suggesting fairness and discipline, it represents the ability to discriminate and to make wise choices. Such choices do, however, require a dispassionate approach, and if this is absent there can be poor judgement or legal trouble.

X. The Hermit
Derived from loneliness, fear, poverty and despondency, this is an isolated character with few possessions. Often shown as a cloaked figure carrying a lamp, he represents the passage of time and especially times of solitude. There is a duality about this card, in that the hermit can rely totally upon himself or can choose to accept alms from other people. We must all spend time alone in order to appreciate the richness of relationship.

XI. The Wheel of Fortune
This is the card of chance, fate and luck. It also represents the wheel of life with its ever-changing fortunes. Usually shown with one figure climbing the wheel and another falling off, it stands for the cyclical nature of life. It is sometimes shown with a figure strapped to it when it stands more for the Karmic wheel – those things in our lives which bind us to a physical existence. Sometimes it represents the unlucky influences that we draw towards ourselves.

XII. Strength
The card of strength depicts the natural energy of willpower and courage. Often shown as a man overcoming a beast, usually a lion, it stands for those inner qualities of passion and dignity that must be tamed before the individual can continue on his journey. Those lower

animal impulses need to be channelled, not with aggression but with compassion and understanding. Only in this way can the seeker of truth recognize 'higher qualities' which will enable him to develop into the person he knows he can be.

XIII. The Hanged Man

This card suggests sacrifice but also an element of dedication. The image is usually one of a man hanging upside down with his hands tied behind his back. However, he never appears to be in distress, having accepted his fate and the need to cast off material values. In the journey towards truth, it is a turning point where limitations are recognized in favour of a simple act of faith. Understanding this brings inspiration and regeneration, but he is no way a martyr, for he recognizes the value of a new life.

XIV. Death

Death in the physical sense is nothing but a new beginning; so the real meaning of this card is actually radical change. Seen as a transition from one stage of life to another, it also stands for liberation and transformation. Usually shown as the figure of the Grim Reaper or as Time, death marks the end of life as we have accepted it until now. Also signifying loss, this card suggests the loss of the ego in favour of something finer and greater.

XV. Temperance

This card represents the first stage of a new existence, picturing life, fecundity and balance. Always somewhere within the image is shown water flowing in two directions – often between two chalices, vessels or cups. This signifies the flow of life between the two dimensions of the physical and the spiritual. Energy in its purest form is an integral part of the way that the traveller empowers himself to move forward, and this card gives the first intimation of future pleasures.

XVI. The Devil

Following the first glimpse of bliss, the traveller then must meet the Devil. This is his own internal gremlin, his base instincts, especially those of a sexual nature. The Devil personifies all his fears rolled into one. The picture, often seen as the conventional devil figure, usually suggests that there is some ambiguity over whether we are ruled by our basic instincts or have power over them. This is again a point of choice where the traveller can either return to the pleasures of the flesh or move towards a more spiritual existence.

XVII. The Tower

The lightning-struck tower demonstrates the breakdown of structure which may have been seen as suitable until now. The image is a powerful one, showing how previously held ideals and concepts can be swept aside by some kind of revelation. Things will never be the same again, and the traveller must accommodate himself to new sensations, feelings and emotional problems. Often seen as a negative card, the outcome of such a breakdown is in fact usually ultimately positive.

XVIII. The Star

After the cataclysm of the Tower, the traveller must now recognize hope and a new aim or objective. The image is regenerative, showing a gentle light cast upon those things which until now have remained hidden. Possibly at a very low ebb, all the energies must now be concentrated into faith in the future and new beginnings. There are, or rather will be, new opportunities to prove our worth. Previous transgressions can be forgiven or left in the past.

XIX. The Moon

The journey of the soul now begins to return to a consideration of aspects of the feminine as part of a greater duality. The moon is often pictured as a mysterious feminine figure with three faces representing the maid, the mother and the crone. In actuality, the moon signifies the unconscious and all of the deeper understanding of life that that entails. She is intuition, limitless knowledge and a sense of inevitability. Since it represents dreams, daydreams and fantasies, it is an ideal card with which to practise creative dreaming. The moon suggests obscurity, but is also the door between the unconscious, inspiration and prophecy.

XX. The Sun

The Sun stands for the energy and power of the consciousness to overcome the darkness. In contrast to the darkness of the moon, the sun stands out in all its bright glory. It is masculine and powerful in its intent. It enables the weary traveller on life's journey to grow in stature and to appreciate the sheer joy of life. Even when adversely affected, it still bodes well. It foretells a time of clarity, trust and optimism – a coming to terms with all that we are.

XXI. Judgement

Before the traveller can take his place within the world, he must stand in judgement on himself – only he can judge his actions, joys and sorrows. The representation is usually of a figure of judgement revealing the skeletons from the past. With new knowledge, we can forgive others and ourselves for our lack of perception and understanding. Past deeds must be looked at and justified in the light of present knowledge before we move on.

XXII. The World

This is the final card in the Tarot journey before the Fool begins again on another cycle of existence; it signifies completion. Usually shown as or named The Universe, the image is one of totality. The problems and difficulties of the journey have been conquered, enabling the individual to take up the position he has won in the cosmic dance. He has attained a state of unity and is within the world, but not of it. He now has the right to a well-regulated life and ultimate success.

Dreaming with the Tarot

Combining the images with the basic meanings gives a starting point for the imagination, and what comes up can then be taken into creative dreaming for further consideration. Over the years, I have found the following method works very well.

This exercise can be done with each card, as many times as feels right. As time goes on, you will find that you are appreciating more and more detail within the card, and will therefore take that detail into your creative dreaming.

- Sit quietly where you will not be interrupted.

- If you are trying to follow the Tarot journey – man's journey through life – take each card in the order set out above. What comes to mind as you do so? Working in this way is a progression in understanding.

- If you prefer to work with random images, simply shuffle the Major Arcana and, asking for an image which is appropriate for you at this point in your life, select a card for consideration.

- Think about your own life at this moment and how the particular card applies to you. How can you apply your knowledge of the meanings of the card to the situations in which you find yourself?

- Contemplate the card for a short time and allow yourself to internalize the energy and power of the image. Try to take in as much of the detail and information as possible.

- Now close your eyes and try to visualize yourself as part of the action of the card. How does it feel to be part of that scenario? What emotions and sensations are you conscious of at this time?

- Now tell yourself that you will have a creative dream about what is most relevant to you or your situation at this time.

- Go to bed, allowing your last thought to be of the card's meaning.

- Remember when you wake up to make a record of your dream whether it is creative or not. You may find that an ordinary dream on one night leads to a creative project or to other creative dreams on a subsequent occasion.

Affirmations

You may like also to use occasionally an affirmation or statement of intent which epitomizes the qualities of each card. Such affirmations can be made the focus of your creative dreaming. We suggest you might like to try some of the following:

The Fool

'My freedom is to be an individual; my task is to use that freedom wisely.'

The Magician

'I have at my command all the tools I need to create the existence that I want.'

The High Priestess
'I hold the secret of all knowledge within and guard it with integrity.'

The Empress
'I am the nurturer of all, the giver of life and of love.'

The Emperor
'I have the power of life and therefore responsibility for all things of the earth.'

The Hierophant
'I am inspired and guided by my highest wisdom for the greatest good, finding it within myself and the world.'

The Lovers
'I love both the feminine and the masculine parts of myself, and wish to share my integration with others by showing how accepting I can be.'

The Chariot
'I conquer my instincts and emotions with the intentions of my higher self and achieve physical goals.'

Strength
'My greatest fears and weaknesses provide the energy which enables me to express my higher self and my dreams.'

The Hermit
'I look within for the guidance of my higher self to elevate my moods and direct me to the light.'

The Wheel of Fortune
'As I experience the fluctuations of my physical, emotional and mental life and accept the process completely, I am enabled to manifest my full spiritual potential.'

Justice
'I am balanced and able to understand the outer manifestations of my inner issues, and subsequently to take the correct action.'

The Hanged Man

'I relinquish my attachments and fears, in the faith that this sacrifice of invalid patterns will open me to a new life.'

Death

'I leave my needs and relationships behind and seek the higher light within myself. The more I let go, the freer and more luminous I become.'

Temperance

'I integrate and blend the diverse polarities of my life to create balance, unity and harmony in creating who I am and manifesting what I do.'

The Devil

'I will transcend the chaos of my darkest fears and transform my weaknesses and vulnerabilities into a clear channel of light penetrating through the gloom.'

The Tower

'Sudden realizations about inadequate past ideas and patterns free me instantly from self-created limitations and physically-binding circumstances.'

The Star

'I am a living, breathing being radiating pure energies and giving sustenance to myself and others through the inspiration of my light.'

The Moon

'I value both my positive and negative feelings as expressions of the world around me, and accept their enrichment and fertilization.'

The Sun

'I understand my physical limitations but look to heaven to find the inspiration to trust and live with my inner child. Personal growth comes through relinquishing my rigid personal boundaries.'

Judgement

'Beyond illusion, reality allows me to doubt and the dream does not allow me to doubt. Illusion does not exist, only reality exists.'

The World

'I am a co-creator of the world, and know that I will be nurtured and supported by it as I acknowledge my identity with all its actions.'

MYTHOLOGICAL FIGURES

Once you have learned to meet and understand those mythological figures associated with the Tarot, you have a further rich source of study in the mythology and legends of your own and other cultures. These can allow you to learn a little of the complexities of both human and divine nature. Using creative dreaming to explore the very deep layers of human nature makes us realize that the mythological stories are as relevant today as they have always been. Somewhere within each of us we are able to find our own version of a beautiful woman such as Aphrodite, a fearless hero such as Jason (of the Argonauts), or a dreadful monster like the gorgon.

When we are learning to put ourselves in touch with the forces of nature we shall no doubt come across the nymphs and satyrs. The former are perceived as semi-divine maiden spirits analogous to aspects of nature, particularly trees and rivers, and the latter as libidinous woodland spirits associated with Dionysus. When we are searching for the more creative side within us we may need to consider the qualities of the Muses. Traditionally these were the nine goddesses who presided over the arts and sciences. They were said to be the daughters of Zeus and Mnemosyne (Calliope, Clio, Euterpe, Terpsichore, Erato, Melpomene, Thalia, Polyhymnia and Urania) and their images form a rich source of material for dreaming with awareness.

This is partly a light-hearted exercise, but also partly serious. As you read the brief entries below, perhaps your imagination will take flight and then you can use your newfound skill of creative dreaming to play out the stories. You may gain a new understanding of how life could have been in those times

You can also apply the essence of the story to your own life today. When thinking of these stories, put yourself in the position first of all of the main character and explore what it feels like to be that character. Use as a basis the IFE technique shown in the Tips and Techniques section but, instead of becoming a dream object, become the mythological character of your choice. You might also try playing out one of the minor characters of the story. With this sort of preparation, you should soon be able to experience a creative dream incorporating your favourite, or most relevant, characters. You may even learn a great deal about yourself in the process!

It does need to be said that the list below is by no means comprehensive and is geared towards Classical mythology. You may wish to build up your own library of favourites or stories which have a particular relevance for you.

Achilles (Greek mythology): During his infancy, in order to make him invincible, his mother plunged him into the Styx, holding him by the heel. Achilles as a soldier withdrew from fighting in the Trojan War after a fierce quarrel with Agamemnon. His friend Patroclus, clad in Achilles' armour, was killed by Hector, whereupon Achilles re-entered the battle, and was later wounded in the heel – the only vulnerable place in his body – by an arrow shot by Paris. He died of this wound.

Adonis (Greek mythology): A beautiful youth loved by the goddess Aphrodite and by Persephone. Killed by a boar, he had, by the decree of Zeus, to spend winters with Persephone in the underworld and summers with Aphrodite. He is often identified with the Babylonian god Tammuz, and his cult involved the celebration of the seasonal death and rebirth of crops.

Amun or Ammon (Egyptian mythology): A god who became identified with both Zeus in Greece and Jupiter Ammon in Rome. As a national god of Egypt, he was associated in a triad with Mut, his wife – a mother goddess – and Khonsu, their son. This triad echoes the interrelationships necessary within a family.

Andromeda (Greek mythology): Her mother Cassiopeia bragged that she herself (or her daughter) was more beautiful than the nereids. Poseidon, god of the sea, thereupon sent a sea monster in retribution to ravage the country. To soften his anger, Andromeda was tied to a rock and offered in sacrifice. She was rescued by Perseus. This story highlights several archetypal actions – the pride of the mother, the sacrifice of the maiden, the anger of the masculine and the heroic rescue.

Antaeus (Greek mythology): A giant, son of Poseidon and Earth, living in Libya. He forced any who crossed his path to wrestle with him. He overcame and killed them all until he was conquered by Hercules.

Anubis (Egyptian mythology): Often represented as having a dog's head, he is the protector of tombs and the god of mummification. He is known to weigh the soul of the departed against a feather. If found wanting, the soul is consigned to the underworld.

Aphrodite (Greek mythology): Identified by the Romans with Venus, she is the goddess of beauty, fertility and sexual love. She is also identified with Astarte, the Phoenician goddess, and the Egyptian Ishtar. Her name probably means 'from the foam' although she is also held to be the daughter of Zeus and Dione.

Apollo (Greek mythology): The son of Zeus and Leto and also brother of Artemis; he is seen as the epitome of masculine beauty. His main responsibilities were with the arts, prophecy and medicine.

Arachne (Greek mythology): A talented weaver who challenged the goddess Athene to a contest. Athene in anger destroyed Arachne's work, whereupon she tried to hang herself. Athene compassionately turned her into a spider instead.

Argus (Greek mythology): There are two beliefs pertaining to this figure; both equally relevant within the sphere of creative dreaming. The first is that he was a watchman with numerous eyes who was slaughtered by Hermes. After his death, Hera took his eyes away to be preserved on the tail of the peacock. The second is that he was Odysseus' dog, who recognized his master on his return from Troy after an absence of 20 years. Both stories focus on the importance of the power of vision in mythology.

Ariadne (Greek mythology): She helped Theseus to overcome the Minotaur (a fabulous beast and also her half-brother) by giving the former a ball of golden thread to help him navigate and escape from the labyrinth. Theseus and she were forced to flee together, but she was abandoned on the island of Naxos. Found by Dionysus, she then married him.

Artemis (Greek mythology): She was the goddess of hunting and is associated with abundance and childbirth. She was identified with the Roman goddess Diana and also with Selene, goddess of the moon. She is often depicted with a bow and arrows.

Arthurian legend: Based on the life and times of Arthur, King of Britain, the legends are a rich basis for creative dreaming. The quest for the Holy Grail, the Round Table and the interrelationships between the various knights and their ladies have all entered folklore as romanticized perfection. Camelot as an idealized environment, Merlin as the archetypal magician and Lancelot as the most courtly of Arthur's knights who ultimately betrayed him with Guinevere, are also well worth considering.

Asclepius (Greek mythology): The son of Apollo, he is a hero and god of healing. Often pictured wearing a staff with a serpent coiled round it – the caduceus – he sometimes also carries a scroll or stone tablet, thought to represent medical knowledge.

Atalanta (Greek mythology): A huntress, fleet of foot and averse to marriage, who would marry only someone who could beat her in a race. One of her suitors won their race by throwing down three golden apples given to him by Aphrodite. These were so beautiful that Atalanta stopped to pick them up and was thereby beaten. This story, and the one which follows, give many triggers for creative dreaming.

Athene (Greek mythology): She is the goddess of wisdom and strategy. She is usually depicted as female, but armed, often carrying an owl – the figure of wisdom. She is said to have sprung, fully armed, from the head of her father, Zeus. She represents that part of woman that is the thinker rather than the intuitive.

Atlas (Greek mythology): As a punishment for wrongdoing he was condemned to supporting the heavens for eternity. Later stories suggest that he was turned into a mountain – the Atlas mountains. This image of him bearing the world on his shoulders is one that will often surface in dreams when someone is under extreme pressure.

Bacchus: A Roman alternative name for Dionysus.

Balder (Scandinavian mythology): A son of Odin and god of the summer sun. Like many other gods, he was vulnerable to one thing only – in his case, mistletoe. Loki, the trickster god, had the blind god Hodur kill him.

Bastet: An Egyptian goddess, usually shown as a woman with the head of a cat, wearing one gold earring. While initially destructive, if you are prepared to challenge her, she is said to work with you and not against you. She therefore forms a useful focus for understanding the negative side of femininity.

Centaur (Greek mythology): A kind of composite creature, a Centaur has the head, arms and torso of a man with the body and legs of a horse. Often representing Sagittarius in dreams, Centaurs are often seen as being uncontrollable and drunken, although this seems to be a confusion with satyrs.

Charon: In Greek mythology there was a belief that the dead soul must be ferried across the River Styx to Hades. This task fell to Charon, an aged ferryman who was paid for his services by a coin being left in the mouth of the deceased. In creative dreaming this image can help us to effect necessary change in our lives.

Chimera (Greek mythology): A Chimera is a composite being composed of several parts of other animals. Such a being is often seen when we first experiment with creative dreaming. This demon or bogey often needs to be confronted before we can progress properly.

Chiron (Greek mythology): Given the task of teaching the gods healing, Chiron was injured by one of his pupils and has become the archetype for The Wounded Healer who is often too proud to allow himself to be healed by others.

Cronus or Kronos (Greek mythology): The leader of the Titans, he was the youngest son of Uranus (Heaven) and Gaia (Earth). He overcame and castrated his father, married his sister, Rhea, and fathered many future gods, including Zeus, by her. Cronus swallowed his male children immediately after their birth because it had been foretold that he would be conquered by one of them. When Zeus was born, Rhea deceived Cronus by giving him a stone wrapped in cloth and took the baby to Crete. Zeus eventually deposed him as ruler of the universe. This story gives many images suitable for working out the dynamics of family relationships.

Cupid: A Roman god who is identified by the Greeks with Eros, the god of love. In both cases he is represented as a naked beautiful boy with wings, carrying a bow and arrows. He wounds his victims by the use of these weapons and is seen most often today in images connected with St Valentine's Day. He represents true, if capricious, love and has been known to appear unexpectedly in dreams.

Cyclops (Greek mythology): In *The Odyssey,* Odysseus escapes from the giant Cyclops Polyphemus by stabbing him in his single eye while he was asleep. It is thought by some that this single eye may be a cross-cultural reference to the Third Eye now recognized in psychic development. In other tales the Cyclops are depicted as one-eyed giants who made thunderbolts.

Daedalus (Greek mythology): Considered to be the instigator of carpentry, he is credited with many works of pure craftsmanship. He is said to have built the labyrinth for Minos, King of Crete, in which to imprison the Minotaur. Daedalus and his son Icarus were imprisoned by Minos, but escaped on wings fashioned by Daedalus. Icarus flew too near the sun and was killed, although Daedalus reached Sicily safely. This story gives some good triggers for experimental flight in creative dreaming.

Demeter (Greek mythology): The corn goddess, whose symbol is often an ear of corn, was the mother of Persephone. She is identified with Ceres and also Cybele; she is said to have mourned the defection of her daughter to such an extent that the world suffered from famine. She thus epitomizes the archetypal Destructive Mother.

Diana (Roman mythology): Goddess of the moon, she was also identified with Artemis and is connected with the principles of hunting and virginity.

Dionysus (Greek mythology): A Greek god who was known originally by the Romans as Bacchus. He was initially a fertility god given to excess and became linked with wild and uninhibited religious ceremonies. He therefore became known as the god of wine and inspiration.

Echo (Greek mythology): Deprived of speech in order to stop her incessant talking, she was left able only to repeat what others had said. Falling in love with Narcissus and being rejected by him, she faded away until only her voice was left. In another version of her story, she rejected the love of the Nature god Pan, who had her torn to pieces, each of which could copy other sounds. This is a good image to consider when working with blockages in communication.

Electra (Greek mythology): In order to gain revenge for the murder of her father Agamemnon, Electra persuaded her brother Orestes to kill her mother Clytemnestra and Aegisthus (their mother's lover). This myth gives rise to the psychological Electra Complex, which is extreme love for the father figure.

Eros (Greek mythology): See Cupid.

Frey (Scandinavian mythology): The god of fertility and giver of rain and sunshine. Brother of Freya.

Freya (Scandinavian mythology): The goddess of love and of the night.

Frigga (Scandinavian mythology): The wife of Odin and goddess of married love and the home, she is often identified with Freya. She gives her name to Friday.

Furies (Greek mythology): The spirits of chastisement, often depicted as three goddesses with hair created from snakes. They carried out the punishments meted out upon criminals, tortured the guilty with pangs of conscience and caused famines and plagues.

Gorgon (Greek mythology): Any of the three sisters with snakes for hair, of whom Medusa was the only mortal one. They had the ability to turn anyone who looked at them into stone. Medusa was killed by

Perseus, who looked at her reflection in his shield in order to find where best to wound her.

Graces (Greek mythology): Goddesses, usually three daughters of Zeus, representing charm, grace and beauty, qualities which they gave as physical, intellectual, artistic and moral attributes.

Hades (Greek mythology): He was a son of Cronus and master of the underworld, the home of the spirits of the dead. He is represented as stern and uncompromising rather than evil – he later gave his name to the place in which he resided. As an image for creative dreaming, such a place or personality gives numerous opportunities for consideration.

Hecate (Greek mythology): A goddess of dark places and destructive femininity, her name means 'the distant one'. She is often associated with spirits and magic and acknowledged by gifts at crossroads. She is sometimes identified with Artemis and Selene.

Helen (Greek mythology): Believed to have been born from an egg, the daughter of Zeus and Leda, the swan. Her beauty was legendary and is said to have caused the Trojan War. Her name connects her with the Hellenic goddess of vegetation and fertility. As a subject for creative dreaming she forms an image of feminine gracefulness.

Helios (Greek mythology): The sun personified as a god. Generally represented as driving a chariot from east to west across the sky on a daily basis, this image is a common one in ancient belief systems, though the names may be different in each system.

Hercules (Greek and Roman mythology): He was a hero of extreme strength and bravery. Known as Heracles by the Greeks, he undertook 12 labours which are said to give us the basis of the zodiac. He therefore offers a potent image for the Hero's journey in creative dreaming.

Hermaphroditus (Greek mythology): He became joined in a single body which retained characteristics of both sexes when the nymph Salmacis fell in love with him and beseeched the gods to be forever united with him. As an image of wholeness, he can appear often in dreams.

Hermes (Greek mythology): Called Mercury by the Romans, he was the messenger of the gods. He is recognizable in mythology through his winged rod and sandals, and by his hat which is often depicted as the sign of infinity. He is sometimes also perceived as a fertility god as well as the god of merchants, thieves and the right to communicate.

Horus (Egyptian mythology): His symbol was the hawk or the eye. As the son of Isis and Osiris, he avenged his father's murder, overcoming evil and in the process himself becoming a god. The Eye of Horus, being a magical symbol, is an effective image in creative dreaming.

Hypnos (Greek mythology): The god of sleep, son of Nyx (Night), gives his name to hypnotism, hypnopompic and hypnagogic states. As mentioned elsewhere these last two states have particular importance in creative dreaming.

Icarus (Greek mythology): See Daedalus.

Isis (Egyptian mythology): Wife of Osiris and mother of Horus, she was initially a nature goddess. After Osiris was killed by his brother, she was required to rescue the disparate parts of her husband's body in order that he could father Horus. Her worship therefore became one of the major mystery religions, re-enacting the rites of death and new life.

Jason and the Argonauts (Greek mythology): The Argonauts were a band of especially chosen companions whom Jason took with him on board his ship Argo in his hunt for the Golden Fleece. Their story is one of the oldest Greek sagas and it is thought that it may possibly reflect early exploration in the Black Sea. Jason had himself tied to the mast of the ship in order to gain passage past the Sirens, so that he could see the way forward but could not be overcome by the Sirens' feminine wiles. As a heroic journey this story can give rise to a great deal of material for creative dreaming.

Juno (Roman mythology): Identified also with Hera by the Greeks, she was originally an ancient Italian goddess. Wife of Jupiter, she was seen as a marriage goddess and the queen of heaven. As an image of the woman of power she is a wonderful icon to work with in creative dreaming.

Jupiter (Roman mythology): Also called Jove, he was originally a sky god. Identified by the Greeks as Zeus, he is associated with lightning, the thunderbolt and excessive actions. The giver of victory, as a creative dreaming image he opens the way to the completion of successful ventures.

Kali (Hinduism): Best known in her destructive aspect, she is the goddess of the graveyard. The wife of Siva, she presents another aspect of herself as Durga, an equally fierce goddess, and as Parvati who is more benevolent. Presenting three aspects of femininity, her story gives plentiful substance for creative dreaming.

Lilith: In Jewish lore she is the first wife of Adam. Capricious and mysterious, she is frequently shown as the murderer of newborn children. In psychological terms, it is this aspect of womanhood that both men and women fear and with which they must come to terms. She can be comfortably confronted through creative dreaming.

Mars (Roman mythology): Initially an agricultural god, he is the god of war and the most significant god after Jupiter. March is named after him; his greatest importance nowadays is in the field of astrology.

Mercury (Roman mythology): See Hermes.

Midas (Greek mythology): Best known for the story of how everything he touched was turned to gold, as an image for use in creative dreaming he epitomizes the folly of ill thought-out wishes and desires. Since he could neither eat nor drink, he then had to subject himself to indignity in order to escape from his own greed.

Minos (Greek mythology): A legendary king of Crete who, having irritated Poseidon, became the father of the Minotaur (half-man, half-bull). Until Theseus was brave enough to challenge this monster, many innocent young men and women were sacrificed.

Minotaur (Greek mythology): See Ariadne, Minos and Theseus. As an image for creative dreaming this creature epitomizes uncontrolled desires and sometimes the Shadow.

Morpheus (Roman mythology): The god of dreams and later also the god of sleep. He gives his name to morphine and its derivatives.

Narcissus (Greek mythology): Traditionally a beautiful young man who fell in love with his own reflection, he illustrates the futility of false self-love. Both the flower that bears his name and his image of beauty can be considered through creative dreaming.

Nemesis (Greek mythology): A goddess usually seen as the bringer of divine justice for misdeeds or arrogance. Following this idea, creative dreaming can be used to confront the principle of retribution through her.

Neptune (Roman mythology): See Poseidon.

Odin or Woden or Wotan (Scandinavian mythology): Usually represented as a wise one-eyed old man. The ultimate god and creator, he is also god of victory and the dead. He gave his name to Wednesday.

Odysseus (Greek mythology): Called Ulysses by the Romans, he is the central figure of the Odyssey, which are tales of his and his followers' exploits. Barred from returning to his home for ten years by Poseidon following the Trojan War, he was forced to travel through the ancient kingdoms, learning much along the way. His is a typical Hero's journey.

Oedipus (Greek mythology): Left to die on a mountain by his father, who had been informed through a prophecy that he would be killed by his own son, Oedipus was cared for by a shepherd. Famed for solving the riddle of the Sphinx, he eventually returned to Thebes, killed his father and married his mother, both by mistake. On discovering what he had done, he punished himself by gouging out his own eyes and banished himself as an outcast. In psychological terms, his name gives rise to the Oedipus Complex (inappropriate love of the mother). The story gives an objective focus for creative dreaming.

Orion (Greek mythology): A giant and hunter, he was changed into a constellation of stars when he died. His myth survives today in the belief that sacred sites all over the world are linked to the position in the sky which is known as Orion's Belt.

Orpheus (Greek mythology): The story of Orpheus and Eurydice echoes many ancient tales of the female being rescued from the dead or the underworld by the male. In Orpheus' case, he rescued his wife and, against instructions, looked back into the underworld and therefore lost her for a second time. Used in lucid dreaming, this story can clarify the mixture of good and evil in human nature.

Osiris (Egyptian mythology): Father of Horus and husband of Isis, he was initially known as a fertility god. His death and resurrection through the persistence of Isis clarifies the concept of continuing life and is a potent creative dreaming image.

Pan (Greek mythology): A shepherd god, he is pictured as half-man, half-goat. Considered by many to be untamed and unregulated, he represents all those forces of nature with which man must come to terms. His music is usually haunting and ethereal.

Pandora (Greek mythology): The first mortal woman. She was given responsibility by the gods for a box. Some say it was filled with blessings, others say with difficulties. Against instructions she opened the box and released into the world many problems. However, Hope was left behind in the box in order help to heal the world. Using this image for creative dreaming helps to give an understanding of wanton behaviour and deliberate misdeeds, but also hidden talents.

Pegasus (Greek mythology): A magical winged horse which sprang from the spilt blood of Medusa when Perseus killed her. Pegasus is said to carry the soul to uncharted realms. As a 'safe' image for flying, Pegasus is an excellent representation for use in creative dreaming.

Penelope (Greek mythology): The wife of Odysseus, Penelope cleverly avoided her many suitors while he was banished from her side by Poseidon. She did so by promising to marry once she had finished her weaving, but in fact she unravelled her work every night. As a symbol of industriousness and strategy, she offers material for creative dreaming.

Persephone (Greek mythology): Called Prosperina by the Romans. She was kidnapped by Hades and made queen of the underworld.

Unwilling to return permanently to Earth, she lied to her mother, Demeter, saying that she had been forced to eat some pomegranate seeds, a symbol of fertility, in the underworld. She had, however, done so voluntarily. In order to appease both her mother and Hades she agreed to spend half the year on Earth and half as queen of the underworld. Her story highlights relationships between mother and daughter and the need for autonomy.

Perseus (Greek mythology): A hero fêted for many daring deeds. On instruction from Athene he cut off the head of the gorgon Medusa and gave it to her. Having Pegasus, the winged horse, as his constant and faithful companion, he rescued and married Andromeda.

Pluto (Greek mythology): The god of the underworld. Also known as Hades, he was a force for transformation and sometimes retribution. Equal in power to Zeus, he often could not be ignored.

Poseidon (Greek mythology): Identified by the Romans with Neptune, he was the god of the sea, water, earthquakes and horses. Often depicted with a trident in his hand, Poseidon is seen as vengeful when thwarted.

Psyche (Greek mythology): A beautiful maiden beloved of Eros, who had been sent to kill her. She disobeyed his instructions to remain in ignorance of his nightly form and thereby he was forced to leave her. This meant she had to perform what seemed to be an impossible task in order to redeem herself. Released from mortal form, she has become the personification of the soul as female. As an image for creative dreaming she puts the individual in touch with those inner qualities which give freedom to self-expression.

Ra (Egyptian mythology): The sun god, worshipped as the giver of life and a supreme deity. Travelling across the sky during the day and voyaging through the underworld at night, he is often shown in his ship with other gods.

Romulus and Remus (Roman mythology): Twin sons of Mars, they were abandoned at birth near to the River Tiber. They were found and nurtured firstly by a she-wolf and then by a shepherd family. Remus was killed before the founding of the city of Rome, which was named after his brother.

Saturn (Roman mythology): Somewhat stern and unyielding, he is an ancient god often identified with Cronus. His festival in December, Saturnalia, marked a turning point (around the time of the shortest day) towards spring in the cycle of the year. This celebration ultimately became one of the components of Christmas.

Sisyphus (Greek mythology): Punished in Hades for his transgressions in life by being doomed throughout eternity to rolling a large stone to the top of a hill, from which it always rolled down again. In terms of creative dreaming this demonstrates the futile task from which there is no escape.

Sphinx (Greek mythology): Originating in Egypt, the myth of the sphinx became known throughout the Mediterranean basin. It had a human head and the body of a lion and was thought by the Greeks to be female. It is said that it killed anyone who could not answer its riddle to do with the three ages of man. When this riddle was solved by Oedipus, the sphinx had no reason for living and killed itself.

Theseus (Greek mythology): Also see Ariadne and Minos. In some accounts, the son of Poseidon, he is most famed for his conflict with, and conquest of, the Minotaur. This depicts a typical Hero's journey. He was helped by Ariadne but later abandoned her in order to complete another heroic task. In some stories, he is also reputed to have married an Amazonian woman who was killed in his stead. Looked at from the perspective of creative dreaming, the stories associated with him can give a view of masculine energy used perhaps unwisely.

Thor (Scandinavian mythology): The god of thunder, he is shown as armed with a hammer. Also the god of agriculture and the home. Thursday is named after him. Used in creative dreaming, he is an image of masculine power and energy.

Tir-nan-Og (Irish mythology): The Irish equivalent of the Greek Fields of Elysium, the Valhalla of Norse legend or the Summerland beloved by

Spiritualists. This is a land or place of total happiness – a state of bliss. It is a good starting point for those interested in Celtic mythology.

Titan (Greek mythology): Also See Cronus. The Titans are any of the older gods who preceded the Olympians and were the children of Uranus (Heaven) and Gaia (Earth).

Trojan Horse and War (Greek mythology): A hollow wooden horse was used by the Greeks to enter Troy towards the end of the Trojan War – the ten-year siege of Troy. The Greeks were striving to recapture Helen, who had been abducted by the Trojan Paris. The horse was apparently abandoned outside the walls of Troy. The Trojans themselves opened the gates of their city. The group of men hidden in the horse overcame the city's defences, thus defeating the Trojans. As a trigger for creative dreaming it is possible to learn much about one's own strategy and to expect the unexpected.

Troll (Scandinavian folklore): A grotesque entity, usually living either in a cave or under a bridge. An image often used to frighten children, in creative dreaming it can be utilized to make sense of negative behaviour.

Tyr (Scandinavian mythology): The god of battle, identified with Mars, after whom Tuesday is named.

Unicorn: A mythical animal, usually pictured as having the body of a beautiful white horse with a single straight horn in the middle of its forehead – thought to represent the Third Eye. The Unicorn had, by common belief, medicinal or magical properties. It is said that only virgins can control Unicorns.

Uranus (Greek mythology): The first ruler of the universe and of uncertain temperament, he was a personification of Heaven. He was overthrown and castrated by his son Cronus. In creative dreaming, he enables us to confront our own uncertain temperament.

Valkyrie (Scandinavian mythology): Odin's twelve handmaidens. They transported those who were slain in battle after performing courageous deeds – and who were deemed worthy by the gods – to Valhalla, the place of eternal glory. As an image for creative dreaming they correspond to the Amazon in the archetypes.

Venus (Roman mythology): The goddess of beauty and sexual love, she is identified with Aphrodite, the Greek goddess of love. Initially the spirit of kitchen gardens, she later came to represent all that was womanly and fine. While herself sexually profligate, she later became the goddess of chastity and was revered in many forms. As an image in creative dreaming she is the idealization of woman with all her charms.

Wayland the Smith (Scandinavian and Anglo Saxon mythology): A smith with supernatural powers, he is a version of the Green Man – the depiction of nature. He is reputed to have his forge in a Neolithic barrow called Waylands Smithy, from where, on clear nights, he can be heard working.

Yggdrasil (Scandinavian mythology): A representation of the Tree of Life, this an enormous ash tree at the centre of the earth. It has three roots, one extending to Niflheim (the underworld), one to Jotunheim (land of the giants) and one to Asgard (land of the gods), thus representing body, mind and spirit. Although it is constantly under threat from an evil serpent gnawing at its roots, as well as deer feasting upon its leaves, the tree is able to survive because it is watered from the well of fate. As a focus for meditation and creative dreaming there are many fruitful images available.

Zeus (Greek mythology): Identified by the Romans with Jupiter. He is the supreme god, the protector and ruler of mankind. Destined to kill his father Cronus, he eventually deposed him as ruler of the universe. All-powerful, he is the distributor of good and evil and the god of weather and atmospheric conditions. He is depicted as mating with both goddesses and humans alike, thereby having many offspring along the way.

ASTROLOGY

Astrology and astronomy are closely linked and are both part of history. The position of the planets helped the ancient peoples, such as the Babylonians, to regulate their lives in ways which sometimes even today we would do well to copy. In the beginning, particularly in an agricultural society, it helped them to know when to plant and when to harvest, and some of the ideas developed then survive today in gardening lore and practices.

As more complicated societies developed, astrology showed leaders when to go to war, when to create festivals and celebrations for their people and when to concentrate on strengthening their ties with other nations. It is more than probable that the soothsayers of old were astrologers and, as they were most likely shamans as well, practised the art of creative dreaming.

The twin sciences formed the bedrock of knowledge of the study of history, science, art and religion, and ordinary people relied on the information they accumulated. In the 17th century, man began to move away from a sense of awe and wonder at his place in the universe. Astrology was the tool of intuition – and intuition was no longer seen as a viable learning tool. Astronomy became a pure science and astrology lost its place of importance. In the new secularization of society, it also became lost to the priests and teachers of religion. However, it survived, and now, as we move forward into hopefully a more spiritual age, it begins to assume a new importance in our drive to understand ourselves.

As with so many of the older practices, it is shown to have a basic common-sense approach to all of those mysteries with which we all struggle. It is interesting that what have become known as the 'outer planets', that is Uranus, Neptune and Pluto, whose influences are seen to be generational (i.e. affecting a generation as a whole), have all been discovered since the Age of Enlightenment began in the late 17th century.

Astrology can provide many rich images for use in the field of self-development as a whole, and this is particularly true for creative dreaming. By knowing the qualities of each planet, you can use creative dreaming to 'fix' the information so that it becomes second nature to use your awareness in everyday life. Initially, having instructed yourself to have a creative dream, concentrate in turn on each of the planets and their qualities. Allow at least three nights for each planet, and within a month, even though you may not have dreamed creatively for each of them, you will have assimilated a great deal of information. Alternatively, you might concentrate only on those planets which intrigue you.

The Planets

The two most important planets of all to astrologers are the Sun and the Moon. From Earth, the Sun by day and the Moon by night are the most visible of our helpers. Knowledge of their qualities shows us the way forward as well as where we have come from.

Below are brief descriptions of each of the planets:

The Sun: The Sun gives light, which draws us forward into what we can be. It gives us our identity, or 'self' within the world. The Sun relates to our will, consciousness, creativity, father and authority figures.

The Moon: The Moon represents emotions, feelings, instincts and day-to-day habits. The Moon in an astrological chart shows the link with the mother and describes how a person is nurtured and how they themselves nurture others. Its house (explained in more detail later) shows the circumstances under which emotions are most likely to express themselves. The Nodes of the Moon (a calculated position used by many astrologers) show our purpose and difficulties in how we make links with the world in which we live. The South Node of the Moon shows old patterns of behaviour and response. The North Node points in the direction of further fulfilment and integration.

Mercury: Mercury represents thoughts, ideas and the mental processes in general. It governs not only ideas, but also the communication of those ideas. All types of communication are in fact ruled by Mercury, recognized by the Romans as the messenger of the gods.

Venus: Venus rules our values and perception of acknowledgement of ourselves. When we make an assessment or appreciate something, whether that is another person or a material possession, Venus is behind it. It is of prime importance in relationships, enjoyment, art and attractiveness.

Mars: Mars is associated with activity, assertion, power or enlightenment. It tells us how we get things started, the way we like to work and how we express rage. Often known as the warrior planet, it gives an indication of how we face conflict.

Jupiter: This planet, often known as the benevolent one, indicates the way we can solve the questions that disturb us. It is to do with how we can make use of fortuitous happenings. The largest planet in the Solar System, it represents development, progress and expansion.

Saturn: Saturn announces the spheres in life where we are bound to learn the hard lessons of the path we have chosen. Saturn, the ringed planet, shows us our boundaries and perimeters but also where and how we need to search for stability in life. Once the lesson is absorbed, we have all the help we need in being able to work with quiet persistence.

Uranus: Uranus highlights our ability to go beyond our boundaries; it is the planet of sudden happenings, of abrupt changes. Uranus offers us opportunities for change – both personal and global. Inventiveness, freshness and freedom are all characteristics associated with this planet.

Neptune: Neptune dissolves boundaries, either self-imposed or otherwise, providing us with the means to blend with the cosmos. It is inspiration, fantasies, perfection, consideration and fellowship. In its more negative aspect it is to do with mystery, delusion and scattered thinking. In many ways, it is the planet most closely linked with the practice of creative dreaming.

Pluto: Pluto is the planet of profound alteration from the very core of our being. Touching as it often does those parts which we do not understand within ourselves and which we would not necessarily wish to change, it encourages us to rethink our values and desires entirely. Pluto is about death, rebirth and transformation.

SIGN	REPRESENTATION	QUALITIES
Aries	The Ram	The starting point – the trailblazer and adventurer. Courage, chivalry and boldness. Independence, impelling force and energy.
Taurus	The Bull	The steady, prudent, resolute response to life. Containing and all-encompassing. Developed impetus.
Gemini	The Twins	Connective, analytical, establishing and drawing together of ideas. Endless search for information. Examination, inquiry, curiosity. Tenseness and anxiety.
Cancer	The Crab	Home and kinship. Demonstrative and sensing. Supervision. Direction. Compassion. Practice and habitual behaviour. Absorption. Intuition prior to identification.
Leo	The Lion	Self-respect. Pride, decision, artistic energy. Declaration and acting. Drama. Bravery. Children. Sports. Humour, regality. Generosity of heart.
Virgo	The Virgin	Anxiety. Virtue, chastity and commitment. Business-like, judicious and faultfinding. Attention to detail. Crafts.
Libra	The Scales/ Balance	Partnership, fellowship, unity. Tactful. Socially skilful. Appraising. On the ball.
Scorpio	The Scorpion	Transformation and regeneration. Atonement and action. Purging. Reduction to the fundamental. Dismissive. Strong protection.
Sagittarius	The Centaur/ Archer	Seeker of understanding. An educator, traveller, risk-taker. Genuineness, forthrightness, philosophy and truth.
Capricorn	The Mountain Goat	Pragmatic vision. Sober and methodical. Control and power. Perseverance and hard work.
Aquarius	The Water Bearer	Objective; works with anyone. Ambitious, essential, humane. Knowledge not action.
Pisces	The Fishes	Anticipation, sympathetic and acceptance. Sacrifice and going with flow. Changeable. Absorbing. Daydreamer. Inclination.

Elements and Modes

The ancients gave each sign an element: Fire, Earth, Air and Water. Fire is active, Earth practical, Air intellectual and Water sensitive. In addition, they also divided the 12 signs of the Zodiac into Modes – Cardinal, Fixed and Mutable. Cardinal initiates, Fixed maintains and Mutable changes. For the purposes of this book, it is only necessary to remember the basic meanings. You only need to remember that Aries, the cardinal fire sign, initiates the cycle of life. Taurus, the fixed earth sign, grounds the life spark. Gemini, the mutable air sign, heeds the surrounding environment. Cancer, cardinal water, chooses to nurture within the home. Leo, fixed fire, expresses creativity. Virgo, mutable earth, then adjusts the physical conditions. Libra, cardinal air, pulls the energy together. Scorpio, fixed water, deals passionately with the relationships so formed. Sagittarius, mutable fire, uses experience to seek meaning. Capricorn is cardinal earth and therefore builds structures. Aquarius, fixed air, sets focuses on more spiritual ideals. Finally Pisces, mutable water, connects to divine inspiration to allow the cycle to begin again.

The placing of your planets, especially your Sun, gives a particular slant to your personality. Astrologers use certain keywords which express the signs of the zodiac in ways which are easy to remember. To enhance your understanding of yourself these keywords give fertile material for dreams – either creative or otherwise. You may like to assimilate them in the same way as you have with the planets, or to use the image on the previous page given for each sign, before you choose to study your astrological chart. Do remember that study of this nature should be fun, and not something that creates a problem for you.

The Houses

If you wish to go even deeper into self-interpretation, you might like to know the meaning of the houses within an astrological chart. The chart represents the space around us and each house suggests a particular area of life. By understanding the effect of each planet in the different houses, you can find out where your pleasures and pains are most likely to occur. Again, dreams – and creative dreams in particular – can help us to a very deep understanding. For example, if a person has Mars in Cancer in the Fourth House you could say that their ambition and drive is expressed in a sensitive and protective manner in matters of the home and family. The houses and the areas covered in life are:

NUMBER OF HOUSE	AREA OF LIFE COVERED
First	Self-awareness. Physical characteristics. Health.
Second	Material possessions. Personal security.
Third	Mental qualities. Relation to environment.
Fourth	Home and family.
Fifth	Creativity. Happiness. Power.
Sixth	Service to others. Work.
Seventh	Partnerships. Personal relationships.
Eighth	Sharing. Legacies. Dealing with death.
Ninth	Travel. Organizations. Philosophy.
Tenth	Social status. Career.
Eleventh	Hopes and wishes. Group objectives. Acquaintances.
Twelfth	Emotions. Sorrows. Inspiration. Deception.

Finally, as a sort of *aide memoire,* here is the way that each of the signs thinks about itself:

Aries	*I Am*
Taurus	*I Have*
Gemini	*I Think*
Cancer	*I Feel*
Leo	*I Will*
Virgo	*I Analyze*
Libra	*I Judge*

Scorpio	*I Desire*
Sagittarius	*I See*
Capricorn	*I Use*
Aquarius	*I Know*
Pisces	*I Believe*

NUMBERS

For those who wish to use creative dreaming to explore symbolism on a much more esoteric level, a great deal of information can be accessed through the use of numbers, which we touched on briefly earlier. A number will often surface in dreams which has intimate significance for us, such as a certain date, or the number of a house that we once lived in. Our minds will often register the importance of the number, both esoteric and otherwise, even though this is not consciously remembered.

Numbers have significance in many belief systems as well as in most religions. Probably the most commonly recognized meanings are those which were considered to be pragmatic and down to earth. Considered by many to be pure fortune telling, the first set of interpretations nevertheless gives rich grounds for investigation when having fun with creative dreaming.

One: You will achieve notable expertise in your work.

Two: Professional or personal relationships need treating cautiously.

Three: Your thoughts for solidity and prosperity will develop.

Four: A stable and protected home is available to you.

Five: A significant disclosure, which will bring transformation, is about to be made.

Six: A meaningful relationship is about to be made possible.

Seven: Internal efforts will help explain inherent difficulties.

	POSITIVE	NEGATIVE
One	Independence, self-respect, purpose, unity of purpose.	Dogmatism, arrogance, narrow-mindedness, humiliation, unwillingness.
Two	Tranquillity and balance, integrity, altruism, sociability, compatibility.	Indecision, apathy, lack of dependability, bloody-mindedness.
Three	Freedom, boldness, fun, eagerness, inventiveness.	Listlessness, restlessness, overconfidence, half-hearted conduct.
Four	Loyalty, imperturbability, orderliness, honesty.	Awkwardness, monotony, conventionality, inflexibility.
Five	Assurance, energy, bravery, health, susceptibility, compassion.	Hastiness, instability, inconstancy, unreliability.
Six	Idealism, honesty, philanthropy, supremacy, faithfulness, trustworthiness.	Softness, abstraction, surrender.
Seven	Wisdom, perception, philosophy, perseverance, observation.	Sullenness, fault-finding, lack of action, antisocial feelings.
Eight	Orderliness, power, business ability, judgement, control, perseverance.	Lack of inspiration, rudeness, aloofness, domination.
Nine	Intelligence, selection, artistry, acceptance, brilliance, lofty moral sense, intellect.	Illusion, laziness, lack of concentration, aimlessness.

Eight: An extraordinary opportunity is about to enter your life.

Nine: Caution needs to be taken not to overextend yourself.

Zero: The cipher suggests that anything is possible.

All numbers can have both negative and positive connotations, and opposite is a table setting out some key words which can act as a focus for further thought or as subjects for meditation before using them as themes for creative dreaming.

   Working with the negative qualities of numbers – or considering that a number is negative for you – is not in itself a bad thing. When a number highlights negative qualities within you and allows you to achieve a balance by recognizing them, you then have at your disposal a means of making your conduct more appropriate to each situation.

'Esoteric' numbers

Spiritually, as we progress, the particular energy which is contained in numbers becomes more available to us. Most numerical systems only have significance up to nine and any other numbers are then reduced to their basics. That is, 13 becomes 4 (1 + 3) and 25 becomes 7 (2 + 5). However, other systems offer choices of a higher degree of spiritual awareness or a return to the more basic meaning. Thus, eleven is a master number for those who are prepared to take responsibility for guiding others but can be reduced to two and thus is an appreciation of duality if that responsibility is not willingly undertaken. We have taken this system of numbers only as far as twelve, since beyond that explanations become more complicated and difficult. The more esoteric interpretations are:

One The self, the beginning; the first; singularity.

Two Duality; hesitancy; balance; masculine v. feminine; two sides to an argument; contrasting elements.

Three The triangle; freedom; independence.

Four The square; vigour; stability; efficiency; the earth; reality; the four sides of human character – perception, feeling, thought, anticipation; earth, air, fire and water.

Five The human body; human emotion in the body; the five senses.

Six Agreement or symmetry.

Seven Cycles of life; mystical, ethereal meaning; human totality.

Eight Death and resurrection; the universe.

Nine Pregnancy; the end of the circle and the commencement of something new; spiritual awareness.

Ten A new beginning; the male and female together.

Eleven Eleventh hour; the master number.

Twelve Time; a full cycle or wholeness.

Zero The feminine; the Great Mother; the unconscious; the absolute or hidden completeness.

In using creative dreaming to understand numbers you might use a statement of intent before going to sleep, such as 'I wish to understand the significance of the number... and its qualities of...'. You should find that your unconscious will then give you the information you need, either lucidly or through ordinary dreams. An extension of working with numbers is to recognize the place of sacred geometry in the overall scheme of things. Dreaming gives us access to ancient knowledge without us actually knowing what we have got hold of. Shape and form are extremely important in this world of ours, and proportion is probably even more so. If something is out of proportion, it enters the realms of the bizarre and even the ugly.

Each shape, and its resultant object – triangle/pyramid, square/cube – also has its own significance. In creative dreaming, we link into something quite profound in our exploration of geometric shapes.

Whereas so many people have had difficulty in learning geometry by conventional methods, experimenting through creative dreaming with shape is a real pleasure. The Tools for Creative Dreaming exercise in the Tips and Techniques section suggests an exercise to help you experiment with shape.

* * *

By the time you have practised the various visualizations and affirmations in this section, and learnt to understand how ancient teachings can help you to understand yourself, you will probably be finding that your attitude to yourself and life in general will be changing quite considerably. Work done with your dreams can help you to decide what you need to do to change those attitudes which you have already identified. These are likely to be those which have inherited from your families, both maternal and paternal, and which may be handed down through more than one generation. Examples of these are poor self-image, Victorian attitudes to sex and sexuality and the inability to communicate.

Such concepts may also have arisen from perceptions you have had as a child of the world around you and which until now you have had no reason to change. Such patterns might be: waiting for attention in a large family; recognizing that one is not going to be listened to; lack of respect; difficulties with authority figures; and displays of anger. You will find that almost imperceptibly these issues have less need of attention in your daily life. They seem not to matter quite so much.

With the help of creative dreaming, you will now be able to accept new possibilities for fresh attitudes which your dreamwork has brought up. Particularly taking into account the wider viewpoints you are developing by having studied life-affirming aspects in yourself, something quite meaningful is happening. You are now able to use intentions, affirmations or actions to change negative – or even less than positive – attitudes. Gradually this will have an effect on the way you understand your dreams and perceptions and you may find that your life begins to feel less burdensome and in many ways much 'lighter'. Having learnt all about creative dreaming it is important that you understand your dream images. For that, you need the Dream Dictionary.

Dream
Dictionary:
Common images

Research shows that a few images continually crop up in dreams. These are animals and birds, environments, journeys and transport, and people and family. It is worth looking closely at their meaning or symbolism because the themes they reveal can often make interpretation simpler. We suggest that you consult this section before you delve into the individual entries listed in the A–Z.

ANIMALS AND BIRDS

Animals are symbols which appear in dreams with such regularity and in so many guises that it is sensible to give them a section all on their own, purely and simply so that the meaning becomes readily available. For ease of interpretation the alphabetical listing has been retained, and we have also included the symbolism which is ascribed to birds. Most of the time the animals represent aspects of the personality which cannot be easily understood except on an instinctive level.

There are some basic interpretations which are important before the symbolism of the actual animal is even considered. These are:

Animal with a cub Represents motherly qualities and therefore the mother.

Baby animal The child-like side of our personality, or possibly children known to us.

The hurt young animal We may perceive a difficulty in becoming mature or facing life. It may be therapeutic to work with dreams as a way of putting ourselves in touch with the inner child, and working through some of the traumas which inevitably occur during childhood. It is worthwhile noting that here we are not talking about child abuse, but about those things that the child has not had enough knowledge or maturity to deal with. This could be such things as illness or death in the family, a change in location and so on. What traumatizes one child will be accepted and assimilated by another.

Cold-blooded animals The hostile, heartless aspect of the instincts is often portrayed by reptiles and other cold-blooded animals. They are usually recognized as being destructive and alien.

Composite animals To dream of composite animals could indicate some difficulty in deciding what qualities are needed in a particular situation. The various characteristics of the different animals of which they are made up need to be assimilated and integrated. There are two potentials for growth in one figure.

Half animal, half man (such as the centaur) Our animal instincts are beginning to be recognized and humanized. This can also suggest the astrological sign of Sagittarius.

Deformed animals Through such a dream we can come to realize that some of our impulses are less than pleasant.

Eating the animal Pagan belief thought that one assimilated, through eating the animal, aspects of it that were superior to ordinary human attitudes. Dreams can illustrate such beliefs. Such a dream could also be about the 'demons' we create which can only be overcome by re-absorbing them in a constructive way. Animals are often symbols of our lower, more primitive urges.

Godlike, talking, awe-inspiring or wise animals, or those with human characteristics It is always important to pay attention to this aspect of animal life in both fairy tales and dreams, since these aspects are an important part of our makeup. It is the part of ourselves that has an instinctive wisdom and grasp of circumstances, but which is often not listened to in the hurly-burly of everyday life. Animals have not yet become mindful of, or have challenged, the 'greater' power from which they came, so the wisdom they show is innocent and simple. They learn to go with the cycle of growth and decay which is a part of nature.

Helpful animals The figures of animals are an easy way for us to accept assistance from the unconscious side of ourselves. This is much seen in the practice of modern day shamanism, where each person develops a relationship with his or her totem animals.

Invertebrate animals These usually represent the more instinctive responses in a person.

Killing the animal may illustrate the need to destroy the energy derived from the baser instincts. We may well be conscious of the fact that our motives are not necessarily of the purest and that part of our personality needs to be suppressed.

Parts of animals (the limbs, eyes, mouth, etc.) have the same significance as parts of the human body. If the four legs are particularly emphasized – possibly in contrast with a three-legged animal – the rounded personality with all four functions of the mind fully developed is being highlighted.

Pets Represent unconditional love, affection and a mutual appreciation. A dead pet can represent the end of childhood or the loss of innocence.

Prehistoric animals A trauma from the past, or from childhood, may be causing difficulty.

Sinister or threatening animals Any threat from animals indicates the fears and doubts we have over our ability to cope with the stirrings of the unconscious.

Taming or harnessing an animal shows the efforts made to control our instincts and, if possible, make them productive and useful. Just as we would domesticate a horse we can tame our instincts for the greater good. When we dream of domesticated animals we are aware of those parts of ourselves with which we have come to terms.

Seeking refuge from animals, whether by building defences or perhaps by running away, is indicative of our struggle with animal instincts, and raises the question as to whether the action being taken is adequate. We may be fearful of those instincts, and conscious of the fact that they can be uncontrollable.

Transformation of animals in dreams, a mutation into an animal or vice versa shows the potential for change within any situation. It may be that consideration should be given to the process of change as much as to the qualities of the animals themselves.

Vertebrate animals When the backbone of an animal is emphasized the interpretation should concentrate on the qualities associated with that animal and tend to repressed emotions.

Wild animals Usually wild animals stand for danger, dangerous passions, or dangerous people. There is a destructive force arising from the unconscious, threatening our safety. Such a dream may be a way of understanding anxiety.

Wounded animals We may be suffering either emotional or spiritual wounds.

Animals appear in dreams whenever we need some sort of understanding of our own psychological urges. Most animals have certain characteristics which are specific to the type, and therefore represent those characteristics in dreams.

Bear The mother appears in dreams in many guises, the bear among them. The image may be of the possessive, devouring mother or of the all-caring mother. If it is recognized in the dream that the bear is masculine the image may then be of an overbearing person, or possibly the father.

Birds Over the years birds have come to represent the Soul – both its darker and its enlightened side. They were once believed to be vehicles for the soul and to have the ability to carry it to heaven. In dreams birds usually represent freedom, imagination, thoughts and ideas which, by nature, need freedom to be able to become evident. Ever since the Stone Age times, man has been fascinated by birds and by flight. As a result, birds were very often invested with magical and mystical powers.

Psychologically, birds' conduct being entirely natural, they can be used in dreams to understand man's behaviour. Thus:

In a man's dream a bird can represent the Anima. In a woman's dream it suggests the Self, in the sense of the Spiritual Self.

A caged bird can indicate some kind of restraint or entrapment.

A bird flying freely represents aspirations and desires and possibly the spirit, set free and soaring towards the Divine.

A display of plumage indicates our facade – the way we see ourselves, or project ourselves to the world.

A flock of birds containing both winged and plucked birds indicates some confusion over conflict between bodily or material considerations and spiritual aspirations. Birds can sometimes denote the feminine, free side of the being.

The golden-winged bird has the same significance as fire and therefore indicates spiritual aspirations.

A high-flying bird represents spiritual awareness or that part in us which seeks knowledge, and needs elevation or ascension to do so.

The two aspects of the Anima or Self may be represented as two opposites. The black bird signifies the dark, unheeded, or hidden aspects, the white the open, clear, untrammelled side.

A pet bird can either denote some dearly loved principle or ideal, or our sense of carefully nurtured happiness, which still is not totally free.

As with animals, birds can suggest various aspects of our personalities which may need to be studied and understood:

Chicken Our imagination is being used to serve a practical function. There is potential for growth, though this may also come about through belonging to a group. The chicken can also represent stupidity and cowardice.

Cock The cock is the symbol of a new day and of vigilance or watchfulness. It represents the masculine principle and so the need to be more upfront and courageous.

Crow Traditionally the crow warns of death but may also represent wisdom and deviousness.

Cuckoo The meaning of the cuckoo is ambivalent, since it can represent deviousness or unrequited love. As the harbinger of spring there is a change from old, stale energy to newness and freshness.

Dove Always taken to mean the bringer of tranquillity after the storm, the peaceful side of man's nature appears in dreams as the dove.

Duck In a dream this can often denote some kind of superficiality or childishness, possibly because it floats upon its own element of water.

Eagle Because the eagle is a bird of prey, in dreams it signifies dominion and superiority. It can also mean keenness and awareness as well as perception and objectivity. If we identify with the eagle our wish to dominate is becoming apparent though there may be some difficulty in reconciling other parts of our nature. If we feel threatened somebody else may be threatening the status quo.

Falcon The falcon as a bird of prey shares the attributes of the eagle. It embodies freedom and hope for those who are being restricted in any way. It can represent victory over lust, arising from the control imposed on it by its owner.

Goose/Geese The goose is said to represent circumspection and love. A flock of geese is often taken to represent the powers of intuition and to give warning of disaster. Like the swan, the goose can represent the dawn or new beginning. The wild goose can represent the soul and often depicts the pagan, wild side of us. Geese were once considered to be witches' familiars.

Hen The hen denotes discretion, mothering and procreation. When a hen crows in a dream it is taken to represent feminine domination.

Ibis The ibis, sometimes taken to be the stork, is the symbol of perseverance and of aspiration.

Kingfisher A kingfisher signifies honour and peacefulness.

Lark A lark is traditionally supposed to represent the transcendence of the worldly self.

Magpie/Jackdaw Because of the belief that magpies and jackdaws are thieves, and that they have an affinity for shiny metal objects, to dream of one may indicate that someone is trying to take or steal something of value from us. The magpie can also denote good news.

Ostrich The ostrich suggests that we are attempting to run away from responsibility, or hide from knowledge.

Owl The owl is sacred to Athena, goddess of strategy and wisdom; therefore in a dream represents these qualities. Because it is also associated with the night-time, it can sometimes represent negative forces.

Peacock The peacock suggests an expansion of understanding from the plain and unadorned to the beauty of the fully plumed bird. Like the phoenix it represents rebirth and resurrection.

Pelican The pelican in dreams is sacrifice and devotion or careful mother love.

Penguin The penguin is thought to represent harmony but also possibly stupidity.

Pheasant To dream of pheasants generally foretells of prosperity and good fortune to come.

Phoenix The phoenix is a universal symbol of rebirth, resurrection and immortality (dying in order to live).

Quail The quail represents ardent behaviour, sometimes courage and often luck. Negatively it can also represent witchcraft and sorcery.

Raven The raven, if it is seen to be talking, often represents prophecy. Its meaning can be ambivalent since it can represent evil and sin, but also wisdom.

Seagull The seagull is a representation of freedom and power.

Sparrow The sparrow denotes business and industry.

Stork The stork is a symbol of new life and new beginnings.

Swallow The swallow seen in a dream signifies the coming of spring and therefore new beginnings.

Swan The swan is the soul of man and is often taken to be the divine bird. It can sometimes denote a peaceful death.

Turkey The turkey is traditionally a food for celebrations and festivals, and denotes that there may be good times ahead.

Vulture/Buzzard Vultures and buzzard scavenge for food. In dreams, they have an association with the feminine aspect in its destructive persona.

Woodpecker The woodpecker is a guardian of both kings and trees in mythology. It is also reputed to have magical powers.

Bull In dreams the bull is recognized as sexual passion or creative power and out-and-out masculinity and assertiveness. However, depending on the other aspects of the dream the bull denotes the negative side of behaviour, such as destructiveness, fear or anger (for example, a bull in a china shop). Slaying the bull is a very powerful image, linking with ancient festivals, and suggests initiation into the world of the mature adult who succeeds in mastering his instincts. The bull can also represent the sign of Taurus in the Zodiac.

Cat To dream of cats is to link with the sensuous side in human beings, usually in women. The refined, but also the powerful yet self-reliant aspect of woman, may also be suggested by the cat. Goddesses, such as Bast the Egyptian cat goddess, are usually represented as having two sides to their natures, one devious and one helpful, so the cat often denotes the capricious side of the feminine.

Chameleon Just as the chameleon is capable of changing in order to fit in with its surroundings so the human must learn how to adapt, and this is represented by a chameleon in dreams.

Cow The eternal feminine, especially the mother or mother figure, is often depicted by the cow. This is partly because it provides milk and nourishment.

Coyote The coyote represents a transformer, usually of negative energy into positive, and also the trickster.

Deer/Reindeer The deer signifies pride and nobility. The herd has an organization, based on rank. We are therefore enabled to recognize our place in the world.

Dog We may recognize either a devoted and loyal companion, a protector, or somebody we cannot get rid of and who might make trouble. If the dog is one that we owned or knew at some period of our life there may be memories associated with that period of our life which hold clues to present behaviour. A dream of a huntress with dogs suggests that we are making a connection with one of the feminine archetypes, that of the Amazon. A dog guarding gates or being near a cemetery indicates the guardian of the threshold, possibly death but usually change.

Donkey The donkey symbolizes patience, or sometimes stupidity and obstinacy.

Elephant An elephant appearing in dreams signifies loyalty, memory, patience and strength. In the more esoteric sense it signifies dazzling wisdom.

Fox A fox tells of dissimulation, cunning and crafty behaviour.

Frog A period or act of transformation (a frog transforms from a tadpole and moves from water breathing to air breathing) may be seen as a frog. There is something offensive which is turning into something of value (for example, a frog into a prince).

Goat It is the symbol for Capricorn in the Zodiac. In its more negative aspect it signifies the darker side of human nature, immorality and overt sexuality. More positively, dreaming of a goat is to recognize creative energy and masculine vigour. The goat may also represent the Devil or Satan.

Hare Because of its affiliation with the moon, the hare can signify the Priestess/Witch aspect of femininity or the Priest/Sorcerer of the masculine – the intuitive faculty, spiritual insight and instinctive 'leaps'. In its positive imagery, it is the radiant hare (often holding its baby in a cave), and thus the Mother of God.

Hedgehog The hedgehog can represent wrong-doing and rudeness, or literally our inability to handle a 'prickly' situation.

Horse The figure of a horse in dreams represents our vitality. Traditionally a white horse describes the state of our spiritual awareness; a brown one the more rational and sensible side, while a black horse is the excitable side of our nature. A pale horse suggests death or change, and a winged horse depicts the soul's ability to transcend the earthly plane. If the horse is under strain or dying there may be a problem with motivation and there may be insurmountable pressure in our life. When the horse is being harnessed we may be focusing too hard on thoroughly practical objectives. In a man's dream, a mare will denote the Anima, a woman, or the realm of the feminine. In a woman's dream, if she is being kicked by a horse, this may indicate her own Animus or her relationship with a man. A horse that can get through any door and batter down all obstacles is a representation of the collective Shadow - those aspects of the personality which most people attempt to suppress. The horse as a beast of burden often signifies the mother, or mother archetype. In modern dreams the car has largely taken over from the horse as a symbol with many of the same associations (See **Journeys and Transport**).

Hyena The hyena is taken in dreams, through its scavenging nature, to signify imperfection, lack of stability and deviousness.

Jackal Esoterically, the jackal is the servant of the transformer, guiding souls from the earth plane into the light. It is often associated with the graveyard, and therefore with death.

Jaguar The jaguar's main qualities are its speed and balance. In dreams it therefore suggests the balance of power between the dark and light forces.

Kangaroo This animal often stands for motherhood, and also strength.

Lamb The lamb is the innocent side of man's nature. It is said that evil cannot withstand such innocence.

Leopard The leopard represents oppression and aggression and traditionally the underhandedness of power wrongly used.

Lion The lion stands for dignity, strength and courage. It can also represent the ego and the feelings associated with it. A lion lying with a lamb suggest that there is a union, or compatibility of opposites; instinct and spirit going hand in hand. If in the dream there is a struggle with the lion there should be a successful development as long we are not overpowered or the lion killed.

Lizard This represents instinctive action or 'one-track' thinking.

Monkey The qualities of mischief, impudence and inquisitiveness all belong to the monkey and are characteristic of the immature, childish and arrested side of our personality.

Mare – See **Horse**

Mole Often taken to represent the powers of darkness, but can also signify the blinkered perseverance and tenacity which enable us to succeed.

Mouse The mouse's quality of shyness can often be addressed in us through dreams, if it is recognized that this can arise from chaos and lack of understanding.

Otter Often suggests the ability to exist in a highly emotionally charged environment.

Ox Depicts the ability to be untiring, and to make sacrifices for others.

Pig Indicates ignorance, foolishness, selfishness, greed and dirtiness. Our better self may be beginning to recognize these unattractive qualities in himself. Without such recognition there can be no transformation or mastery of them. Big litters of piglets can represent fruitfulness, although sometimes without result, since the sow can depict the Destructive Mother.

Rabbit Rabbits have an obvious connection with fertility in dreams, or the trickster aspect of the personality could be coming to the fore. A white rabbit may show the dreamer the way to the inner spiritual world and as such act as a guide.

Ram A symbol of masculine potency and authority, and, by association with those qualities, of the sign of Aries in the Zodiac.

Rat Signifies the contaminated and devious part of us or of a situation in waking life. It can also represent something that is repellent in some way. Traditional symbolism suggests that we may be experiencing disloyalty from a friend or colleague.

Reptiles To dream of reptiles indicates that we are looking at our more frightening lower attitudes. We may have no control over these, and could therefore be easily overcome by them.

Seal Dreaming of a seal suggests that we are in touch with the elements in which we live but may not have progressed too far away from an instinctual reaction to circumstances.

Serpent – Also see **Snake** The serpent is a universal symbol which can be male or female or it can be self-created. It can signify death or destruction or conversely life and also rejuvenation. It is the instinctive nature and is also potential energy. When the power of the instinctive nature is understood and harnessed we come to terms with our own sexuality and sensuality, and are able to make use of the higher and more spiritual energies which become available. In a man's dream a serpent may appear if he has not understood the feminine or intuitive part of himself, or when he doubts his own masculinity. In a woman's dream the serpent may manifest if she is afraid of sex, or sometimes of her own ability to seduce others. Because of its connection with the Garden of Eden the serpent is the symbol of duplicity and trickery, and also of temptation.

Sheep The sheep is renowned for its flock instinct, and it is this interpretation which is most usually accepted in dreams. The helplessness of the sheep when off-balance is also another recognizable aspect, as is the apparent lack of intelligence. The god-fearing, 'good sheep' and also the passive and 'sheepish' may have relevance within the context of a dream. To dream of sheep and wolves, or of sheep and goats, is to register conflict between good and evil.

Snake Serpent dreams usually occur when there is an aspect of sexuality or emotional passion that has not been understood and there is a need to come to terms with our instinctual side. The most primitive urge is sexuality and if this part of the personality has been suppressed and thwarted the image of the snake or serpent as sustained power is the most effective at drawing attention to the problem. On a more basic level this has direct connotations with the penis. The serpent is always taken to signify evil, as in the Garden of Eden, yet it actually represents uncontrolled passion. The serpent suggests temptation, yet also signifies the search for the spiritual. A snake entwined around the body or limb indicates some form of entrapment, possibly being enslaved to the passions. A snake, or worm, leaving a corpse by its mouth can represent the sexual act, but can also signify our control of our libido. A snake in the grass denotes disloyalty, trickery and evil. With its tail in its mouth, this image is one of the oldest available to man and signifies completion, and the union of the spiritual and physical. Being swallowed by a snake shows the need and ability to return to the ultimate, and lose our sense of space and time. Because snakes are such a low form of life, while also being in some cases poisonous, they have become associated with death and all that man fears; this is symbolized by the mythical figure of Medusa, the snake-haired goddess, who if looked at directly would turn men into stone. A staff or similar object twined around it is called the caduceus. This is universally represented as two snakes entwined round a central staff and is now known to be a symbolic representation of the basic form of DNA, the 'building blocks' of life. It signifies that the unconscious forces that are released once we reconcile the opposing sides of ourselves create healing, rebirth and renewal. The colours of the snake may give additional insight into the meaning of the dream.

Squirrel The squirrel represents the possessive aspect of our personalities but may also suggest our ability to guard for the future.

Tiger The tiger signifies royalty, dignity and power and is both a creator and a destroyer.

Toad Implicit in the ugliness of the toad is the power of mutation and growth into something beautiful. To dream of toads is to connect with whatever we may consider ugly in life, yet also to recognize the power of transformation. For a toad and an eagle to appear is to note the difference between earthly and spiritual values.

Vermin In the sense that they are unwanted and invade others' space vermin represent a negativity that needs to be got rid of.

Whale The whale, because it is a mammal which lives within water, indicates the power of resurrection and rebirth – man's ability to come back from the dead and to handle more than one set of circumstances at a time.

Weasel The weasel traditionally highlights the devious, more criminally oriented side of ourselves.

Wild Boar The wild boar depicts the archetypal masculine principle, and therefore the negative Animus in a woman's dream. We may be trying to escape from an issue that should be confronted and dealt with more daringly.

Wolf Dreaming of wolves may indicate that we are being threatened, whether singly or in a pack. We may have cruel sadistic fantasies in dreams without taking responsibility for them. The she-wolf represents not only the hussy, but also the carer for orphans and rejected young.

Zebra This animal has the same significance as the horse, but with the additional meaning of balancing the negative and the positive in a very dynamic way.

ENVIRONMENTS

Often the setting or environment in a dream can give an insight into the state of mind that we are in. A particularly dark and depressing atmosphere can illustrate the feelings that we have over our situation at that particular moment, or be a warning of conditions to come. A bright airy space may suggest happiness and potential, and may also be a representation of our own way of looking at life. A room, for instance, may show a facet of our overall personality, while a building indicates our overall feeling about ourselves. (In dreams the house has particular significance since it is said to represent the soul.)

Interpreting the attributes of certain places as they appear in dreams gives us a perception of our own 'inner landscape'. So, a landscape that becomes fertile or lighter in the course of the dream indicates that an aspect that we have not previously appreciated – or have found unpleasant – is now developing possibilities and potentials, possibly for spiritual development. Equally, dreary and unfriendly landscapes, or tranquil favourable places, may well refer to our subjective view of the world.

The country where the dream takes place or the destination we are pursuing may have a certain resonance for the dreamer. For example, America for many people will signify a rather brash, commercially oriented culture. England tends to be seen as inhibited and dutiful. France will represent the temperamental masculine and so on. Such a dream may also be highlighting cultural differences or wish fulfilment.

The countryside can suggest a particular mood or feeling, especially of freedom. An urban environment may well suggest stress or bustle and hurry, while quickly changing scenes may graphically depict the theme of the dream.

Places which are familiar to us will evoke certain moods connected with previous experiences, though the details may have changed, perhaps to depict a change in our appreciation of that particular memory. For instance, the dreamer's birthplace suggests a secure space but if it now feels oppressive it may no longer be a sanctuary.

Unknown or unfamiliar places are aspects of ourselves of which we are not yet aware. A place that seems familiar and yet is unknown to us signifies a situation we are continually rerunning in our lives without being able to resolve it. A sheltered space offers peace and tranquillity, and a sense of safety, whereas wide-open spaces offer us freedom of movement.

Buildings

Buildings can represent the structure we try to give to our everyday lives. The attitudes and beliefs we have formed, built from experience and perception, and even from the beliefs and perceptions of others round us such as our families, can often appear in dreams as buildings. In real life we learn a lot about a person from his personal environment, and dreams reflect our character, hopes and concerns, often by highlighting such things through the environment of the dream itself. The features of the building often mirror the features of our personality. For example, a house with a door that is difficult to open might signify a natural shyness and difficulty in getting to know people.

Buildings can become composite, and therefore confusing. In understanding our dream, we should interpret the main appearance of the building first, and the secondary appearance as qualities to be recognized. Various buildings have certain meanings:

Boarding house/hotel A boarding house or hotel indicates a situation which is of a temporary nature or shows that we may be aware of our own insecurities and may not feel particularly grounded.

Castle/Citadel/Fortress As a defended space, such an image can variously represent the feminine nature, or a place of safety and our innermost selves.

Church, tabernacle, temple etc. Any religious building will suggest a place of sanctuary and refuge, where we may be at peace with our beliefs. A sacred space or one which has been consecrated is often that part of ourselves where we can communicate with our idea of divine power. Such a building in dreams allows us to understand the raising of our own vibration to a more spiritual level.

House A house nearly always refers to the soul and the manner in which we set up our lives. If we are initially aware that the house is not empty – that there is something in it (e.g. furnishings) – it indicates some aspect of us which needs to be considered. There being someone else in the house can mean that we are feeling threatened by an aspect of our own personality. If there are different activities going on, particularly if they are very different, this suggests antagonism between two parts of our personality, possibly the creative and the intellectual, or the logical and intuitive. The front of the house portrays the facade we present to the outside world. Going into or out of the house means we are in a position to decide whether we need at that time to be more introverted or extroverted. Being outside the house depicts the more public side of ourselves. In a dream of an impressive, awe-inspiring house we are conscious of the Self or the Soul, the 'higher' aspects of ourselves. Moving to a larger house implies that there is need for a change in our lives, perhaps to achieve a more open way of life, or even for more emotional space. If a small house is seen, we are seeking security, or perhaps the safety of childhood, without responsibility. If we find the smallness of the house constricting, we may be feeling trapped by responsibilities, and need to escape. Work on the house such as cementing, repairing, and making changes shows that relationships may need to be worked on or repaired, or perhaps we need to look at health matters. We should take note of the damage or decay that has occurred in our lives.

The different rooms and parts of houses in dreams indicate the diverse aspects of our personality and experiences. For example:

Attic Dreaming of being in an attic is to do with past experiences and old memories. Interestingly, it can highlight family patterns of behaviour and attitudes which have been handed down.

Basement/cellar The cellar most often represents the subconscious and those things we may have suppressed through an inability to handle them. A basement can also highlight the power that is available to us provided we are willing to make use of it. We may not have come to terms with our own sexuality and prefer to keep it hidden. It can also represent family beliefs and habits, particularly those that we have internalized without realizing it.

Bathroom In dreams our attitude to personal cleanliness and our most private thoughts and actions can be shown as the bathroom or toilet.

Bedroom The bedroom portrays a place of safety where we can relax and be as sensual as we wish.

Hall The hallway in a dream is representative of how we meet and relate to other people, though it is also indicative of how we make the transition from the private to the public self and vice versa.

Kitchen Being the 'heart' of the house, this shows how we nurture and care for others.

Library Our minds, and how we store the information we receive, can appear as a library.

Rooms Rooms in a dream can describe various parts of our personalities or levels of understanding, but often signify either the womb or the mother figure. A sitting room or lounge would be the more relaxed comfortable side which seeks ease and comfort.

Igloo Because of its shape, the igloo stands for completeness and sanctuary. It is warm on the inside and cold on the outside and therefore signifies the difference between the internal and the external.

Pyramid The pyramid is considered to be a focus for power, so for one to appear in a dream is to be concentrating on the power within. Being a construction of triangular shapes it may represent body, mind and spirit.

Tower (obelisk, steeple, lighthouse, etc.) Any image of a tower is representative of the personality, and the Soul within. While there are obvious connotations that connect it with masculinity, it is more correct to perceive it as the Self within a wider context. When thought of in this way, attention can then be paid to other attributes of the tower, such as where windows, doors and staircases are placed. This leads to a greater understanding of the Spiritual self.

Warehouse The warehouse, being primarily a place for storage, has the symbolism of being a repository, either for spiritual energy or for spiritual rubbish. It will depend on our own personal beliefs how it is regarded.

Features of buildings can also be significant aspects of the dream:

> ***Balcony (or ledge, sill, etc.)*** A balcony indicates both support and protectiveness. It can also represent the Mother in her protective aspect.

> ***Chimney*** As a conduit from one state to another and a conductor of heat, in dreams the chimney can indicate how we deal with our inner emotions and warmth.

> ***Doors*** Doors refer to the openings of the body and therefore, by default, one's sexuality. The front door and back door signify the vagina and the anus respectively, but may also suggest how we allow people to approach us, and how vulnerable we can become. Breaking down the door means that we are now ready to tackle inhibitions and an unwillingness to face the issues over sex and relationships. It can also represent rape or abuse. Opening and closing the door, while often taken to stand for intercourse, can show our attitude to sex, and our ability to be open and broad-minded over all sorts of issues. Refusing to open the door shows an innocent approach to sexuality, but also sometimes a narrow-minded approach to life. A door between the outer and inner rooms shows

there may be a conflict between the conscious and the unconscious, or our inner private self and our public personality. Barring the door denotes our need for self-protection, although if the door is barred to us there is some block to progress around. If an animal or person forces his way in and destroys the lock our own protective mechanisms have let us down. Escaping by another door indicates that we need to find a different solution to the one we thought would solve a problem. Someone knocking on the door signifies that our attention is being drawn to an external situation in our waking lives.

Hall/Passages Any passages can stand for the passages within the body, the vagina or the anus, the intestines and so on. Equally, on a psychological level, they signify how we allow our personal space to be penetrated. Passages also represent the transitions between the various stages of our lives.

Lift A lift usually indicates how we deal with information. For instance, a lift going down would suggest going down into the subconscious, while a lift going up would be moving towards the spiritual. It is believed that in the sleep state we leave our bodies, and this can be reflected in dreams of lifts or elevators. Thus, descending in a lift and getting stuck represents the entrapment of the spiritual by the physical body, and going up in a lift and getting stuck can suggest that we are too geared towards the material world.

Rooms While the function of each room is important – see above – rooms can have significance in dreams in other ways. A small room with only one door or a basement with water in it is a very direct representation of the womb, and may suggest a need to return to the womb-like state, or a consideration of issues to do with pregnancy. A series of rooms refers to the various aspects of femininity, and often to our whole soul. Something in an upstairs room denotes an idea or concept belonging to the spiritual or intellectual realms. Leaving the room and going into another one suggests leaving something behind in order to bring about change on whatever level is appropriate. Such a change need not necessarily be for the better. If a room is empty, something, such as comfort or support, is lacking in our lives.

Stairs Stairs are often an indication of the steps we must take in order to achieve a goal. Climbing the stairs is illustrative of the effort that we must make in order to have access to the more mystical, spiritual side of our being. It can more simply be the exertion we practise in everyday life. To have access to the hidden, unconscious side of ourselves we need to 'go down' into the unconscious, thus going downstairs. A golden staircase is such a basic image, with so many interpretations, that particular attention needs to be paid to other aspects of the dream, and also our spiritual state of mind at that specific time. Largely it represents a 'death', though not necessarily a physical one. It is more the realization that we no longer need to be trapped within the physical, but can move towards a more fulfilling life. It is a way out of the everyday mundane.

Walls A wall signifies a block to progress and the nature of the wall will give some clue as to what the block is. Construction or demolition of a wall or building suggests that we all have the ability within us to construct successful lives, and equally an ability to self-destruct. A dream that highlights construction or demolition gives us access to those qualities and abilities within ourselves. For instance, an old wall suggests an old problem, whereas a glass wall would indicate difficulties with perception. A dream where walls close in could describe the remembered feelings of birth, but is more likely to represent a feeling of being trapped by the lifestyle we have. A brick wall, rampart or dividing wall all signify the difference between two states of reality, often the inner psychological state and the exterior everyday world.

Water

Water is usually taken in dreams to symbolize all that is emotional and feminine. Deep water suggests either being out of our depth, or entering our own subconscious. It also represents cleansing, being able to wash away the things which deeply affect us in everyday life. In baptism, water is a cleanser of previously held 'sins', often also those habits, beliefs and concepts inherited from the family. So, to dream of a baptism may suggest that it is time to let go of these 'inheritances'.

Water can also stand for our potential and our ability to create a new life in response to our own inner urgings.

The representation of water appears so often in dreams, with so many different meanings, that it is possible only to suggest some probable ones. Thus coming up out of the water indicates a fresh start. Deep water suggests the unconscious; flowing water signifies peace and comfort or going with the scheme of events. Going down into water indicates a need to renew our strength, while being immersed in water can suggest pregnancy and birth. While rushing water denotes passion, shallow water reveals a lack of essential energy. To be on the water (as in a boat) can represent indecision or a lack of emotional commitment, while to be in the water but not moving signifies inertia.

Other images associated with water are as follows:

Bathing is associated with purification, both emotional and spiritual.

Canals may symbolize the process of birth, but also attempts to regulate our emotions.

Diving into water can be interpreted as trying to find the parts of ourselves which we have suppressed. It can also suggest taking risks which we might not normally do.

Drowning indicates that we may not be in control of our emotions properly and could be in a situation where we can be overcome by them. We are pushing ourselves to the limit.

Floods, being by their nature chaotic and destructive, symbolize the uncontrollable 'welling up' of emotion which can destroy our known way of life. Eventually there has to be some sort of cleansing process.

Fountains are always taken as symbols of womanhood, in particular the Great Mother in her most giving sense.

Lake A lake, like a pool, can signify a stage of transition between the conscious and the spiritual Self, as in the story of King Arthur. The unexpected image of a lake denotes the need to consider our emotional responses very carefully. To see ourselves reflected in a pool suggests that we need to come to terms with the Shadow. We have to understand that there is a part of ourselves that we do not appreciate but which, when harnessed, can give much energy for change.

Obstacles such as dams, islands and driftwood symbolize both our conscious efforts to control the force of the water (and therefore our emotions) or difficulties which are being put in our way.

Rivers or streams, like roads, denote our life and the way that we are living it at that moment. It will depend on our attitude or state of mind as to whether we see our lives as a large river or a small stream. If the water in the river appears to be contaminated we are not deciding on the best actions for ourselves, and may be letting others affect our judgement. Crossing a river means there will be great changes, but can sometimes suggest death, either of the self or of the old. If the river is very deep we should perhaps be paying attention to how we relate to the rest of the world, and our feelings about it. If the river is rushing by we may feel that life is moving along at too fast a pace. If we can see the sea as well as the river, we may be aware that a great change must occur, perhaps an expansion of consciousness, or that greater attention must be paid to the unconscious within. If the river causes fear we are creating an unnecessary difficulty for ourselves by not understanding our emotions.

Sea or ocean The original chaotic state from which all life emerges is often pictured as a sea. It usually depicts cosmic consciousness, that is a state of total knowledge, although that may be obscured by our fear of 'the deep'. We need not fear that which we understand. A shallow sea suggests insincere emotion. The waves in the sea characterize emotion and lust. A calm sea suggests a peaceful existence, while a stormy sea signifies passion, either negative or positive. To be conscious of the rise and fall of the tides is to be conscious both of the passage of time and of the rise and fall of our own emotions.

Waterfall In former times, the waterfall was taken to represent an orgasm, although today it more often represents any display of emotion that is powerful and yet under control. It can also suggest some kind of spiritual cleansing.

Waves signify the ups and downs of everyday life.

JOURNEYS AND TRANSPORT

The idea of a journey standing as a metaphor for the story of our lives is perhaps one of the most powerful ones there is. Not only does it describe our everyday lives, in a purely practical sense, but also our path to an understanding of ourselves in the spiritual. Dreams often show us how we are progressing by using the symbolism of a journey, and showing obstacles in our lives as difficulties on that journey. Often the symbolism is highly graphic, giving us the opportunity to work out what is holding us back, or often what is around to help us to move forward. The dreaming mind will have at its disposal the totality of our experience to date, and will call on that to highlight particular patterns of behaviour, courses of action or recognizable scenes which help us to manage our lives. The image of a journey becomes more apparent as time goes on and major transitions approach. We become more aware of reaching our final destination.

If we accept that any journey consists of moving between two points there is much to be learnt by that process. Indeed, if we translate our dreams in terms of a journey we can often uncover fresh insights into our motivation and various agendas.

Arriving at a destination gives some idea of how we have succeeded in what we are attempting to do in our waking lives. If we do not know where we are, then it is perhaps important that we take time to re-orientate ourselves within a new environment. A sense of anticipation may show we are capable of moving on confidently, whereas a feeling of dread suggests that we should try to manage our fears better. If we feel that we have arrived but have forgotten something along the way, we are perhaps not recognizing the effort we have put in, or the help we have had. If we sense that a difficult journey is now behind us, then we have come through the problem and pitfalls of the past.

When the destination is known or becomes apparent, it will give some indication of the aims and objectives we have. It is often enough just to have a plan for that particular section of the journey. Because our aims and objectives can alter according to our ability to accommodate change, we may discover through dreams that we actually need to change the way we are functioning in order to focus on a new goal. Our declared desires and intentions may not correspond with those we subconsciously have – our inner motivation may be totally different from our outer behaviour – and dreams will highlight this discrepancy. The exact nature of our objective is often not known to us until after we have confronted the obstacles and challenges along the way.

In fact, obstacles ahead in dreams may indicate that we are, or need to be, aware of the difficulties which may occur. We do need to be aware that we ourselves can cause the problems. Our own attitude to life is perhaps responsible. When we find ourselves turning a corner, we have accepted the need for a change of direction. We may have made a major decision. To be stopping and starting suggests that there is conflict between laziness and drive. When we are at a standstill we are being prevented, or are preventing ourselves, from moving forward. This interpretation needs handling with care, since to stop may also be appropriate.

Departing Any dream which deals with departures, whether from home, stations or airports and so on, usually suggests new beginnings. Formerly all departures were interpreted as death, but today it is mostly to do with some form of transition which leaves behind the old and allows room for the new. In many circumstances, to dream of wanting to leave, but not being able to, suggests that there is still further work to be done before we can begin the new. To be conscious of the time of departure might suggest that we are aware of a time limit within some circumstance in our lives.

Driving The whole of the symbolism of driving in dreams is particularly obvious. It represents our basic urges, wants, needs and ambitions. If we are driving we are usually in control, though we may be aware of our own inadequacies, particularly if we do not drive in everyday life. If we are uncomfortable when someone else is driving we may not have confidence in that person, and may not wish to be dependent on them. When someone else takes over driving, we are becoming passive in our relationship with them. If we are overtaking the vehicle in front, we are achieving success, but perhaps as an aggressor. When we are overtaken, we may feel someone else has got the better of us. Once again the way we are in everyday life is reflected in the dream. Our drives, aggressions, fears and doubts are all reflected in our driving.

Engine This represents the sexual impulse or instinctive drives, the life force or our basic motivation. Something wrong with the engine may indicate the beginning of a health problem.

Passenger In dreams, if we find that we are a passenger in a car the image most likely denotes that we are being carried along by circumstances, and have not planned for all eventualities. Travelling with one other passenger indicates that there may be a one-to-one relationship on the horizon, while carrying passengers suggests we may have knowingly or inadvertently made ourselves responsible for other people. This last image could suggest that other people are not pulling their weight in circumstances round us.

Road Just as each individual vehicle demonstrates the dreamer's body and external way of being, so the road reflects the dreamer's way of doing things. For instance, a road which meanders all over the place may indicate that we have no real sense of direction. Any turns in the road, particularly a blind corner, will suggest changes of direction; cross-roads will offer choices, while a cul-de-sac would signify a dead end. Any obstacle in the road will reflect difficulties on the chosen path, and if a particular stretch of road is accentuated it may be a period of time, or may mean an effort. Going uphill will suggest extra effort, while going downhill will suggest lack of control.

Traffic accidents and offences may all be to do with sexuality or self-image, or the way we handle aggression or carelessness, both in ourselves and others. A collision might suggest, therefore, a conflict with someone. Road rage would signify not being in control of our emotions. Avoiding an accident would typify being able to control our impulses.

Transport
To be aware of our mode of transport in dreams suggests how we are moving through this specific period of our lives. Previously the horse was used as an image to depict how we dealt with life. Nowadays the car, the aeroplane and so on have been substituted. The vehicle which appears in our dreams often conforms with the view we hold of ourselves. For instance, we may be driving a very basic type of car or a

Rolls Royce. We may be driving a workaday vehicle or a sports car. Such an image can represent either our physical body or our personality. If we are with friends the suggestion is that we may wish to look at group goals. If we do not know the other people, we may need to explore our ability to make social relationships.

Aeroplane and airport An aeroplane suggests a swift easy journey with some attention to detail being necessary. Interestingly, the aeroplane can also symbolize both a new sexual relationship and a new awareness of spiritual matters. An airport signifies a state of transition and an airman or pilot is either a romanticized picture of the Animus or of the Self, that part of ourselves which will 'get us there'.

Bicycle As a representation of duality the bicycle epitomizes youth and freedom, and perhaps the first stirrings of sexual awareness. A bicycle can also denote some kind of effort which needs to be made to succeed.

Boats It will depend on what kind of boat is depicted. A small rowing boat would suggest an emotional journey which requires a great deal of effort; a yacht might suggest a similar journey done with style, whereas a large ship would suggest creating new horizons but in the company of others. A speedboat might represent an adventurous spirit, a canoe a different, personally challenging, way of working.

What happens to the boat in the dream will have relevance as a reflection of our waking life. Running aground, pulling into harbour and so on are easily interpreted. Disembarking shows the end of a project or period, successful or otherwise. Making a long sea voyage suggests leaving friends and family, as would running away to sea. If we miss the boat we have not paid enough attention to detail in a project in our waking lives, or we do not have enough information to proceed. Any narrow waterway or river signifies the birth experience. A ship usually represents the feminine because of its capriciousness. A ferry holds all the symbolism of the journey across the River Styx after death. It is the giving up of selfish desires. After this we may be 'reborn' into a better life, or way of life. It may also represent a transition in our lives.

Bus A bus journey is that part of our lives where we are aware of the need to be on the move, but particularly to be with other people, with whom we have a common aim. Such a journey has a great deal to do with our public image. Trouble with timetables (e.g. missing the bus, arriving too early, missing a connection etc.) denotes that we are having difficulty with our external lives and perhaps should re-evaluate how we want to live our lives. Getting on the wrong bus or going the wrong way means that there are conflicting needs and desires and we need to listen to our own inner intuition. This is usually a warning of a wrong action. Dreaming of not being able to pay the fare shows that we do not have enough resources to set out on a particular course of action.

Car The car is a reflection of us, how we handle life, and the image we wish to project to other people. It also mirrors the physical body, so anything wrong with the car will alert us to a problem. Any part of the car will be of consequence. For instance, if the engine is not working properly we are literally feeling 'run down'. If the starting motor was not working, this would suggest that we need help to start a project, or lack motivation. You should be able to decipher the symbolism with relevance to your own life. The back tyres might suggest your support structure, the steering wheel the way you control your life and so on. If the brakes are not working you are not exerting proper control over your lives. Too many people in the car would suggest that you feel overloaded by responsibility.

Lorry/Commercial vehicle A lorry in a dream will mean the same as a car, except that the drives and ambitions will be linked more with work and how we relate on a business basis to the outside world.

Motorbike/Motorcycle Imaging independent behaviour, blatant masculinity and daring, a motorbike also can stand for the sexual act. It can also be a symbol of freedom. If the rider is a woman the motorcycle can suggest androgyny, while a Hell's Angel would suggest some kind of anarchical behaviour.

Train A train, as a method of public transport, brings our attitude to social behaviour and relationships with other people into prominence and elucidates our attitude to ourselves. A steam train would denote old-fashioned behaviour, although rather romantic, whereas a modern-day train might suggest speed and efficiency. Underground trains indicate exploring the unconscious.

We have successfully achieved a certain goal and circumstances have gone our way when we dream of actually catching the train. If we miss the train, however, we may be missing an opportunity and do not have the resources to enable us to succeed. Equally we may feel that external circumstances are imposing an element of control over us. Often, dreams of missing a train and then in the same dream catching either it or a later one suggest that we are managing our inner resources better. Dreams of missing a train alternating with dreams of catching one show that we are trying to sort out our motivation. Getting off the train before its destination means that we are afraid of succeeding at a particular project. This can also signify premature ejaculation. Getting off the train before it starts suggests we have changed our mind about a situation in waking life. Not wanting to be on the train might suggest we feel we are being unduly affected by outside events. Arriving at the station by train indicates we have completed that stage of our life journey. It may be that we now feel ready for new relationships and experiences. The carriages on a train suggest the various facets of our lives and the way we feel about them. For example, if a carriage is untidy or dirty, we should be aware that we need to 'clean up' an aspect of our lives.

Railway lines and tracks will have relevance as ways of getting us to our destination. Being conscious of the way the track is laid, for instance whether it turns right or left ahead, may give us an inkling as to what direction we are going. Recognizing the signals in front of us would have the same meaning. Coming off the rails might suggest doing something unbecoming to our nature.

Tram Trams may be seen by many as out-dated transport, yet they combine the best of several types. In dreams, therefore, they will indicate controlled movement as well as a reachable goal.

Walk If in our dreams we are conscious of walking as opposed to using a mechanised form of transport, it usually suggests that we are capable of carrying out a project in our lives on our own. Going for a walk (a symbol of a short journey) shows that we can enjoy the process of recharging our batteries and clearing our minds.

PEOPLE AND FAMILY

For those who only want to understand the relevance of the characters in their dreams, this section gives an easy to consult listing. Family members will display better known characteristics than strangers.

People appear in dreams in many guises. Sometimes they appear simply as themselves, because the dream scenario requires a particular set of circumstances. This may range, for instance, from shopping with our mother to climbing a mountain with an old friend. A person's appearance in a dream may be significant because of the ordinariness of the occasion, because their behaviour is bizarre, or because our dreaming self wishes to highlight a particular aspect of either our character or actions. They may be reminders of earlier, happier times or emphasize characteristics of our occupation or indeed may offer explanations of past actions. Only you can be certain of the significance.

In order to extract the 'information' which each character brings to us as dreamers, it is often necessary to decide what or who each one makes us think of. This is one area where free association comes into its own. That way we are able to reveal the deeper meanings and connections that we make. As an example, one particular old school friend of mine appearing in a dream invariably suggests some form of religious fervour, simply because of that person's teenage behaviour. An individual from the past can also link us with that period of our lives, or with certain memories which may, or may not, be painful.

Sometimes, rather than trying to unravel the meaning of a dream it is enough to look at what bearing the dream character's actions have or could have on our everyday life. To interpret why we have elected to have our characters adopt a particular role in our 'dream play' it would be necessary to know a little bit more about their lifestyle. A member of someone else's family may, by association, suggest our own family members or possibly unresolved issues of some kind.

Also, we are more likely to dream about people when there is some conflict between love and discord. Often in dreams there may be a noted difference between two of the participants in order to clarify two sides of our thoughts and feelings. Similarly, there may be a marked contrast in the way we handle a situation with two of our dream characters. It is as though two options are being practised.

As with composite animals, the composite character will emphasize more than one characteristic or quality in order to draw our attention to them. Not being able to decide if the dream character is one person or another may suggest a common characteristic – the fact that it is not just one person emphasizes the many-faceted human being. Every character who appears in our dreams is ultimately a reflection of a facet or part of our own personality, and can often be better understood if we put ourselves in the position of that person in the dream.

Below are some common figures which appear in dreams:–

Adolescent Dreams of ourselves as an adolescent concentrates on the undeveloped, perhaps immature, side of our personality. Dreaming of an adolescent of the opposite sex often means having to deal with a suppressed part of our development. The emotions associated with adolescence are very raw and clear and to get back to such innocence is often possible only through dreams. There may be conflict over freedoms both given, and taken, by others.

Ancestors Our conformity, ways of behaving, ethics and religious observances are all handed down from generation to generation. When we become conscious of our ancestors in a dream we are focusing on our roots, and perhaps questioning them. We may also come to an understanding of ourselves through our relationship with the past, either our own or others'.

Authority figures (judges, police, teachers etc.) Our impression of authority is first developed through our relationship with our father or father figure. Often depending on how we were treated as children, our view of authority will be anything from a benign helper to an exploitative disciplinarian. Most authority figures will ultimately lead us back to what is right for us, although not necessarily what we might consider good. Authority figures in dreams initially appear to have power over us, though if worked with properly will generate the power to succeed, and may come to be viewed in terms of the Higher Self. Dreaming particularly of police can indicate a kind of social control and a protective element for us as members of society. Often a policeman will appear in dreams as our conscience. We may feel that our wilder, more renegade side needs controlling.

Baby To dream about a baby that is our own indicates that we need to recognize those vulnerable feelings over which we have no control. We may be attempting a new project or way of life which is literally 'our baby'. Dreaming of a foetus rather than a fully-formed baby suggests that the project or idea has not yet been properly formed, sufficient for it to survive on its own. If the baby is someone else's in the dream we need to be aware of that person's vulnerability, and to recognize that we cannot interfere in a certain situation, or that they may be innocent of something. Psychologically we are in touch with the innocent, curious side of ourselves, with the part which neither wants nor needs responsibility. Dreaming of a baby can indicate that, on a spiritual level, we have a need for a feeling of purity.

Boy To have a dream about a boy shows the potential for development through new experience. If the boy is known he reflects aspects of our personality which we are learning to understand. Emotionally, we may need to be in touch with ourselves at that age and with the unsophisticated naïveté and passion that a boy has. We are contacting our natural drives and ability to face difficulties.

Boyfriend To dream of a boyfriend, whether present or former, associates with the feelings, attachments and sexuality connected with him, and our concept of how he expresses himself. To dream of having as a boyfriend someone whom you would not anticipate, e.g. someone you do not like, indicates the need to have a greater understanding of the way you relate to men, and particularly that type of individual. Consideration may need to be given to the loving, nurturing side of masculinity. We are still searching for the ideal lover.

Child (who could be one of our own children) Dreaming of a child gives us access to our own inner child. We all have parts of ourselves which are still child-like and inquisitive. When we are able to get in touch with that side of ourselves we are giving ourselves permission to clarify a capacity for wholeness which we may not previously have recognized.

Dictators (Hitler, Stalin, Napoleon etc.) If we have had a domineering father, a known dictator may appear in dreams as representing that relationship. Such a character may also represent a distrust of overtly strong masculinity.

Carers such as nurses, nuns etc. This suggests the more compassionate, nurturing, feminine side of ourselves. Often it is that part of the personality which has been 'called' or has a vocation. Usually there is also, for men, the idea of a non-sexual relationship.

Crowd Crowds in dreams can suggest how we relate to other people, particularly socially. Oddly, a crowd may signify the many varying aspects of our personalities as a group. They may indicate how we can hide ourselves, or indeed how we hide parts of ourselves and do not single out any one attribute. We may also be attempting to avoid responsibility. A huge crowd suggests information which we may not be capable of handling properly.

Emperor or Empress – See **Authority Figures**, and also **King** and **Queen**

Girl When a girl of any age appears in our dreams we are usually attempting to make contact with the more sensitive, innocent, intuitive, feminine side of ourselves. If the girl is known to us we probably are aware of those qualities, but need to explore them more fully. If she is unknown, we can acknowledge that a fresh approach would be useful.

Girlfriend When a girlfriend or ex-girlfriend appears in a man's dream there are usually matters to do with the relationship between the masculine and feminine, whether in himself or in his environment. There may also be fears to do with sexuality. If a girlfriend appears in a woman's dream, there can either be a concern about her in the dreamer's mind, or she (the dreamer) needs to search for - and find - qualities belonging to the friend within herself.

Hero (any heroic figure) In a man's dream the figure of the hero can represent all that is good in him, the Higher Self. In a woman's dream he will suggest the Animus. When the hero is on a quest, the dreamer is struggling to find a part of him or herself which is at this time unconscious (Also see **Quest**). It is important that the darker forces in us are conquered – but not annihilated, since they cannot be totally eradicated without harming the Wise Old Man. In other words, our eventual integration still needs the challenge of the negative. In dreams the hero's failure may be brought about inadvertently. We all have a weak point through which we can be attacked, and we may be being warned of an element of self-neglect. To have such a dream indicates that we are not paying attention to the details in our lives or to that part of ourselves we tend not to have developed. The death of the hero can often suggest the need to develop the more intuitive side of ourselves, to be born again to something new. A conflict between the hero and any other dream character suggests a basic disharmony between two facets of our own character. The hero often appears in dreams as an antidote to some hated external figure within our everyday life.

High Priest, Astrologer, or anyone with similar esoteric knowledge The Higher Self often presents itself in dreams as a character who appears to have knowledge of magical practices or similar types of knowledge. It is as though we can only become aware of this deeper knowledge by meeting our teacher first.

An inadequate person It is a lot simpler to encounter our own shortcomings in the dream state, where we are safe. Often this is the first occasion we have to meet the Shadow. We dare not ignore this aspect of ourselves nor can we afford to reject such an image when it does appear. We must learn to deal with a sense of inferiority.

Intruder The intruder in a woman's dream is often an image of her own inner masculinity, i.e. the Animus (See Archetypes). In a man's dream it personifies the Shadow. A change in our attitude brings about a better and more meaningful relationship with ourselves.

King A king surfacing in a dream usually represents the father or father-figure. When the king is old or on the point of dying the dreamer will be able to discard old-fashioned family values. An emperor may indicate that some of the father's attitudes are alien to us.

Ministers of all religions Ministers of all religions are vested with a certain type of authority that many people find daunting. When such figures appear in dreams there seems to be an aura about them which highlights moral and correct behaviour.

Man Any masculine figure which appears in a dream demonstrates an aspect or facet of our personality so that we can recognize it. There is a particular group of behaviour patterns within each of us that makes us recognizable. In dreams these patterns and characteristics can be magnified so that they are easily identifiable – they can often appear as personalities. Much energy and power can become available once their significance is understood. A man in a dream can identify the Shadow (the negative side of himself) for a man, and the Animus for a woman. Even when we are threatened by a negative character trait, we still have the ability to access room for improvement.

> *An older man* (particularly if the man is white-hairded or holy) can represent the innate wisdom we all have. Such a person can also signify the father in dreams.

> *A large man* appearing in our dreams indicates either our appreciation of the strengths, certainties and protection which our basic beliefs give us, or suggests that we may be threatened or made apprehensive by those very qualities.

> *A man in a woman's dream* highlights the more logical side of her nature. She has, or can develop, all the aspects of the masculine which enable her to function with success in the external world. If the man is one she knows or loves she may be trying to understand her relationship with him. An unknown man is generally that part of our personality which is not recognized. In a woman's dream it may be the masculine side of herself, and in a man's dream it is The Self.

Any member of an ethnic minority suggests any part of ourselves which is unconventional or different, highlighting what we see as cultural characteristics. For instance, an Egyptian may represent magical knowledge, or the ability to barter, depending on our experience.

Old people In dreams, old people can represent either our ancestors or grandparents, hence wisdom accrued from experience. If the old person is male – depending on the gender of the dreamer – he will stand for either the Self or the Animus. If female, then she will signify the Great Mother or the Anima. All father figures, or representations of the father, will often appear old as if to highlight their remoteness. A group of old people often appears in dreams. Usually this signifies the traditions and wisdom of the past – those things which are sacred to the 'tribe' or family. Older people usually stand for our parents even though the dream figures may bear no relationship to them.

Pirate Dreaming of a pirate suggests there is an aspect of our personality which destroys our emotional connection with the soul, or steals away some basic attribute.

Prince (Hero) and Princess As well as standing for the archetypal figures, these represent those parts of ourselves, or other people, which exist by right. That is, they are those aspects which have been brought into conscious awareness and authority. As the Hero has taken responsibility for his own journey, so the prince and princess take responsibility for the lives they live.

Queen (Not only the present queen, but a historical one such as Victoria) Such a figure most often represents our relationship with our mother, and thus with women in authority generally.

Stranger – Also see Shadow under Archetypes in the Enhancing your Dreams chapter – The stranger represents that part of ourselves which we do not yet know. There may be a feeling of reverence or of conflict which we need to deal with before we can progress.

Twins (including the mirror-image of a figure in the dream) Twins can suggest two sides of our personality. If they are identical, we may be coming to terms with our indeterminate feelings about ourselves. If not identical they suggest the inner self and the outer reality. Twins may also signify our projections into the world of our own personalities.

Woman In a woman's dream a female family member or friend is often representative of an aspect of her own disposition, but often one she has not yet fully integrated. In a man's dream such a figure describes his relationship with his own feelings and with his intuitive, softer side. It can denote how he relates to his female partner.

A goddess or holy woman signifies more spiritually the highest aspect of the feminine that can be attained, and the need to work for the greater good. It can also suggest intuitive wisdom.

Oriental women appearing in dreams usually suggest the enigmatic side of the feminine. In a woman's dream they will reveal her own intuitive and exquisite powers. In a man's dream such figures will often reveal his attitude to his own sexuality.

An older woman most often represents the dreamer's mother and her sense of inherited awareness.

An unknown woman in dreams will represent either the Anima in a man's dream, or the Shadow in a woman's. It is the quality of surprise and intrigue which allows us to explore further the relevance of that figure. We can gain a great deal of information because the figure is unknown, and therefore needs to be carefully considered.

Occupations

When we begin to work spiritually to develop ourselves, it can be seen that there is a huge store of knowledge which can be worked on and with to enhance our lives. Below are some occupations which frequently appear in dreams, along with some possible explanations. It cannot be stressed too strongly however that people appearing in dreams in this way are more than likely to have a particular significance for the dreamer.

Actor Dreaming of an actor suggests that we need to take responsibility for our actions and for who we are. Performers of one kind or another may also serve in dreams as a projection of the type of person we would like to be. We may, for instance, in real life be shy and withdrawn, but need to be admired and loved.

Analyst/Therapist We may well be in contact with our own 'inner analyst' – our instinctive knowledge of our own actions.

Artist Such a figure often represents the creative force within us.

Bailiff This oppressive figure usually represents a particular kind of authority figure, especially one of retribution.

Baker This old-fashioned figure symbolizes nurture and caring, and our ability to change our circumstances by our own means.

Ballerina This figure symbolizes our search for balance and poise.

Banker A banker in dreams suggests that part of our personality that we have entrusted with our resources, both emotional and material, in an effort to conserve them or use them well.

Barber/hairdresser In dreams the hairdresser or barber may appear as the part of ourselves that deals with self-image and the way we feel about ourselves. On another plane, the connection between self-image and beauty is obvious. We cannot progress unless we can first like ourselves.

Beggar/tramp Emotional drives and thoughts in waking life can become starved and appear in dreams as a beggar. The tramp, more properly, personifies the 'drop-out', wanderer or freedom-lover in us.

Burglar/intruder To dream of a burglar or intruder suggests that we feel threatened in some way – possibly sexually – but we may also need to defend ourselves against a violation of personal space. On another level, the intruder can represent that part of us that has trouble dealing with doubt and fear.

Butcher Previously taken to represent the Grim Reaper or a sign of death, nowadays he tends to represent the correct division of resources, which may require some experience and skill.

Chemist Psychologically, the chemist represents the part of ourselves which is capable of making changes and is concerned about bodily health.

Doctor or physician A doctor in our dreams may suggest a known authority figure, or someone who has our best interests at heart. Such a figure may represent a healer.

Estate agent An estate agent suggests that part of ourselves which needs a secure base from which to operate successfully within the world.

Fisherman Whenever one of our dream figures is carrying out a specific action we need to look at what is represented by that action. Often a fisherman will represent a provider, or perhaps bravery, as with a deep-sea fisherman, whilst a fresh-water fisherman may indicate the need for rest and recuperation. Because of the Christian connection, a fisherman can suggest a priest in dreams.

Gardener The gardener can represent the insights which we have gathered through our experience in life and can equally represent wisdom, but of a particular sort. Often the gardener indicates someone on whom we can rely, who will take care of those things with which we do not feel capable of dealing.

Hermit The hermit is a lonely figure with principles, who in dreams may suggest that side of ourselves which finds itself unable to make successful relationships. The hermit can also suggest the Wise Old Man.

Huntsman Traditionally representing death, or more properly the inevitability of an ending, the huntsman can also indicate a vendetta.

Inventor Dreaming of an inventor connects us with the more creative side of ourselves – someone who is capable of taking an idea and making it tangible. When we dream of an inventor, we are also linking with that side of ourselves that is wiser, but at the same time perhaps more introverted than our waking selves.

Jailer This is another aspect of an authority figure, but one which is restrictive in its intent.

Judge/magistrate Also an authority figure, the judge suggests power vested in him by the people, and therefore that part of ourselves which monitors our behaviour.

Leper This is that part of us which feels cut off and alienated from normal society, but perhaps also recognizes its own mistakes.

Monk This links with the more reclusive spiritual side of our lives.

Official An official in a dream often links back to someone who has been given authority (see Authority Figures) or status by others. Someone in uniform may suggest a 'service' element to the dream.

Organist The co-ordinator of our life force or vibration is often seen as an organist. Occasionally such a figure may also suggest a healer or therapist.

Optician This most often represents the need for clarity and wisdom, or rather, knowledge applied.

Osteopath As with a doctor, such a person in dreams may suggest that part which is capable of manipulating our lives towards success.

Outlaw This suggests the anarchic, rebellious side of us.

Pope To meet the Pope in a dream is to meet the side of ourselves which has developed a code of behaviour based on our religious or spiritual beliefs. He may be benign or judgemental depending on how the figure of the Pope was presented in childhood. The Pope often appears in dreams as a substitute for the father, or as a personification of God.

Prostitute This indicates some kind of need, whether it is to understand an extrovert side of the personality, or to understand the Siren.

Sailor The sailor in dreams, as with other uniformed figures, is a romanticized representation of the hero, the masculine exploitative side.

Tailor It is perhaps more important to decide what significance the tailor has to us before attempting an interpretation. Any professional person develops certain talents, such as, in this case, the ability to do precise work and to 'fashion' something new. To dream of a tailor alerts us to these qualities within ourselves.

Waiter/Waitress The interpretation of this dream depends on whether we ourselves are waiting at a table, or whether we are being waited upon. If we are in the role of waiter, we are aware of our ability to care for other people. If we are being waited on, we perhaps need to be nurtured and made to feel special.

Family

Images of the family, being the first people we relate to, have a great deal of significance in dreams.

Beyond the womb, the family structure is the first secure image that a child latches on to. Sometimes, through circumstances not within their control, that image can become distorted, and later dreams will either attempt to correct this image or will confirm the distortion. Therefore, we may dream of arguing with a family member, but the significance depends on both the the the dream and our everyday relationship with that person. All our future relationships, both intimate and platonic, are influenced by the ones we first develop within the family.

The struggle, as it were, for individuality should happen within the relative safety and confines of the family unit. This, as we know, does not always happen. In dreams we are able to 'control' family images in order to work through our difficulties without harming anyone else. It is worth mentioning that one person, working on their own dreams, can have a profound effect on the interactions and unconscious bonding between other members of their family. Almost all of the problems we come across in life are mirrored within the family, so in times of stress we will dream of previous problems that the family has experienced. In a nutshell, dreams about the family are so prominent because many of the conflicts and problems in life are experienced first within that environment. It is as though a pattern is laid down which, until it is broken willingly, will continue to appear.

There are numerous variations when it comes to interpreting dreams relating to the family, beginning, though, with the fairly common dream of a man's mother being transformed into another woman. We know that generally a man's first close relationship with a woman is with his mother.

So, depending on the particulars of the dream, such a change can be either positive or negative. It can be a sign of growth and maturity, time for him to realize, through dream, that he can let mother go. This transformation suggests some change in his understanding of women.

Similarly, a woman's first relationship with the male is usually with her father. Therefore in a dream where a woman's father, brother or even lover turns into someone else she must become more independent (and in the case of the lover, walk away completely) from that relationship in order to progress towards more rounded relationships.

When a man's brother or a woman's sister appears in a dream, it often symbolizes what is known as the Shadow. It is often simpler to project the negative side of our personalities onto members of the family. If this projection continues, it can cause all sorts of problems with family relationships later on in life. The solution can, and will, present itself in dreams to enable us to come to terms with our own image. The aggressive pattern between family members is fairly distinctive, but it is somehow easier to work through in dreams than in everyday life.

If in a dream the images are confused – for example, a mother's face on a father's body – then this suggests that we may be having problems in deciding which parent is more important to us – we must decide if it is even relevant to make such a decision. Family members suffering from injury or appearing to be distorted in some way may reflect our fear for, or about, that person. If one of the family continually appears in dreams, or maybe does not appear when expected, then the relationship or concept we have of that person needs to be better understood. Dreaming of an incestuous relationship, which is not so in waking life, may signify that you have become obsessed, not necessarily sexually, with the other person. It highlights how dangerous such an obsession might be. Such a dream can also suggest the need to integrate the best loved qualities of the other person into our own lives If we dream that our parents are suffocating us and thus forcing rebellion, then we need to break away from childhood behaviour and develop as an individual; dreaming of a parent's death can also have the same symbolism. If a parent appears in our own environment it denotes we have learnt to change roles within the parent/child relationship and can possibly accept our parents as friends. If, within a dream, it appears that our parents are behaving in an inappropriate way, then it indicates our need to acknowledge that they are not as perfect as we had first imagined.

Very early on in a child's life it moves through extreme self-involvement and interest to an almost exclusive relationship – usually with mother. It is only later that he or she acknowledges the need for a different relationship. This relationship can sometimes cause the child to doubt his or her own validity as a person. When this question is not sorted out successfully it can show in the dream image as a conflict or a rivalry with either one or both parents.

To dream of a conflict between a loved one and a family member denotes we have not really differentiated between our needs and desires for each person. Learning how to love outside the family is a necessary sign of maturity. The idea of a family member intruding in dreams signifies that family loyalties can obstruct our progression in everyday life.

Rivalry between siblings, a common problem in life and in dreams, usually reverts to a feeling of insecurity and doubt, possibly relating to whether we feel we are loved enough within the family set-up.

Individual members Individual members, and their status within the family, can symbolize the various archetypes. With that in mind the father represents the masculine principle and that of authority, while mother signifies the nurturing, protective principle.

A brother can represent the dual feelings of parity and rivalry. In a man's dream an older brother indicates experience coupled with authority, while a younger, less experienced brother suggests vulnerability and possibly immaturity. In a woman's dream a younger brother represents, again, rivalry, but also vulnerability – whether her own or her brother's. An older brother can denote her outgoing, confident self.

When the relationship with a daughter is emphasized in dreams, it often represents the outcome of the relationship between husband and wife. In a woman's dream, the relationship with the daughter suggests a jointly supportive one – although rivalry and jealousy can arise that, of course, needs to be dealt with. In a man's dream his daughter may bring into prominence his fears about his own ability to handle his vulnerability.

When members of the extended family – cousins, aunts, uncles, etc. – appear in dreams it typifies the many parts of ourselves that are discernible.

If the relationship with father is a good one in waking life, the image of father in dreams will usually be a positive one. Father also represents authority and all the conventional forms of law and order. In a man's life the father generally becomes a role model, though it is often only when the individual discovers that he is not being true to his own nature that dreams can point the way to a more fruitful life. In a woman's life father is the standard on whom she bases all later relationships. When she appreciates that she no longer needs to use this standard, she is then able to work out in dreams a more suitable way to have a mature relationship. If the relationship with father has been a difficult one, there may be some opposition to resolving the various conflicts that will have arisen – often this can be accomplished in dreams.

Grandparents appearing in dreams indicate not only our attitude to them, but also to the traditions and beliefs handed down by them, of which there are usually many. It could be said that grandparents do not know whether they have done a good job of raising their children until their sons and daughters have children of their own.

Within the husband/wife relationship lie the crucial feelings a wife has about her own sexuality and intimacy of body, mind and spirit. Her view of herself will have been formed by her connection with her father, and any ensuing relationship will be tinted by that bond. If her doubts about validity are not expressed correctly, they will appear in dreams in the guise of the loss, or death, of her husband. They can, on occasion, also be projected onto other women's husbands.

Primary in a child's development, is its relationship with mother. In the main it is the first relationship that the child develops, and should be perceived by the child as a loving, caring one. If this does not happen, anxiety and mistrust may arise, which can result in men perpetually having relationships with older women, or, in some cases, completely denying the right to any relationship. In a woman's life her ability to relate to others depends on her relationship with her mother. She may feel she has to look after the needy male, or form relationships with both men and women that may not be totally fulfilling. In the use of dreams as therapy there are many ways of working through relationships with the mother figure if one dares; much material and spiritual success can be attained.

The sister in dreams represents the feeling, sensitive side of ourselves. Through being able to understand our sister's personality we have the ability to make connections with that part of ourselves. If she is older in a man's dream the sister allows the ability to show the capacity for persecution but also for caring. If she is younger, then she can highlight the more vulnerable side of his personality. Women dreaming of a younger sister suggest some kind of sibling rivalry. If older, the sister stands for aptitude and capability.

The son appearing in dreams can suggest our need for self-expression. He can also signify parental responsibility. In a mother's dream he may characterize her ambitions. In a father's dream he can highlight unfulfilled hopes, dreams and desires, depending on how the dream develops.

The wife/husband relationship is based on how good the man perceives himself to be as a husband or the woman as wife. If he has formed a relatively good, if not entirely successful, relationship with his mother, he will try to prove himself a good husband through his dreams. He will also experience the potential loss and death of his partner in the same way as he experienced the loss in emotional terms of his mother.

A

Abandoned

Akin to the sense of being rejected, being abandoned is in many ways one of the first experiences we have as a human being. It represents a sense of how we experienced the first severance from our mother. How the child experiences this severance can traumatize it to the point where in later life that abandonment and severe sense of loss occurs in dreams. More positively, to be without restraint – to act in an abandoned manner – suggests a need for freedom.

Abortion

Abortion suggests the need for effort to get rid of what is no longer needed. One can reject a sensitivity, emotion, conviction or philosophy, which could be troublesome in some way. Abortion in dreams can represent the sudden termination of a favourite project. In a woman's dream abortion can suggest some fear of childbirth.

Aboriginal

By allowing ourselves to be in touch with natural forces we can make use of them rather than fight them. In dreams, the aboriginal, or other tribal society, often suggests to the western mind elements of the unsophisticated. This is a basic raw energy which can put us in touch with the real meaning of life without all its material attachments and desires.

Absence

To be aware of the absence of something in a dream can suggest some kind of loss. The unexpected often occurs in dreams and frequently we have an awareness that not everything is as it should be. For something to be missing shows that there is a feeling of impermanence. For instance, to be in a room with no door could indicate that there is no way out, whereas no window might show that there needs to be more openness in a situation.

Absorb

A great deal of the process of understanding takes place through absorption of information. In dreams to be absorbed into something represents the need to belong to a greater whole, or to make efforts to integrate various parts of our lives. We often experience states in dreams which are not feasible in everyday life and absorption is one of these. To be absorbed in what we are doing suggests focusing our attention.

Abyss

An abyss suggests that we recognize within ourselves the so-called bottomless pit or void. There is a fear of losing control, of a loss of identity, or of some type of failure. We must take a risk without knowing what the outcome is going to be.

Accident

Dreams of an accident suggests an element of the unexpected in some circumstance within our lives. We are usually receiving a warning or highlighting anxieties to do with safety or carelessness. It may be that we need to be aware of a lack of forethought in other people.

Acid

Psychologically, there is an awareness that self-confidence and our usual sense of well-being is being eroded by outside influences. There is perhaps a corrosive issue in our life which is bad but may eventually be cleansing. There could be the perception that we are being eaten away by some inappropriate feeling.

Acorn

Life, fertility and immortality are symbolized by the acorn, as is the androgynous. A huge growth process is starting to emerge from small beginnings. The germ of an idea is present but patience is needed. When such a fundamental symbol appears we are literally returning to our roots.

Addiction

We all have our own everyday needs, be it alcohol, drugs, exercise or anything that we feel that we can't do without. If we dream of being addicted, then some obsession needs to be acknowledged and action needs to be taken. A release of some kind is needed, be it from a substance, a person, or a certain situation. If we are not normally of an addictive personality, then perhaps our human pleasure-seeking capabilities should be recognized. Fear of addiction in dreams suggests we have a fear of being swamped or overcome by someone or something.

Address – Also see **Letter** and **Parcel**

An address is usually a place of safety and security. However, the relevance of a particular address to us is probably significant. If that place was safe, then we are is probably harking back to something from that period that is missing; if unhappy, we want to escape from the past, and are being reminded of how we dealt with the situation we were in then. Comparisons are being drawn to enable us to act appropriately. A new address may suggest radical change.

Advertisement

There comes a time in all our lives when we need recognition for our efforts – being aware of advertisements in dreams signifies this need for something to be publicly recognized. We are perhaps acknowledging also that we have undersold ourselves and need to sell ourselves better in order to achieve the goal for which we are aiming.

Advice

Inner awareness often manifests itself as a figure which is giving advice. The Wise Old Man or Woman is an archetypal representation of the part of us that knows what we should be doing. Receiving advice from someone may highlight a need to listen to others.

Affair

We need to come to terms with our own sexual needs and desires for excitement and stimulation. Dreaming of an affair allows us to release such feelings. We may feel the need to do something naughty or to take emotional risks. Such a dream may also indicate the need to integrate a perhaps unrecognized part of ourselves or to learn to love that part of us represented by the lover.

Alcohol – Also see **Drunk**, **Intoxication** and **Wine**

Everybody needs to experience pleasure at some point, and to dream of alcohol or of being drunk often represents the need for this pleasure-seeking venture. We are often more honest and open in the drunk state but are so in an uncontrollable manner. Therefore to dream of being drunk can signify a need to be more honest but to be aware of the consequences of our actions. As a symbol alcohol suggests a means of changing consciousness.

Alien

Dreaming of aliens usually suggests that we are in touch with a part of ourselves which is unknown and frightening, and which needs to be faced. There is the potential for experiencing ourselves – or a part of ourselves – as not belonging.

There are increasing numbers of people who dream of being abducted by aliens. Often these dreams contain an element where the physical body is being explored or changed in some way, often from a sexual point of view. Some women believe they have become pregnant because of this, and thus do, in fact, become different from other people. Whether this is some kind of hysterical reaction, a genuine step on the path of self-development, or is in fact real is difficult to evaluate. Most alien figures do seem to have certain characteristics in common, and may be linking with an archetypal impression.

Alone

Being single, isolated or lonely in dreams can suggest issues to do with independence. Loneliness can be experienced as a negative state, whereas being alone can be positive. In dreams a feeling can be highlighted in order for us to recognize whether it is positive or negative, and whether we can deal with our own emotional makeup without the help of others. Often being alone in a dream suggests that there is a wholeness about us which indicates a degree of self-sufficiency.

Altar – Also see **Religious Imagery** and **Table**

There is usually some religious significance in dreaming of an altar. Since pagan times an altar has represented the surface from which a sacrifice of some sort is made and thus an altar can also signify a dedication to a cause or objective. An altar thus becomes a symbol of the public acknowledgement of our efforts or beliefs. In more esoteric terms an altar represents the meeting of the physical and spiritual realms, and the communion or coming together of like-minded people.

Amputation

Amputation in dreams suggests some kind of loss of power or ability, or some disfigurement of the perfection of each individual. When we speak of something 'costing an arm or a leg' we are aware that the price of something is exorbitant, and this type of imagery can pop up in dreams. Giving away our power or integrity may be too great a price to pay within a particular situation in our lives. To dream of amputating someone else's limb indicates our ability to deny others their right to self-expression. Many sayings evolve from acts to do with amputation e.g. 'I'd give my right arm for that'.

Anaesthetic

Trying to avoid painful emotions, and feeling overpowered by external circumstances can lead to dreams of being anaesthetized. It may be that we are trying, or being forced, to avoid something that we cannot or do not want to face. We would rather cut the situation off painfully than face the consequences. Occasionally such a dream will indicate the need to be quiescent and let events unfold around us.

Anchor

The necessity to remain stable in emotional situations often means that we need to catch hold of a concept or idea which will give us a point of reference in difficult situations and an anchor is such an image. We have to become grounded in order to weather the storm. An anchor can also sometimes suggest a spiritual concept which represents hope and sanctuary.

Antlers – Also see **Horns**

Traditionally supernatural powers, fertility and nobleness of spirit are represented by antlers. More mundanely, antlers will suggest masculine supremacy and power, intellectual or otherwise. In many supposedly more primitive societies powdered antler horn enhanced sexual prowess, or gave one the power of the animal concerned.

Anvil

The anvil is an image which belongs to the mists of time, and will probably therefore not come to consciousness, unless perhaps we are learning about basic forces, or studying mythology. It contains within the symbolism the idea of creating a spark, and therefore new life, or of tempering a basic energy into something useable and more highly polished.

Apple – Also see **Food**

Apple blossom is a Chinese symbol of peace and beauty. Spiritually an apple suggests a new beginning and a freshness of approach. The apple obviously has connections with Eve's temptation of Adam, and all the imagery that may suggest, although it is believed that the fruit used was in fact a fig.

Apron

The apron is such a symbol of domesticity that its original function as a protective garment or even a badge of office (as in Freemasonry) has largely been lost. In many cases, dreaming of an apron suggests ties with our mother or the more nurturing side of the personality.

Appointment

Normally in dreams time has a strange way of lengthening or shortening according to the demands of the particular scenario. Therefore to be aware of an actual appointment in a dream, such as going to the dentist or a solicitor, suggests having an aim or objective in mind, perhaps to do with acting professionally or appropriately. Using time effectively may be important to us.

Arch

Passing through an arch or doorway in dreams usually indicates some kind of initiation or rite of passage. We move into a new phase of life, perhaps taking on new responsibilities, learning new skills and meeting new people. There may be some kind of test, but the way is not barred to us: we simply are required to make the effort.

Arena

An arena suggests a ritualized conflict. Today sport is used as a release from tension and difficulty. By creating a specific environment where conflict can be dealt with we allow more space for self-expression and creativity. The old-style arenas were usually circular and tiered in order to preserve a hierarchical system.

Armour

Armour in dreams signifies chivalry, protection and the need to protect or be protected, possibly from something we feel is threatening us. It may be that there is a degree of old-fashioned rigidity in our makeup which prevents us from moving into new situations.

Arms – Also see **Body**

Arms – in the sense of weapons – are used to protect and defend. There was quite a series of rituals to do with the Page becoming the Knight and making the transition from the arms-bearer to the user. In dreams we may be defending ourselves, fighting, being held or acknowledging.

Arrow

Arrows as weapons suggest power, energy and expertise - they can also symbolize words in dreams. We could either hurt or be hurt by directness, and there is the need to be aware of the consequences of our actions. In today's world of signs and symbolism the arrow can indicate the direction our lives should take.

Ascension

Ascension is an altered state of consciousness which can occur as a result of meditation and spiritual practices. In dreams it is seen as acceptable and real, and is often accompanied by symbols of paradise. Esoterically, ascension frequently follows the experience of a descent into the underworld.

Asceticism

To meet an ascetic or holy man in a dream is to meet our higher self, and to recognize the part of ourselves which is continually seeking union with the ultimate or whatever our idea of the divine is. There may be conflict with natural drives, such as a search for celibacy. We are looking for clarity and purpose.

Ashes

When a situation has outlived its usefulness and there is nothing more to be learnt we may dream of ashes. When a relationship or affair ends, ashes whether dead or hot can indicate sorrow. These are what remains of our experience which will enable us to make the best of a situation.

Attack

The interpretation of the dream will depend on whether we are being attacked or are the aggressor. Being attacked in a dream indicates a fear of being under threat from external events or internal emotions. Impulses or ideas which we do not fully understand force us into taking a defensive position. If we are the attacker we need a more positive form of self-expression.

Audience – Also see **Actor** and **Stage**

We need to be carefully considering some aspect of our lives, particularly one which takes place in public. We are the creators of our own play, and an audience may also represent the various parts of our own personality we have created.

Aura

The aura is an energy field which surrounds the physical body and is a representation of the power we hold within, the force field with which we repel and attract people. It is an expression of the spiritual Self, particularly if we are undergoing a period of self-improvement. To perceive an aura in a dream indicates how powerful we consider ourselves – or others – to be.

Avalanche

Psychologically, we need to regain control of forces either within or outside ourselves. The power of frozen emotions could overwhelm us and we may therefore be in danger of not appreciating those around us.

Axe

Esoterically, the axe represents power, thunder, conquest of error and sacrifice. So in dreams we become aware of the destructive force which may be needed to take us out of a particular situation. The axe is often also a symbol of time.

B

Back/Backbone – Also see **Body**

If the backbone is particularly noticeable in our dream we need to consider our main support structure, and also either our firmness of character or perhaps some rigidity in our personality. Someone else's back may suggest that they are not giving us sufficient support, though it may also signify that a particular situation no longer has a place in our lives.

Backwards

Regressive tendencies can cause us to move backwards into previous behaviour patterns. To dream of going backwards indicates that we may be slow to learn, and should withdraw gracefully from a situation. Continuing with our present course of action may be detrimental and impede our progress.

Badge

Dreaming of a badge shows our need to be accepted not just as ourselves, but also as part of a greater whole, and to belong to a group of special people while still maintaining our own identity. We are aware that certain qualities in us need to be recognized and the wearing of a badge is showing the world those qualities.

Bag

We may be having problems with the feminine or more secret elements in our identity. Everybody needs a certain amount of privacy, and a bag allows us to carry around our emotions in public without openly displaying them. Any container tends to signify the more feminine attributes and therefore, by association, intuition and hidden meanings.

Baggage

An indication of our feelings of sorrow can manifest in dreams as baggage. We are under some psychological stress, carrying past hurt or trauma, and may be carrying an extra load, either emotional or practical.

Bailiff

The bailiff in dreams signifies spiritual retribution or Karma of some kind. When a bailiff appears in our dream we doubt our own ability to manage our resources and are perhaps accepting that we need to be more accountable for our actions especially to figures of authority. We have put ourselves at risk and have not fulfilled our obligations. We could be 'punished' by material loss and loss of status.

Bait

There is an aspect of our lives which needs to be enticed out into the open. In a woman's dream putting down bait can be an indication of her doubts about her own ability to attract a partner. The bait could be an action or the use of a particular emotion in order to achieve the end result.

Balance

In dreams balance and all symbols associated with balance are to do with maintaining our equilibrium in the face of difficulty. The circumstances we find ourselves in will demonstrate what the difficulty may be and show us how we need to weigh things up in order to act appropriately.

To be looking at financial balances or at balancing the books generally means a consideration of the resources we have available to us.

Balcony – Also see Buildings

Psychologically we are searching for power within a situation in which we feel powerless. To dream of being on a balcony indicates that we are searching for a higher status than we have at present, or are aware of the fact that within a particular situation we have a degree of competence and wisdom.

Bald

Priests used to shave their heads to show they had nothing to hide, and thus showed both their humility and their spirituality. Dreaming of being bald can be somewhat difficult to interpret since, for a woman, loss of hair can suggest a loss of femininity, whereas for a man baldness can suggest intelligence and the wisdom of maturity.

Ball

A ball connects with the playful, childlike side of ourselves and our need to express ourselves with freedom. In dreams the sphere also suggests perfection and completeness, that is both structure and freedom. Solar and lunar festivals are symbolized by games with balls, when there is much laughter and fun. This of course then leads us to the ball in the sense of a formal party, again allowing us to mark a special occasion, or rite of passage.

Ballerina – Also see Dance

We are aware of the creative side of our personality, and the need for controlled movement through music, grace and the inner aspect of feeling. Also we are searching for balance and poise.

Balloon

A balloon is a recognizable symbol for joy, and in dreams it may introduce a note of fun and light-heartedness amid seriousness. It may often make us aware of our 'humanness' but also our search for the spiritual, or more free-spirited side of our personalities, often a feeling of 'light-spirited' joy, or indeed the spirit rising. Very often it is the colour of balloons in our dreams which is important (see Colour in the Dream Interpretation chapter).

Bamboo

Man is symbolized by bamboo, perfect, but also pliant or yielding. In Chinese lore the bamboo suggests enduring strength, and being a hardy plant signifies the ability to survive. The pliability of bamboo indicates yielding but enduring strength.

Ban

To be excluded from anything is perhaps one of man's biggest fears, since this ties in with a basic feeling of rejection. To be banned from a favourite place in dreams suggests that we have not come up to scratch in some way, or are not conforming with authority. Banning someone ourselves signifies that we do not approve of an action or feeling.

Band

Some kind of band or tape suggests that we are marking (or need to mark) some kind of limitation within our life. Perhaps there is some kind of restriction or exclusion operating, which needs to be acknowledged.

A musical band or group in dreams indicates the basic harmony which can exist in each of us, but could also suggest the type of behaviour to which we aspire – maybe recognition for talent, or suitable remuneration for our efforts.

Bandage

Bandages signify preservation or a protective healing process. There may be hurt feelings or emotional injuries which need attention. If a bandage is being applied in a dream this shows the beginning of a healing process, which may be self-motivated. If it is being taken off, the healing process is over, and we are free of restriction.

Bank

For many, a bank will suggest resources held in reserve for use as we need them. A bank also indicates a secure spiritual space, from which we can manage whatever resources we have – which may be material, emotional, mental or spiritual. On a more mundane level, for a bank to appear in a dream can simply indicate that we need to pay attention to our finances.

A river bank would suggest the boundary between our emotional and practical selves.

Banner – Also see **Flag**

A banner appearing in a dream can stand for some kind of ideal, which may for instance be a certain standard of acceptable behaviour. An old fashioned banner – as used in mediaeval battles – indicates a need to consolidate thoughts and actions as a group, and perhaps agree on a particular course of action. Such a crusade may require some statement of commitment.

Baptism – Also see **Religious Imagary**

Baptism is a rite of passage, and as such is symbolic of many things – initiation; death and rebirth; regeneration; renewal. The basic link of all these is the feeling of optimism that it brings. We are probably aware of moving into a new phase of existence, perhaps having made a promise or vow along the way.

Bar – Also see **Public House**

The bar is a symbol of our spiritual power, and power in everyday life. We need to handle ourselves with strength of purpose, but when we dream of a bar, such as an iron bar, we should look at how rigid or aggressive we are being in our behaviour.

A bar, in the sense of a public house, can represent masculinity or perhaps behaviour which is designed to give us relaxation and fun. This will depend of course on our conscious beliefs about such places.

Barefoot

Being barefoot at one time indicated great humility. When Christ wished to show that he was no different from other men he washed his disciples' feet. Depending on the circumstances of the dream, to be barefoot can indicate either poverty, humility or the recognition of sensual freedom. A common dream is to have lost one's shoes, which has a great deal to do with appropriate behaviour.

Basket

An old-style interpretation of a dream of a basket full of bread suggests nurturing and sharing – as in a sacramental meal. By association a basket therefore represents the feminine, nurturing, fruition and abundance.

Bat

A flying bat symbolizes discernment or obscurity of a spiritual, sometimes occult, kind. There may be some idiosyncrasy within ourselves, of which we are very afraid. Popular belief has it that bats are evil, which actually arises from their association with witchcraft, and bats attacking us in dreams can indicate the need to confront our fears of what we do not understand.

Other types of bat, such as those used in ball games, suggest aggression.

Bath/Bathing

To dream of bathing someone shows the need to nurture or to have an intimate connection with that person. When we dream of being in the bath, it may indicate the need for cleansing of some old feelings, the need to relax, to let go. We have an opportunity to contemplate what has occurred in the past and to adopt new attitudes.

Interestingly ritual bathing and cleansing is said to enhance the ability to dream.

Bay

To dream of a seashore and be conscious of a bay or inlet is said to show we are aware of a woman's sexuality and receptiveness. The wolf baying at the moon shows the overcoming of basic animal instincts. To be keeping something at bay indicates a need to be on our guard.

Beach

The sea usually suggests emotion, so in dreams to be on a beach shows our awareness of the boundary between emotion and reality, our ability to be in touch with the elements. Depending on our actions and state of mind in the dream, dreaming of a beach usually means relaxation and creativity.

Beacon

Beacons in our dreams may highlight our search for spiritual enlightenment and spiritual sanctuary. They can also show, variously, a warning, the need for communication or a strongly held principle by which we live.

Bean

To be storing beans, which in ancient folklore signify immortality and magic power, in a dream may show a fear of failure, or lack of confidence in our ability to carry through a mission, or the need to create something in the future. To be planting beans would suggest faith in the future, and a wish to create something useful. Traditionally the bean was supposed to be capable of feeding, clothing and providing an object of exchange for barter.

Beard

Spiritually there are two meanings in interpreting the symbol of the beard and the meaning will depend on our own culture. It may mean wisdom and dignity, or it may mean deceit and deviousness. To dream of a man with a beard means we must guard against cover-up and deceit. We also need to consider more masculine attributes in ourselves or others.

Beating

If in dreams we are taking a beating, humility, anguish and grief are symbolized. To be beaten either physically or in a game indicates submission on our part to a greater force. The act of beating something or someone represents our need for 'power over' by our aggression and brute force, and possibly an anger in us which cannot be expressed properly in waking life.

Bed

A bed can represent a form of spiritual sanctuary and a sense of purity. To be going to bed alone in a dream can indicate a desire for a return to the safety and security of the womb. To dream of a bed made up with fresh linen indicates the need for a fresh approach to those thoughts and ideas that really matter to us.

Bee/Beehive

The bee symbolizes immortality, rebirth and order. As something to be feared, as well as trained and used, the meaning of bees in dreams can be ambivalent. Folk-tales, such as the one about telling our troubles to the bees, can surface in dreams without us necessarily recognizing what they mean. The beehive is said to represent an ordered community and therefore the ability to absorb chaos.

To be stung by a bee is a warning of the possibility of hurt, but can also suggest penetration. Being attacked by a swarm indicates we are creating a situation which may become uncontrollable. To dream of tending a beehive alerts us to the need for good management of our resources, and an awareness of the need for hard work.

Beetle – Also see Insects

The scarab beetle in Egyptian mythology represents protection from evil, and its ability to cleanse an environment represents hard work. Thought by many to be dirty, in a dream the beetle carries the same symbolism as all insects – that is, something which is unclean or not properly attended to.

Bell

Traditionally, to hear a bell tolling in a dream was to be warned of disaster or of a death. Bells can also indicate the conscience, and our need to seek approval from others. By forewarning us of risk or danger they alert us to potential mistakes.

Belt
A belt may be an insignia of power particularly if it seems ornate in the dream. Additionally we may be 'hide-bound' through outdated material, attitudes and duty.

Birth
We tend to dream of birth at the beginning of a new way of life, a new attitude, new ability, or a new project – also when we become aware of the death of the old.

Bite
Being bitten in a dream may show that we are experiencing aggression from someone else, or conversely that our own aggressive instincts are not under control.

Blindfolding
In spiritual terms, blindfolding is a rite of passage. It is a transition between two states. If we are conscious in a dream of a blindfold there may be something we are deliberately not seeing or being shown (this ties in with the interpretation of blindness).

Blindness
Spiritually, blindness is a form of ignorance. It can suggest the irrational. It is also a form of initiation, as in the blindness of St Paul on the road to Damascus. In dreams it may be that we are choosing not to use knowledge appropriately.

Body
The body in dreams signifies us as individuals and all that we are. In dreams, the body often represents the Ego. The body forms the prime source of information about ourselves, and often highlights problems we may have on a physical level. Those aware of other systems of belief will often find knowledge fed to them through dreams about the body. Psychologically, most of what happens to us is translated into feelings about the body, and therefore becomes a fertile source of symbolism in

dreams. When emotions cannot be faced in ordinary everyday life, they very often become distorted dream symbols.

Different aspects of the body can have various meanings in dreams. For example, to dream of the upper part of the body is to link with our intellect and the spiritual aspects of our character, while the lower part of the body represents our inborn emotional aspects. An adult's head on an immature body, or a child's head on an adult body, is an indication that we need to recognize the difference between mature thought and emotion. If there is conflict between the upper and lower part it indicates that there is disharmony between the mental faculties and instinctive behaviour. The right side or hand being especially noticeable in dreams signifies we should take note of the logical side of our personality, whereas the left side or left hand indicates we need to be aware of our intuitive, creative side.

Body parts can have relevance as follows:

Abdomen/stomach/belly When the dream appears to concentrate on the abdomen, there is a need to focus on emotions and repressed feelings.

Anus – Also see **Excrement** In dreams, the mind often returns to the initial gaining of the control of bodily functions as evidence of self-realization, self-reliance and control but also of suppression and defence. Such a dream therefore is indicating an aspect of childish behaviour or egotism.

Arms We use our arms in all sorts of different ways. In dreams, as in waking life we may be defending ourselves, fighting or being held. We may also be showing some kind of passionate commitment to a cause.

Back Dreaming of seeing someone else's back suggests we should identify the more private elements in our own personality. Other people may not at this present time wish to share their thoughts with us, or indeed may suggest contempt or disapproval. We may also be exposed to the unexpected happening. If we dream of turning our backs we are rejecting the particular feeling being experienced in the dream.

Backbone If the backbone is particularly noticeable in a dream, we should consider the main support structure in our lives. Intellectually, we need to consider our firmness of character.

Becoming fat or thin To dream of a change in body shape suggests the possibility of change in our personality or in the way we handle emotional difficulties.

Blood Many people fear blood, and thus a dream about blood can highlight the need to handle such fears. On a more spiritual level it represents the blood of Christ or martyrdom, and that a sacrifice is being made. This links into the ancient belief that the blood somehow contained the life of the spirit, and therefore spilt blood was sacred. It can also represent renewal of life through its connection with menstruation.

Breasts Usually, breasts in dreams indicate our connection with the mother figure and our need for nurturing, which may or may not be conscious. Such a dream can also depict a wish to return to being an infant without responsibilities.

Constipation Withholding in dreams signifies an inability to let go of the past or of previous patterns of behaviour, and shows our fear of the inability to perform adequately.

Excrement We may not have gone beyond the feeling that anything to do with bodily functions is dirty and self-centred. There may be an element of rebellion in our waking life. Playing with excrement can represent money and value, so in a dream this can highlight anxiety about money, as well as a fear of responsibility. If the excrement is transformed into living animals, maybe rats, we are coming to terms with the fact that we are responsible for managing our own impulses. Excrement in its more spiritual meaning belongs to the realm of feelings and we may simply be trying to get rid of bad feelings. Those bad feelings can be turned into something worthwhile. Evacuation of the bowel usually highlights our need to be free of worry and responsibility, or possibly the need to learn how to be uninhibited. It can also in dreams signify the sexual act.

Eye Any dream to do with the eye is to do with observation and discrimination. It has a connection with the power of light and, in ancient times, of the sun-gods. Through its connection with Egyptian symbolism, the eye is also a talisman. Loss of eyesight suggests loss of clarity, and depending on which eye can be either the loss of logic (right eye) or loss of intuition (left eye). Regaining the eyesight can indicate a return to the innocence and clear-sightedness of the child.

Hair The hair represents strength and virility. In dreams, to be combing the hair is to be attempting to untangle a particular attitude we may have. To be having our hair cut is to be trying to create order in our lives. To be cutting someone else's hair indicates we may be may be to be curtailing an activity. (It is possible that there may be some fear or doubt connected with sexuality.) To be bald in a dream is to recognize our own intelligence or wisdom.

Hand The hands are two of the most expressive parts of the body and signify power and creativity. The two hands contrasted with each other, perhaps a different object in each hand, shows there may be some conflict between our belief and our feelings. A hand on the breast signifies submission. Clasped hands indicate union or friendship, while clenched hands suggest a threat. Folded hands suggest a state of rest. Hands covering the eyes generally represent shame or horror, while hands crossed at the wrists suggest that we feel we are being bound. The open hand represents justice, and the laying-on of hands signifies healing and blessing (particularly if the hand is placed on the neck). Hands placed together signify defencelessness, while placed in someone else's are an indication of a kind of surrender. When hands are raised this can indicate either adoration, prayer or surrender; if the palms are turned outwards a blessing is being given, while when they are raised to the head we should give a great deal of thought and care to our situation. Washing hands suggests innocence or rejection of guilt, while wringing the hands signifies distress. A huge hand, particularly from the sky, suggests that we have been 'specially chosen'. The right hand is the 'power' hand, while the left is passive and receptive. Sometimes in dreams the left hand can represent cheating.

According to ancient belief which is now again in vogue, each finger suggests a certain quality: first finger – expansion, second finger – restriction, third finger – the self and little finger – communication. Thus a pointing finger can suggest a way forward or a special kind of selection.

Head The head is the principal part of the body. Because it is the seat of intellect, it denotes power and wisdom. Dreaming of the head suggests that we should look very carefully at the way we deal with both intelligence and folly. To dream of the head being bowed suggests prayer or invocation. When the head is covered we may be covering up our own intelligence or acknowledging somebody else's superiority. A blow to the head in a dream can indicate that we should reconsider our actions in a particular situation.

Heart The heart is the centre of the being and represents 'feeling' wisdom rather than intellectual wisdom. It is also representative of compassion, understanding and love.

Heel This suggests the part of ourselves which is strong but, at the same time, vulnerable.

Jaw The jaw depicts our way of expressing ourselves. Spiritually, it is also thought to signify the opening to the underworld.

Kidneys The kidneys are organs of elimination; therefore to dream of them is to be aware of the need for cleansing.

Knees The knees are symbolic of prayer and entreaty, and of emotional commitment.

Limbs In dreams any limb can be taken to mean sexuality and fears associated with gender issues. Being dismembered can be taken in its literal sense – we are being torn apart. Sometimes this can suggest the need to restructure our lives and begin again. At other times it can indicate that there is a way in which we are being threatened to the very core of our existence.

Liver The liver is representative of irritability and suppressed anger.

Lungs In Chinese medicine the lungs represent grief. They are also involved in decision making. Spiritually, the lungs are the seat of righteousness, and the source of thoughts concerning the Self. Highlighted in dreams, they can represent the breath of life.

Mouth The mouth represents the devouring, demanding part of ourselves, and by implication the feminine, receptive side. The other aspects of the dream should give a clue to the most relevant interpretation.

Nose The nose in dreams can stand for curiosity, and also for intuition. Sometimes it is also representative of the penis.

Penis Dreaming of a penis – either one's own or someone else's – usually highlights the attitude to penetrative sex.

Skin Skin in a dream stands for our persona, or the protective camouflage we create for others.

Teeth Teeth are said to stand for aggressive sexuality. Teeth falling or coming out easily means we are going through some form of transition, e.g. from childhood to maturity, or from maturity to old age and vulnerability. If we are anxious about teeth dropping out it suggests there is a fear of getting old and undesirable, or an anxiety about maturing. In a woman's dream, if the teeth are swallowed this can signify either the wish for, or pregnancy itself.

Throat Dreaming of the throat denotes awareness of our vulnerability and also of the need for self-expression.

Thumb Dreaming of a thumb suggests awareness of how powerful we are. The thumb pointing upwards represents beneficial energy, but pointing downwards is negative. Paradoxically, the former was used as the death signal for Roman gladiators.

Tongue The tongue in dreams may be associated with our

understanding of information that we wish to pass on to other people. We may have deeply felt beliefs we wish to share, but need to know when to speak and when to remain silent. Another explanation that is much more basic is that of the symbolism of the serpent and the phallus, and hence sexuality.

Urine Urine in a dream often indicates our feelings about emotional control. We may either yield to emotion or bottle it up. How we deal with urine often also tells us a great deal about our own sexuality.

Vagina Most often, dreams of the vagina are to do with our self image. In a woman's dream, it highlights her receptivity. In a man's dream it suggests his need to be penetrative, both mentally and physically.

Womb The womb represents a return to the beginning. We all have need of security and shelter, and freedom from responsibility. Dreams of the womb can signify our need to satisfy those requirements. On a slightly more esoteric level, the womb represents our connection with the Great Mother or Mother Earth. Dreams of returning to the womb suggest a reconnection with the passive, more yielding side of our nature. We may need a period of self-healing and recuperation.

Bomb

In dreams bombs appearing suggest that our own emotions are likely to get the better of us. We may be in some kind of explosive situation with which we need to deal. A bomb actually exploding is usually an unexpected event. Dreaming of such an explosion would suggest a fear of sudden death or unexpected change.

Bonfire – Also see **Fire**

To be lighting or tending a bonfire in a dream indicates passions that are not confined by rigidity and custom, while at the same time suggesting that such passion needs to be given space in one's life. To be burning rubbish suggests a need for cleansing some aspect of our lives. Reflecting the power of the sun, burning also represents encouraging the power of good as well as Solar festivals.

Book – Also see **Novel** and **Reading**

Our search for knowledge and the ability to learn from other people's experience and opinions is symbolized in dreams by books and libraries. To dream of old books represents inherited wisdom and spiritual awareness – sacred ones, such as the Bible or Koran, signify hidden or sacred knowledge. To dream of account books indicates the need or ability to look after our own resources.

Border

To have our attention drawn to the edge or border of material often indicates changes we will make in the material world. To be standing on a border between two countries would show the need to be making great changes in life; perhaps physically moving our place of residence or making decisive changes in the way we think and feel. Meeting new experiences may give us the sense of crossing a barrier or border. Psychologically we may need to make decisive changes.

Bottle

To a certain extent it depends on which type of bottle is perceived in the dream. To see a baby's feeding bottle would indicate the need to be successfully nurtured and helped to grow. A bottle of alcohol would show the need to celebrate, or to curb an excess, while a medicine bottle might symbolize the need to look at our own health. A broken bottle could indicate either aggression or failure.

Bow

Since bowing is indicative of giving someone else status, to be bowing to someone in a dream would indicate our sense of inferiority. To perceive a bow, as in Cupid's bow, within a dream can indicate the need to be loved – the union of masculine and feminine. To see a bow made of ribbon in a dream is making a connection to the feminine principle and to beauty – it may also represent some form of celebration.

Bowl

The bowl is one of the oldest dream symbols known. A bowl of water represents the feminine, fertility and the receptive principle or our capacity for emotion. A bowl of food represents our ability to nurture and sustain others. A bowl of flowers can represent a gift or a talent.

Box

Various types of boxes perceived in a dream can represent different aspects of the feminine personality. This arises from the old symbol of the square representing the physical aspect of the feminine.

To feel boxed in in a dream is to be prevented from expanding in an appropriate way, while to dream of packing things in a box suggests that we are not able to deal with feelings or thoughts which are giving us difficulty. If we are opening a box, we need to be aware of opportunities in waking life, but also not to act too rashly. Spiritually it represents the feminine containing principle.

Bread – Also see **Food**

Dreaming of bread connects us with our need for basic emotional and biological satisfaction. Bread is symbolic of life itself. It is food of the soul and can also represent the need to share.

Break

To dream of something being broken symbolizes loss or damage. If we actually dream of breaking something, action needs to be taken in order to break a bond or connection in our waking life. If a favourite object is broken we must make changes and break from the past or give up a cherished principle.

Breeze

Psychologically, for most people a breeze indicates happy times. Symbolically, wind is usually considered to belong to the intellect, so by this association a gentle breeze indicates love, while a stiff breeze can indicate a degree of abrasiveness.

Bridge

A bridge in a dream signifies the emotional connection between us and other people or various parts of our lives. It is one of the most commonly found images in dreams and almost invariably indicates the crossing from one phase of life to another, some kind of rite of passage, and for this reason it is sometimes taken to indicate death. The bridge may be depicted as weak or strong, sturdy or otherwise, which gives an indication of the strength of connection necessary to make changes in our waking life.

Bridle

Symbolically a degree of spiritual restraint or control is often needed. To be bridled in a dream, as in being yoked to something, indicates the need for focused effort. If the bridle is made of flowers it indicates a more feminine way of imposing control. If the bridle is harsher – such as one of metal and/or leather – we perhaps need to be harder on ourselves or on someone we love.

Brightness

A bright light symbolizes our move towards spiritual illumination, and to experience brightness in a dream means that some part of our life needs illuminating, often by an external source.

Broken – See **Break**

Brotherhood

In dream interpretation the Priesthood is often represented by a brotherhood and suggests the need to belong to a group of like-minded people. This could be something in the nature of a trade union, or of the Freemasons – something which allows us to work with our peers.

Brutality

Brutality manifests itself in demonic acts of evil. Unrestrained passion – whether sexual or otherwise – can appear as brutality and cruelty in our dreams. To experience some form of brutality in a dream can be frightening until we realize that we are connecting into the darker, more animal side of ourselves. We may need to deal with fears associated with that side of ourselves.

Bubble

Bubbles as beautiful but fragile objects remind us of the transitory nature of human existence, that nothing is permanent. We may dream of bubbles as part of our need to have fun in a child-like way. We often become aware of the temporary nature of happiness, and our need for illusion.

Buckle

A buckle can have a double meaning in dreams. It can represent a protective element against the forces of evil; it can also help us take the strain and not 'buckle' under pressure. To be fastening a buckle in a dream shows that we accept responsibility for what we do.

Buddha/Buddhist

If we dream of being Buddhist when we are not, we need to look at the difference between Western and Eastern religion. This is usually to do with spiritual clarity and the denial or loss of ego. There is a saying that goes, 'If you meet the Buddha on the road, kill him.'

Burial – Also see **Death**

To have a dream about being buried either alive or dead indicates a fear of being overcome, possibly by responsibility, or of repressing parts of our personality in ways which are harmful. To be attending a burial in our dreams shows the need to come to terms with loss, particularly of something that we value.

The obvious spiritual symbols of death, loss and pain are relevant here. This is not necessarily a negative meaning; we should look at resurrection and the positive elements that it can bring.

Butterfly

When seen in dreams or meditation, the butterfly represents the freed soul and immortality. There is no need for the soul to be trapped by the physical body, although psychologically, the butterfly can indicate a lack of ability to settle down or to undertake a protracted task. On a practical level, when seen in dreams, the butterfly represents light-heartedness and freedom.

C

Cage/Cell – Also see **Prison**

The cage normally represents some form of trap or jail. To dream of caging a wild animal alerts us to our need to restrain our wilder instincts. To dream that we are in a cage indicates a sense of frustration and perhaps of being trapped by the past.

We are also being warned that we are enforcing too much restraint on our hidden abilities. We could be allowing others to hold us back in some way.

Calendar

Time is a self-imposed limitation, so when anything that marks time appears in a dream we are being warned of the potential for limitation. Our attention may be being drawn to the past, present or future and a significant event in our lives.

Calf – See *Baby animal* under **Animals and Birds**

Camera

To be using a camera in a dream means we are recording events or occasions which we may need to remember or take note of more fully. Being filmed indicates that we need to look more carefully at our actions and reactions to certain situations.

Canal

Because a canal is a man-made structure, a dream about a canal usually indicates that we are inclined to be rigid insofar as the control of our emotions is concerned. We may be introducing too much structure into our lives at the expense of our creativity.

Cancer

To dream of a cancer, one of our most primal fears, indicates that we are out of harmony with our body. It indicates fear of illness and equally can represent something 'eating away' at us – usually a negative idea or concept. Intellectually we may have worked through our fears but still be left with attitudes and beliefs that cannot be cleared away, and very often this appears as cancer in dreams.

There is also the astrological sign of Cancer to bear in mind – The Mother and The Moon.

Candle

To dream of candles indicates that we are trying to clarify something that we do not understand. Candles on a birthday cake can therefore indicate that we are marking a transition from the old to the new. Lighting a candle represents using courage and fortitude or asking for something that we need. Psychologically, candles can represent knowledge or wisdom that has not fully crystallised. They can also represent our control of personal magic. On another level candles suggest illumination, wisdom, strength, and beauty.

Cane

Because many people associate the cane with some form of punishment or sadism, it can represent self-punishment or masochism. It is more likely, however, that we are trying to come to terms with some form of childhood trauma. Because a cane also represents pliability, we may be trying to achieve a balance between our willingness and our unwillingness to accept a situation.

Cannibalism

Cannibalism in dreams represents inappropriate behaviour. To be aware of eating human flesh may indicate our dislike of unsuitable foods or actions. There is often a part of ourselves we have not 'internalized' which we need to absorb. Eating human flesh in a dream can also mean that we are taking in wrong information in waking life. It also symbolizes the absorption of powers or qualities belonging to someone else.

Canoe

To dream of a canoe indicates that we are handling our emotions in isolation, though we are possibly making efforts to control their flow. We are aware that we are capable of making changes but only by our own efforts. We may be protected from our emotions, but we should consider whether this is appropriate.

Canopy

Dreaming of a canopy suggests that we need protection, shelter or love – or possibly all three. As a canopy protects the head – the seat of intellect – we may have a need to draw attention to higher ideals or aspirations.

Car – Also see **Journeys and Transport**

The car is representative of our own personal space. To dream of being in a car usually alerts us to our own motivation. Therefore, driving the car can indicate our need to achieve a goal, while being a passenger could indicate that we have handed over responsibility for our lives to someone else. Dream scenarios involving cars are often more to do with what we are doing to ourselves on a psychological or emotional level. Being alone in a vehicle indicates independence, while dreaming of the brakes of a car shows our ability to be in control of a situation. The car engine indicates the essential drives with which we have to deal. A crashing vehicle suggests fear of failure in life, while a car on fire denotes stress of some sort, either physical or emotional. To be in a car which is driven carelessly, either by us or someone else, marks a lack of responsibility, while a feeling of being left behind would be shown by your car being overtaken. To dream of reversing a car registers a feeling that we are slipping backwards or having to reverse a decision.

Cards (Greeting)

To dream of giving or receiving a card such as a birthday card alerts us to the need for a specific kind of communication with the addressee. Our subconscious may be registering concern, either about ourselves or others. On another level, there may be a need for visual communication, that is, the ability to convey a message spiritually.

Cards (Playing)

In a dream, playing cards highlight our ability to be open to opportunity or to take chances. The cards that we deal, or are dealt, in a dream may have significance as to number or as to suit: Hearts indicate emotion and relationship. Diamonds represent material wealth. Spades represent conflict, difficulties and obstacles. Clubs represent action, work and intelligence. The King portrays human success and mastery. The Queen indicates emotional depth, sensitivity and understanding. The Jack represents impetuousness, creativity or an adolescent energy.

Carriage – Also see **Journeys and Transport**

Dreaming of a carriage, such as a horse-drawn one, could be suggestive of old-fashioned attitudes to modern thinking. A train carriage would indicate that we are taking a journey that is slightly more public in character than a car journey. Any symbol that signifies our being moved in some way usually draws attention to our ability to make progressive changes in our lives. The carriage is also a symbol of majesty and power.

Carried/Carrying

To be aware of carrying an object suggests we need to look at what is being accepted as a burden or difficulty. If we dream of being carried we may feel that we are in need of support. To dream of carrying someone registers the fact that we may be accepting responsibility for someone else and that this responsibility is a burden.

Castrate – Also see **Sex**

Any dream containing sexual trauma is alerting us to our inner fears. The violent act of castration in a dream indicates the damage we are doing to ourselves in denying such fears. Conventionally, there may be some difficulty in coming to terms with the conflict between the masculine and feminine within.

Caterpillar

A caterpillar in a dream indicates that we need to go through a major change in order to progress. However, we must ensure that we remain flexible in our attitudes; that way we will be more open to the potential we have.

Cauldron – Also see **Kettle**

The cauldron symbolizes abundance, sustenance and nourishment; the magic cauldron represents feminine power and fertility. On another level, it may be that we need to acknowledge our intuitive abilities.

Cave

A cave represents a doorway into the unconscious. While initially the cave may be frightening, an exploration can reveal strong contact with our own inner selves. Passing through the cave signifies a change of state, and a deeper understanding of our own negative impulses.

Cemetery

A cemetery in a dream can mean both the part of ourselves that we have no use for and also our thoughts and feelings about death. Both things need to be handled, though the latter also entails dealing with the fear we may have surrounding death.

Centaur

The Centaur is half man and half beast, and is associated with the Zodiac sign of Sagittarius. To have a Centaur appear in a dream demonstrates the unification of man's animal nature with his qualities of human virtue and judgement. The symbol of a Centaur in a dream represents our ability to unite two complete opposites in an acceptable way.

Centre

To dream of being at the centre of something highlights our awareness of our ability to be powerful within a situation; that everything revolves around us. To be moving away from the centre indicates that part of our lives may be off balance. Psychologically, to be at the centre or in the middle of a situation shows we need to be aware of both our ability to control that situation and our ability to be flexible. Moving towards the centre shows our need for integrity in our day-to-day life.

Ceremony

When we dream of taking part in a ceremony, we are conscious of a new attitude or skill that is needed or an important major change that is taking place in our lives. We may need new order in our lives, or a deeper sense of awareness, and this is symbolized by a ceremony.

Chain

To dream of chains in any form indicates a type of restriction or dependency. The links in a chain can very often symbolize the communication that we need to free ourselves from stifling attitudes. Bondage and slavery, dignity and unity are all symbolized by chains and highlight their ambiguity.

Chariot – Also see **Journeys and Transport**

To dream of a chariot would possibly imply the necessity for old-fashioned methods of control within the situations surrounding us. The chariot may represent basic urges before they have been altered by conditioning.

Charity

To dream of giving or receiving charity has a lot to do with our ability to give and receive love and care. Charity comes from the word 'caritas', which means 'caring from the heart'.

Chased

This is a common dream theme and is often has to do with escaping responsibility or any sense of fear or failure we may have. To be chased by an animal generally indicates we have not come to terms with our own passion.

Chasm

When dreaming of a chasm we are being alerted to situations which hold unknown elements or are in some way risky. We will need to face the situation and eventually make decisions one way or another.

Chess

The game of chess originally signified the 'war' between good and evil, so in dreams it may still express the conflict within. It may also indicate the need for strategy in our lives. Playing chess and losing indicates that we have undertaken an activity in our waking lives that cannot be successful. We have not got the wherewithal, or perhaps the knowledge, to pit ourselves against greater forces.

Chest – Also see **Box**

A chest appearing in a dream symbolizes the way in which we hide or store our emotions or our important ideals. It may also store the best in us. Also in dreams a box – whether plain or otherwise – will show how we handle life.

Chimney

Any opening in a roof represents an awareness of change and growth. It also symbolizes an escape from the ordinary. On another level, a chimney and the passage of smoke portray the channelling of energy in a more productive way than is presently occurring.

Choking

When we find ourselves choking in a dream we are coming up against our inability to express ourselves appropriately. There is some conflict between our inner and outer selves, perhaps some indecision over whether we should speak out or remain silent. It is also possible that we are being stifled by people or circumstances and are not in control of either.

Christmas tree

For most people the Christmas tree is associated with a time of celebration, so to have one appear in a dream signifies the marking of a particular period of time, perhaps a new beginning. It may also indicate a time of giving, and by association the ability to enjoy the 'present'. We may recognize in a Christmas tree the lightening of a situation that so far has been either oppressive or depressive.

Churning

Most dreams in which there is a liquid being churned, boiled or made to move in some way are linking back to a very primitive sense of chaos (lack of order), and this indicates we may need to reassess our creative abilities to make use of the energy available to us. We very often need to become conscious of a very deep-rooted chaos in ourselves in order to become appreciative of our capacity for order.

City

Dreaming of a city indicates that we are trying to comprehend our sense of community or neighbourhood. We may need to socially or emotionally interact better. A deserted city may portray our feelings of having been neglected by others.

Cliff

To be on the edge of a cliff in a dream indicates we are facing danger or an unknown situation in our waking lives. It shows the need to make a decision as to how to deal with the situation, and possibly be open to taking a risk. There may be a step we need to take which will psychologically prepare us and put us 'on edge' in such a way that we must overcome our own fears in order to proceed through our own limitations.

Climbing

To dream of climbing is to dream of getting away from something, possibly of escaping – we may even be avoiding trouble. It also suggests that we are trying to reach new heights in our lives, possibly having to make greater efforts than before to succeed. On a more spiritual plane, climbing symbolizes ascension, in the sense of climbing to achieve enlightenment.

Cloak

A cloak can suggest warmth and love, but also protection. This protection can be either physical or emotional, or the spiritual protection of faith. Fear of losing the cloak can suggest the fear of losing faith or belief.

Clock

When a clock appears in a dream we are being alerted to the passage of time. We may need to pay more attention to our own sense of timing or duty, or to recognize that there is a sense of urgency in what we are doing. The clock hands in a dream may be indicating those numbers that are important to us. If an alarm clock rings we are being warned of danger or impending difficulties.

Clouds

There are various meanings in dreams about clouds. One indicates an uplifting experience; another can indicate that we are feeling overshadowed by someone; a third may also suggest that we have a hidden worry or difficulty that can be dealt with only after it has been given form in a dream.

Clover

Traditionally the clover plant is considered to be lucky, and therefore denotes good fortune is on its way. We need to look at our ability to bring the various parts of ourselves back into harmony with one another.

Club (People)

When we dream of being in a night club we are highlighting the right of every human being to belong. Psychologically we are not able to be part of a group until we have a certain level of maturity, so to dream of being with a crowd can denote our awareness of ourselves.

Club (Weapon)

To dream of using a weapon to club someone denotes an inner violence that has remained unexpressed. It may also depict our violence against ourselves, or our displeasure at something we have done. Conversely it shows we have great strength at our disposal, for which we need to find an outlet. On another level, a club signifies masculinity, although somewhat crudely expressed.

Coffin

When we dream of a coffin we are reminding ourselves of our own mortality. We may also be coming to terms with the death of a relationship and feelings of loss. We are also, perhaps, shutting our own feelings away, and therefore causing a part of ourselves to 'die'. On a spiritual level redemption, resurrection and salvation are all personified by the coffin.

Cold

To be conscious of cold in a dream is to be aware of feeling neglected, or of being left out of things. We can very often translate our inner feelings or our emotions into a physical feeling in dreams – to feel cold is one such translation.

Comb

A comb often signifies the need to tidy something up in our lives – we need to tidy up our thoughts. In a man's dream it can indicate seduction or sensuality. We may be conscious of the fact that we need to work with our self-image. Fertility, the rays of the sun, entanglement and music are all represented by the comb.

Comet

To dream of seeing a comet is to recognize the possibility of circumstances arising very quickly over which we have no control – the outcome may be unavoidable. It may also symbolize the answer to a problem coming to us with the speed of light. On another level, a comet symbolizes a deep impact, Armageddon, fire or danger.

Compass

Dreaming of a compass means we are attempting to find a direction or activity in our lives. We need to be able to understand the differing directions offered to us, and to follow the one that is right for us. The compass can also represent the source of life, or sometimes justice. On another plane, when we are trying to find direction, and sometimes our own limitations and boundaries, we need a compass.

Computer

The computer and other high technology images are now such a part of people's lives that it very much depends on other circumstances in the dream as to the most relevant interpretation of this image. If we work with computers a great deal it may simply be an everyday tool, whereas in other cases it will be a reminder of potential or abilities. It may also be that we are making a link with past memories or stored information.

Contraceptive – See Sex

Cooking

If we are cooking in a dream, then we are trying to satisfy a hunger – it may be ours, it may be someone else's. It does not necessarily have to be a physical hunger. Cooking can suggest the need to blend certain parts of our life with a view to success; after all, cooking is creative.

Cord

Within any relationship there are certain restrictions or dependencies, and these may be depicted in dreams as cords or ties. These emotional bonds can be both limiting and freedom-giving. We need to appreciate the ties of duty and affection. Spiritually, it is the symbolism of the Silver Cord – the subtle energy that holds the life force within the body.

Corn

Dreams containing images of corn or wheat symbolize fertility or fruitfulness. They may also represent new life or new developments in other ways. To be harvesting corn is to be reaping the rewards of hard work. We may be linking with some very primeval needs and requirements. It is worth knowing that The Great Mother in her nurturing aspect is always shown with corn.

Corner

If we turn a corner in a dream, then we have moved forward into a new experience or phase of our life. If we can note the direction, then turning a right-hand corner indicates a logical course of action; to turn a left-hand one indicates a more intuitive approach.

Corridor – Also see *Hall/Passages* under **Buildings**

When we dream of being in a corridor we are usually in a state of transition; possibly moving from one state of mind to another, or between two states of being. We may be in a disagreeable situation, but not be able to make decisions except to accept the inevitable.

Cosmetics – Also see **Makeup**

If we are using cosmetics in a dream, then it could be that we want to cover up our features or, conversely, enhance them. If we are using cosmetics on someone else, then it suggests that we need to enhance that relationship. Another meaning relates to our image and whether or not we are happy with it and want to make changes.

Countryside – Also see **Environments**

Dreaming of countryside puts us in touch with our own natural spontaneous feelings. It can help us to relax or may even provoke a certain mood. The countryside may also signify a need to clarify our own feelings about our lifestyle – particularly in terms of freedom.

Cradle

To dream of a cradle can represent new life or beginnings or, for a woman, pregnancy. In a man's dream a cradle can represent the need to return to a womb-like, protected state. An empty cradle can represent a woman's fear of childlessness or her fears of motherhood, depending on the other aspects of the dream. On another level, the physical as opposed to the spiritual body is sometimes represented as a cradle.

Crack

There may be a weakness or a flaw in our lives and this is symbolized by the notion of a crack appearing in a dream. It can also represent the irrational or unexpected. Another meaning is our inability to mentally 'keep it together' or our fear of not being able to do so.

Crooked Line

When a line appears in a dream as crooked, there is usually the need to register the oddity as being out of balance or off kilter. Another signification is acknowledging our own ability to be directed away from truth and honesty, and in some cases from what we consider to be normal.

Cross – See **Religious Imagery** and **Shapes**

Crossing

To dream of crossing a road is recognizing the possibility of danger or fear. We are perhaps pitting ourselves against the majority, or something that is bigger than us. To be crossing a field could suggest having a false sense of security – we may need to bring our feelings out into the open. On another plane, crossing a river or chasm often depicts death, not necessarily a physical death but possibly a spiritual change.

Crossroads

Dreaming of crossroads indicates that we are going to have to make choices in our lives, often to do with career or life-changes. Turning left at a crossroads can indicate taking the wrong route, though it can indicate the more intuitive path. To turn right can obviously mean taking the correct path, and can also mean making logical decisions.

Crowd

Dreaming of being in a crowd can symbolize the fact that we do not wish to stand out, or that we do not have a sense of direction at present – we may wish to camouflage our feelings from others. We may need to retain our anonymity, to create a facade for ourselves. A crowd, on another level, suggests popular belief, or common religious feelings.

Crown

To dream of a crown is to acknowledge our own success, and to recognize that we have opportunities that will expand our knowledge and awareness. It can also represent that we are about to receive an honour of some sort. The crown can represent victory and dedication particularly to duty. Another signification of the crown is victory over death, suggesting eventual spiritual attainment.

Crucible

Dreaming of a crucible suggests receptivity, intuition and creativity. It can also signify the great power we have, which, when released, allows us to take responsibility both for others and ourselves. A crucible can symbolize the potential of psychic energy.

Crutch

When we dream of crutches we are experiencing the need for support, although it may also be that we need to support others. We may find others inadequate and need to readjust our thinking; we may disapprove of other people's shortcomings or weakness. In our development we become aware of our various dependencies, whether these are alcohol, drugs, patterns of behaviour or people.

Crucifixion – See **Religious Imagery**

Cube – See **Shapes**

Cul-de-sac

When we find ourselves trapped in a cul-de-sac it symbolizes futile action, but perhaps also a state of idleness. Circumstance may be preventing a forward movement, and it may be necessary to retrace one's steps in order to succeed. If we are stuck in old patterns of behaviour, then we may be being threatened by past mistakes.

Cup

The cup contains much symbolism, especially indicating a receptive state that accepts intuitive information. Often the feminine is offering some opportunity from the unconscious. Intuitively if we are open to the more feminine side we are able to both give and receive help and assistance. The feminine awareness of the draught of life, immortality and plenty is intuitively and sensitively used.

Cymbals

Cymbals are connected with rhythm and sound, so for them to appear in a dream is an indication of the need for a return to a basic vibration. We are reconciling passion and desire. In another meaning cymbals signify two inter-dependent halves.

D

Dagger – Also see **Knife**

The dagger, as a weapon, is usually understood as a symbol of aggression or masculine power. Having the same significance as a knife, it will depend how it is being used as to the interpretation. Used to attack,we might become aware that we have something to eradicate in life. Used to defend suggests that we are being threatened in some way, but can be more assertive in reply. Any form of attack highlights our vulnerability.

Dam – Also see **Water** under **Environments**

Any symbol which suggests a bottling up of great energy can be interpreted as a natural expression of difficulty or frustration. The association with water suggests that we may be bottling up our own emotions and drive, or conversely we could be trying to stop somebody else's emotional outburst from happening. When we build a dam we are putting up defences but if a dam is bursting we may feel we have no control over emotional situations around us.

Dance/Dancing

Spiritually, dance signifies the rhythm of life, and the freedom of spirit which comes about through co-ordinated movement. In many cultures dance movements are symbolic of actions which were necessary for survival, such as the conflict with animals, or represented patterns of creativity. Dance is also used to portray extreme emotion, and it is this symbolism which often comes across most strongly dreams.

Danger

A dangerous situation in dreams will usually reflect in a graphic, rather exaggerated, form the anxieties and dilemmas of everyday life. Dreams often highlight danger or insecurities in symbolic form, such as conflict, fire or flood. Often such a dream contains a warning of inappropriate action which may harm us or others. Dreaming of being in a dangerous or precarious position can also indicate spiritual insecurity.

Dark

When the setting in a dream is dark it usually suggests some kind of negativity, a state of confusion or the depressed, hidden side of the personality. It can also suggest the Shadow, or a part of ourselves with which we have not come to terms.

Date (Day)

When a particular date is highlighted in a dream, we are either being reminded of something particularly significant – or possibly traumatic – in our lives or perhaps to consider the symbolism of the numbers contained in the date itself.

Date (Fruit)

Fruit, and particularly the date, is often associated with fertility and fertility rites. In Roman times dates, because of their luscious taste and spiritual connections, were often used as an aphrodisiac during pre-nuptial activities. Because dates are an exotic fruit, when we dream of dates we are becoming conscious of the need for the rare or exotic in our lives. Equally, we may need sweetness and nurturing. We need to be cared for and looked after in a way that is different from normal.

Dawn

A new dawn can bring a great sense of hope. To dream of a dawn or a new day represents a new beginning or a new awareness in circumstances around us. We are looking for different, perhaps more spiritual, ways of dealing with old situations.

Day

Time has no real meaning in dreams, so to note that time is measurable suggests that we are actually looking at the length of our lives. It will perhaps be a period of time before something can happen. Dreaming of a specific day of the week may also be a way of alerting us to our state of mind.

Death

Death is a transition from an awareness of the gross physical to the more spiritual side of one's nature. To dream of death, particularly our own, usually heralds some major change in life, the death perhaps of an old outdated way of being, necessitating a move into the unknown. Dreams of death often occur during those periods in life which were formerly handled by ceremonies and rites of passage, such as puberty to adulthood, maturity to old age. Many women dream of death during the menopause, and this is thought to be because the role of becoming a mother is no longer valid, and the woman must re-evaluate her life. Because in the past death held great dread, it also depicted catastrophe, in the sense that nothing would ever be the same again. Depending on personal belief, and whether one believed in life after death, it was something that had to be experienced and faced up to rather than understood. Dreaming of death therefore often became a symbol for birth, as a way of coping with it. In these present times, as people's attitudes change, death in a dream indicates a challenge which must be confronted. We need to adjust our approach to life and to accept that there can be a new beginning if we have courage.

Defecate – See **Excrement** under **Body**

Demolition
If we are carrying out the demolition we need to be in control, but if someone else is in charge we may feel powerless in the face of change. We may be conscious of a build-up of emotional energy within ourselves which can only be handled by a breakdown of old attitudes and approaches.

Devil
In previous times, the figure of the Devil was one to be feared and hated. It personified evil, and all of those things which cause conflict between higher ideals and the lesser self. As the wilder, more pagan side of ourselves, the conventional figure with horns and a tail will often appear in dreams. It is almost as though it has been given 'life' by the way that people concentrate on it. Once it is understood as something to be confronted, as something belonging to all of us, it loses its potency.

Devour
Clearing evil – or taking in good – is symbolized as devouring it. Kali, as the keeper of the graveyard, symbolizes this, as do the devouring Gods. It is a way of returning to source.

Digging/Excavation – Also see **Mine**

Often, when we begin the process of learning about ourselves, we need to uncover those parts we have kept hidden, and this is shown in dreams as excavating a hole or digging up an object.

Dinosaur

When we dream of monsters or prehistoric animals of any type we are touching into very basic images which have the power to frighten and amaze us. Because they are considered to be so large, we need to be aware of whether it is their size or their power which is frightening – our basic urges, if they remain uncontrolled, can threaten our everyday existence, by either their size or power.

Dirty

Evil or negative impulses are often shown in dreams as things or people being dirty.

Disk

A computer disk in a dream could suggest a great deal of information and knowledge is available to us. A compact disc can have a similar significance except that its content, being musical, is more recreational than work-oriented. This could indicate that in waking life we need to be aware of our need for relaxation. Divinity and power are represented spiritually by the disk.

Doctor

It will depend what sort of doctor appears in our dream as to the correct interpretation. A surgeon would suggest the need to cut something out of our lives. A physician would indicate that careful consideration should be given to our general state, whereas a psychiatrist signifies the need to look at our mental state. If the doctor is known to us he may stand as an authority figure.

Doll

A doll depicts how the dreamer felt as a child, a need for comfort or the reappraisal of childhood experiences which we have forgotten. Only 'coming alive' when played with, a doll may also express some undeveloped part of our personality.

Donkey – See **Animals and Birds**

Door

A door in a dream expresses the idea of a movement between two states of being. It can gain us entry into a new phase of life, such as puberty or middle age. There may be opportunities available to us about which we must make deliberate decisions.

If the door in the dream is shut or difficult to open it indicates we are creating obstacles for ourselves, whereas if the door is open we can have the confidence to move forward.

Dove – See **Animals and Birds** and **Flight**

Dragon

There is a heroic part in each of us which must face danger and conflict in order to manage the lower side of our natures and reach our inner resources. Seen as both frightening and yet manageable, the dragon under some circumstances will represent in us the 'wild' side of ourselves. We must come to terms with our own passions and chaotic beliefs in order to become custodians of our own future.

Dragonfly

The dragonfly represents immortality and regeneration. In dreams the dragonfly shows the need for freedom, but equally the recognition that freedom can be short-lived. Our reactions are instinctive rather than logical.

Draught

Typically a cold draught when working psychically indicates a visitation by Spirit. To feel a draught in a dream is to be aware of an external force which could affect us, or a situation we are in. It also suggests a communication from a hidden part of ourselves.

Draughts/Checkers – See **Games**

Drink

Drinking in a dream may indicate our need for comfort and sustenance, and to be taking something in or absorbing it. Spiritually there is a belief that the drinking of wine is, or symbolizes, the imbibing of Divine Life and power.

Drowning – Also see **Swimming**
We have allowed ourselves to be put in a situation over which we have no control and where we can be overwhelmed by emotions we cannot handle. We are unable to handle an emotionally stressful situation around us at the time of the dream. In more esoteric terms drowning symbolizes an immersion in the Sea of Life, and therefore a loss of ego.

Drum – Also see **Musical Instruments**
We may be seeking a more basic form of expression than the normal, everyday methods we use. We are becoming conscious of the natural rhythm which lies behind all life, and using sound and vibration to seek divine truth.

Drunk – Also see **Alcohol** and **Intoxication**
Being drunk in a dream indicates the need to make contact with a part of ourselves which is able to let go of restriction and inhibition. In previous societies it was an accepted part of life that, at certain times, drunkenness was allowed as a way of celebration or as a release of tension – hence the term a 'Bacchanalian revel'. There is the need to achieve a change of consciousness.

Dwarf/malformed figure – Also see **People**
A dwarf may signify a small part of ourselves that needs consideration. This may be a stunted aspect of our personality, not yet integrated or which has been left undeveloped and does not become apparent until we are prepared to take responsibility for it.

E

Earth

In dreams, earth is often a symbol for the natural support and nurturing which we all need. It can also suggest the mechanisms and networks which we have established in everyday waking life, and therefore take for granted. If we are trapped in earth, or buried in some way, it may be that the unconscious drives and needs which have been of value up to now are tending to overwhelm us. We should perhaps look to listening to our conscious thoughts more.

Earthquake

Old opinions, attitudes and relationships may be breaking up and this is causing concern. There is upheaval occurring in our lives, which may be on an emotional level, and we need to be prepared to deal with it carefully. A dream of this nature is almost bound to reveal hidden insecurities, but growth can take place, provided we are prepared to get rid of the debris – emotional or otherwise.

Easter egg

The Easter egg tends to be a symbol of spring, and suggests renewal or undeveloped potential. In dreams we are taken back to childhood feelings of promise and wonder. It may also alert us to the passage of time, since the mind will often produce symbols of times and seasons rather than actual dates.

Eating

Being eaten in a dream suggests being attacked by our own – or possibly other people's – emotions and fears. Being eaten by a wild animal shows the likelihood of us being consumed by our more basic, carnal nature or by our internal drives. Hunger is a basic drive and only once such a drive is satisfied can we move forward to satisfying our more aesthetic needs. To be eating in a dream shows that we are attempting to satisfy our needs or hunger. To refuse food suggests a rejection of growth and the opportunity to change.

Eclipse – Also see **Moon**

On a spiritual level, an eclipse in dreams can represent a loss of faith and fears and doubts about our own ability to succeed. Our light is being dimmed by others more able or talented than we are.

Education

Dreaming of education often takes us back to a former state, and indicates that we need to apply the knowledge we have gained from the experiences we have had to a present situation. To dream of a place of education, such as a school or college, suggests that we should be considering our own need for discipline or disciplined action. In terms of psychic development dreaming of education of some sort can symbolize new knowledge becoming available to us.

Egg

The egg is the symbol of potential, of opportunities yet to come; we have not made fully conscious our natural abilities, and are therefore not yet perfect. To be eating an egg in dreams demonstrates the need to take in certain aspects of newness before we can fully explore a different way of life. We may have to stand back and observe before we can undertake new learning experiences.

Egypt – Also see **Environments**

Faraway places in dreams usually signify the exotic. Egypt in particular in dreams is always seen as magical, mysterious or connected with ancient knowledge, though to what extent depends on our own knowledge of the country.

Ejaculation – Also see **Sex**

Our attitude to sex and sexuality often becomes apparent in dreams through the sexual act, and to ejaculate in a dream may be an effort to understand negative feelings, such as fear and doubt. It could also simply be indicative of the need for release, and the satisfaction of sexual needs.

Electricity

Electricity symbolizes power, and it will depend on the context of the dream which aspect of our energy is being highlighted. To dream of electrical wires is to be aware of our capabilities, which may have had to remain hidden for a time. Dreaming of switches shows we are aware of the ability to control. To receive an electric shock suggests that we are not protecting ourselves from danger of some sort, and need to be more aware.

Eloping/elopement

Elopement suggests some kind of union which is not accepted as valid by those around us. This may be an actual relationship, or some kind of partnership which by its nature needs to be kept secret. Dreaming of eloping, particularly with someone you know, is trying to escape from a situation in which our actions are not understood, but may lead to some kind of integration within ourselves.

Embryo

The core of being is the embryo, an extremely vulnerable part of ourselves, and therefore the centre of Creation. We may have the beginnings of a project in mind, or a new situation developing which needs careful nurturing. We are working towards conscious knowledge.

Employment

Employment dreams are often to do with how we assess our own worth among our peers, and what we mean by being gainfully employed. This can be as much to do with status as with reward. Such dreams may also have relevance to the way we perform tasks, with a high degree of focus or not, and also to how we perform in teams.

Empty

In a dream where there is emptiness this may reflect a day-to-day lack of pleasure and enthusiasm, or a sense of isolation There is an inability to realize expectations, and we have nothing left to give us a sense of security. Empty boxes or rooms might signify having got rid of outdated material, but having nothing to put in its place.

Enchantress

As the negative aspect of the feminine, the enchantress can appear in dreams as a woman meets her self-destructive side. She is to be understood rather than feared.

The enchantress is such a strong image within both the masculine and feminine psyches that she can appear in dreams in many guises. Morgan le Fay in the story of Arthur epitomizes the enchantress. She is the feminine principle in its binding and destroying aspect; the evil witch or the beautiful seductress. She has the power to create illusion, and the ability to delude others.

Enclosed/enclosure

Spiritually, any enclosure represents the protective aspect of The Great Mother. In dreams the defence mechanisms we put in place to prevent ourselves from deeply feeling the impact of such things as relationships, love, anxiety or pain can often manifest as an enclosed space. Restraints and constraints can appear as actual walls and barriers. Aspects of ourselves which are we too frightened give full expression are often perceived as enclosed spaces.

End

When in life we come to an ending there is also usually a new beginning. Thus when we dream of being at the end of a situation the signs are that it has run out of energy, and it is time to move on. Such a dream can suggest the attainment of a goal, or a point where change is inevitable. We need to decide what we can leave behind, and what must be taken forward. Endings can be both positive and negative.

Engineering

Often in dreams engineering of any kind will suggest the control and management of the inherent power we have, both within the spiritual and the physical realms. It suggests our ability to create a structure and use forces which are not normally available to us, through techniques and mechanical means. These will allow us either to progress or will make life easier for us. Dreaming of engineering works – as in roadworks – is to recognize the need for some adjustment in part of our lives so we can move on.

Enter/entrance

An entrance in a dream has the same relevance as a door, suggesting new areas of experience, the need to make changes, to create new opportunities. It is often worthwhile to note whether the entrance opens inward or outward, since this may give an indication as to how we handle ourselves in states of transition. An entrance which has two parts to it, such as a porch or an airlock, may be interpreted as the need to balance two aspects of ourselves before proceeding.

Escape

Escape suggests our need for spiritual freedom, of attempting to move beyond – or to avoid – difficult feelings. Many anxiety dreams have an element in them of the need to escape, either the situation itself, or something that is threatening us. We may also be trying to escape from something we know we must tackle, such as a responsibility or duty.

Evaporation

By raising our consciousness the energy within a situation can be changed for the better. We have it within our power to create opportunities for transformation, once we can deal with passionate feelings (water). They do not go away, they simply change state.

Evening

Evening in dreams signifies old age and wisdom. It also suggests twilight, and the boundaries of our conscious mind. Evening or evening light also means that we should take time for ourselves – perhaps by relaxing and remaining peaceful.

Evil

A sense of evil occurring in a dream usually suggests that there is something which is misplaced or corrupt. Evil usually brings with it a sense of dread, foreboding or disgust, particularly if it is accompanied by inappropriate action from other people. To experience evil in a dream is usually to be conscious of our own urges, which we have judged to be wrong.

Exams/being examined – Also see Tests

Dreaming of taking or being barred from examinations is a fairly typical anxiety dream which has a great deal to do with the standards we set ourselves, and our need for achievement. We have a need to be accepted for what we can do, so some of the occasions which first give us anxiety as children are used by the dreaming self to symbolize other such occasions. Being examined by a doctor or an alien may be in the first place alerting us to concerns over health, though this need not necessarily be physical, and in the second our own need to come to terms with our sense of our own body.

Excrement – Also see **Body**

The power of the person is said to be contained in his excrement, since we often need to let go various aspects and experiences of our lives, in order to make room for the new. Dreaming of experiencing pleasure in our own excrement returns us to a very deep innocent type of self-expression.

Explosion

A dream is a safe space in which to accomplish the cleansing which occurs through the release of anger and fear, and an explosion can symbolize such a process. It enables us to make room for more positive expression of what we are feeling and thinking.

Eye – See **Body**

F

Face

Faces appearing in dreams by themselves often seem to be random snatches of what many might call the psychic or astral content of our dreams. It often strikes us that the faces are particularly beautiful or by contrast hideously ugly, and since there is an element of disembodiment about them we are most likely being alerted to particular types of personality. We may be seeking knowledge or information not otherwise available to us. To concentrate on somebody else's face in a dream is an attempt to understand the outward personality. When the face is hidden from us, which can happen frequently as we choose to begin to develop psychic powers, we can make the assumption that certain information is being hidden from us until we are able to deal with it. We also at that stage probably need to look at how we are presenting ourselves within the everyday world.

Failure

Failure in a dream may not necessarily be personal. If, for instance, lights fail or refuse to work we may need to be aware of a lack of energy or power. Personal failure can indicate a degree of competitiveness or can offer alternatives in the way we need to act. The fear of failure is an almost universal fear, and to dream of failure may give us the opportunity to face that fear in an acceptable way. It does not necessarily mean that we will fail in waking life.

Fairground

The fairground has a dreamlike quality of its own. It is a sort of enclosed world of fantasy, and may alert us to the way in which we handle the child-like aspects of ourselves. Roundabouts might, for instance, suggest the daily round of existence, while swing-boats might signify the ups and downs of fortune.

The Ferris wheel is often a representation of the Wheel of Life. It is possible that we need to lose some of our inhibitions and as a result we will be able to take more pleasure out of life.

Fairy

Fairies are known to be capricious, and in dreams may represent the spontaneous elemental side of our being. It will obviously depend upon which type of fairy appears in our dreams, since each type will have a different significance. They may suggest mischief, or the more malign side of the coin, as in goblins and elves.

Fall/falling

The sensation of falling in dreams can arise during the hypnogogic or hypnopompic states. It may be interpreted as the need to be grounded, to take care within a known situation. Equally we may be harmed by being too pedestrian. Falling has also come to be interpreted as sexual surrender and as moral failure, not being as one should. We may not feel that we are properly in control of our lives.

Fame

The ego craves recognition, and dreaming of being famous or of achieving fame within a chosen field signifies that we ourselves need to recognize and give ourselves credit for our own abilities. If we are trying to make decisions as to how to move forward within our lives, we have to recognize our potential to stand out in a crowd. Being treated as a famous film star suggests our ability to be acknowledged by others, often in a slightly more glamorous way than normal.

Fan

A fan often suggests sensuality and sexuality. There was at one time a recognizable language associated with the fan, so such an article has come to represent the capricious feminine personality. Particularly in a woman's dream, the fan can be used as a symbol for openness to new experience and creativity. Waving a fan is reputed to clear away evil forces.

Fare

A dream in which we are having to pay a fare occurs when we feel that what we have done has not been given due acknowledgement, and that there is a need to come to terms with the demands that may be being made on us. To be paying a fare in a dream is acknowledging the price that is paid in order to succeed. A taxi fare would indicate a more private process than a bus fare.

Fasting

To be fasting in a dream may be an attempt to come to terms with some emotional trauma, or to draw attention to the need for cleansing in some way. If we have a grievance, fasting may be a way of making it known. Fasting is a way of changing consciousness, and also a move towards spirital realization through resistance to temptation.

Fat

To dream of being fat alerts us to the defences used against inadequacy. Equally we may also be conscious of the sensuality and fun side of ourselves we have not used before. Depending on how we think of our bodies in the waking state, we can often use the dream image of ourselves to change the way we feel.

Fax machine/fax

Messages from a hidden source or part of ourselves are often brought to us in dreams in a totally logical way. Thus, while the message itself may be unintelligible, how it is initially received is not. We may be aware that someone is trying to communicate with us but, because we are distanced from them, the transmission has to be mechanical. In a dream, a fax machine can have spiritual undertones in that it can be a way of transmitting messages from 'beyond'.

Feather

Feathers in a dream could denote softness and lightness, perhaps a more gentle approach to a situation. We may need to look at the truth within the particular situation and to recognize that we need to be calmer in what we are doing. Feathers often represent flight to other parts of the Self, and because of their connection with the wind and the air, can represent the more spiritual side of ourselves. To see feathers in a dream perhaps means that we have to complete an action before allowing ourselves to rest.

Fence

Dreaming of fences signifies that we are aware of boundaries – maybe class or social – it could also be a boundary within a relationship. It may be that we find it hard to express ourselves, in which case we need to put in a bit more effort. In terms of a fence, we have to get over it.

Ferry

To dream of being on a ferry indicates that we are making some movement towards change. Because the ferry carries large numbers of people it may also represent a group to which we belong that needs to make changes. The ferry is associated with death; there is the story of being ferried across the River Styx to death. This would indicate a major change is on its way.

Field

When we dream that we are in a field we are looking more at our field of activity – that is, what we are doing in everyday life and whether we feel we are achieving our goals. It may also be a play on words in that it is to do with the feeling state and is to do with the freedom from social pressure. It may also be an indication that we need to get back to nature, to basics, as it were.

Fiend – Also see **Devil**

To dream of a fiend or devil usually means that we have got to come to terms with a part of ourselves that is frightening and unknown and which we are yet to explore. We need to confront this part and make it work for us rather than against us. It is said that there is sometimes little difference between 'friend' and 'fiend'. We may find it worthwhile to look close to home for the answers if we suspect some kind of evil or misbehaviour.

Fig

The fig, because of its shape, is connected to sexuality, fertility, masculinity and prosperity. If we are eating figs in a dream, then it may be that a celebration is in order. The fig is also associated with the Tree of Knowledge and the deeper awareness that comes with that. On another level, it can represent a psychic ability and a direct connection with the beginning of physical life.

Fight

If we dream that we are in a fight, it usually indicates that we are confronting our need for independence. We may also need to express our anger and frustration and the subconscious desire to hurt a part of ourselves.

File

Dreaming of an abrasive file – such as a metal file – would suggest that we are capable of being too abrasive with people.

In modern times to dream of files or filing and thus putting order into our lives is to make sense of what we are doing and how we are doing it. A chaotic situation can now be dealt with in an orderly manner.

Film

To dream of being at a film indicates we are viewing an aspect of our own past or character that needs to be acknowledged in a different way. We are attempting to view ourselves objectively or perhaps we may be escaping from reality. Film as recording images is an important part of modern man's makeup and to be put in a position of viewing film within a dream is to be creating a different reality from the one we presently have. If we are making a film (if it is not our normal occupation), we may need to question the reality we are creating.

Finding

If we dream of finding something we are becoming aware of some part of ourselves that is – or will be – of use to us. To find something without much effort shows that events will take place that will reveal what we need to know. More esoterically, we may be close to finding something that will enable us to move forward.

Fire

Fire in a dream can suggest passion and desire in its more positive sense, and frustration, anger, resentment and destruction in its more negative. It will depend on whether the fire is controlled or otherwise as to the exact interpretation. To be more conscious of the flame of the fire would be to be aware of the energy and strength that is created. Being aware of the heat of a fire is to be aware of someone else's strong feelings. Psychologically, fire often appears in dreams as a symbol of cleansing and purification. We can use the life-giving and generative power to change our lives. Sometimes fire indicates the need to use our sexual power to good effect. To dream of being burnt alive may express our fears of a new relationship or phase of life. We may also be conscious of the fact that we could suffer for our beliefs. Baptism by fire signifies a new awareness of spiritual power and transformation.

Fireworks

Fireworks are generally accepted as belonging to a happy occasion or celebration, though they may also be frightening. So when we dream of fireworks we are hoping to be able to celebrate our own or someone else's good fortune. Fireworks can also have the same significance as an explosion. A release of energy or emotion can have quite a spectacular effect on us, or on people around us. In another meaning there could be an excess of spiritual emotion that needs to be channelled properly.

Fish

To dream of fish links in with our emotions – more specifically our ability to be wise without being methodical. We should all have awareness and knowledge, and to be dreaming of fish indicates that the common experience, as it were, is now more available to us than ever. Two fish swimming in opposite directions represents Pisces.

Flag – Also see **Banner**

A flag in a dream will have the same meaning as a banner – that is, a standard or a place round which people with common aims and beliefs can gather. It may also represent old-fashioned principles and beliefs.

Flail

Any instrument used to beat us in dreams is a recognition that someone has power over us, and can use force rather than giving us the power to act for ourselves. The flail would reinforce our ideas about authority. In older times the Jester would use a pig's bladder to flail the king to remind him of his need for humility. A flail can also represent spiritual supremacy and Supreme power that can be available to us.

Fleas

Fleas are an irritation, and in dreams signify just that. There may be people or situations in our lives that are causing us difficulty and we need to go through a process of decontamination in order to be free. We may be aware that we are not being treated properly and that people who should be our friends are not being fair. Fleas are symbolic of the type of evil that is likely to hurt, rather than destroy – such as gossip. We should recognize that we have the ability to deal with it.

Fleece

We may be word-associating as in the sense of being 'fleeced' or cheated. The fleece of a sheep also represents security, warmth and comfort, and will often signify those creature comforts we are able to give ourselves.

Flies

Flies are always associated with something nasty, which does not allow for the fact that they also devour rotten material. So to dream of flies is to be aware that we have certain negative aspects of our lives that need dealing with.

Flight/Flying – Also see **Journeys and Transport**

Conventionally to dream of flying is to do with sex and sexuality, but it would probably be more accurate to look at it in terms of lack of inhibition and freedom. We are releasing ourselves from limitations that we may impose on ourselves. To be flying upwards is to be moving towards a more spiritual appreciation of our lives, while to be flying downwards is to be making an attempt to understand the subconscious and all that it entails.

Floating

Floating in a dream was considered by Freud to be connected with sexuality, but it is probable that it is much more to do with the inherent need for freedom. Generally we are opening to power beyond our conscious self, when we are carried along apparently beyond our own volition. We are in a state of extreme relaxation and are simply allowing events to carry us along. Because we are not taking charge of our own direction, we are being indecisive and perhaps need to think more carefully about our actions and involvements with other people.

Flogging

Any violent act against the person usually indicates some form of punishment. To dream of being flogged would indicate that we are aware that someone is driving us beyond our limits, often in an inappropriate manner. Flogging ourselves would highlight a type of masochism in our own personality.

Flood

Although flood dreams are sometimes frightening they mostly indicate a release of positive energy. Often it is an overflow of repressed feelings, which, if we are in the middle of a flood, are also feelings that we have been overwhelmed by. On the flipside, floods do sometimes suggest depression.

Flowers

Flowers in a dream usually give us the opportunity to link to feelings of pleasure and beauty. We are aware that something new, perhaps a feeling or ability, is beginning to come into being and that there is a freshness about what we are doing. To be given a bouquet means that we are being rewarded for an action – the colour of the flowers may be important (See Colours in the Dream Interpretation chapter).

Formerly each individual flower had a meaning in dreams:

Anemone Your present partner is untrustworthy.

Arum Lily An unhappy marriage or the death of a relationship.

Bluebell Your partner will become argumentative.

Buttercup Your business will increase.

Carnation A passionate love affair.

Clover Someone who is in need of finance will try to get in touch.

Crocus A dark man around you is not to be trusted.

Daffodil You have been unfair to a friend; look for reconciliation.

Forget-me-not Your chosen partner cannot give you what you need.

Forsythia You are glad to be alive.

Geranium A recent quarrel is not as serious as you thought.

Honeysuckle You will be upset by domestic quarrels.

Iris Hopefully, you will receive good news.

Lime/Linden This suggests feminine grace.

Marigold There may be business difficulties.

Mistletoe Be constant to your lover.

Myrtle This gives joy, peace, tranquillity, happiness and constancy.

Narcissus Take care not to mistake shadow for substance.

Peony Excessive self-restraint may cause you distress.

Poppy A message will bring great disappointment.

Primrose You will find happiness in a new friendship.

Rose Indicates love and perhaps a wedding, within a year.

Snowdrop Confide in someone and do not hide your problems.

Violet You will marry someone younger than yourself.

Flute – Also see **Musical Instruments**

Many musical instruments – particularly wind instruments – indicate extremes of emotion, enticement and flattery. Because of the shape the flute is often taken as a symbol of masculine virility, but it could also be taken to stand for anguish. As a way of expressing the sound of the spirit, and therefore harmony, the flute can be used as a symbol of happiness and joy. It may also indicate celestial music and all that's associated with it.

Fog

To dream of being in a fog marks our confusion and inability to confront, or often even to see, the real issues at stake in our lives. To be walking in a fog is often a warning that matters we consider important can be clouded by other people's judgement and it may be wiser to sit still and do nothing at this time.

Following
If we are following someone in a dream we may need a cause or crusade to help give us a sense of identity. We could be looking for leadership or are aware that we can be influenced by other people. It also indicates that, particularly in a work situation, we are perhaps more comfortable in a secondary position rather than out in front. When we dream of being followed we need to identify if what is following us is negative or positive. If it is negative, we need to deal with past fears, doubts or memories. If positive, we must recognize our need to take the initiative, or to identify what drives us.

Food – Also see **Eating** and **Nourishment**
Our need and enjoyment of food fulfils certain inherent needs. The meanings are as follows:

Bread When we dream of bread we are looking at our experiences and our basic needs.

Cake This signifies sensual enjoyment.

Fruits We are representing in dream form the fruits of our experience or effort, and the potential for prosperity. The colour could also be significant.

Ham/Cured Meat Our need for preservation is represented by cured meats.

Meals Depending on whether we are eating alone or in a group, meals can indicate acceptance and sociability.

Meat Physical or worldly satisfaction or needs are shown often in dreams as meat. Raw meat at one time signified misfortune.

Milk As a basic food, milk will always signify baby needs and giving to ourselves.

Onion The different layers of us are often shown as an onion (Also see individual entry).

Sweets These tend to represent sensual pleasure.

Vegetables These represent our basic needs and material satisfaction. They also suggest the goodness we can take from the earth and situations around us. The colour may also be important (See Colour in the Dream Interpretation chapter).

Footprints

To see footprints in a dream indicates that we are needing to follow someone. If those footprints are stretching in front of us there is help available in the future, but if they are behind us, then perhaps we need to look at the way we have done things in the past. They usually indicate help in one way or another, and certainly consideration. If we see footprints going in opposite directions we need to consider what has happened in the past and what might happen in the future.

Forest

Dreaming of forests or a group of trees usually means entering the realms of the feminine. A forest is often a place of testing and initiation. It is always something to do with coming to terms with our emotional self, of understanding the secrets of our own nature.

Fork

A fork, particularly a three-pronged one, is often considered to be the symbol of the Devil and therefore can symbolize evil and trickery. In dreams a fork denotes duality and indecision. Psychologically, the fork can signify the same as a barb or a goad – something that is driving us, often to our own detriment. We may have come to a fork on our spiritual path and development and need guidance as to which direction to take.

Forge

When the forge and the blacksmith were a part of normal, everyday life this particular dream would indicate some aspect of hard work or desire to reach a goal. Now it is more likely to mean a ritual action. The forge represents the masculine and active force. It also represents the power of transmuting that which is base and unformed into something sacred. To dream of a forge indicates that we are changing internally and allowing our finer abilities to be shown.

Fountain

To dream of a fountain means that we are aware of the process of life and 'flow' of our own consciousness. Because of its connection with water it also represents the surge of our emotions, and often our ability to express this. The fountain can also represent an element of play in our lives, the need to be free-flowing and untroubled.

Fraud

When fraud appears in a dream, particularly if we are the one being defrauded, there is the potential to be too trusting of people. If we are the one committing fraud, then we are running the risk of losing a good friend.

Friend

A friend appearing in our dreams can signify one of two things. Firstly we need to look at our relationship with that particular person, and secondly we need to decide what that friend represents for us (for instance: security, support, or love). Often friends highlight a particular part of our own personality that we need to look at, and perhaps understand or come to terms with, in a different way.

Funeral

To dream of being at a funeral indicates that we need to come to terms with our feelings about death. It may also indicate a time of mourning for something that has happened in the past and this time of mourning can allow us to move forward into the future. Dreaming of our parents' funeral indicates a move towards independence.

Furniture

The furniture which appears in our dreams, particularly if it is drawn to our attention, often shows how we feel about our family and home life, and what attitudes or habits we have developed. It can also give an indication as to how we feel about ourselves. For instance, dark heavy material would suggest the possibility of depression, whereas brightly painted objects could testify to an upbeat mentality. Sometimes the furniture which appears in a dream can highlight our need for security or stability, particularly if it is recognizable from the past.

Different articles can represent different attitudes:

Bed/mattress This can show exactly what is happening in the subtle areas of our close relationships. We can get an insight into how we really feel about intimacy and sexual pleasure. For some people the bed is a place of sanctuary and rest, where they can be totally alone.

Carpet Often when carpets appear in a dream we are looking at our emotional links with finance. The colour of the carpet should be noted (See Colour in the Dream Interpretation chapter).

Chair A chair can indicate that we need a period of rest and recuperation. We may need to deliberately take time out, to be open to other opportunities.

Cupboard/wardrobe Cupboards and wardrobes may depict those things we wish to keep hidden, but may also depict how we deal with the different roles we must play in life.

Table For a table to appear in a dream is often to do with communal activity, and with our social affiliations (Also see individual entry and **Altar** under **Religious Imagery**).

G

Gall

Gall in old-style symbolism represented bitterness and disgust. To find something galling is to find it irritating, often without being able to do anything about it. In dreams this can be translated into slime or goo which is overwhelming. Recognizing this feeling through dreams can result in us being able to express whatever is irritating us.

Gale – Also see **Wind**

Being in a gale in dreams indicates that we are being buffeted by circumstances that we feel are beyond our control. We have got ourselves into circumstances over which we have no control. We must make decisions as to whether we are going to confront the forces of nature, or perhaps our own inner spirituality, and harness the energy that we have, in order to fulfil a task.

Games

Playing any game in our dream indicates that we are taking note of how we play the game of life. If we are playing well we may take it that we are coping well with circumstances in our lives. If we are playing badly we may need to reassess our abilities and to identify which skills we need to improve in order to do things better. Games and gambling can also represent not taking life seriously. They can show how we work within the competitive field and give us some kind of insight into our own sense of winning or losing.

Specific games such as football, baseball, rugby and cricket, which are team games, represent for many the strong ability to identify with a 'tribe' or a group of people. Because they are mock fights they can be used as expressions of aggressiveness against other people, in the way that wars and localized tribal fights were used previously. They indicate the way in which we gain identity and how we connect with people. In dreams, games which require the power of thought and strategy – such as chess or draughts – often give some idea of how we should be taking a situation forward (See **Chess**). Decisions may need to be made where we have to gauge the result of our action, and take into account our opponent's reaction.

To dream of gambling indicates that we may need to look at something in our lives that is figuratively a gamble; we may need to take risks, but in such a way that we have calculated the risks as best we can.

Garage

A garage is the workshop from which we move out into the world, having done what we need to do in order to repair and conserve the symbols of our success. In dreams a garage is representative of the way we look after and maintain our drive and motivation, and how we look after the resources that we have.

If we are having to pay a visit to a professional garage, it can suggest an expertise that we do not have, or a source of energy that needs to be properly maintained.

Garbage

Garbage or rubbish in our dream suggests that there are certain parts of our lives that can now be thrown away or discarded. We have perhaps still retained 'left-over' feelings and concepts that may have nurtured us in the past but no longer do so. It will often depend on the type of garbage that is being thrown away as to the symbolism. The remains of food preparation would make us look at nurturing, while throwing out old furniture might suggest discarding something that no longer brings comfort.

Garden

In dreams a garden can represent a form of paradise, as in the Garden of Eden, and is often a symbol of the feminine and qualities of wildness. Dreaming of a garden can be illuminating, because it can indicate areas of potential growth in our own lives, or it can be that which we are trying to cultivate in ourselves. A closed garden suggests virginity or purity. It also often signifies our inner life and that which we totally appreciate about our own being.

Garland

Psychologically a garland can represent honour and recognition, some sort of accolade for work done or a task completed. Such a thing in dreams would suggest approval by our peers, rather than self-congratulation. Garlands as decoration of a space or building are a rather old-fashioned representation of a time of celebration and merriment.

Garlic

Garlic in olden times had a great deal of importance, particularly in the use of magic. It was often seen as a symbol of masculine fertility and because of its smell it was seen as protection against evil forces. Dreaming of garlic may therefore connect back to either of these meanings, unless of course it is being used in cooking when the meaning may be altered by the symbolism of the other ingredients.

Gas

Gas can have the same significance as air and wind in dreams but usually is taken to be slightly more dangerous. It may suggest intellectual power, which when controlled is useful but dangerous when misused. As something supplied to us from an external source it is a precious useable commodity which requires discretion and thought in its application. To dream of not being able to turn the gas on, for instance, would suggest that there is a lack of energy in a particular project.

Gate

A gate in dreams signifies passing through some kind of barrier or obstacle in order to continue on our way. It marks a transition or change from one stage to another. Often the awareness of change is highlighted by the type of gate. For instance, a utilitarian gate such as a factory one would tend to indicate a work change, whereas a garden gate might represent pleasure. Dreaming of a gate usually signifies some kind of change, often in awareness. The gate between the physical and spiritual realms has a long established existence, and may suggest death.

Genitals – Also see **Body**

The child becomes aware of his or her own genitals, particularly as a source of pleasure – at a very early age, so to dream of our own genitals could suggest a need for child-like comfort, or some problem with our sexuality. To dream of being mutilated around the genitals could refer to either past or present mistreatment, either sexual or emotional, or a blow to our self-esteem. Dreaming of someone else's genitals either indicates our involvement with that person's sexuality, or, if of the opposite sex, our need to understand the hidden side of ourselves.

Ghost

When we dream of the dead they usually appear as quite substantial figures, so it is unlikely that dreaming of a ghost actually represents a spirit entity. It is much more likely to signify old memories, feelings, or hopes and dreams, which may be somewhat insubstantial. By putting ourselves in touch with what is now defunct we can take appropriate action in the here and now. Oddly, ghosts in dreams can also suggest perhaps previous incarnations or spiritual states. The shadowy figure so often perceived in dreams is a representation of the Shadow – those parts of ourselves that we have suppressed.

Giant

Giants and ogres in dreams often represent an emotion that is big and uncontrollable. It is often unconfined primordial power, and takes us back to the helplessness we may have experienced as a child in an adult world. We may also become conscious of ourselves as being larger than life as we begin to develop spiritually, and need to become aware of the shifts in perspective that are necessary. Dreaming of giants helps us to handle such change without too much trauma.

Gift – Also see **Present**

In a spiritual sense, dreaming of a gift may be highlighting our creative talents, of which we may not have been aware. To receive a gift within a dream is to recognize our talents and abilities. Each of us has a store of unconscious knowledge which from time to time becomes available, often through dreams. Depending on the other elements in the dream, we are acknowledging what we receive from others.

Gig

Today, the gig, concert, or rave has taken the place of the dance or tea party. In dreams, therefore, it can represent an opportunity for freedom and movement, a social occasion or a gathering of people who are on the same wavelength as ourselves. This then signifies our need for us to 'let go', if only for a short time.

Girdle

A girdle represents wisdom, strength and power, and also the inevitability of the cycle of life and death. In a woman's dream the girdle may depict her sense of her own femininity, for instance whether she feels bound or constricted by it. In a man's dream it is more likely to show his understanding of his power over his own life.

Giving

Giving is all about the internal relationship with ourselves or the environment and with others. We all need to share aspects of ourselves with others, and to be conscious of giving in a dream shows our need to share our (perhaps excess) energy.

Glass

Glass is a barrier but it is transparent and therefore allows us to see that which we cannot reach. If we dream of breaking glass we are probably ready to break free from emotional ties and enter a new phase in our lives. Any barriers that we or others put up can be dealt with successfully. Glass also signifies the barrier of death.

Glasses/Spectacles

Glasses or spectacles indicate an association with our ability to see or to understand. Psychologically, when we are able to wear glasses we are more able to look at that which is external to ourselves rather than turning inwards and becoming introspective. In the spiritual sense, a dream of glasses or spectacles may be urging us to take a different viewpoint. Equally, if someone is unexpectedly wearing glasses, it is to do either with our lack of understanding or perhaps their inability to see where we are coming from.

Globe

A globe symbolizes our need for wholeness or the approach to wholeness. To dream of looking at a globe, particularly a world globe, indicates our acknowledgement of the need for a wider viewpoint. We can cultivate a more globally aware perspective. We have certain powers within us that will enable us to create a sustainable future for all, and for this we need to be able to understand and take a world view.

Goad

If we are goading somebody to do something they do not want to do in a dream, we must take care that we are not creating circumstances that could turn around and control us in our waking lives. We may be trying to force people to take action to move forward but we must also be aware that we need to be in control of that particular movement. Psychologically, we are all goaded by our own more aggressive and negative parts. Often a dream can reveal how we are making things difficult for ourselves and can represent which parts of ourselves are taking authority over the others.

Goal

To dream of scoring a goal may indicate that we have set ourselves external targets. In achieving those targets we may also recognize that the goals that we have set ourselves in life are either short or long-term and we may need to adjust them in some way. If we miss a goal, then we may need to reassess our abilities to make the grade – but we can still aspire to great things.

Goblet

In dreams the goblet represents the feminine, receptive principle and our ability to achieve enjoyment in different ways. We may be able to make a celebration out of something that would appear to be quite ordinary. To be drinking from a goblet indicates allowing ourselves the freedom to enjoy life to the full. To dream of a set of goblets, indicates several different ways in which we can make our lives enjoyable and fun.

Goggles – See Glasses/Spectacles and Mask

Gold

Gold signifies the best, most valuable aspects of ourselves. Finding gold indicates that we can discover those characteristics in ourselves or others. Burying gold shows that we are trying to hide something. Gold in dreams can also represent the sacred, dedicated side of ourselves. We can recognize incorruptibility and wisdom, love and patience. In this context it seldom stands for material wealth, being more the spiritual assets that we have.

Golf – Also see **Games**

The game of golf can represent belonging to a team, but conversely it can also represent our own individual achievement. To be playing such a game indicates that we need freedom of movement and clarity of vision. Playing golf can often represent our need to show our prowess, to be able to drive as far as we can, and often is used within the context of business acumen.

Gong

If we hear a gong sounding then we need to recognize that a limitation has been reached, or that we are summoned to success. If we are striking the gong, then this represents a need for strength. Overall a gong symbolizes that something requires recognition.

Gossip

To be gossiping in a dream can mean that we are spreading information, but in a way that is not necessarily appropriate. To be in a group of people and listening to gossip generally means that we are looking for some kind of information, but perhaps do not have the ability to find it alone. Thus, to be gossiping in a dream may mean that we have to complete certain actions before moving on.

Grail

The Holy Grail is such a key image that in dreams it can appear as something miraculous, something that fulfils our wish and allows us to move forward into our full potential. Often it signifies the achievement of spiritual success, but can also represent the cup of happiness. The grail appearing in a dream indicates that we can expect some form of satisfaction and change to occur within our lives. We are searching for something that we may feel is unattainable, but by putting ourselves through various tests may eventually be attainable.

Grain

Dreaming of grain can indicate some kind of a harvest. We have created opportunities for ourselves in the past that now can come to fruition. Provided we look after the outcome of these opportunities, we can take that success forward and create even more abundance. To dream of grain growing in a field can indicate that we are on the point of success, that we have tended our lives sufficiently to be able to achieve growth.

Grasshopper

The grasshopper is a symbol of freedom and capriciousness, and in dreams it can often indicate a bid for freedom. The expression 'a grasshopper mind' shows an inability to settle to anything, and will be seen in dreams as a grasshopper. On another level, in Chinese history the grasshopper is often associated with enlightenment.

Grave – Also see Death

Dreaming of a grave is an indication that we must have regard for our feelings about, or our concept of, death. Such a dream may also be attempting to deal with our feelings about someone who has died – part of our personality may have been killed off, or is dead and buried to the outside world.

Gravel

Often our attention is drawn to the size of an article within a dream. Gravel in this context is simply an indication of small particles; we perhaps need to pay attention to the small details in life. Such a dream may also bring back memories of a particular time or place, and remind us of happier times, such as those of childhood. Skidding on gravel signifies that we should avoid taking risks in everyday life.

Grease

In a dream, grease is the word that indicates that we have not taken as much care over a situation as we should have. It suggests that we should use better judgement lest we put ourselves at unnecessary risk. Grease can also signify making things easier for ourselves.

Guillotine

A guillotine in a dream indicates something irrational in our personality; we may be afraid of losing self-control. We could be aware of an injury to our person or to our dignity. There is the potential for us to lose contact with someone we love, or with the part of ourselves that is capable of love. By way of its physical action, a guillotine represents a severance of some kind.

Guitar

Guitar music in a dream can indicate the possibility of a new romance, but can also indicate the need for caution. If we are playing the guitar we are making an attempt to be more creative with our talents. Any musical instrument characterizes our need for rest and relaxation and for harmony in our lives.

Gun

In dreams the gun has masculine and sexual connotations. If a woman is firing a gun she is aware of the aggressive side of her personality. If she is being shot at she perhaps feels threatened by overt sexuality. It will depend on the other circumstances in the dream as to how we interpret the use of a gun. We may, for example, be using it as a protection of those things we feel are important to us. The symbolism here also reverts to a more base attribute – that of straightforward masculinity.

Guru

A guru appearing in a dream is a representation of the wisdom of the unconscious. As that wisdom becomes available we often bring it through to conscious knowledge. Psychologically, we all need a symbol for a father figure and this is one such symbol. In searching for knowledge of a specific sort, we need an external figure with whom to relate. In Eastern religions, this is the guru – who performs the same function as the priest in Western religion. For many of us, God is too remote for us to be able to have a personal relationship with him. A guru therefore becomes the personification of all wisdom made available to us through his perception. He will assist us in accessing our own innate wisdom.

H

Hail

Because it is frozen water, hail signifies the freezing of our emotions. It would appear that the damage created by these frozen emotions comes from outside influences rather than internal feelings. Hail has a particular part to play in the cycle of nature. We need to appreciate that there are times when numbing our emotions may be appropriate – though not indefinitely.

Hair – See **Body**

Ham – See **Food**

Hammer

Dreaming of hammers indicates a more aggressive, masculine side of our nature. There may be the feeling that part of our personality needs to be crushed or struck for us to be able to operate properly. The double-sided hammer also has particular symbolism. The two sides are justice and vengeance. You should consider carefully which one is relevant to you.

Hand – See **Body**

Handcuffs

Dreaming of being in handcuffs denotes that we are being, or have been, restrained in some way, possibly by an authority figure, or possibly by our own doubt or fear. If we are putting handcuffs on someone, we may be attempting to bind that person to us, which at the same time smacks of possessiveness.

Hanging

Hanging is a violent, sometimes misjudged, act against a person; if we witness a hanging in our dream, then we are open to violence, and perhaps need to reconsider our actions. If we ourselves are being hanged, we are being warned of a problem – possibly the prospect of taking the blame for someone else's actions. Alternatively, there may be a hang-up in our lives. If something is hanging over us, then we are being threatened or suppressed by some circumstance around us.

Hare – See **Animals and Birds**

Harem

For a man to dream that he is in a harem suggests that he is struggling to come to terms with the feminine nature. For a woman, it shows that she is understanding her own flamboyant, sensual side. On a different level, she is also recognizing her need to belong to a group of women – a sisterhood.

Any group of women appearing in dreams will signify femininity in one form or another, and a detailed interpretation will depend on whether the dreamer relates to a particular person in the scenario.

Hat

A hat frequently suggests knowledge.

Harp

Dreaming of a harp indicates that we need to find the correct vibration within our life to create a harmony. If we are 'harping on' then we need to be listened to. The harp sometimes signifies the ladder to the next world.

Harvest

We are going to reap the rewards of all the hard work we've put in - if the symbolism for harvest has its way. To dream of a harvest can actually have two meanings. In can mean looking back into the past and reaping the rewards, or it can mean looking towards the future in order to use what has happened previously.

Hash

To dream of hash, as in marijuana weed, indicates we are using substances to raise consciousness and we probably need to recognize that it's time to look at things from another direction and perspective.

Hay

Hay, hayfield and haystacks often indicate fun, relaxation and girls and boys who like to have fun. There is a warmth surrounding the symbolism for hay as it also can conjure up good memories and feelings.

Head – See **Body**

Hearse

Obviously linked to death, the hearse denotes we are concerned about a lack of time. However, it may be that time is running out, not necessarily for us, but for a project or relationship. If we connect with the latter, then it may be best to leave things as they are rather than try any kind of resurrection.

Heart – See **Body**

Hearth

To dream of a hearth or fireplace is to recognize the need for security. This may be of two different types. One is knowing that the home is secure. The other is recognising the security of the inner self. We may be, or need to be, linking with our own passionate wilder nature.

Heaven – See **Religious Imagery**

Hedgehog – See **Animals and Birds**

Heel – See **Body**

Hell – See **Religious Imagery**

Hen – See **Animals and Birds**

Hermaphrodite – Also see **Sex**

When we dream of a hermaphrodite, we may be uncertain about our own gender, or about our ability to adjust to the roles played by our own sex. As we learn more about ourselves, we attempt to achieve a balance between the logical and the sensitive sides of our nature.

Hermit

There is a type of loneliness within many people that prevents them from making relationships on a one-to-one basis. This may manifest in dreams as the figure of the hermit. In dreams if we meet the hermit, we are discovering the dimension in ourselves that has a spiritual awareness.

Hero/Heroine – See Archetypes in the Enhancing Your Dreams chapter

Hill

To be on top of a hill indicates we are aware of our own expanded vision. We have worked hard to achieve something and are able to survey and assess the results. To be climbing a hill in the company of others often indicates that we have a common goal – that a journey we thought was ours alone is actually not – and we can use their knowledge to help us. To dream that we are going downhill would indicate we are feeling as if circumstances are pushing us in a certain direction.

History

To acknowledge a sense of history in a dream suggests we are linking with the past and past aspects of our personality. It may be that we are looking back and assessing the person that we may have been, and that can either be a positive or negative thing.

Hive

The hive usually represents an area of work where there is considerable activity – and where the best use is made of all resources in order to move out and move on. To dream of being near a hive can represent the effort that is needed to be made to create fertility for ourselves. The hive can also represent protective motherhood.

Hole

A hole usually represents a difficult situation. If we are falling into a hole then we are getting into the unconscious side of our fears, that is, getting beneath the surface of our personalities. A hole above our heads can signify a way through to spiritual understanding. A round hole represents the Heavens; a square hole represents the Earth.

Holiday

To be on holiday in a dream indicates a sense of relaxation and of satisfying our own needs without having to take care of others. It could also be a suggestion that it is time to take a break from everyday life.

Hollow

Dreaming of feeling hollow connects with our feelings of emptiness, lack of purpose, direction and control in our lives. We may also be lacking motivation. To dream of being in a hollow would indicate that we need some kind of protection from what is going on around us.

Holy Communion – See **Religious Imagery**

Home

The home, and particularly the parental home, can stand for shelter, warmth and nourishment. To dream of being at home signifies a return to the standards we learnt as a child. The home can also represent sanctuary – that is, a place where we can be ourselves without fear of reprisal.

Homosexuality – Also see **Sex**

If, in a dream, we are attracted to someone of the same sex, then the suggestion is that we have a conflict, or are anxious about our own gender. It may also indicate that we need a different kind of love other than sexual, sometimes needing to love ourselves in a specific way. In another way, to dream of homosexuality is an attempt to come to terms with opposite aspects of ourselves – we are making ourselves more whole with a view to more success in relationships.

Honey

Honey represents pleasure and sweetness. To dream of eating honey can be to recognize that we need to give ourselves pleasure. Equally, it can indicate the very essence of our feelings. Honey has links to fertility and virility. So, in a dream this would indicate that we are perhaps entering a much more actively sexual or fertile time.

Horse – See **Animals and Birds**

Horseshoe

The horseshoe is a lucky symbol and, traditionally, if it is turned upwards it represents the moon and protection from evil. When turned downwards the power is reputed to 'drain out', bringing bad luck. The horseshoe is also connected as a lucky symbol to weddings. In former times, to dream of a horseshoe indicated that there would shortly be a wedding in your family.

Hood

A hood has a menacing air to it and it may indicate that there is a part of us that feels threatened in some way. More likely is the idea that part of our personality may be invisible to us and needs to be uncovered in order for us to function. Traditional interpretation said that for a woman to be wearing a hood indicated she was being deceitful. If a man is wearing a hood, it suggests that he is withdrawing from a situation.

Hook

When we dream of a hook we are understanding that we have an ability to draw things towards us that are either good or bad. It can also indicate that we are being 'hooked', and therefore not being allowed the freedom we want. In childhood dreams the hook can represent the hold that a parent has over us. This symbolism can continue into adulthood, depicting the way that we allow people to take control within our lives.

Horns – Also see **Antlers**

Horns suggest the idea of the animal within the human. Following on from that horns also denote masculine sexuality, and possibly the desire to hurt.

If it is a hunting horn, then it is either a warning or a summoning of some kind. More spiritually, horns can suggest the search for divinity.

Hospital – Also see **Operation**

Depending on our attitude to hospitals, when one appears in a dream it can either represent a place of safety, or a place where our very being is threatened and we become vulnerable. It can also represent that aspect within ourselves that knows when some kind of respite is needed, possibly in order to re-evaluate a situation.

Hot

Good feelings can be translated in dreams to a physical feeling. To dream of being hot indicates warm, passionate feelings. To be aware that our surroundings are hot indicates that we are loved and cared for. Now and again, extreme emotion can be interpreted as a physical feeling – so anger, jealousy or other such feelings can be experienced as heat. Experiencing something as hot that should be cold indicates that we are perhaps having difficulty in sorting out our feelings.

Hotel – Also see **Buildings** under **Environments**

If a hotel crops up in dreams, then we may need to escape from a situation for a while. Alternatively, it may be that our current situation is only temporary.

Living in a hotel signifies a basic restlessness and unsettled aspect of the dreamer's character, who may be attempting to escape from himself.

Hourglass

In dreams time is irrelevant. To experience something that measures time is often to alert us to the need for measuring our activities more precisely. When we are under stress we can be overly aware of the running out of time, that it can become an enemy – this can be symbolized as an hourglass. The hourglass used to be taken as a symbol of death. More properly, it is a symbol for the Passage of Life.

Hunger

Apart from actually being hungry, to experience hunger in a dream suggests that our physical, emotional or mental needs are not being properly satisfied – every human being has needs that require fulfilment.

Hunt

Dreaming of being hunted is mostly taken to be to do with our sexuality. Its even older meaning is linked with death, particularly a death containing an aspect of ritual killing or sacrifice. By association, therefore, to dream of a hunt is to register the necessity for a change of state in everyday life.

Hurricane

When we experience a hurricane in a dream we are sensing the force of an element in our lives that is beyond our control. A hurricane can also be symbolic of our passion – we may need to figure out if we can control it – with the consequences for others being of importance.

Husband – See **People and Family**

Hyena – See **Animals and Birds**

I

Ibis – See **Animals and Birds**

Ice-cream

Ice-cream appearing in a dream deals with the sensual tastes that we have. Normally it is a pleasurable experience, and very often reminds us of childhood. To be eating ice-cream indicates that we may be accepting pleasure into our lives in a way that we have not been able to do before. To be giving other people ice-cream indicates that we are giving other people pleasure. However, we must bear in mind that the pleasure, like the ice-cream, can melt away.

Icon – See **Religious Imagery**

Igloo – Also see **Buildings** under **Environments**

An igloo can represent both a cold exterior containing a very warm interior, or the coldness of the construction itself. It can appear as though someone is uncaring and therefore creating an icy home environment, although there is warmth within that person. On another level an igloo can symbolize the feminine, particularly the womb.

Illness – Also see **Sickness**

Dreaming of illness may alert us to the fact that all is not well either with ourselves or our environment. The nature of the illness may give some indication as to what is amiss, or it may highlight what needs to be done in order to make a situation improve.

Imitation

To dream of being imitated can mean that we are aware that whatever we have done is the correct thing to do and that other people can learn from our example. It can equally mean that other people are seeing us as being leaders, when we ourselves do not necessarily feel that it is the correct role for us. Imitating someone else suggests we are aware of their greater knowledge and wisdom.

Immersion

To be immersed in water indicates the way we handle our emotions. We could be trying to find that part of us that is forever innocent. We are attempting to clarify situations, ideas and attitudes that have been suggested to us by other people.

To be immersed, that is in the sense of being focused, reveals we need to concentrate on one thing only in order to understand ourselves.

Immobility

To be made immobile in a dream is to suggest that either the energy has run out of a particular situation, or that there is nowhere else to go.

Imp

An imp appearing in a dream usually indicates disorder and difficulty. The imp often has the same significance as the Devil in tormenting us, creating difficulty and harming us. The imp can also represent the uncontrolled negative part of ourselves, that part that instinctively creates chaos and takes great joy in doing so. It is perhaps an aspect of loss of control.

Incense – See **Religious Imagery**

Incest – Also see **Sex**

Incest is such a taboo subject that to dream of it seldom refers to the physical act. It usually represents the need and desire we have to be in control. It may occur in dreams because as a child we had not been allowed to sort out our feelings so far as the family were concerned. Since self image and sexuality are so closely connected, however, incest in dreams is much more likely to be an effort to sort out our feelings about ourselves.

Income

The income we earn is an important part of our structure, so any dream connected with this will tend to signify our attitude towards our wants and needs. To dream of an increased income shows we feel we have overcome some obstacle in ourselves and can accept that we have value. A drop in income signifies our neediness, and perhaps our attitude to poverty. Dreaming of receiving a private income suggests we perhaps need to look at our relationships with other people.

Indigestion

To experience indigestion in a dream shows that there is something in our lives that we do not agree with or cannot tolerate. Equally, it may indicate that we are actually suffering from indigestion, and this is recognized in the dream state – there is a belief that certain foods can trigger off intense dreams.

If something is indigestible in a dream, it may be that we recognize that we have some sort of mental block to deal with. Perhaps we need to do things in a different way, or in smaller steps.

Infection

Dreaming of having an infection suggests that there is the possibility of us having internalized negative attitudes from other people. However, it greatly depends on which part of our body we see as infected. If, for example, the leg is infected, then this will denote we are being held up somehow. On another level, it may be that we are being negatively influenced.

Initiation – See **Religious Imagery**

Injection

If we are given an injection, then we are feeling as though our space has been penetrated. To dream of giving an injection suggests that we are attempting to force ourselves on other people – this may have sexual connotations. An injection may also be our way of healing, thus making ourselves better. More negatively, an injection can indicate short-term pleasure rather than long-term gain.

Insects

Insects in dreams can reflect the feeling that something is bugging us – something we could do without. It may also indicate a feeling of insignificance and powerlessness. It will depend on the particular insect in the dream as to the interpretation. Thus, a wasp might indicate danger, whereas a beetle could mean either dirt or protection.

Inscription

Any inscription in a dream is information which will need to be understood. Reading an inscription can suggest that something is understood already, whereas not being able to read an inscription suggests that more information is required in order to complete a task.

Insomnia – See Sleep Disorders in the Sleeping and Dreaming chapter

Intestines – See **Body**

Intoxication – Also See **Alcohol** and **Drunk**
When we are intoxicated in a dream it can be important to decide why we are so. Being drunk can indicate a loss of control, whereas a change of state brought about by drugs can represent a change in awareness. The changes that occur in consciousness through intoxication can be mirrored in a dream. Sometimes that change can be depressive – suggesting a need to explore the negative in our lives; sometimes they can be euphoric – showing our ability to reach a state similar to a kind of mania.

Invisible
If we are invisible in a dream, then it denotes that there is something we want to put behind us and forget. If something is invisible, then we just need to recognize the presence of something without having to look at it too closely to begin with.

Iris – See **Flowers**

Iron
When iron appears in dreams, it usually represents our strengths and determination. It can perhaps also signify the rigidity of our emotions or beliefs. When we dream of using a clothes iron we are often attempting to make ourselves more presentable. We may also be trying to 'smooth things over'. Iron in a dream can also signify the part of ourselves that requires discipline.

Island
Dreaming of an island signifies the loneliness we can go through. An island can also represent safety in that, by isolating ourselves, we are not subject to external demands. Occasionally we all need to recharge our batteries, and to dream of an island can help, or warn, us to do this,

which will in turn help us to function better. A more esoteric meaning is that an island can signify a retreat – somewhere that is cut off from the world – which will allow us to contemplate our inner self.

Ivory

Ivory is something that should be protected and preserved, thus, to dream of ivory is to be looking within to discover what is worth preserving. To dream of an ivory tower can signify the way we shut ourselves off from communication.

Ivy

Dreaming of ivy denotes, on one level, celebration and fun. However, it can symbolize the clinging dependence that can develop within relationships. Because ivy has the symbolism of constant affection, we can recognize that we are in need of love and affection. On yet another level, ivy symbolizes immortality and eternal life.

J

Jailer

A jailer in a dream can suggest a strong sense of restriction either by some part of our personality or by an external force. There may arise a period of loneliness and a sense of being trapped in an ongoing situation. The spiritual side of our nature may give us the ability to break out of the situation, or bring us to a realization that we must remain within the particular situation for the time being.

Jar

In old-style symbolism a jar, or any kind of hollow container, represents womanhood. For a woman it can represent her ability to be a mother and in a man it can represent the principle of 'mothering'. On a slightly more esoteric note a jar can suggest the more sensitive side of our nature, so being jarred or shaken up represents being hurt by what is happening. If the jar is broken then we have received some deep hurt from which we wish to recover.

Judge/justice – Also see Judge under Authority Figures and Jury

Often when we are attempting to stabilize two different states or ways of being, the figure of justice or balance can appear within a dream. This is to warn us that we may need to use both the physical and spiritual aspects of ourselves successfully. Since justice is usually to do with the correct way to do things according to group belief, we may feel that there is the need to conform with others – that we are doing, or are about to do, something which goes against the grain.

Judgement

Being able to use judgement, whether good or otherwise, is a skill which comes with maturity. In dreams we may find ourselves making the types of judgement which we would not normally do in waking life. For instance, we may pride ourselves on not being judgemental and find that, in dreams, that part of ourselves which judges behaviour works completely differently.

Jungle

A jungle can often represent chaos. This chaos can be either positive or negative, depending on other elements in the dream, and may suggest some kind of obstacle or barrier that has to be passed through in order to reach a new state of understanding. Being trapped in a jungle suggests we may be trapped by negative and frightening feelings from the unconscious, though having come through a jungle would indicate that we have passed through, and overcome, aspects of our lives which we have previously found difficult. In mythology and fairy tales, cutting through the jungle often represents overcoming the impenetrable defences created by feminine awareness.

Jumping

The act of jumping can be somewhat ambiguous in a dream. Repetitive movement usually suggests the need to look at what we are doing and perhaps to express ourselves in a different way. Jumping up can indicate reaching for something that is above us, beyond our reach and requires effort to achieve, whilst jumping down can mean exploring the unconscious or those parts of ourselves which we have not yet examined. Jumping up and down can indicate frustration or joy.

Jury

A group of people in dreams sitting in judgement suggests that we are having to deal either with issues of peer pressure – that is, how others think of us, or with our own estimation of ourselves. We may be questioning the values which we have adopted, or feel that we or a part of us have not been true to our own ideals – we have been found wanting. Being a member of a jury calls into question our ability to belong to a group of like-minded people or not. For example, we may not feel we can go along with the group decision. Provided we adhere to our own inner truth, we cannot be judged.

K

Kaleidoscope

A child is fascinated by the patterns that a kaleidoscope creates – no two being the same and yet each one being regular in its repetition and reflection within itself. The dream image of a kaleidoscope can introduce us to our own creativity, which may become trapped. It connects us with our childlike selves, and with the beauty of basic patterns such as the mandala and the intricacies of creativity. We become aware of our own 'smallness' within the larger scheme of things.

Keepsake

Any object which evokes memories reminds us of what we have been capable of doing or being. Keepsakes which traditionally were exchanged between lovers are indicative of the love and respect there is between two people.

Kettle – Also see **Cauldron**

A kettle is often taken to symbolize transformation and change. In dreams it will have an almost magical significance and indicate practical, pragmatic learning to do with change. In some instances, like all hollow objects, a kettle can represent femininity and home-making.

Key/keyhole – Also see **Lock and Prison**

Keys often appear in dreams; they have obvious significance in that it locks or unlocks that which needs opening or closing. This may be our potential or perhaps old memories, experiences or emotions. For instance, if the key opens a door something will be revealed – usually to our advantage, whereas if it locks the door we are trying to shut something away, perhaps the past or situations we do not wish to handle. To dream of a bunch of keys suggests the need to 'open up' the whole of our personalities to new experiences. Sometimes the material the key is made of will be significant. The more mundane the material, the more mundane is the solution. We hold within us many of the answers to our difficulties, but often need a down-to-earth worldly symbol to trigger off our ability to work out solutions we have previously hidden. Silver and gold keys represent – respectively – transient and spiritual power.

Looking through a keyhole suggests that our vision and understanding is restricted in some way, or that we are being excluded from activity. Being unable to fit a key into a keyhole indicates inappropriate behaviour. If the size of the keyhole is wrong, we have the choice of adjusting, in waking life, our knowledge (represented by the key) or the way we apply that knowledge (the keyhole). Noticing that there is no keyhole indicates a problem in reconciling our inner and outer self. Conventionally the keyhole has been taken to represent the feminine, more sensitive side of our personality.

Kick

Aggression is often shown in dreams in an easily recognizable form. A kick is a way of propelling something, such as a ball, forward and therefore represents our need for motivation – either within ourselves or with others. Kicking someone else suggests there is an unresolved frustration either with the other person or ourselves, while being kicked highlights our ability to be a victim.

Kidnap

Within any situation we can find that our own fears and doubts cause us to be victims at various times in our lives. Being kidnapped in a dream highlights our ability to be taken over and forced to do, or be, something against our will. To be the kidnapper shows that we are trying to influence someone else and need to moderate our actions.

Kidneys – See Body

Killing

Killing is an extreme answer to a problem. It indicates the violent ending to a predicament. Killing someone in a dream is attempting to be rid of the power they have over us. Dreaming of being killed suggests that factors with which we are dealing are making us, or part of us, ineffective in everyday life.

King – See People and Family

Kingfisher – See **Animals and Birds**

Kissing
Kissing someone in a dream usually suggests acceptance, approval or respect. Dreaming of kissing someone whom we do not like in real life may indicate having to come to terms with qualities within ourselves which we actively dislike in others. Kissing also suggests that we are sealing a pact, or coming to an understanding. Being kissed on the forehead indicates a lack of sexual involvement and counts more as a blessing.

Kitchen
In dreams, the kitchen can often represent the mother, or rather the mothering function, highlighting the housekeeping or nurturing aspect. The kitchen is the place from which we go out into the world, and to which we return. It is also the place in which transformation can take place. Perhaps the best illustration which shows this is the way in which Cinderella is transformed into a princess within her own domain.

Kite
The kite represents freedom, particularly freedom from responsibility, but at the same time suggests that our activities should have an element of control about them. The expertise needed to fly a kite is only learnt through experience. In Chinese lore, the kite symbolizes the wind and can suggest our spiritual aspirations.

Knapsack
Any burden that we carry in dreams represents either the difficulties we have accumulated, or the resources we have with which we can deal with problems. It will depend on whether the dream generally has a positive or negative tone which interpretation is correct. A knapsack, being small, would suggest a short period of emotional difficulty. If you believe in reincarnation, the knapsack is also reputed to carry those things we have brought forward from a previous life, or those experiences we must assimilate in this.

Knee – See **Body**

Kneeling

Kneeling usually suggests submission or sometimes supplication. Initially, kneeling represented giving someone or something status in our lives – that is, putting ourselves on a lower level. In dreams, this is the most frequent explanation. If kneeling is taken as simply a way of being in contact with the earth it will indicate the need to be in contact with the basic aspects of life.

Knife

A cutting implement in a dream usually signifies some kind of severance, whether from a person, relationship or situation. We may need to cut out what is non-essential. It can be important in a dream about a knife to notice what type is being used, and what the action is. A stabbing action suggests penetration, whereas a slashing action suggests the violent removal of unwanted material. In a woman's dream this is probably more to do with her own fear of penetration and violation, whereas in a man's dream it is highlighting his own aggression.

Knight

It will depend whether the knight appears in a woman's or a man's dream as to the correct interpretation. There is the standard interpretation for the female, that of the knight in shining armour, and therefore a romantic relationship – a search for the perfect partner. A man may be looking for the heroic part of himself; the part that will take risks because they are there to be taken. In both cases the knight may represent the spiritual side of our nature. A 'black' knight is often taken as a figure of evil, whereas a 'white' knight is a fighter for the good of all. Psychologically, the knight in a dream signifies the guiding principle.

Knob

There are many interpretations which can be given for a knob. Just as a key can represent an answer to a problem, so also can a knob suggest a particular course of action for a dreamer. This may be a turning point in one's life, a new way of accessing information or a different way of regarding the situation. Not being able to turn a doorknob can suggest an obstacle which stands in our way. In some dreams, taking note of the slang term, the knob will represent the penis or masculine principle.

Knock

Hearing knocking in a dream is often a warning of some kind of difficulty. Our attention needs to be refocused on the matter in hand. For example, if in a dream we are knocking on a door, it may be that we are wanting some attention or approval. We may be feeling excluded from a particular situation or event. It could also suggest that we are trying to be with someone – to be part of their lives – but do not feel particularly confident of our right to be there.

Knot

A simple knot seen in a dream could represent a blockage in the natural flow of events or the need to take a different direction in a project. To be untying a knot suggests solving a problem which is more complex than we first appreciated, and which may take time to undo. In more symbolic terms, a knot can suggest a maze or labyrinth which itself represents the complex feminine makeup. A more complex knot could indicate that we are bound to a situation by a sense of duty or guilt. To be feeling knotted up inside suggests being under some emotional strain.

L

Label

A label is a means of identification, of establishing our right to own some object or of differentiating between several different categories. Dreams can often highlight basic human instincts and our sense of identity is one of the most important instincts we have. To be able to label or mark our possessions in some fashion gives us a place in the world, a right to belong, to mark up our successes or failures. To be re-labelling something suggests that we have rectified a misperception.

Labour

'Hard labour' suggests self-flagellation or self-punishment in what we are doing. However, if a woman dreams of being in labour she perhaps has an issue with her wish and desire to be pregnant, or with that of mothering. It may also be that she is bringing a scheme or project to fruition, and is about to achieve a long cherished goal.

Laboratory

Dreaming of a laboratory indicates we need to make an impartial appraisal of what is happening to us. If we are specimens in a laboratory we may feel that we are being judged in some fashion, whereas being the scientist or technician suggests that we may need to look more carefully at the situation highlighted by the dream. Being in a laboratory suggests a more objective approach to life, and often seems to be a feature of dreams about alien beings.

Labyrinth – Also see **Maze**

In undertaking our own journey of discovery and exploring our deeper personality, we open ourselves up to all sorts of potentials, some of which will lead us to new experiences and some of which will lead us into cul-de-sacs. It is often at this point that we dream of exploring a labyrinth or a series of underground interlinking passages. Often such a dream will force us into confronting our own fears and doubts, and overcoming the Shadow, or that part we most dread and have difficulty in understanding. The labyrinth is also the representation of the hidden feminine mysterious part of our personality.

Ladder

The ladder represents our ability to move from one phase of existence to another and denotes how secure we feel in moving from one situation to another. Such a dream may occur during career changes and can signify promotion. The most well-known ladder dream is Jacob's Ladder, told in the Bible. This signifies the transition between earth and heaven, and the ladder shows the ability to move from the physical realms of existence into an awareness of the spiritual dimension in life. In spiritual development such a dream is fairly commonplace.

Lagoon/lake – Also see **Water** under **Environments**

The unconscious side of ourselves – an abundant source of power when it can be properly accessed and understood – often manifests in dreams as a lake or lagoon. The home of the darker, more occult side of femininity and sensitivity – as seen in the Arthurian legends – gives rise to both the sword as a weapon of protection and the more negative beautiful witch as Morgan le Fey. The lagoon as part of a wider sea is also a potent symbol of deep emotion.

Lamb – See **Animals and Birds**

Lame/lameness

A loss of confidence and strength suggests that part of our personality is not functioning correctly. This will often manifest in dreams as lameness. As we become more proficient in interpretation, lameness on the left side will show difficulty with the softer, sensitive feminine whilst on the right it will suggest problems with the masculine assertive side of the personality. In mythological terms, lameness is taken to represent the imperfections of the physical realms which are a necessary part of existence.

Lance

Any type of lance, being both a cutting and penetrative instrument, has the same meaning in dreams as a knife. It suggests masculine power and therefore sometimes the sexual act. Lancing a boil or cutting out bad flesh creates a sense of releasing negative energy or contamination.

Language

Hearing foreign or strange language suggests that there is something within us which we do not yet understand. Just as a child must sort out and learn to make sense of what it hears, so in dreams a fresh idea or concept may not present itself with clarity initially, but as a series of increasingly better understood words. Recognizing in dreams that we understand a strange language suggests that we have internalized such an idea or concept. Various aspects of our personalities may present themselves as speaking in foreign languages, and in waking life this may give rise to the phenomenon of 'speaking in tongues'.

Large – See **Size**

Lark – See **Animals and Birds**

Late

Being aware of being late in a dream suggests that we are not totally in control of the situations around us. Psychologically, such a dream is said to represent the search for perfection and the feeling that we have, or maybe will, let someone down. If someone else is late in a dream, we may be conscious that there is a lack of communication in some way.

Laugh/Laughter

Laughter in the spiritual sense signifies pure joy. If we ourselves are laughing we may be experiencing a release of tension. Often the object of our entertainment will give a clue to the bearing of the dream on everyday life. Being laughed at in dreams suggests we may have a fear of being ridiculed, or may have done something which we feel is not necessarily appropriate.

Lava – See **Volcano**

Lavatory – See **Toilet**

Lead (Metal)

The conventional explanation of lead appearing in a dream is that we have a situation around us which is a burden to us. It can indicate that the time is ripe for transformation and transmutation. In spiritual symbolism lead stands for bodily consciousness, and has connotations with the process of alchemy, of the transformation of the base into the pure.

Lead and Leading

Leadership qualities are not necessarily ones that everybody will use. Often we can surprise ourselves in dreams by doing things that we would not normally do, and taking the lead is one of them. This suggests taking control of a situation around us. Leading someone in a dream presupposes that we know what we are doing and where we are going. Being led indicates that we have allowed someone else to take control of a situation around us. Dreaming of a dog lead would symbolize the connection between ourselves and our lesser nature, and the necessity to introduce some kind of controlling element into our lives.

Leaf/leaves

A leaf very often represents a period of growth and fertility and can also indicate time. It will depend on the look of the leaves as to how they are interpreted. For instance bright green leaves can suggest hope and new opportunities, or the springtime. Dead leaves signify a period of sadness, barrenness or autumn (See **Seasons**).

Leak – Also see **Water** under **Environments**

Dreaming of a leak suggests we are wasting or losing energy in some way, and may indicate that we are being careless with our personal resources. Someone may be draining us emotionally and we need to be more responsible in our actions.

Leather

Depending on the circumstances in our waking life, leather is often associated with protection of one's physical body. It may also suggest some kind of recognizable clothing creating a rebellious or different image. Leather can also be connected with control such as in the use of whips, bridles or harnesses. In today's climate leather can also be associated with 'real' goods rather than man-made.

Left – See Position in Dream Interpretation chapter

Leg – See **Body**

Lens – Also see **Glasses/Spectacles**

Using a lens in dreams suggests that more attention needs to be paid to the details of our lives. Something needs to be closely examined. It may be that detail needs to be enlarged, so that we can see things more clearly (See **Magnifying Glass**).

Lemon – See **Fruit**

Lending

In spiritual terms, the concept of lending is connected with healing and support. If in a dream we are lending an object to someone we are aware that the characteristic that object represents can only be given away temporarily. If someone is lending us an article then we are perhaps not responsible enough to possess what it represents on a full-time basis. Conversely, we may only need it for a short time. If we are being lent money we need to look at the way we are managing our resources, but also at what guidance or support we need to do this. If we are lending money, we are creating an obligation within our lives.

Leopard – See **Animals and Birds**

Leper

Spiritually, a leper in a dream can suggest that we are having to deal with a moral dilemma which takes us away from our usual compassion and caring. We may feel that our lives have been contaminated, or that we have been rejected by the society in which we live, or that conversely we are having to accept or reject some kind of impurity in others. The other aspects of the dream, as well as what is occuring in your waking life, should give you the most relevant explanation.

Letter – Also see **Address**

At its simplest, a letter suggests communication of some sort. An official letter may represent information we need or have, a bill may indicate that some action we propose to take has a cost, while a love letter may mean that we are aware of how much we are cared about by others. If we are sending a letter we need to be clear about our own way of communicating.

Level

Dreaming of a level road or surface would indicate our way ahead is fairly straightforward, suggesting ease and comfort. A level crossing suggests that we are approaching a barrier, or hindrance, to our progress which requires attention. We may not, at this stage, have enough information to take avoiding action.

Library – Also see Buildings under Environments

A library in a dream can often represent the sum total of our life's experience. It suggests both the wisdom and skills that we ourselves have accumulated, and the collected wisdom available to all humanity. It can also represent our intellectual capacity and the way we handle knowledge. Additionally, in those who have, or are developing, clairvoyance it is often taken as the Akashic records – the spiritual records of existence.

Lice – See Insects

Light

Any kind of light in a dream usually means illumination. It is also much to do with confidence. In dreams it is often the quality of the light which is important. For instance, a bright light suggests intuition while a dim light might suggest the potential for unease. To feel lighter signifies feeling better about ourselves. The lamp in dreams often signifies guidance, and wisdom, particularly from a divine source. An old-fashioned lamp will represent ancient wisdom, often of a personal kind rather than universal. A candle is often used in meditational practices, and therefore in dreaming, becomes an archetypal symbol of the soul.

Lighthouse

Spiritually a lighthouse highlights the correct course of action to help us achieve our spiritual goals. It can act as a shaft of light which can lead us into calmer waters. A lighthouse is a warning system, and in dreams it tends to warn us of emotional difficulties.

Lightning

Lightning in a dream reveals unexpected changes, often occurring through some type of sudden realization of a personal truth, or of a more universal awareness. It can also indicate a revelation which knocks away the structures we have built in as safeguards in our lives. There is often a discharge of tension or passion, which may initially seem destructive, but ultimately clears away the debris of outmoded ideas and principles. Lightning can also in the more spiritual sense suggest a visitation by the Holy Spirit.

Lily – Also see **Flowers**

Spiritually lilies are a symbol of resurrection and of everlasting life. Because of their association with funerals, for many lilies can signify death. They can, however, also symbolize purity (and hence virginity), nobility, grace, and other aspects of femininity.

Line

Spiritually in dreams a line can have great importance. The straight line can represent time and the capacity to go both forward and back. In more mundane terms a line marks a boundary or the division between two spaces. A straight line will suggest a degree of rigidity, while a curved line perhaps a more easy-going approach. A line can also demonstrate some kind of connection between two dream objects.

Linen

Linen in dreams on a purely practical level can suggest an appreciation of fine things. Spiritually, fine linen signifies purity and righteousness. It was the cloth used to wrap Christ within the tomb, and therefore suggests reverence and love. This symbolism would be carried through in a dream of a family celebration in which, for instance, linen tablecloths figured. Formerly, a woman's dowry consisted of the finest cloth and clothes that she could afford and fine linen was therefore a sign of status.

Liniment

Using liniment in a dream suggests the need for healing or perhaps for nurturing and caring. The method of application may also be important.

Liquid

One of the symbols of liquid is to do with liquidity – that is, having resources or equity which can be realized. This can be on either a physical or emotional level. Liquid in dreams can have more than one meaning. Water has its own meaning, but other liquids will lend themselves to different interpretation. Orange juice, for instance, might suggest looking at matters of health.

Because liquid is always connected with 'flow' the idea of allowing feelings to flow properly is one which needs to be considered. A strong symbol in spiritual development is golden liquid, which can represent both power and energy.

Liver – See **Body**

Lizard – See **Animals and Birds**

Lock/locked – Also see **Key** and **Prison**
A lock appearing in a dream may highlight the need to free up whatever we have shut away. To force a lock would indicate that we perhaps need to work against our own inclinations to lock things away in order to be free of inhibitions. We may also be trying to bring about a situation which requires a good deal of force or energy to succeed. To recognize in a dream that a part of our body has become locked suggests that we are carrying extreme tension. It is possible that we need to release that tension in a physical way in order to be healthy.

Loom
The loom in spiritual terms means fate, time, and the weaving of destiny. A loom also symbolizes creativity, whether more mechanical or craft-oriented, and signifies the ability to create our lives according to a set pattern. We are more likely to dream of such a creative tool if we are an artist or weaver.

Lorry – See **Journeys and Transport**

Lost
The search for the lost object or the lost chord (in the sense of a missing vibration) epitomizes the search for enlightenment. To have lost something in a dream may mean that we have forgotten, or are out of touch with, matters which could be important. To have suffered some kind of loss or deprivation may mean that part of ourselves or our lives

is now dead or defunct and we must learn to cope without it. This may be an opportunity, a friend or a way of thought which has previously sustained us. We may have lost the ability or the motivation to make clear decisions and must remain in a state of confusion. Often this type of dream is classified as an anxiety dream.

Lottery

Nowadays the lottery has a great deal of significance in people's lives. It is a sort of legitimized gambling or taking of risks, and in dreams epitomizes the achievement of all that we could wish for. It also signifies the principle of luck operating on our behalf. Rather than the effort we are prepared to put in to gain some kind of profit, we instinctively recognize the element of chance or happenstance in our lives. A lottery ticket suggests the recording of our desires. Spiritually the lottery represents the ability to take chances, to rely on fate rather than good judgement.

Low – See Position in Dream Interpretation chapter

Luggage

Luggage will often symbolize what we feel may be important or necessary for our future progress. Sometimes having the same meaning as baggage, those things we have picked up on life's journey but must now decide whether we still need to carry with us, luggage can also suggest a temporary situation which we must continue to endure. Spiritually if we are to travel 'light' we must often find a way of unburdening ourselves. Luggage in a dream can help us to envisage this.

Lungs – See **Body**

M

Machine

Machinery in dreams often focuses on the mechanical processes within our bodies which enable us to survive. These functions are those associated with the automatic nervous system which continue with the minimum of maintenance. Machines can also suggest a mechanistic way of looking at life, of creating a universe which meshes together but without the back-up of a creative process. Perceiving a large machine such as a tank in dreams can suggest an unstoppable force.

Mad/Madness

Madness in dreams is slightly different from madness in the waking state, which can be seen as inexplicable behaviour. The former can suggest an uncontrolled and uncontrollable part of ourselves which is not being integrated into the present situation. This may be frightening, or may suggest some kind of intense feeling – the other circumstances of the dream will indicate the correct interpretation.

Maggots

Maggots in dreams may reflect our own fears about death and illness, but can also suggest impurities within our body or within a situation around us. For most people maggots cause such a reaction of distaste that they will tend to represent something that we 'cannot handle'.

Magic

Magic in dreams speaks of our ability to link with our deepest powers. They can be the powers of sexuality or the powers of control, or of power over our surroundings. We are all intrigued by mystery or the inexplicable, and have the need to make things happen – a symbol to do with magic can alert us to our own inner talents.

Magistrate – Also see Authority Figures under People and Family

Magistrates and judges appear in dreams as representatives of authority figures and therefore of the people we first knew in that capacity – our parents. They also can suggest that part of ourselves which knows right from wrong and allows us to act within the norms and laws of the society in which we live.

Magnet

The magnet has the ability to create a 'field' round itself, a field of magnetic energy. This energy is similar to the energy field that clairvoyants and psychics perceive around other people, and often a magnet appearing in a dream alerts us to the intrinsic power that we have, which seems to be inert until such times as it is activated by greater knowledge. We all have within us the ability to attract or repel others, and often a magnet appearing in a dream will highlight that ability. Since of itself the magnet is inert, it is the power it has that is important. We often need to realize that the influence that we have over other people comes not only from ourselves, but also from our interaction with them.

Magnifying Glass – Also see Lens

When anything is magnified in a dream it is being brought to our attention. To be using a magnifying glass indicates that we should be paying attention to the details of our lives. We should be able to act in full awareness of what we are doing – making what we are looking at conscious. When the magnifying glass itself and not what we are looking at is important, we are recognizing our own abilities, our own power within a situation.

Magpie – See Animals and Birds

Makeup – Also see Cosmetics

To be aware of makeup in dreams is to acknowledge that we have a choice as to the sort of person we want to be. We can choose the image we wish to project, and can create whatever facade we choose. Our use of makeup in dreams may depend on how we use it in everyday life. It can be used to create beauty or to cover up imperfections.

Mansion – See Buildings under Environments

Mantis

The mantis, as with most insects, can often show the trickster part of us that can create problems when things are effectively working out for us. We may be the trickster or perhaps we are the one being tricked. This is usually on an emotional level and, by and large, if we are completely honest we will know the genuine meaning of the dream.

Manure

Some of the experiences which we have to go through can be distressing or difficult. If we cannot understand what is going on and do not utilize it as part of the development we all go through, those experiences remain with us and cause difficulty later on. These bad experiences may appear as manure within a dream, ready to be dealt with by natural processes.

Map

A map in dreams can represent the help we need in our quest to find the way forward. It often indicates the clarification of the direction we should be taking in life. It is worth remembering that we need to read the map ourselves, and therefore we are our own guides. Not being able to read a map might therefore indicate confusion, while knowing we needed a map but not having one might suggest a lack of information.

Marble

Marble can represent spiritual firmness, permanence and stability. Its particular quality of long-lasting beauty is a symbol of those things which are meant to endure. Slightly less positively, it can also suggest rigidity and inflexibility.

Mare – See **Horse** under **Animals and Birds**

Marigold – See **Flowers**

Market/marketplace

A market complete with stalls tends to be somewhat impermanent or temporary and can be interpreted in dreams as such. It can also suggest that we need to become more commercial in the work that we are doing, or perhaps to be more creatively influenced, rather than doing something purely and simply because it is commercial. A marketplace can also be viewed as a place of spiritual exchange. The stock market or a scene associated with it suggests that we probably need to pay attention to the way we handle our resources, financial or otherwise.

Marriage/Wedding

To dream of a wedding or marriage can often give an indication as to how we feel about relationships. For instance, a teenager may dream of marrying her father, as she learns how to handle relationships with other people. On a subliminal level the human being is always looking for someone to complement him or herself, to supply qualities which he or she feels are not present within themselves, so to dream of a wedding can give an indication of the potential for growth by uniting two particular parts of us which need to come together in order to create a better whole.

Marsh – Also see Swamp

Dreaming of marshy ground very often represents difficulty on an emotional level. It may be hard to feel secure and properly grounded in the middle of these problems. It may be that we lack either the self-confidence or emotional support that we need to move forward. Literally there is some way in which we are feeling 'bogged down'.

Martyr

Dreaming of being a martyr suggests that there is the potential for us to turn ourselves into some kind of sacrificial victim, perhaps doing things out of a sense of duty rather than love. Not feeling that we can refuse to fulfil what others expect of us – or rather what we think they expect – can lead to the type of behaviour that may be seen, for instance, in the over-possessive mother who expects her children for lunch, but then grumbles because she spends all morning cooking. Additionally, dreaming of religious martyrs can suggest behaviour we admire or some kind of fanatical act in order to prove a point.

Mask

Dreaming of a mask often makes us aware of either our own or other people's facade – the public face. Most people are capable of concealing their true selves from other people and when it is no longer appropriate behaviour this conduct can appear in dreams as a mask. This mask can be perceived as either a positive or negative more frightening mask. In primitive cultures to wear a mask such as that of an animal gave the wearer the powers of that animal.

Masturbation – See **Sex**

Masochism – See **Sex**

Mattress – Also see **Bed** under **Furniture**
Similar to a bed, the mattress can suggest one's private space. To dream of a mattress indicates the feeling we have about a situation we have created in our lives, whether it is comfortable or not. Interestingly, dreaming of a mattress may also suggest the temporary nature of a relationship we have.

Maypole
The maypole in a spiritual sense is a representation of the phallic, of masculine spirituality and of life-giving energy. It is the central axis of the world that we create for ourselves; thus to dream of a maypole may have sexual connotations, but also may indicate the way in which we handle our own lives.

Maze – Also see **Labyrinth**
A maze often represents a confusion of ideas and feelings. Psychologically, the maze in a dream may suggest the variety of opinions and authoritative beliefs that we come up against in our ordinary, everyday world, and which may represent blocks to progress. There are conflicting drives and assumptions and we often discover that in attempting to find our way through the maze we have learnt something about our own courage, our own ability to meet problems. Often there is the apparently irrational fear and doubt that arises from not being able to find our way in and out of the maze. This can allow us to release feelings of self-doubt and fear through dreams.

Meander
Since meandering is a kind of aimless wandering, often without a particular purpose in mind, experiencing such a thing in dream can suggest variously a lack of purpose, or a freedom of movement not

normally available to us. The emotions associated with the action will give some inkling of the correct interpretation. Often we need to go with the flow.

Medal
Human beings appreciate feeling good about themselves. A medal being awarded in a dream acknowledges our abilities and/or successes – not just in the immediate moment – but gives a tangible reminder of what we have done.

Medicine
Sometimes an incident in waking life can be unpleasant at the time, but ultimately results in some kind of healing, and is finally good for us. In dreams medicine can stand as such a symbol. Medicine also may suggest a health problem, or a circumstance which can be changed from the negative to the positive.

Meditation
Interpreting the act of meditation will depend on whether you meditate in waking life. In someone who does, it will suggest a discipline that is helpful to you, putting you in touch with intuition and spiritual matters. In someone who does not, it may indicate the need to be more introverted in order to understand the necessity to be personally responsible.

Medium
Mediumistic aspects in a dream can represent our wish to be in contact with those who have passed over, whether literally, or figuratively, in the sense of not being available to us. It may be that we need to have some sort of deeper contact with our own unconscious, or with the dead. Interestingly, there may be a play on words, and the middle way is called for.

Memorial
A memorial is a tangible representation of homage and esteem, and in dreams may represent a memory which needs to be treated with respect and reverence. Such a memory deserves its proper place before we can move on.

Menstruation – Also see **Blood** under **Body**

All that is mysterious in women can be symbolized by menstruation. It is only in a patriarchal society that such a natural process is seen as unclean. Thus to dream of menstruation may be linking with the creative side of ourselves which can conceive new ideas and can create new and more wonderful 'children' out of simple material. Dreams of menstruation tend to occur as a woman goes through the various rites of passage associated with her life, such as puberty or the menopause, and can therefore sometimes stand as a symbol for opportunities lost.

Mermaid/merman

Traditionally, the mermaid or merman belongs to the sea as well as being able to exist on land. This symbolically represents an ability to be deeply emotional and also entirely practical, and to need to spend some time in the dark recesses of the emotional self in order to exist within the natural world. A merman or mermaid appearing in a dream is usually a call to integrate the material and emotional sides of ourselves, in order to function more effectively. Until these two separate parts are properly integrated, the human being cannot fully exist in either realm.

Metal

Any metal appearing in dreams represents the restrictions and constraints of the real world. Most metals have symbolic meanings, often connected with the planets and their qualities. Sun is represented by gold (masculine), the Moon by silver (feminine), Mercury by quicksilver (communication), Venus by copper (love), Mars by iron (drive or determination), Jupiter by tin (expansiveness), Saturn by lead (heaviness).

Microscope

A microscope appearing in a dream very often indicates that we need to pay attention to detail, or to be aware that some aspect of our personality needs to be expanded in some way. Also we may need to be somewhat introspective and more objective in order to achieve a particular personal goal.

Milk – See **Food**

Mill/millstone

The two stones in an old-fashioned mill are said to signify will and intellect, the tools we use in self-transformation. We are able to extract from our experiences in life what is useful to us and can convert it into 'nourishment' i.e. information to help us move forwards. Symbolically a millstone in dreams may also represent a heavy burden that we carry (as in 'a millstone round my neck').

Mine

Dreaming of a mine signifies bringing the resources of the unconscious into the light of day. This is one of those symbols which can actually be a word play. The things in the dream are 'mine.' It shows you are able to use the potential available.

Mirror

The mirror suggests self-realization backed up by wisdom. Dreaming of a mirror suggests concern over our self-image. We are worried as to what others think of us, and need self-examination or reflection in order to function correctly. There may be some anxiety over ageing or health. By association it may be that our behaviour needs adjusting. Magically, mirrors can be used to reflect back onto someone their past misdeeds or difficulties, and as one becomes more aware of personal magic, a mirror in a dream can assume this significance.

Miscarriage

Dreaming of a miscarriage suggests that we are conscious of the fact that something is out of order, not quite right, or has been brought to an end too quickly. In a woman's dream it will depend on whether she has actually suffered a miscarriage, since nowadays she may well not have given herself time to grieve for the loss of her child.

Dreaming of a miscarriage can also suggest the loss of work, a project or even a part of ourselves, and we need time to acclimatize.

Mist

Mist in a dream is a symbol of loss and confusion – particularly emotionally. It also represents a state of transition or initiation in the move from one type of awareness to another. Symbolically mist can also signify the passage of time.

Moat

A moat in dreams can be an emotional barrier or defence. It is a representation of our defences against intimacy. In dreams we often gain an insight into how we build or dig those enclosures. We can also decide what steps we need to take to remove them. Often it is the water in the moat which gives us an awareness of our emotional state.

Mole – See **Animals and Birds**

Money

Money in dreams represents our own personal resources - whether material or spiritual - and our potential for success. In some circumstances a dream of money can be linked with our view of our own power and our sexuality. It does not necessarily represent hard currency, but more the way in which we value ourselves and our own resources. This symbol appearing in dreams would suggest that we need to assess that value more carefully, and maybe to be aware of what is the 'cost' of our actions and desires. This is one of those symbols which can only be fully interpreted within the context of a dreamer's own life.

Monk – See **People and Family**

Monkey – See **Animals and Birds**

Monster

A monster in dreams usually stands for our negative relationship with ourselves and fear of our own emotions and drives. Something which we have allowed to grow out of all proportion comes back to haunt us and to highlight the frightened child within. Often by choosing to work with the dream image we can overcome the actual fear itself.

Moon – Also see **Planets**

The Great Mother, in her guise as the darker, unknown side of Self, is symbolized by the moon, and therefore represents the unapproachable. The moon has, even in pagan times, represented the emotional and feminine self. To dream of the moon, therefore, is to be in touch with that side of ourselves which is dark and mysterious. It is the intuition, the psychic, love and romance. Often in dreams the moon can also represent one's own mother or the relationship with her.

Mortuary

Death and dying even in today's more enlightened times holds much fear for many people. When a mortuary appears in a dream, we are usually having to consider our fears and feelings about death. In fact, this may not only be in relation to physical death, but may suggest that a part of ourselves has died or ceased to be vibrant. The mortuary may stand for a transition state between two ways of existing, a sort of halfway house.

Moses – See **Religious Imagery**

Moth

Just as the butterfly symbolizes the emerging soul, so the moth stands for the Self, but perhaps in its darker sense. It represents the hidden transient side of our personality, the night time self and therefore sometimes the dreaming self.

Mother – See **People and Family**

Motorbike – See **Journeys and Transport**

Mound – Also see **Hill**

The Earth Mother or the entrance to the Underworld is symbolized by the mound, and connects back to our very early childhood needs and the comfort that mother's breast brought. As human beings, the need for comfort and sustenance continues throughout our lives. At the same time, need to come to terms with our dependence on the feminine, nurturing aspects of the personality. Dreaming of mounds as opposed to mountains helps him to understand this.

Mountain

The symbol of the mountain, as an archetypal representation of difficulties to be overcome, offers many alternatives and choices. In dream sequences it most often appears in order to symbolize an obstacle which needs to be overcome. We are able to challenge our own inadequacies and to free ourselves from fear. To reach the top is to achieve our goal. Because the symbol of a mountain is common to meditation and dreamwork, it is often possible to work through with this image what our course of action needs to be.

Mourning – Also see Funeral and Weeping

Psychologically, we need a period of adjustment when we have lost something, so the process of mourning is an important one in all sorts of ways. We not only mourn death but also the end of a relationship or a particular part of our lives. Since sometimes mourning or grieving is seen as inappropriate in waking life, it will often appear in dreams as a form of relief or release. Through dreams we may find that we can help ourselves to create a new beginning through our mourning for the old. Often some kind of a ritual is needed to mark the ending of an old phase and the beginning of a new.

Mouse – See Animals and Birds

Mouth – See Body

Movement

The way we move in dreams can indicate a great amount about our acceptance of ourselves. For instance, to be moving quickly might suggest a smooth acceptance of the necessity for change, whereas being moved would signify being moved by outside circumstances or at the wish of other people. Being conscious of movement in dreams highlights certain options of action which are available to us. Moving forward suggests an acceptance of one's abilities, while moving backwards signifies withdrawal from a situation. Moving sideways would suggest a deliberate act of avoidance.

Mud

Spiritually mud represents the very basic primordial material from which we are all formed, and the need to go 'back to basics'. Mud in a dream suggests that we are bogged down, perhaps by not having separated the practical from the emotional (earth and water). Mud can also represent past experiences or our perception of them, which has the ability to hold us back.

Mummy (Egyptian)

The Egyptian mummy symbolizes death, but also preservation after death and therefore the afterlife and new beginnings. However, we may be trapped by old concepts and belief systems, from which we need to be set free. The Egyptian mummy in dreams can also symbolize our feelings about someone who has died.

The most obvious connection between mummy and mother is a play on words. In many ways, for full psychological health, our mother must 'die' to us, or rather, we must change our relationship with her, in order for us to grow and mature.

Murder/murderer

To be angry enough to wish to kill suggests that we are still holding some kind of childhood anger, since it is quite natural for a child to wish somebody dead. If we are trying to murder somebody else in a dream, we first need to understand what that person represents to us before recognizing the violence of our own feelings.

We may be denying, or trying to control, a part of our own nature that we do not trust. We may also have feelings about other people which can only be safely expressed in dreams. If we ourselves are being murdered, a part of our lives is completely out of balance and we are being destroyed by external circumstances.

Museum

A museum in dreams can represent the sub-conscious, that part of ourselves which we only approach in an effort to understand who we are and where we came from. It can also signify the past, or old-fashioned thoughts, concepts and ideas. It also shows that those things which are most interesting are worth preserving.

Music/rhythm/musical instruments – Also see **Orchestra**

Sacred sound has always been used in acts of worship, often to induce an altered state of consciousness, and music and rhythm are both an expression of our inner selves and of our connection with life. Music in dreams can equally represent a sensuous and sensual experience.

Musical instruments can symbolize the way we communicate with others. For instance, wind instruments tend to suggest the intellect. Percussion instruments suggest the basic rhythm of life.

Mystic Knot

Spiritually the mystic knot suggests Infinity, since it has no beginning and no end. In dreams in terms of self-development, it suggests a problem which cannot be solved by conventional means.

N

Nail

Almost immediately the notion of bonding comes to mind - bonding and thus 'holding together' – and therefore it is not difficult to correlate that with relationships, particularly sexual ones. The same can be applied if dreaming of a finger or toe nail along with the idea of 'holding on' within a relationship. A nail related to the Cross also signifies sacrifice and pain, which of course are both part and parcel of relationships.

Nakedness – See Nude

Name

Hearing our own name in a dream is quite rare. We should be alerted to our own self-sense, to our own nature as well as our desire to belong. Conversely, hearing another person's name may lead us to look at what qualities they have in order to find a new aspect to ourselves: an aspect that will, hopefully, lead us to a more Essential Self, and to a more contented state of being.

Narrow

A sense of narrowness in a dream often suggests that a restriction or a limitation, possibly regarding communication, may be being placed on us. However, we need to differentiate between a negative and positive restriction; it may be that we should not be moved from our current path of finding.

Native American

A Native American signifies a strength of which we may or may not have been aware, that of natural instinct and wisdom. We should now be prepared to look at our spirituality further, and be able to deal with a new type of energy and inner power.

Nausea

Almost certainly a dream of nausea indicates something needs to be expelled from the system, either physically or emotionally. If emotional, find out who or what it is that is making us nauseous and give them short shrift. Physically, it could well be an alert to something pending.

Necklace

A woman who dreams of a man giving her a necklace should beware, as it was once thought to be a pre-cursor to a marriage proposal. However, if her feelings about the dream border on anticipation, it is worth noting that this is a very old interpretation and is open to a degree of scepticism. More seriously, a necklace can represent a deep abundance of feeling or emotion because of its often special meaning to its owner.

Needle

Dreaming of a needle can signify a healing power, through penetration. However, we must be alert to the aspect of 'needle dependency' so to speak, particularly if the needle is being used on us rather than by us. All in all, though, to dream of a needle indicates that we need to apply some sort of insight into our own being that is 'penetrative' and healing.

Nest

We should look at our emotional state with regard to our home life and our dependency on that – or maybe non-dependency. A nest symbolizes the safety of home life, so it is not surprising that women often dream of this prior to giving birth.

Net

Dreaming of a net is often linked to the feeling of being trapped, or more broadly, claustrophobia. You should try to figure out which parts of your life is being stifled – that is, where you cannot 'move' one way or another. Alternatively, being 'under a net' could be a good thing, giving a feeling of security, maybe within a relationship.

Nettle

In real life nettles are something to be avoided, so when nettles appear in a dream we are being warned that a prickly situation could be about to befall us and we should do our utmost to steer clear. Nettles can symbolize 'wildness'. We should look at that with regard to ourselves and what constitutes wild behaviour for us through to the point of losing control. We must decide if a degree of healing or rejuvination can or cannot take place through this, since nettles are also a symbol of healing.

New

When, during a dream, a sense of 'newness' is felt, it usually represents new beginnings, new ways of progressing, or possibly even new relationships. It is also a time to look at how we can learn anew, or maybe even re-learn old rules and evaluate from there.

New Year

To dream of the New Year, as with dreaming of something new, is to recognize the potential for a fresh start. The New Year is a time when plans are laid and we feel full of hope and excitement. It may be that we have moved out of a darker time, and are now ready to face the future.

Newspaper

In the waking world a newspaper tells us what's going on around the place – with varying degrees of style and accuracy. Hence, in dreams, different newspapers mean different symbolism. A tabloid paper will suggest low-level information. A broad-sheet will invariably mean better, 'quality' advice. A Sunday paper often points to knowledge gained in and through rest, and a local rag symbolizes that the news we need is just around the corner.

Niche

When we have found our niche, in everyday life, we feel protected and safe; therefore, in dreams we are being alerted to this and it may be that we just need to recognize where we are in life or what outside influences can help us get to where we want to be.

Night

Night is usually the time we can gather strength and relieve ourselves of the day's torment. The antithesis is one of fear and restlessness. We must rid ourselves of the latter symbolism in order to use the night as a forerunner to a 'new day' and a fresh approach. It must also be said that night can symbolize death, so we must look closely at the dream to determine whether this is so, and if it is what we can do about it. It does not have to be negative: it could be, for example, the 'death' of a situation or relationship that will ultimately move us on.

No

'No' has a number of interpretations in the dream world, though all are more or less similar. To be saying no, that is to be resisting, is a sign that we can now make decisions without the consequence of guilt. In a relationship, it is now possible to face rejection positively and without trepidation – along with the added bonus of knowing that it is right for us to do so.

Noose – Also see **Hanging** and **Rope**

Apart from the obvious link to death, the symbolism of a noose centres around being, or feeling, trapped. We need to find out if we are in danger of trapping ourselves or if we are being manipulated by others into a potentially 'tight' situation. If the latter is the case, we must assert and express ourselves, as it could also be an attempt to curb self-expression.

Nourishment/Nurturing – Also see **Food**

We must look at what we need – both physically and emotionally – as the symbolism of nourishment pertains to our basic needs and wants. It is also linked to our relationship with the mother figure and, following through from that, the feminine side of our nature/nurture.

Novel – Also see **Book** and **Reading**

If, in a dream, we are conscious of reading a novel, we must try and establish its theme, as this will have a bearing on the symbolism. For example, if the novel is an adventure story this might suggest the need to take a risk, to 'go where angels fear to tread' as it were. It follows then that we may need new stimulation to help move us forward.

Nuclear Explosion – Also see **Bomb**

If we have been anxious or even afraid of the future, or of change, then it is common to dream of an explosion. We may fear that things are going to change too quickly when we would prefer a more measured route. Change is imminent, and we must be ready to handle it lest another element of symbolism come into play – that of destructive energies.

Nude/naked

Dreaming of being naked has various connotations but most revolve around self-image or self-expression and the need to be seen for what we are, not what is projected. Nudity is also linked with innocence and with that the desire to be open and honest. This could tie in with the need for a new start; in effect – and bearing in mind we are born naked – a rebirth.

Nugget

A nugget is the best part of a larger, usually less bright, situation. So it may be that we have to find some piece of information or understanding in order to be inspired. It can also signify that there is something that we must find within ourselves – something that can, for example, give us confidence.

Numbers

When numbers are brought into focus in dreams they can have a personal and/or a symbolic significance. Often a number will turn up which has personal meaning, such as a relevant date, or the number of a house we may have lived in. Our minds will retain the significance of the number, even though we do not always consciously remember it ourselves. It is also worth noting that numbers are infinite and that mathematics is the link between man and science.

Nut

If the nut in question is of the metal variety, then this indicates a construction or reconstruction of our life in such a way that it will hold together more securely.

A nut – the edible kind – is seen as being a way of taking in wisdom, in other words, nourishment to the brain; this in turn can also feed, and thus enhance, any psychic power we may have.

Nymphs

It is excellent indeed for a man to dream of nymphs, as they represent beauty, youthfulness, innocence and purity. For both men and women who dream of nymphs, it would be necessary to look at those aspects along with their own sense of femininity. We must figure out what areas we may need to progress in or highlight about ourselves.

O

Oak – See **Tree**

Oar

An oar can be seen as a way of guiding us to our goal – but we must be aware that it takes skill and judgement. In other words, we are in control of our own destiny.

Oasis

All around the world an oasis is viewed as a place of sanctuary, where we may live forever in peace and contentment whilst receiving emotional invigoration. Our worries and anxieties should cast no shadow, until they eventually fade away into a distant blur. We then feel fully refreshed and can come together, step out, and roll with whatever life throws at us.

Oats

Oats are a crucial source of nourishment – simple and effective – and because of this they have come to represent homeliness, warmth, comfort and strength. The alternative symbolism surrounds sexuality – sowing our wild oats: it might be that we need to decide whether to branch out of a relationship or not, we should consider our decision very carefully.

Obedience

There are two sides to the concept of obedience. If we are aware of being obedient then we are acknowledging a higher authority, possibly even a 'higher power'; if we expect or demand obedience from others, then we are allowing ourselves to be powerful, though hopefully not in a despotic way. If this is the case we should look closely at our actions.

Obelisk

A carved stone appearing in a dream signifies we are now looking at how we have shaped our own fundamental nature. The more basic it is, the more space we have for improvement; the more elaborate it is, then the more successful we are at using our creative energies and instincts.

Obligation

Obligation in a dream relates to our sense of duty, usually to another person. It may well transpire that we have to carry out a task that we do not particularly want to, or have been putting off, but as the old saying goes, 'duty calls'.

Obscenity

We are more able to deal with whatever obscene inclinations we may have via the dream state than in waking life. If in dreams we are seen to be involved in an obscene exploit, then we should be aware of how this is being kept in check; if it is being performed against us, then maybe we are being deceived or victimized.

Obsession

In waking life obsession is often dangerous, but if it comes up in dreams it may be an indication that there are anxieties that simply need working through. Obsession can also translate into repetition of actions, and it is likely that we are being encouraged, by the unconscious mind, to fully appreciate and understand a real situation.

Obstacle

In dreams, as in wakefulness, obstacles, whether the physical or emotional kind, have to be scaled, yet that is generally easier said than done. However, how we overcome obstacles in a dream is often a pointer to how we can handle such things as self-doubt and indecision in real life.

Occult

The literal meaning of occult relates to things being 'hidden from view'. So for someone to dream of the occult, when they have no inkling of the subject, often suggests the need to address their hidden fears. Yet it may also be pushing towards revealing a wisdom that has remained hidden in us for too long.

Ocean – See **Water** under **Environments**

Octopus

An octopus can move around freely and in any direction at any given time, so the symbolism here appears straightforward. We need to be aware that we can have the same unrestricted movement in all senses – if we want it. More esoterically, the octopus picks up on the symbolism of the mandala, and the Buddhist eightfold way of life.

Odour – Also see **Perfume** and **Smell**

Suffice to say that if we sense a pleasant odour in a dream it indicates good things; if it is bad, then we need to be aware of negativity. It can also be an odour that takes us back to another time or place, and if so we need to determine what that situation means to us both then and now.

Offence

If in a dream we offend someone, then we need to be more aware of people's feelings. If we take offence, then we are tapping into our emotional sensitivity and its place in our everyday life. In another sense, if we are committing an offence, then we have to look at our behaviour – particularly the moral aspect.

Office

An office or work situation sometimes, in dreams, represents a place where we are comfortable (in a formal way). We would look at our feelings regarding work and authority and assess if this is so, and if not, what to do about it. An office scene can also point to our feelings about responsibility and the need to have or relinquish it.

Officer/official – Also see **Authority Figures** under **People and Family**

Here we should look at the part of ourselves that directs our life and puts it into 'order' to establish if a good job is being done. It may be our desire to fit into an organized group that causes us to dream of an officer or an official figure, or the need to be guided, or sometimes told what to do.

Ogre – See Archetypes in the Enhancing your Dreams chapter

Oil

The specific type of oil determines what symbolism is to be applied. For example, cooking oil indicates a removal of dissension, whereas massage oil indicates an easing away of tension by love and care. Engine oil, on the other hand, highlights just that – our ability to keep our own engines in good working order.

Ointment

Ointment relates directly to the caring and healing process – that is, our ability to heal or need to be healed in some form or other. Also the preservation of our system and prevention of disease can be significant in the dream world.

Old/ancient/antique

In a dream, when we have a sense of things being old, it is an indication that we need to bring some past knowledge to the fore, or maybe some old wisdom or advice needs to be re-assessed. If the 'oldness' takes the form of a man, then this could be a sign that we should take a look at our feelings surrounding time, and more specifically, death.

Onion – Also see **Food**

The onion is understood to be a symbol of wholeness – albeit a complex multi-layered one – as our own personalities are. So if we dream of an onion we need to look at, and, in a manner of speaking, 'into' ourselves.

Opal – See Crystals in the Sleeping and Dreaming chapter

Opera

Operatic symbolism centres around the dramatic. If we dream we are at the opera, then this indicates that we are looking at the 'dramas' around us; to be actually taking part in an opera indicates that we need more drama in our lives or we may need to express ourselves more dramatically.

Operation – Also see **Hospital**

To dream of an operation, particularly if it is being performed on us, is to allow ourselves to come to terms with our fear of illness and pain. It is, as well, the recognition that we need to get better, and that our need for that is greater than our fear. We may need to have something which is wrong for us cut out of our lives.

Oracle

Most people want to know what is going to happen to them in the future; they like also to be told what to do next – to an extent. So dreaming of an oracle links us with that perceptive part of ourselves, the part that knows what our next move is. More spiritually, the oracle represents Hidden Knowledge.

Orange – See Colour in Dream Interpretation chapter and **Food**

Orchard

An orchard signifies our ability to look after our interests. If the orchard is showing flowers, then we have what is required to be a success. If it is a fruit orchard, then we are being reassured that the work we are doing will come to fruition. Another branch of orchard symbolism is fertility; indeed, any collection of trees can signify fertility, but an orchard suggests a more orderly way of going about things.

Orchestra – Also see **Music**, **Musical Instruments** and **Organ**

For us to function correctly we must work in harmony with others. Dreaming of an orchestra is a pointer to how we can bring elements together to achieve a wholeness. We will need to orchestrate the moves, to take some degree of control, to 'conduct', which means listening and understanding as well as being listened to and understood.

Ore

Ore is a crude material which requires working with, so a dream of this kind is alerting us that our opinions and ideas, though resourceful, can be somewhat crudely put and need refining. It may also be suggesting that we do not fully comprehend our own thoughts and we need to evaluate before speaking.

Organ

In traditional Chinese medicine, the various organs of the body depict different qualities. For example, the gall bladder handles our ability to make decisions, while the liver is the foundation of irritability. In dreams, therefore, being aware of a bodily organ would require us to be alert to what is bothering us and dealing with it in an appropriate way.

An organ in the sense of a musical instrument suggests grand sound and therefore one of high vibration.

Orgy

To dream of being involved in an orgy, aside from the physical effect it may have on us, relates to excess energy, and particularly the release of sexual energy. It can also make us aware of our need to relate and inter-relate with others, perhaps with one eye on our own sense of, or even fear of, non self-control.

Orient

For many people, the Orient and Oriental lifestyle seems somewhat exotic. Dreams of this way of life remind us that we don't need to get caught up in the 'ordinariness' of our everyday lives and can allow ourselves to daydream. We can set free the emotions that we may have suppressed. In the West we tend to think of the Oriental way of life as more intuitive than ours; we are perhaps being shown that we can use our more intuitive side in waking life.

Ornament

Ornaments, whether religious or secular, become part of our personal space, though the original intent was to enhance that space. In dreams it is this symbolism which is important. It may be, for instance, within a relationship that we feel under-valued and somewhat taken for granted, like an ornament. If so, we should act quickly to rectify the situation. On the other hand, it may be that we have something of meaning and worth that we wish to elevate to a better position. This of itself signifies that we need to use our own time and space more constructively in order to bring greater success.

Orphan

We all at some point in our lives feel deserted, unloved and vulnerable. It is not uncommon at these times to dream of an orphan. However, if we sense that we have been orphaned ourselves, then this might indicate that we need to stand on our own two feet more and take more responsibility. In another sense, if we are taking care of an orphan, then it could be that we are trying to look after, or heal, that part of us that feels un-cared for.

Ostrich – See **Animals and Birds**

Otter – See **Animals and Birds**

Ouija Board
A Ouija board – an unrefined device used to contact the 'other side' - allows us to tap into the unknown which can sometimes become the dangerous unknown. So to dream of one suggests we need to explore the things we don't understand, to take risks and to confront our fears.

Ouroboros
The ouroboros represents the Whole. Illustrated mostly as a serpent that is eating its own tail, it symbolizes infinite energy and power. It will usually appear in dreams when the dreamer is ready to deal with, and comprehend, total spiritual self-sufficiency.

Outlaw
To dream of being an outlaw suggests we are aware of that part of us that feels it is beyond the laws of other men, both legally and morally. It has to do with that element (that most of us have) which aspires to be rebellious and anarchic. We must, however, endeavour to keep things in perspective.

Oval – See **Shapes**

Oven
When dreaming of an oven we are being made aware that we can transform some of our less developed traits into something more accessible and cultured. The old 'bun in the oven' saying does actually have some weight, as an oven can represent the womb as well as birth and gestation.

Owl – See **Animals and Birds**

Ox – See **Animals and Birds**

Oyster
Although there is no absolute scientific evidence that the oyster

encourages sexual desire, we should not dismiss the connected symbolism – all things sexual – that relates to it through dreams. The oyster also symbolizes spiritual change. We can focus and build on negative qualities in our lives without trying to erase them completely.

P

Packing – Also see **Wadding**

When we dream of packing suitcases, as though going on a journey, we are highlighting the need to prepare carefully for the next stage of our lives. There is a need, or want, to get away from old ideas and difficulties. It also suggests we need to get some sort of order in our lives.

Padlock

Dreaming of locking a padlock would mean that we are attempting to shut something – maybe an emotion – away. This links with another piece of symbolism – the need to defend ourselves from fear or possessiveness. Alternatively, if we are opening a padlock we may be trying to open up to new experiences.

Pagoda – See **Buildings** under **Environments**

Painting

Because painting has a lot to do with creative talent and self-expression, the way that we are painting in a dream may be important. If, for example, we are painting on a small canvas we may need to concentrate on detail. If we are painting large pictures we may need to adopt a wider perspective. Colour in a painting also has a bearing on interpretation.

Pairs

The unconscious mind has a knack of sorting information by comparing and contrasting. So when we are aware of conflict within ourselves, we may dream in pairs. Note also that in dream interpretation looking at the opposite meaning to the obvious can give us greater insight into our mental processes.

Palace – See **Buildings** under **Environments**

Palm

To see a palm tree in a dream is most often to do with chilling out –

maybe it's time to take a holiday. The palm of the hand is significant as a symbol of generosity and openness.

Pan

In dreams a pan signifies nurturing and caring. It can also suggest a receptive frame of mind. Just as a cauldron can be taken to indicate the transformative process, so a pan can suggest the ability to combine several 'ingredients' in our lives to make something different.

Pantomime

A pantomime often appears in dreams as a reminder of happy times – usually childhood. In a dream a pantomime can be used to draw our attention to something – that something would be seen as larger than life.

Paper

Paper is an image that, in dreams, is dependent on the circumstances in our waking life. For example, in a student's life paper would suggest the need to pay attention to the studies. For a postman, there may be job anxieties, whereas festive wrapping paper could indicate the need for celebration. On a more universal level, paper can indicate a potential for learning and creativity.

Parachute

To dream of a parachute suggests that, whatever is happening to us in waking life, we have the protection that will see us through. It may also indicate that we are able to face our anxieties and still progress. A parachute can also denote a freedom of spirit.

Paradise

To dream of paradise is to link with the dreamer's inborn ability to be perfect. We can experience total harmony within ourselves. From another standpoint, paradise is that part of ourselves that is enclosed within, and does not need to be available to anyone else.

Paralysis

When paralysis is felt in a dream we are experiencing some kind of fear or suppression. Feelings that are emotionally based are felt as paralysis; this is to highlight the physical effect those feelings can have. The imagination can play tricks on us, and when we experience as real some kind of reaction we would not normally allow ourselves, it comes across as paralysis. ﹒

Parasites
Lice, fleas or bugs in a dream suggest that we may be aware that someone is attempting to live off us in some way. In another way, we may feel unclean in some aspect of our lives, which makes us ashamed or uncomfortable. We are aware that we cannot exist without support. We realize that we are not satisfied with our own lives and why we may be living vicariously.

Parcel/package – Also see **Address**
If we receive a parcel, then we are being made aware of something we have experienced but not really explored. If we are sending a parcel, then we are releasing our energy into the wider world. Both parcels and packages indicate potential and skill.

Parliament
If we dream of parliament, then we may need to make important decisions. Parliament also symbolizes our recognition of a higher authority.

Party
When we dream we are attending a party, we are alerted to our social skills – or lack of them. In waking life we may be shy and dislike such gatherings, but in dreams, if we are coping with the groups involved, we have a greater awareness of our own belonging. On a more obvious level we may need a celebration of some sort.

Passport
The passport in a dream links with our own identity and self-image. It may also suggest, particularly if we have recently undertaken a new project, that we are allowing ourselves a passport to a better life.

Path
A path signifies the direction we have to take. This is pretty much all-encompassing as it may represent the path of relationships, career, etc.

We should try to identify if the path is smooth or rocky, winding or straight, as this will have a bearing.

Pattern – See Shapes

Pawn-shop
Dreaming of a pawn-shop can indicate that we are not being sufficiently careful with the resources, whether material or emotional, that we possess. Also, it may be alerting us to other people taking what is ours, leaving us with nothing.

Pedestal
When we become conscious in a dream that something has been placed on a pedestal we have obviously attempted to make that thing special. We have elevated it to a position of power and worship – we have to decide if this is appropriate or not.

Pen/pencil – Also see Ink
If a pen or pencil appears in a dream we are expressing or recognising the need to communicate with other people. If the pen will not work we do not understand information we have been given. If we cannot find one we do not have enough information to proceed with an aspect of our lives. The difference between a pen and a pencil is that a pen suggests permanence, whereas a pencil is more transient.

Pendant – See Necklace

Pentacle/pentangle/pentagram – See Shapes

Pepper
From a herbal point of view, pepper has the ability to 'spice things up', so to dream of it shows that we probably need to put energy into a situation in our waking life to make it more interesting. In any case, pepper suggests that a radical change could be on the cards. More esoterically, it represents spiritual warmth and love.

Perfume – Also see Odour and Smell
It is likely that a certain perfume will remind us of a particular person or

time – whether that is good or bad depends on the individual. Also, intuitive information is often recognized because of a particular perfume.

Perspiration

When we experience fear in a dream, the physical manifestation – such as rapid heartbeat and sweating – is often absent. It is only on awakening that we realize that we have reacted physically. When we realise we are perspiring in a dream, we are aware of our reactions to external stimuli. We are alerted to the need to handle our own emotions and fears.

Pet – Also see **Animals and Birds**

A pet appearing in a dream means we are linking in with our natural desire to give and receive love. We may need to 'look after' someone (or something), possibly more vulnerable than us.

Petrol

In dreams, petrol symbolizes the energy we need to go places. Whether we are giving or receiving petrol will depend on whether we are reciprocating the energy.

Photographs

Photographs conjure up past occasions and memories – not all good, of course.

If we dream of looking at photographs we are often looking at some aspect of ourselves. To be given a photograph of oneself would indicate that we need to be taking an objective view of stuff around us or perhaps of ourselves within that situation – we need to stand back and look closely at what is going on.

Physician – See **Doctor**

Piano

A piano appearing in a dream signifies our potential creativity – though we will have to practise a great deal. It may be that we need to look at our workaday situation in the light of making something happen in order to use our best potential.

Picture

A picture in a dream is usually an illustration of something that is part of our lives. It will depend on whether it is painted, or a print of another picture, as to the interpretation.

The condition of the picture may be important, as may also the colours in the picture. The subject matter may give us suggestions as to what we should be 'looking at' in our lives.

Pier

Dreaming of a pier would suggest happy times and memories to most people. We may have an association with a particular town or it may simply be that a seaside pier signifies rest and relaxation. It may also indicate the end of a journey.

Pilgrim/pilgrimage

When we undertake a pilgrimage in a dream we recognize the purposeful, directed side of our personality. We have a goal in life, which may require faith to achieve. A pilgrim can often represent that part of our personality that is secure, and does not need external input; we have the ability to direct our lives provided we create the correct circumstances.

Pillar

One symbolism of a pillar relates to phallicism. Another, though, is probably more accurate. We are able to create stability and support and can stand firm in the presence of difficulty. In dreams, to find that we are a pillar of the community suggests that we should be taking more responsibility for our actions.

Pillow

Pillows, both in life and in dreams, indicate comfort and support. Sometimes, when we are going through a period of self-denial, we deny ourselves any comfort symbolism and so our pillow may disappear. To dream of a pillow fight indicates a mock conflict.

Pimple

For most people the way they view themselves is important. To be overly conscious of something like a pimple in a dream is to indicate some worry as to how we come across to others. A pimple can also represent some kind of blemish in our characters which at some time or another will have to be handled.

Pin

Here it depends whether the pin is holding something together or is being used to pierce us or some object in our dreams. If it is holding something together it indicates the emotional bonds we have. If it is piercing an object a trauma is suggested, although hopefully it will be quite small. Sometimes in dreams we are reminded of a feeling we have in everyday life. To experience pins and needles in our dream suggests that we are not ensuring an adequate flow of energy in a situation around us.

Pine cone

If the pine cone does not have a personal connection for us – such as a childhood memory – it denotes good fortune. The shape of the pine cone and the fact that it contains many seeds gives an obvious connection to the phallus and masculinity.

Pipe

On a practical level a pipe symbolizes many things. A water pipe can give information as to how we might handle our emotions. A tobacco pipe or chillum might suggest a means of escape, whereas a musical pipe indicates our connection with the rhythm of life.

Pistol – See **Gun**

Piston – Also see **Engine** under **Journeys and Transport**

A piston in a dream can mean sexual drive or activity. In this context it is more of a mechanical action than a loving act, and may show our attitude to sex. A piston may also suggest a person's drive for success. We may need to assess the amount of effort that is necessary for us to be able to achieve our goals.

Pit – Also see **Abyss**

People often talk about 'the pit of despair' and the feelings attached to it. A pit in a dream makes us more conscious of this particular feeling. We may be in a situation that we cannot get out of, or may find that if we are not careful we will put ourselves in such a situation. The pit, like the abyss, can represent death – not necessarily a physical death, but more a death of the old self.

Placenta

The baby in the womb will use the placenta as a source of nourishment, so for us it will indicate that we are reliant on others, those we are connected to. In another meaning, one of the biggest traumas to be gone through is separation from our mother, and the placenta acts as a cushion in this process. Dreaming of a placenta indicates our need for such a cushion at times of separation.

Plague

If we dream of a plague it suggests that we have an imbalance from which we will suffer – whether it is physical, mental or emotional - within ourselves. The plague has obvious links with religion, so on a spiritual level it signifies divine retribution.

Planets

Dreaming of planets is to do with those subtle energies that surround us and affect us, even though we may not be aware of it. The significance of the various planets is as follows: Jupiter suggests growth and expansion. Mars indicates activity and war but also ambition. Mercury signifies communication and intuition. Moon represents our emotions and our links with our mother. Neptune works with illusion coupled with inspiration. Pluto rules the unconscious and transformation. Saturn is a restraining influence and rules the past. Sun usually symbolizes the energy that we have. Uranus governs sudden changes. Venus highlights love and beauty.

Plank – Also see Wood

To dream of walking the plank suggests taking an emotional risk. A plank of wood appearing in a dream can indicate that something needs repairing, or that we feel safer carrying our own means of support. If the plank is to be used in flooring, the symbol is one of security, but if to be used as a door or as decoration on a wall, it signifies an adornment of our inner space.

Plants – Also see **Weeds**

Due to the natural process of growth and decay that plants go through, they become a symbol for progressive change. If the plants are cultivated, we should note our ability to create potential. If they are uncared for, the energy might quite literally have gone out of a situation in our waking lives.

Plate

A plate can be simple or elaborate. In dreams the interpretation will depend on the decoration. On another front, in the old days plates were often only owned by the rich. So to own a plate suggests that we have achieved a certain level of awareness.

Play

When in a dream we are watching a play, we need to decide whether it is a drama, a comedy or a tragedy or if it's good or bad. This is because we often are trying to view our own lives objectively. More practically, it links with our creative side.

Ploughing

Ploughing symbolizes working at getting ready for new growth and being able to prepare for change – we may be in the process of creating a new opportunity for ourselves. By looking at our lives from a different perspective we can creative opportunities for ourselves.

Plumage

In a dream plumage being drawn to our attention can often stand for a display of our power and strength in achieving what we want. It may also be a signal of defiance, and we need to stand firm and show our colours, as it were.

Plumbing

Dreaming about plumbing is to look at the way we direct our emotions. It indicates how we make use of our emotions by avoiding obstacles and creating security for ourselves and thus controlling the flow of emotions within. Another interpretation is that of the internal plumbing. Often, to dream of plumbing in this sense alerts us that we need to pay attention to health matters.

Plunge

To dream of plunging into something is to recognize that we are facing uncertainty. We are taking a risk and going into the unknown. That risk will often take us into our emotional depths and we will learn new things about ourselves which we will then be able to make use of. Also, to dream of plunging is to recognize that we have the ability to go forward.

Pocket

To dream of a pocket is to be dealing with our personal secrets or thoughts – those things that we have deliberately chosen to hide rather than share. Following on from that, and on another level, a pocket can symbolize the Occult.

Point

Anything pointed in a dream refers to male sexuality. To be aware of the point of decision is to come to the conclusion that something has to be done – we must bring about change in one way or another and at that particular 'point'. In other words, until we decide to take action nothing will be happen.

Pointing

When we dream of someone pointing, normally we are having our attention drawn to a particular object, feeling or place. We need to take note of both who is pointing it out to us and equally what they are pointing at – after all, it may be an indication of the right direction for us. Alternatively, we may feel that we are at the receiving end of something – often pointing can be an aggressive act.

Poison

To be able to recognize poison in a dream means that we need to avoid an attitude, emotion, or thought which will not be good for us. It indicates that there may be something about to contaminate us and therefore hold up our progress.

Poker

A poker has obvious links with masculinity and the sexual, but it also links with rigidity. In dreams a poker can therefore suggest aggressive action, but also rigid attitudes and behaviour that we have to deal with.

Pole

It will depend how the pole is being used in the dream as to its meaning. It is seen as an expression of the life force – as in a maypole – but also as a stabilizing force or rallying point, as in a flagpole. It can also be a support mechanism.

Pool – Also see **Water** under **Environments**

Dreaming of a pool deals with our need for the understanding of our own emotions and inner feelings – we might need to submerge ourselves in our emotions to understand them. Other interpretations are: a pool in a wood suggests the ability to understand our own need for peace and tranquillity; an urban swimming pool might signify our need for structure in our relationships with other people whereas a pool in the road would suggest an emotional problem to be got through before carrying out our plans.

Poppy

The poppy symbolizes forgetfulness. In spiritual terms the soul must forget all it knows in order to reincarnate and rediscover its own awareness. The Great Mother as the Goddess was, and is, responsible for that forgetting – hence the poppy signifies the Great Mother.

Postures

Body language is an important part of dreams. Our dream character may develop exaggerated movements or posture to highlight certain information that we need to recognize, for example, an exaggerated posture will indicate the emotion within a dream.

Poverty

To encounter poverty in a dream highlights a sense of being deprived of the ability to satisfy our fundamental needs. If it is more to do with poor surroundings, then we have to look at things around us, rather than be introspective.

Prayer – Also see **Religious Imagery**

Prayer denotes the idea that we need to help ourselves by seeking outside help. We may need someone else's authority to succeed in what we are doing. Psychologically, the human being has always needed to feel that there is a greater power than himself available to him.

Pregnancy

Dreaming of pregnancy suggests a fairly protracted waiting period necessary for something, possibly the completion of a project. Oddly, to dream of pregnancy seldom actually means one's own pregnancy, although it can indicate pregnancy for someone around us. Another meaning centres around being patient and waiting for a natural process to take place so that we can fulfil a task.

Present

When a present appears in a dream, it can be a play on words. We are being given a 'be here now' – we are being reminded to live in the moment, and not the past or future. If we are receiving a present we are being recognized, as well as gaining from the relationship. If we are giving a present, we appreciate that we have characteristics we are able to offer other people. A pile of presents in a dream can signify as yet unrecognized talents and skills.

Prison – Also see **Key** and **Lock**

Prison, in dreams, denotes the traps we create for ourselves. We sometimes create a prison for ourselves through duty – for example, in relationships – or by guilt. And at this time, we can often see no way out.

Prize

In dreams to win a prize is to have succeeded in overcoming various obstacles.

In another meaning, gaining a prize in a dream means having used our instincts and intuition in harmony in order to be able to use inspiration.

Procession

Often a procession is hierarchical, with the most important people either first or last. This could be important in a dream in enabling us to adopt priorities and intentions for ourselves.

Propeller

A propeller acknowledges the drive and ambition behind our journey of progression and discovery. Recognizing our needs, we also need to understand how to move forward. The action of a propeller is to give us 'lift', which suggests being able to use the intellect.

Public House

To be in a pub in a dream and aware of our behaviour indicates how we relate to groups and what our feelings are about society. A public space where we can drop inhibitions has links with our need for celebration. As a meeting place where generally few judgements are made, it becomes a place in which people can co-exist.

Pulling

If, in a dream, we are pulling, then this suggests a positive action. We are being alerted to the fact that we can do something about a situation. If we are being pulled we may feel that we are having to give in to outside pressure. In slang terms, pulling means picking up a potential partner. In dreams this can actually translate itself into a physical feeling. We may also, in everyday life, be being pulled in a certain direction – against our wishes – by our emotions and feel that we are powerless to resist.

Pulse

A pulse is the essential rhythm to life: without it we die. To be aware in sleep of one's pulse may indicate some kind of anxiety. In dreams this may translate itself into a rhythm that is external to ourselves. There could also be health worries.

Punishment

Later on in life, when there is fear of retribution from an external source, we will often dream of being punished. Self-punishment occurs when we have not achieved the standards we expect of ourselves. If there is conflict in our lives, and we cannot resolve it, we will often dream of being punished.

Puppet

When a puppet appears in a dream there is often a sense of being able to manipulate circumstances or people around us. If someone else is working the puppet, we may feel that it is we who are being manipulated. If the puppet is manipulating us, then we need to be aware of some sort of official difficulty. We may also sense that, as the puppet, we are part of something bigger.

Purse

In dreams a purse takes on a value of its own, because it holds what is valuable to us – usually money. The old saying, 'You cannot make a silk purse out of a sow's ear' has relevance in dreams as well as life. The mind can play tricks and manifest an apparently inappropriate image – one that needs to come under further inspection.

Pushed/pushing

When in waking life we are aware of pressure, this can be symbolized in dreams as being pushed and can sometimes highlight our fear of illness. In certain forms of mental illness, the patient experiences a feeling of being pushed around and made to do something he does not want to do. Now and again, when experienced in dreams, this can actually be a form of healing.

Pyramid

A pyramid is an extremely strong image. In dreams it exists on different levels; on a physical level, it is a building of wonder; on a mental level, it is a structure of regeneration: on a spiritual level, it is a guardian of power. It will depend on our own level of awareness as to which interpretation it relates to.

Q

Quarantine

Dreaming of having to put an animal into quarantine suggests our inability to look after a vulnerable part of ourselves, or others. When in normal life we feel isolated, this may translate itself in dream language as being in quarantine. It would seem that 'authority' has taken over to manage this isolation.

Quartz

Quartz seen in dreams tends to represent the crystallization of ideas and feelings. It touches into our internal process, often enabling us to express that which we have found impossible before. Really, to dream of quartz signifies a recognition of developing power.

Quarry

To dream of a quarry is to be plumbing the depths of our personality, searching for any positive knowledge and intuition we may have hidden, in the hope of bringing it to a more conscious plane.

Quest

The Hero's Quest is an archetypal image that can appear in many guises in dreams. To be searching for something usually signifies that we are aware that we must undertake a frightening task in order to progress. Many fairy stories and mythological tales have as their main theme the search for something magical. Such themes can be translated into dreams on a personal level.

Question

To be asking questions in a dream indicates a degree of self-doubt. To have someone asking us questions shows us we are aware that we have some knowledge to share. If the question cannot be answered, we may need to seek the answer ourselves in waking life. If we have a question in waking life that needs answering, by keeping it in mind before going to sleep we may often find the answer through dreams.

Queue – See **Line**

Quicksand

Quicksand signifies a lack of security, possibly in all aspects of our life. To find ourselves trapped in quicksand suggests that we have been put in a difficult situation that is not necessarily of our own making.

Quilt

To dream of a quilt (or duvet) is, on all planes, to identify our need for security, warmth, care and love. A particular quilt may have a special significance. For instance, a childhood quilt in an adult dream would suggest the need for some kind of reassurance.

Quip

When we become aware of a joke or quip by someone else in a dream, we are recognizing that we can allow ourselves to be affected by other people's sense of humour. If we are the ones who are communicating through wit or sarcasm, we may often be surprised by our own ability.

Quiver

Quivering symbolizes extreme emotion. It may be an emotion that has surfaced because of a past experience and now needs addressing. On a more physical level, it could be that we are feeling the cold.

Quote/quotation

To be giving a quote – as in a building estimate – can signify the value that we put on our talents. If we have difficulty with the accuracy – or the acceptance – of the quote we need to reconsider our own self-image. To hear a quote would suggest we should 'listen' to the sentiment being expressed. On a more esoteric level, a quotation signifies Truth.

R

Rack

A rack indicates that we may need some order in a small part of our lives. In another meaning, to be 'on the rack' suggests we may have done something that we regret or feel guilty about. Either that or we have got into the position of being victim of someone else's mistaken actions.

Radar

To dream of radar indicates that we have now come to terms with our intuitive faculty, and maybe it is now also being picked up by others and appreciated, and vice versa. Radar can also suggest a degree of clairvoyance is available to us.

Radiance

If something is distinguished by its radiance it has a special significance or quality that we should look at more closely, with pure thought and wisdom our main concerns.

Radio

Heading the symbolism here is communication. There may be information or ideas available to us that we need to listen to and understand more fully. The radio also signifies 'a voice of authority', so we should find that person whom we look up to and whose opinions we can take on board.

Raffle

To dream of a raffle – particularly of taking part in one – might suggest that we want to gain something in an easier fashion than by effort or hard work. Alternatively, we may feel that we are due a bit of luck that our work deserves.

Raft

On an emotional level a raft represents a certain kind of safety and stability – for the time being – during a difficult time. It will give us the required security, but in time we will need to have a more solid foundation on which to make the necessary transition.

Railway – Also see **Journeys and Transport**

Dreaming of railways indicates that we have some tiny indecision on our mind. That is, we are wondering if, in life, we are on the right track and if not which way to go. If, in the dream, we can see only one track, then there may be only one way to go. If we can see more than one, then we have more opportunities and need to take more time choosing our way ahead.

Rain

Appropriately, rain indicates tears and the releasing of pent-up emotions. If we have been feeling low, then we are being made to realize that now is the time to let go. Rain as itself, as well as symbolically, can refresh and wash away. It may be that we need to clean ourselves of someone or something. is also sometimes taken to represent the sexual act.

Rainbow

To dream of a rainbow is normally a good thing as it is an indication of better things on the horizon. It can also mean that we have been hoping for, and now we are literally dreaming, of something better, something 'over the rainbow' as it were. From an esoteric standpoint, a rainbow is said to depict the seven steps of awareness necessary for true spirituality.

Rape – See **Sex**

Razor

Which interpretation is appropriate depends on the type of razor of which we have dreamt. A safety razor suggests a less risky method is needed to help us reveal the truth about ourselves. An electric razor suggests that we need to pay more attention to the image we have made and put across in everyday life – and then, if necessary, make changes. A cut-throat razor has the same symbolism as a knife, that is, cutting through the unnecessary. Dreaming of a razor can also show that we need to 'sharpen up' our attitude about something.

Reading

Reading a book indicates that we are actively seeking knowledge or information. Also, to be aware that we are reading a novel is to begin to understand our own need for fantasy. Reading a list suggests that we are attempting to give some order to our lives, whereas reading a letter indicates we are awaiting news. A psychic reading often uses many basic dream images. To dream of having such a reading suggests a need to understand ourselves on a deeper level.

Reading, or being in a library, appears in dreams as a form of spiritual realization.

Reaping

In the song 'Perfect Day', Lou Reed sings 'you're going to reap just what you sow', and to dream of reaping indicates just that, that there is a way to gain from work done. Also, if we dream of 'reaping a reward' for something we have done, we are approving of our own activities. On a more negative tack, a hurtful act could return to haunt us. Possibly even more negative is The Grim Reaper, often pictured with a scythe; he is said to reap in the dead.

Red – See Colours in the Dream Interpretation chapter

Red Indian – See **Native American**

Reflection

A reflection seen in a dream has a lot to do with the way we see ourselves or our self-image at that particular moment. It could also be a warning against self-worship. Also, we may at this time be attempting to understand our inner working and the way in which we deal with everyday life.

Refrigerator

On a practical level it could simply be that the bedroom is cold. A refrigerator is also a symbol of self-preservation – you may literally have gone cold emotionally as well as sexually. This could be a result of stored-up resentment, and therefore emotions will not grow. To dream of rotten food in a refrigerator suggests we feel we are not being sustained adequately – emotionally or physically.

Reins – Also see **Bridle**

Reins indicate intelligent control and will. However, as a form of guidance and restraint they show that we need to be in control of the power and energy available to us.

Psychologically, to be 'reined' suggests some form of inhibition – either our own or other people's.

Religious Imagery

We all hold within ourselves a personal basic truth. Religious imagery, because it is so universal, helps us to link back to that basic 'truth'. Despite cultural differences there are certain aspects of this imagery which are universally recognized. An icon – a statue or a painting – though more often thought of within orthodox religion, is actually an illustration of a religious concept. For instance, the statue of the Virgin Mary in Christianity has the same inherent meaning as Durga, the goddess of devotion in Hinduism.

When such symbolism begins to appear in dreams it is time for us to begin to access the inner truth or spirituality which we all possess, and to take responsibility for our life. Depending on our culture and/or knowledge the images will often be startlingly specific in their symbolism. Christian images will tend to appear more readily for people within a society whose law is based on the Ten Commandments. Other systems of belief will manifest their own images.

Although many images may appear, below are those types which most often appear:

Angels It is important to distinguish between the 'higher-self' and the angelic form. Angels tend to be androgynous and to represent pure being and freedom from sin. When the image of a 'dark' angel appears in dreams it usually suggests that we are being alerted to some kind of spiritual wrong-doing that has probably already taken place. Angels are seen as messengers from the gods.

Baptism This is a rite of initiation into the family of man, and in dreams suggests a ceremony or ritual of welcome, marking a particular stage of development.

Bible/religious texts If we dream of a Bible or other religious book, it usually means that we are aware of traditional moral standards. We need a code of conduct which helps us to survive and there is such a resource available to us.

Buddha The figure of Buddha in dreams highlights our ability to experience life to its fullest extent, and those qualities of 'being' which are necessary to be able to do this.

Ceremony Ceremony and ritual form an integral part of religion and also mark the various rites of passage which are necessary as we grow towards maturity. In dreams, taking part in such ceremonies usually denotes a change in attitude, belief or awareness.

Christ Christ personifies 'perfect man' demonstrating the reconciliation of the spiritual and the physical – God and man. Seen in his various aspects, such as appearing on the cross, he represents that part of us which is prepared to suffer for our beliefs.

Churches, chapels, synagogues, temples etc. In dreams any religious building suggests sanctuary, our feelings of awe and wonder or a place where we can share our beliefs. In some dreams it may also represent the human body.

Crucifixion Often represents sacrifice made in the name of principle.

Demon/Devil Seen as temptation, such figures can signify suppressed sexual drives and desires. For most, such figures are the personification of evil.

Feathered Sun This symbol appears in a number of cross-cultural religious images, drawing together the symbols of the Sun and the Eagle. It indicates the universe and the centre of ourselves – the universal centre and solar power.

Festivals In waking life festivals were developed by religious leaders as an opportunity for people to meet together for celebration and sharing. They continue to have this meaning in dreams, as well as pinpointing the various times of year at which the festivals take place. Pagan festivals such as Beltane were adopted by conventional religions in order to give continuity to worship rituals.

God/Gods When we dream of God we are acknowledging to ourselves that there is a higher power more knowing and able than we are. Throughout one stage of development there is comfort and security in believing that there is a paternal God who will care for us and approve of us, and the forceful emotions we sometimes encounter may be linked with our childhood need for love and parental approval. In a woman's dream, dreaming of mythical gods will help her to understand various aspects of her own personality. In a man's dream he is linking with his own masculinity and his sense of belonging to himself, and therefore to the rest of humanity.

Often these emotions can be personalized and recognized in the figures of the mythical gods. In the Enhancing Your Dreams chapter, there is a great deal of information on mythological figures – male and female. However here we give some brief meanings for you. In Greek and Roman mythology, Adonis signifies health, beauty and self-adoration. Apollo signifies the Sun, and taught Chiron the art of healing. Heracles was taught the art of healing by Chiron, but when he accidentally shot Chiron the latter was not able to accept healing from him. Mars as the god of war symbolizes the drive we require to succeed. Mercury (or Hermes) suggests communication, often of a sensitive sort. He is the patron of magic. Zeus is the king of the gods, and signifies fathering in both its positive and negative forms.

Christian belief holds to one God, although manifesting in three forms – Father, Son and Holy Ghost. (Jehovah, in the sense of a vengeful god, alerts us to the negative side of power.) Other religions attribute the powers to various Gods. As we grow in understanding, we can appreciate the relevance of both beliefs and can begin to understand God as an all-pervading energy.

Goddess/Goddesses Dreaming of goddesses connects us with our archetypal images of femininity (See Archetypes in the Enhancing your Dreams chapter). In a woman's dream a goddess will clarify the connection through the unconscious that exists between all women and female creatures. It is the sense of mystery, of a shared secret, which is such an intangible force within the woman's psyche. In the waking state it is that which enables women to create. To dream about goddesses, therefore, is to accept our right to initiation into a sisterhood or network in order to bring about a common aim. In a man's dream the goddess figure signifies all that a man fears in the concept of female power. It usually also gives an insight into his earliest view of femininity through his experience of his mother.

There are many goddess figures in all cultures. There are those perceived as being destructive, such as Kali, Bast and Lilith, and also beneficent ones such as Athena and Hermia. The beneficent ones which women most closely relate to are given here. Aphrodite, goddess of love and beauty, moves women to be both creative and procreative. She governs a woman's enjoyment of love and beauty. Artemis, who is the goddess of the moon, personifies the independent feminine spirit whose ultimate goal is achievement. She is often pictured as the huntress. Athena is goddess of wisdom and strategy. She is logical and self-assured and is ruled by her mental faculties rather than her emotions. Demeter, the maternal archetype and goddess of fertility, highlights a woman's drive to provide physical and spiritual support for her children. Hera, the goddess of marriage, denotes the woman who has her essential goal of finding a husband and being married as paramount and any other role as secondary. Hestia, goddess of the hearth, manifests the patient woman who finds steadiness in seclusion. She emits a sense of wholeness. Persephone, who is ultimately queen of the underworld but only through having rejected her status as Demeter's daughter, gives expression to woman's tendency towards a need to please and be needed by others. Her submissive behaviour and passivity must change to an ability to take responsibility for who she is.

Through her understanding of the goddesses, and often through dreams which highlight such figures a woman will come to terms with her own essential nature.

Hell The old-fashioned image of hell suggests a state of illusion, where nothing is ever as it seems. In dreams, to be aware that there is such a place suggests that the dreamer is beginning to understand his or her chaotic nature.

Heaven In dreams, heaven is represented as a place of high energy, where there is no suffering. Such an idea is seen in most religions, and manifests when the individual is becoming more spiritually orientated.

Holy Communion/manna/spiritual food Any image in dreams of sharing food, particularly bread, in a religious setting, has the symbolism of holy communion, a sacred sharing of the power that belongs to God. This has its roots in the pagan belief that all power and energy can be shared.

Incense This symbolizes a request and a prayer offered to God or to the gods, through perfume and smoke. For those who have knowledge the perfume used may be important.

Mother These images in dreams such as that of the Virgin Mary signify the whole essence of feminine nurturing and holiness associated with the figure of the mother.

The Holy Man or Woman The holy man or woman appearing in dreams signifies the inner guidance which is available to all.

Pope Often to meet the Pope in a dream is to meet the side of ourselves which has developed a code of behaviour based on our religious beliefs. He may be benign or judgmental depending on how the figure of the Pope was presented in childhood. The Pope often appears in dreams as a substitute for the father, or as a personification of God.

Priest or prophet Such a figure in dreams indicates an inner awareness of a belief system, sometimes in the future.

Religious service or ritual

Most dreams which have overtones of ritual or ceremony highlight the idea of certain of the actions having meaning whether individually or in sequence. Indeed, it is often the cumulative effect of the actions which is seen to be important. It is also necessary to understand the effect of group behaviour in such services.

Rent

Whenever we undertake a personal responsibility in waking life, it is often symbolized by dreaming of paying rent in some way. Receiving rent, on the other hand, indicates that we have entered into a negotiation that will benefit us in the long run, that we have understood material value. It is also a symbol of security.

Reptiles

Reptiles in dreams connect with our basic and instinctive reactions and responses. When there is a need to understand why we do things we first need to control, understand and manage our basic drives.

Rescue

When we are rescued in a dream we are aware that we are then indebted to our rescuer. The knight rescuing the maiden symbolizes the notion of the untouched feminine being rescued from her own passion. On another level it could be that we feel lost or desperate and need rescuing from ourselves.

Resign

In dreams, to resign signifies, literally, to give up. We need to know if this a good or bad thing. It could be that we cannot face the music that life presents to us. If this is the case we need to assure ourselves that no further effort can be put in. It may be that we need to try harder or have more belief in ourselves.

Restaurant

If we fear being alone, then we sometimes dream of being in a restaurant or cafe as it suggests a need for company. It follows then that we require emotional support with which food is connected. We may also be conscious of the need for a 'relationship'.

Ribbon – See Bridle

Rice

Rice as an image in dreams suggests food, and therefore sustenance both for the mind, body, and spirit. It can also suggest abundance. Rice is also supposed to be magical and symbolizes spiritual nourishment.

Ring

A ring is continuous and self-perpetuating, so, appearing in a dream, normally suggests a relationship of some sort. Because of this there are different meanings for different rings. A signet ring would imply setting the seal on something. A wedding ring symbolizes commitment. A 'family' ring would represent tradition and value. An engagement ring hints at a more tentative promise of devotion. An eternity ring would be a long-term promise.

Ritual – Also see **Ceremony** under **Religious Imagery**

Rituals are actions that are carried out repeatedly, in order to achieve a required result. The ritual, for example, of getting up in the morning, because it is a habit, simply has the purpose of getting us focused. On the religious front rituals help bond the power of the many, and in dreams usually have this significance.

River – See **Water** under **Environments**

Road – See **Journeys and Transport**

Robe

If we dream of, say, a bath robe this indicates two things. One is the covering up of nakedness, the other is a sense of being at ease. To be dressing someone else in robes is to be protecting them. In another way a robe can symbolize our thoughts, relationships and sex, with clean and dirty being the operative words. In the magical sense, a robe can suggest status and power; the white robe is innocence, and the seamless robe represents holiness.

Rock

To dream of rock might indicate that we need a more solid foundation in the real world. We may need to recognize various qualities within ourselves that are connected with rock, such as reliability, coldness, rigidity, and then deal with them appropriately. On another tack, seaside rock – that is edible – can remind us of happier more carefree times. Dual rocks through which we must pass suggest the same image as the passage between two pillars, that is, passing from one state of being to the next.

Rocket

On a basic level the rocket is connected with male energy and sexuality. A rocket is also a symbol of power, so we may need to look at whether or not we can do things better then we previously thought. A rocket can also represent a search for something more spiritual and 'out of this world' in our lives.

Rocking

Rocking in dreams can be a comforting activity, like a child who will rock himself to sleep. Rocking can also suggest infantile behaviour, from the point of view that it puts us in touch with the natural rhythms of life. This gentle movement also helps us touch in with our own centre, but is also a symbol of transition.

Rod

In the biblical sense a rod can suggest support and encouragement. More mundanely a rod indicates rigidity and impassivity. It can also signify punishment.

Roof

To dream of being under a roof allows us to acknowledge the shelter and protection it gives. Obviously if the roof is leaking or we are on the roof, then we are leaving ourselves open to emotional attack. The sheltering aspect of the feminine as the guardian of the hearth is sometimes represented as a roof.

Room – See **Buildings** under **Environments**

Root – See **Tree**

Rope

A rope can indicate strength and power. The power, however, can, if we are not careful, turn against us.

If the rope is made of an unusual material there is some special bond to which we need to pay particular attention. If we are tied to the rope, something is holding us back from expressing ourselves. Being tied by a rope to something else means we need to look at the relationship between us and what we are tied to.

Rose

The rose in dreams, as in life, often represents love, admiration and perfection; it can also suggest fertility and virginity. Through its own cycle of growth and decay the rose can symbolize the cycle of life. It also represents the 'heart-centre' of life.

Round Table

A round table, like the symbolism of a ring, suggests wholeness – but more essentially the idea that everyone is equal. The table also indicates a centre, but one from which all things can begin.

Ruins

When something is left in ruins we have to ascertain if it is through carelessness or vandalism. If the former, the suggestion is that we need to concentrate on getting things together. If the latter, we need to look at how we are allowing ourselves to be vulnerable.

If we have deliberately ruined something we need to acknowledge the self-destructive element in us.

Running

When running occurs in a dream we need look at what else is happening as this will have a bearing on the symbolism. As an example, one of the most common 'running' dreams is that of actually not being able to run away from somebody; this indicates fear and an inability to do something – a common element in anxiety dreams.

Rush

We need to learn how to control time successfully and ideally with the minimum of fuss, and to be rushing in a dream suggests that we are not doing so. It may be that we have to contend with outside pressure – but that is all about control and management.

Rust

Rust symbolizes neglect and lethargy, both emotionally and physically. To dream of rust means we have to clean up our act before we can progress. If we don't, we will suffer. Rust can also signify outdated attitudes.

S

Sackcloth
Sackcloth appearing in dreams represents humiliation (as in sackcloth and ashes). Because of that, it can also signify repentance – we may want to reveal to the world that we are ready to repent of an action that, in turn, has humiliated us.

Saddle
A saddle appearing in a dream will indicate a need to exercise control over someone. For a woman this is often sexual control; for a man it is more likely to be control over his own life.

Sadism – See also **Sex**
Sadism often surfaces because of anger held over – but suppressed – from childhood pain. It is the wish to hurt or provoke a reaction – often in someone we love. In the dream we have to recognize if we are being sadistic or having a form of sadism inflicted upon us. Both can represent parts of ourselves.

Sailing – See also **Journeys and Transport**
Sailing suggests a sense of freedom and the chance to use our intellect. It can also bring into focus the way we are directing our lives. If we are sailing in a yacht there is more of a sense of immediacy than if we were sailing, say, in a liner. The first is more to do with one-to-one relationships, while the second suggests more of a group effort.

Sails – Also see **Sailing** and **Wind**
Sails can suggest that there is power available that we can use. Sails also represent the spirit – as in a force that moves us. If we combine the two it may be that the power to progress is within us.

Sailor
A sailor represents freedom of movement and spirit as he is in total

control of his own destiny. For a woman the sailor can appear as the Hero; for a man it is more to do with being given permission to run free.

Salad

In dreams, most food indicates a need to be nurtured and stimulated – that is, we are probably lacking nourishment. Salad, because it is food in its simplest sense, takes us right back to nature and simple values.

Salt

In dreams, salt highlights the refined qualities we bring to our lives, those things we do to enhance our lifestyle. We run most of our lives through our emotions but the more subtle aspects are just as vital. As a symbol of permanence and incorruptibility salt is also important in dreams.

Sand

Sand in a dream suggests instability and a lack of emotional security; it can also represent impermanence. It may be that the foundations we are working from do not have a solid enough base, and are likely to 'shift' at any moment.

Sap

In dream terms sap indicates that we are now ready to undertake new work or perhaps even a new relationship. We are aware of our own strength and vitality and are prepared to take on a new challenge. In another way a 'sap' is a more affectionate term for 'wimp'. It may be that we need to get a bit of backbone into our lives.

Sarcophagus

To dream of a sarcophagus is, amongst other things, to recognize the importance of death and the rites of passage associated with it. It is likely that we are in a state of transition in waking life. It can also indicate that there are parts of our ego that we need to keep in check.

Satellite

A satellite signifies communication. It suggests an efficient, effective way of contact and relating to others. A satellite can also appear in a dream to alert us to a dependency that one person can have upon another – though this need not be a bad thing.

Satyr

The satyr, in one form, represents the male spirit at its most basic link with nature. It is that part of nature which is uncontrollable and potentially anarchic. However, if we see it as being destructive then it will be. Conversely, if we see it as being helpful then it will be so.

Savings

Our savings may represent resources, either material or emotional, which we have hidden away until such times as they are needed. It usually suggests that we need to plan ahead in order to call upon another energy at an appropriate time.

In another sense, savings suggest an ability that we already have or have developed, but have not yet utilized.

Saw – See **Tools**

Scaffold

A scaffold in a dream will normally indicate that there is some kind of temporary structure in our lives. If a hangman's scaffold appears this will suggest that a part of our lives must come to an end. Either way, a scaffold denotes that some change needs to occur in our lives.

Scales

Scales (astrologically represented by the sign of Libra) in a dream suggest the need for balance and self-control in our world. The type of scale we see in our dream will determine the meaning. Bathroom scales would suggest a more personal assessment is required, whereas a weigh-bridge might suggest that we need to take our whole lives into consideration. If they were doctor's scales we may be alerting ourselves to a potential health problem.

Scalp – See **Head** under **Body**

Scapegoat

If in our dream we are the scapegoat for someone else's deeds, then we are being made the victim – other people may be trying to make us pay for their misdemeanours. If we are making another person a scapegoat, then this denotes a shift in blame. It is worth looking at the idea of co-operation and understanding, as this may be what is needed to rectify a situation in our waking lives.

Scar

A scar in a dream tells us that there are old wounds that have not been fully dealt with. These may be emotional as much as physical. It is often important which part of the body is scarred, as our nervous system has ways of giving information through our dreams.

Sceptre

The sceptre can represent a magic wand and in dreams can indicate our right to use such magic coupled with authority. It also signifies the transference of divine power from above, rather than below. Thus it is masculine power – the sceptre also has the same phallic symbolism as most other rods.

School

In situations where we are learning new abilities or skills, the image of a school, or 'school of life' will often appear in dreams. However, we may also be learning about the nature of people and relationships. Alternatively, a school will often appear at a time when we are attempting to get rid of antiquated ideas and concepts.

Scissors

In dreams, scissors denote cutting the non-essential out of our lives. These may be things that we simply cannot deal with, and it is now time to cut them out. On a more esoteric level, scissors have ambivalent significance. They can cut the Thread of Life, but can also represent unity and the coming together of the spiritual and physical.

Screw

It rests on what culture we belong to as to how we are going to interpret a screw. In criminal circles a screw will mean a prison officer or jailer. To the younger element in society it is used, along with a number of others words as slang for sex. So we need to look out for word play, even if the object seen is a proper screw. Screws can also suggest a task that, in itself, we may consider pointless, but which becomes more significant in a wider context.

Scroll

If we dream of a scroll we are endorsing the knowledge or information that has been given to us, so that we can now enhance our lives. A scroll can also represent hidden knowledge as well as the passing of time.

Scythe – Also see **Sickle**

The scythe is a cutting instrument, and has a similar symbolism to that of a knife. Its appearance will alert us to some very deeply held notions and ideas. The scythe, as used by the Grim Reaper, also represents death – do remember that in dreams 'death' can also mean great change.

Sea – See **Water** under **Environments**

Seal – Also see **Animals and Birds**

A seal can represent hidden knowledge, authority and power. In dreams, the ownership of a seal gives us the authority to take responsibility for our own actions. If we are seen to be breaking a seal, then this might indicate we are betraying a confidence.

Seance

Dreaming of being at a seance denotes a need to examine the psychic side of our nature. Remembering that 'psychic' means 'being in touch with self', this can suggest being aware of our intuition. However, it may well be that we also need to take time out of our normal routine to relax and be still.

Searching

To be searching in a dream is to be attempting to find a solution to a problem. If we are searching for someone we may be aware of our loneliness. If we are searching for an article then there is something, we want or need that we have yet to find. In another area, a move towards enlightenment often stems from a feeling of searching for something.

Searchlight

If a searchlight appears in a dream, then we need to focus our attention and concentrate more fully on matters that concern us. A searchlight is used to show the way ahead, as is a torch.

Seasons

When we are made aware of the seasons of the year in dreams, we are also connecting with the various periods of our lives. Spring signifies childhood; summer, young adulthood; autumn, middle age; winter, old age. It could also be alerting us to the need for enjoyment, as the seasons are also connected with celebration and festival.

Seed

A seed symbolizes our potential. For a woman, though, it may also suggest pregnancy, or her thoughts about pregnancy. A seed can also indicate the validity of something we are planning. We need to have the right conditions in which to grow and mature.

Sex

A child's first appreciation of itself is as a separate entity from its mother which has to cope with the separation from her. It becomes aware of its need to be protected, comforted and loved.

A crucial stage of its development is its fascination with its own body, and what feels comfortable and good, whether it is nice to touch or be touched, or indeed if touch is permissible. A fear of being touched may reveal itself in dreams, and be recognized as a sexual problem even though the original trauma may have been kept hidden. It is when the individual is no longer afraid of the curiosity that allows an innocent exploration of his own body, that real growth can begin. Dreams will often allow us to explore this physicality in a safe and very personal way.

The complete range of our sexuality can be revealed in dreams. If we ignore our own sexual nature and fail to acknowledge our life force, then the negative aspects will make themselves known in dreams – this is nature's attempt at levelling out the waking state where this awareness may be over-intellectualized or over-dramatized. Interaction with others then becomes essential, and this need will often make itself apparent in dreams.

There are many aspects of sex and sexuality to be interpreted and explained, beginning here with bi-sexuality. As individuals we carry both masculine and feminine potential and responses. One is often more obvious than the other, and there can additionally, in some cases be conflict between the internal and external. This sometimes shows itself in dreams as bi-sexuality or a need for some kind of bond with members of both sexes.

Dreaming of castration indicates a fear of losing our masculinity or even our sexual prowess – a common fear amongst men.

To dream of clothing in a sexual context can have specific relevance to our perception of ourselves. For example, dreaming of being fully clothed during sex would signify some degree of guilt, either on our part or of someone close to us.

Contraception can indicate a fear of pregnancy or of the responsibility for both men and women. More specifically for women there might be a fear of giving birth.

In dreams, fetishes – fixations on an external object without which there can be no sexual act – can highlight fear, immaturity and lack of capability. There is evidence substantiating the belief that, at an unconscious level, man would go for a life of celibacy and that by focusing his energies onto an object he relinquishes responsibility for the sexual act.

Dreaming of a hermaphrodite (who has both masculine and feminine sexual organs) can indicate either bi-sexuality, or androgyny – the ideal balance within one person of masculine and feminine qualities.

Universally, homosexuality is understood as the desire for sexual relations with a partner who is the same sex. However, a more correct definition is the desire for someone who is the same, or very similar, to oneself. It is this element that comes across in dreams. If, on reflection, we can identify similarities in ways which are not purely sexual the dream can be interpreted more fully.

Images appearing in a dream preceding orgasm can signify the real nature of your attitude to sex and sexuality. The conflicts and problems which arise in you because of your sexual desire for someone can be dealt with in the dream state through dreaming of emission or orgasm.

Incest in a dream usually symbolizes the desire to express love or have it expressed in a warmer more tactile way. More obviously, dreaming of incest can highlight guilty feelings about one's parents or members of the family.

The need to be able to communicate properly with someone, on a more intimate level, can show itself as intercourse in a dream. If intercourse is interrupted you may have inhibitions of which you are not consciously aware. Also intercourse in a dream can denote the integration of a particular part of your personality – if a child is then born that integration has been, or can be, considered a success.

A kiss can indicate a mark of respect, or a desire to stimulate the dream partner. It indicates we should be aware of what arousal we need for ourselves.

The desire to hurt ourselves or to be hurt through sex in dreams highlights masochism. This often arises from two causes. The first is to play the martyr – to suffer for our sins. The second is to feel exceptional emotion of one sort or another. It may be we are not allowing ourselves to feel deeply in waking life.

Dreaming of masturbation is to do with the need for comfort and, for a younger person, the excitement and innocence of exploration.

When some kind of image that we as the dreamer consider to be sexually perverted appears we are avoiding or attempting to avoid issues to do with closeness and bonding.

If ideas of rape appear in a dream, then it can be as much to do with violation of personal space as with the sexual act. Sexual rape is unlikely to appear in the dreams of sexually abused children, though the adult may later suffer from nightmares. Rape itself may only manifest when the adult is ready to deal with the trauma. Most rape dreams are based around the need for, or perception of, power issues between the male and female.

Sadism appearing in a dream highlights a counter-balance to our conscious way of being in the world. In everyday life we may be either very placid, in which case it is an escape valve; or if we tend to be dominant and controlling in everyday life the unconscious is showing its need for freedom.

Dreams have a crazy way of throwing up pictures of primitive rites and practises of which we may have no conscious knowledge. Semen is the sign of masculinity and physical maturity and is often seen in dreams as other milky fluids. The spilling of such fluid can represent the sexual act as in primitive times.

Feeling desire for someone else – most often of the opposite sex – is a basic urge for closeness with that person. It seems that we are looking for a part of ourselves and the other character represents the closest that we can get to it. If we were fully integrated as people we would have no need for sex with someone else, but for most of us there is a desire to be united with everything which is not part of our own ego. Such a dream, which highlights the feelings we are capable of experiencing, provides a basis that enables us to understand our own needs.

Transvestism in dreams signifies a confusion so far as gender is concerned.

A dream where we are conscious of venereal disease suggests an awareness of some kind of infection. This need not always be of a sexual nature; it may also be emotional.

Overall, sexual activity is either the highest expression of love and spirituality between two people or, if purely physical, is entirely selfish. It is up to you to decide for yourself which it is.

Shampoo

The need to clear our minds and our heads in order to see and think clearly is often symbolized in a dream by shampoo. In another, more lyrical way, it could be that we quite literally need to 'wash someone out of our hair' to lessen their influence on our lives, so to speak.

Shapes

If and when geometric shapes appear in a dream, then we are given a greater understanding of the abstract world – depending on what stage of development we have reached at that point. It is as though the ancient perception of form is beginning to take on a new meaning and signification. It is important to note as much detail as possible about the dream, as the number of sides the shape has will be significant, as will the colours. Generally, though, we can accept the nature of things as they are, and can take time to look at the basic structure of our own nature. We can appreciate the shape our life is taking without placing emotional inhibitions in the way.

The various shapes and patterns likely to appear in dreams are interpreted as follows: beginning with the centre – the point from which everything starts. In regard to shape, it is the point from which the pattern grows.

The circle symbolizes the inner being or the Self. It is also totality and perfection. A circular object – such as a ring – shares much of the meaning of the circle. A circle with a dot in the centre can signify the soul in completion. It is also sometimes taken to represent femininity.

The crescent (including the sickle and crescent moon) also signifies the feminine – that is, the mysterious power that is intuitive and typically non-rational.

Any cross appearing in a dream stands for the realization (in the sense of making real) and moving of spirit into substance. Travelling through the symbol of the sword to the equal-armed cross, from there to the cross of suffering and crucifixion, and finally to the Tau of perfection, the soul learns through experience to conquer the barricades, thus enabling spiritual progression. The hung cross with the figure of Christ symbolizes the sacrifice of self for others. The four arms of a cross pointing in opposing directions signify conflicts, sorrow and torment, but these are ultimately necessary in order to reach perfection. The three upper arms are said to stand for God the Father, Son and Holy Ghost, though more clearly any Divine Trinity. The intersection signifies the reconciliation of opposites.

The diamond shape suggests that there will be an increase in opportunities culminating in intense 'peak experience' with both positive and negative implications.

A hexagram symbolizes the harmonious development of the physical, social and spiritual elements of human life and its cohesion in creating a perfect whole.

Symbolic of the womb is the oval shape, which also suggests feminine life. Called the *Vesica Piscis*, it is the halo that totally encircles a sacred figure.

In dreams, patterns such as mosaic or kaleidoscope which appear as part of the dream scenario can classify how we handle repeated patterns of behaviour in our lives.

The sphere has a similar meaning to the globe, and denotes perfection and completion of all possibilities.

The spiral, meanwhile, is the ideal path to evolution and growth. Doctrine states that everything is continually in motion, but also continually rising or raising its vibration. If the spiral is towards the centre of something, it shows we advance towards our own centre by a roundabout route. A clockwise spiral, moving outward to the right is a movement towards consciousness and enlightenment. If counter-clockwise, the movement is towards the unconscious, probably regressive behaviour. There is also a link with the navel or solar plexus, as the centre of power and energy.

The square or cube symbolizes the manifestation of the spirit into the physical. It represents the earthly realm as opposed to the heavens. A square within a circle suggests the act of 'becoming' or taking on form. The figure within a square is the Self or perfect Man. Any square object signifies the enclosing and feminine principle.

The star, especially if it is a bright one, denotes those things we all reach for – hope, aspiration, and ideal. The five-pointed star or pentagram evokes personal magic, and all matter in harmony. To be accurate, the star should point upwards. In dreams it symbolises our awareness of our own magical qualities and wishes. If it is pointing downwards it symbolizes the antithesis – evil and witchcraft. Twelve stars signify both the Twelve Tribes of Israel and the Apostles. The six-pointed star, or Star of David, is made up of one triangle pointing upward and another pointing downward. Here, the physical and the spiritual are united in harmony creating wisdom.

The swastika, with its arms moving clockwise, portrays Ideal man and the power he has for good. In eastern symbolism it signifies the movement of the sun. Moving counter-clockwise the swastika in this form signifies all that is sinister and wrong. In this respect it is not known whether Hitler – who had aspirations towards dark magic – deliberately chose this reversed swastika.

The triangle portrays standing man, with his three parts of being – body, mind and spirit. It also symbolizes consciousness and love revealed through his physicality. If the triangle points upwards, human nature moves towards the divine. If it is pointing down it is spirit seeking expression through the physical. The triangle can also represent family relationships – that is, father, mother and child.

There is a game based on shapes in which you draw a square, a circle and a triangle, and then get someone else to elaborate each of the basic shapes into a drawing. Whatever he makes of the square is supposed to relate to his outlook on the world, the circle to his inner being, and the triangle to his sex life.

Shave

If it is a man dreaming of shaving, (it is likely he'll be shaving his face) this suggests that he is trying to change his image. If it is a woman, she is likely to be shaving other parts of her body in order to create a more beautiful image. Both indicate removing an unwanted layer – that is, a facade that has been created. On another tack, if we sense that we have had a 'close shave' then it is possible that we are taking too many risks.

Shawl – See **Cloak**

Sheaf

A sheaf, which is not often seen nowadays, can represent a number of things: harvest, hard work, good husbandry and consolidation, but sometimes also old-fashioned ways. As a symbol of Demeter, the sheaf also symbolizes the nurturing mother. It represents the 'dying world', in that Demeter refused to nurture 'her' humans when Persephone was kidnapped by Pluto.

Shears – See **Scissors**

Shells

A shell, in life as in dreams, is a form of defence that we use to prevent ourselves from being hurt emotionally. It can also be seen as a magical symbol that holds within it the power of transformation. A shell can also indicate that there is wisdom within us – a 'pearl' of wisdom.

Shelter

Shelter of any kind signifies protection. If we are giving shelter to someone in dreams, we may be protecting a part of ourselves from hurt or difficulty. If we are being given shelter we are conscious of the fact that there is protective power in our lives.

Shield

A shield is a symbol of preservation and growth. In our development as human beings, the shield may appear as a symbol of a particular stage of growth. It is at this point that we need to acknowledge that we have control over our own destiny. Often this symbol first appears in dreams representing this stage of development.

Shivering

To be aware of shivering in dreams can represent either a fear of conflict or of coldness of emotion. It may also suggest that we are getting nearer to a release of unconscious behaviour.

Shoes

These allow us to become grounded and in touch with life. Strange shoes, or shoes that don't fit, suggest some changes should be made.

Shop

In dreams, a shop signifies something that we feel we want or need. If it is a shop we know then we are most likely aware of what we want from life. If it is an unknown shop, then we may have to search our minds for what we want. If we are out on a shopping spree, then we need to satisfy our desires and are willing to pay large amounts for it.

Shot/shooting – Also see **Gun**

When we are shot in a dream this indicates that our feelings have been hurt recently – or we are a target for others' rage. If we are shooting something, we may be having to deal with our own fears. We could be guarding against meeting parts of our personality we do not like.

Shovel/spade

A shovel in a dream will signal a desire to dig into past experiences for information – possibly from an introspective point of view. A garden spade would suggest a degree of pragmatism, whereas a fire shovel would symbolize a need to take care.

Shrinking

Firstly, on a psychological level we can learn to handle who we are by recognizing both how necessary, and also how small, we are in the bigger picture. The latter can be accompanied by a feeling of shrinking. Therefore we become less threatening to ourselves and others. This also links with a possible need to return to childhood.

Shroud

A shroud is obviously linked with death, and can signify that we do not fully understand the subject. The image can sometimes be quite frightening, though if we are aware that by shrouding we are hiding something, then it becomes less so.

Sickness – Also see **Illness**

To feel, or to be, sick signals that there is something we need to get rid of; we may be 'sick' of something or somebody. When something is not right in our world, on any level, we need to abolish it. Sickness is one way of doing this.

Sickle

Now that we have moved from an agricultural to a more technological way of thinking, the sickle is no longer such an important image. What we are left with is the old symbol of the sickle representing mortality and death. As so often happens, this is not necessarily a physical death, but represents the 'death' of part of ourselves, or the changes occuring in our waking lives.

Sieve

In dreams a sieve indicates our ability to make the right decision, the ability to sort the good from the bad. It can suggest that we have the knowledge available to know how to get the best out of ourselves.

Signature

Our signature in a dream signifies that we have an appreciation and a recognition of ourselves and our mark in the world. If our signature appears to be illegible, then this might suggest that we are not sure if we are going about things in the right way.

Silence

In dreams silence can suggest apprehension and expectation. If we are being silent, then this indicates that we are, at this time, unable to voice our thoughts and feelings. Conversely, it may be that there is no need for sound, leading us to the old saying of silence being golden.

Silver

On one level silver can represent money or financial affairs – certainly something of value. On a totally different level silver symbolizes the qualities of the moon. It could be that we want to reach for something but we may now need to consider it only a remote possibility – however, if we make the effort, we will be successful.

Singing

Singing is to do with self-expression. If we are singing, then we are expressing our happiness with life. We may also be aware of our skill in expression. If we are chanting, then this suggests we are in touch with a higher vibration.

Sinking

To be sinking in a dream suggests we have lost confidence and are feeling afraid or hampered by a situation. Someone else sinking suggests we are aware of a difficulty that perhaps needs our assistance. What we are sinking into is often relevant. To be sinking in water would suggest a particular emotion is threatening to drown us. To be sinking in sand indicates that we feel there is no safe ground for us.

Siren

When we hear a siren in a dream, then we are being made aware of impending events. A Siren, in the sense of an alluring woman, indicates deception and distraction of man from his purpose. For a woman, the Siren can be a destructive thing if not acknowledged.

Size

To be conscious of size in a dream highlights how we feel in relation to a person or object, remembering that in dreams size is relative. Big might suggest important or threatening, whereas small might indicate vulnerability and a degree of insignificance.

Skeleton

A skeleton in a dream indicates the 'bare bones' of something, perhaps an idea or concept. A skeleton in a closet represents a past action or shame we wish to hide. A skeleton alerts us to our own feelings about death. We are aware that the physical must 'die', but there is a framework – a reminder – left.

Skin – See Body

Skull

There is varied skull symbolism in dreams: to be aware of our own skull is to recognize the structure that we have given our lives. To perceive a skull where there should be a head suggests that part of the person has 'died' or changed. To be talking to a skull is recognizing the need to communicate with people we have not heard from in a while. When a skull is talking to us, a part of us that we have rejected is beginning to come back to life. If we believe in life after death, we may feel that spirit is talking through the skull.

Sky

In dreams the sky can represent the mind. It can also signify our potential. If the sky is dark it may reflect our mood of gloominess; if it is bright, our mood of joy. Floating or flying in the sky can have two meanings: it can indicate that we are trying to escape the ordinary or that we are exploring different areas of potential.

Smell – Also see Odour and Perfume

To be aware of a smell in a dream usually reminds us of a time and a place that holds certain memories. Whether the smell is good or bad indicates the nature of its association.

Smoke/Smoking – Also see Fire

Smoke in dreams suggests danger around the corner, especially if we cannot locate the fire. If we are smoking, we are attempting to control anxiety. If we smoke in real life, but recognize in dreams that we no longer do so, we have overcome a difficulty. Smoke, on another level, can signify prayer rising to heaven.

Snake – See Serpent and Snake under Animals and Birds

Snow

Snow represents a crystallization of an idea. If the snow is melting, then this could suggest the idea or project is fading away, but it is more likely to symbolize something different, and that is the softening of the heart.

On the emotional front snow can indicate coldness, and it may be that we need to thaw out a bit ourselves.

Soap

In dreams, soap signals the idea of being cleansed. It could be that we need to clean up our act in order to progress. Also, we may feel a sense of having been made dirty by an experience and our dream is alerting us to the fact that we need to deal with it.

Sowing

Sowing can signify the sexual act, as well as suggesting good management of resources. It can also represent the beginning of a new project. We need to decide which is the most relevant for us.

Sowing in another sense suggests creating the correct environment in which growth can take place. It is the creative act.

Space

If we are aware of space, then we are in touch with our potential for learning – but we may need the space to carry out the process. An acknowledgement of space can broaden our current view of the world.

Spade – See Shovel

Spark

A spark in a dream represents a beginning. It is a small thing that gives rise to a much bigger picture. It can be perceived as our creative potential. A spark can suggest fire and from there love – so look closely, as we don't want to extinguish a potential match!

Spear

The phallic imagery of the spear relates to the masculine. A great warrior holding a spear is a more aggressive male image. The spear is also that part of ourselves which is fertile and dominant. Whether in a man's or a woman's dream, it allows us to be conscious of the need to get straight to the point.

Spectacles – See Glasses

Speed

Speed in dreams identifies an intensity of feelings that is not usually available in waking life. Travelling at speed suggests trying to achieve a fast result. Speeding – as in a traffic offence – suggests being too focused on an end result, and not the method of getting there.

Sphinx

A sphinx symbolizes some kind of mysterious, enigmatic feeling. The sphinx also stands for vigilance, power and wisdom, as well as dignity.

Spider

The spider, via the horror movie and its scuttling movement, is associated with all things scary and in dreams we can add deviousness to that list. More positively a spider can represent a perfectly woven pattern that both nurtures and protects us.

Spine – See **Backbone** under **Body**

Spirits – Also see **Ghost**

We all have fears and feelings about death, and the appearance of a spirit helps us to come to terms with these. It will depend on our own belief as to whether we feel they are actual spirits or not. When we are conscious of a kindly spirit we are aware that we can move on. When we see the spirits of dead people we usually need reassurance.

Spiral – See **Shapes**

Spire

To see a spire in a dream is to recognize a landmark. In previous times, people used the church as a meeting place. These days, the pub tends to be a marker, but in dreams the spire still persists in the communal sense of recognition.

Spittle

Negatively, spittle represents disgust. On a positive note spittle can be a sign of good faith – the old spitting on the palms routine to close a deal, and thus a bonding through the exchange of bodily fluids.

Splinter

A splinter can symbolize an irritation, albeit a minor one. Of greater significance is the suggestion that splinters represent painful words or ideas. If we sense we are part of a splinter group, then we are saying to ourselves that it is alright to break away from conventional or mainstream thinking.

Spring

Springtime indicates new growth and opportunity and now could be the time to set in motion some idea or project. Spring is a symbol of progression, particularly insofar as emotion is concerned. We can make a new beginning. A metal spring can signify a huge leap forward.

Sprinkle/sprinkling

Sprinkling as a symbol in dreams signals an attempt to make a little go a long way. Possibly we need to get the best out of situations around us, by putting a little effort into a lot of things. Bearing this in mind, sprinkling can also symbolize impregnation.

Square – See Shapes

Squirrel – See Animals and Birds

Stab – Also see Knife

To be stabbed in a dream indicates we are open to being hurt. To stab someone is, conversely, being prepared to hurt. Since a stab wound is penetrative it obviously has connections with aggressive masculine sexuality, but also with the faculty of being able to get straight to the point. When we make ourselves vulnerable we are open to being hurt. Often a stab is a quick way of achieving a result.

Staff

A staff signifies support – that is, the support we need to help us through life. It symbolizes the journeying and pilgrimage we must undertake; we will not have to do it alone, we shall receive help in some way.

Stage

'All the world's the stage', so to dream of one indicates that we want to make ourselves visible or known to the world – maybe we have envisaged our potential to succeed; if so, play on.

Stake

To have a stake in something is to have made a commitment, either on a material or emotional level. On another level, the stake is also a symbol of torture or death by fire, so can indicate there is some unpleasantness around.

Stairs – See Buildings under Environments

Star – See **Film** and **Shapes**

Statue
Dreaming of a statue is to be linking with the unresponsive, cold side of human nature. However, the statue may also represent an ideal, so we must identify what that is by taking in its surroundings and its contours and see how it relates to our waking life.

Stealing – Also see **Thief**
To dream of stealing suggests just that, that we are taking something without permission. If someone we don't know is stealing from us, it is likely to symbolize a part of ourselves that we don't trust. 'Stealing' is an emotive word, and it will depend on our background as to how we feel about inappropriate behaviour. This image also comes up frequently when dealing with the emotions; for example, a 'needy' person may feel they are stealing affection.

Steam
Steam in dreams can suggest emotional pressure and transformation from negative to the positive. Also, we are passionate about something without necessarily knowing what it is. In another sense, it could be that we are looking at, and are aware of, the power of the Spirit.

Steeple – See **Spire**

Steps – Also see **Buildings** under **Environments**
Steps in dreams almost always suggest the effort we need to put in to succeed. Going up steps suggests trying to make things better, whereas going down means going either into the past or the subconscious. Either way, there is a change in awareness necessary.

Sterilization
For a woman to dream of being sterilized, either by an operation or otherwise, may be associated with her feeling of powerlessness. In a man's dream sterilization may suggest sexual dissatisfactions or doubts about his self-image. Sterilization can also have ambivalent spiritual symbolism. It can either suggest cleanliness of spirit, or an aspect of the self that is unable to grow.

Stone

Dreaming of stone can suggest stability but without feeling. Stone has many connotations on an emotional level; for stone to be broken up signifies being badly hurt whereas being turned to stone suggests that we have had to harden up our attitudes. Being stoned could have two meanings depending on our lifestyle. One is being punished for misdemeanours; the other is being under the influence of marijuana.

Storm – Also see Lightning and Thunder

A storm indicates an emotional outburst stemming possibly from anger rather than, say, frustration. When we are in difficulty, for instance in a relationship, a storm can bring release. When an argument is not appropriate in waking life, in dreams a storm can clear our 'emotional air'.

Strangle

To dream of strangling someone is an attempt to stifle our emotions. To dream of being strangled shows we need to get a grip on ourselves. Strangulation is a violent act of suppression – emotionally, our more aggressive side may not allow us to act appropriately in some situations.

Straw

Straw in dreams highlights weakness and emptiness. A straw house – being a temporary structure – would suggest a state of impermanence is present in our lives. When we say something is built on straw, we are aware that it does not have a proper foundation. We need to look at what we feel is permanent in our lives and build on it.

Stream

Dreaming of a stream suggests the awareness of the flow of our emotions. To be in a stream suggests being in touch with our sensuality. Emotionally if we are to function properly we must feel loved and appreciated. To be in the stream of things suggests being part of a social group which will enable us to interact with people.

Submarine

In dreams a submarine suggests we have deep feelings within us that we can now access. This can help us understand some of our subconscious urges a necessary process if we are to feel more comfortable with ourselves.

Suffocating

When we feel we are suffocating in a dream, it may be that our own fears – possibly of sexual and personal relationships – are threatening to overwhelm us. It can also indicate that we are not in control of our own environment. To be suffocating another person may mean we are overpowering them in waking life. If we don't know them in waking life, we need to look at if we are, as a rule, overbearing.

Suicide

Dreaming of suicide alerts us to a violent end to something, perhaps a business project or relationship. Primarily, it is also a sign of anger against the Self.

Emotionally, when dreams of suicide occur, we may have come to the end of our ability to cope with a particular situation in our lives.

Suitcase – See **Baggage** and **Luggage**

Summer

To be conscious of summertime in a dream indicates the good times in our lives – and we may even be able to look forward to success around us. Summer also suggests the potential to relax for a while.

Sun – Also see **Planets**

The sun in dreams suggests happiness, warmth and conscious awareness. If we are looking at the sun, then we are looking for enlightenment in waking life. The sun is also a symbol of essential life energy. In another variation, if we are taking part in a sun dance, then we are, in effect, using the energy of the sun for guidance and vitality.

Swallowing

Swallowing in a dream indicates we are taking something in. This could be knowledge or information, though if we find it is hard to swallow then this shows we are hindered in some way. Swallowing can also suggest suppressed emotion.

Swamp – Also see **Marsh**

A swamp in a dream symbolizes feelings that can threaten our confidence and well-being. To be swamped is to be overwhelmed by a feeling or emotion. On an emotional level, when a swamp appears it indicates that we are linking with our most basic feelings.

Swastika – See **Shapes**

Sweeping

There may be certain elements of confusion, or attitudes, which we need to clear away. It is common to dream of sweeping in this instance.

Sweets – See **Food**

Swimming – Also see **Drowning**

In dreams, swimming in water is symbolic of the emotions. However, there are different variations; to be swimming upstream would indicate that we are going against their own nature. Swimming fish can have the same symbolism as sperm, and therefore can indicate the desire for a child. Swimming in clear water indicates being cleansed, whereas dark water could symbolize the possibility of unhappiness.

Swinging – See **Rocking**

Sword

A sword can suggest a powerful weapon, but it also indicates strength, courage and justice. For the image of a sword to appear in a dream points to an element of warrior in us, and that we are prepared to fight for our beliefs.

Synagogue – See **Churches** under **Religious Imagery**

Syringe – See **Injection**

T

Tabernacle – Also see Religious Imagery

A tabernacle is a place where a sacred object is kept for safety and also represents a temple. To dream of one is therefore to be trying to understand our own need for sanctuary, permanence and safety.

Table

A table as a focus for a meeting is recognized in dreams as a symbol of decision-making. As a place for a family gathering, we may consider meals to be an important ritual. To dream of tidying with a table instils a sense of order. It represents our ability to create order out of chaos. On another level a table can represent judgement and legislation.

Tablet

As with the Tablets of Moses, there is access to esoteric and magical knowledge. Taking, or being given, medicinal tablets in dreams suggests the need to be healthy. If we are giving tablets to someone else we may be aware that their needs – or that part of ourselves represented by them – are not being satisfied.

Tadpole

In a woman's dream tadpoles may signify either her wish, or her ability, to become pregnant. Spiritually, the tadpole represents the Germ of Life and so dreaming of tadpoles links to a focus on the simplicity of life, and perhaps the beginning of a new phase.

Talisman

Man has a deep connection with objects he believes to be sacred, and which are a protection against evil or difficulty. In most pagan religions, objects such as stones and drawings were given special powers. While consciously we may not believe, unconsciously we are capable of linking with ancient magic, so dreaming of a talisman can suggest that our own mental powers are not sufficient to protect us from fear and doubt. We need help from others.

Talking

If we are aware of people talking in a dream, then we are linking with the ability to communicate, which, in normal life, we may find difficult. We are perhaps afraid of not being listened to properly, and this anxiety can express itself through hearing someone else talking.

Tame

To dream of taming an animal indicates our ability to control or develop a relationship with the animal aspect of ourselves. To dream of being tame signifies the need for restraint in our lives. To find that something is tame – in the sense of something dull or half-hearted – suggests that we should reconsider the way we live our lives. Another symbol is of self-control – in C.S. Lewis' Narnian chronicles Aslan, the Great Lion, despite not being tame, displayed self-control and discipline, and thus ruled with the same. For us, in order to progress, we must do the same.

Tangled

Sometimes when we are confused in everyday life, we may dream of an object being entangled with something else. Often the way that we untangle the object indicates the action we should take. When something like hair is tangled, we need to be aware that our public image is coming across to other people as distorted.

Tank

Dreaming of a water tank is putting ourselves in touch with our inner feelings and emotions. Dreaming of an army tank connects us with our own need to defend ourselves, but to be aggressive at the same time. Such a dream would indicate that we are feeling threatened in some way. Often in dreams we become aware of our need to overcome objections and difficulties – the image of a tank helps to highlight our ability to do this without being hurt.

Tap

A tap symbolizes our ability to make use of worldly resources. If we dream of not being able to turn a tap on or off, then this alerts us to our ability – or lack of ability – in controlling things we consider to be ours by right. It may also indicate our need to deal with our emotions better.

Tape

If we dream of a tape measure, then we need to measure our progression in life. Or we need to consider how we 'measure up' to others' expectations. Equally, if we are doing the measuring we may be trying to create order in our lives. Dreaming of a recording tape would suggest that we are aware that the way we express ourselves is worth remembering.

Tapestry – See **Weaving**

Tar

Road tar suggests that we may be trapped somehow, while on the move. Beach tar indicates that we have allowed our emotions to be contaminated. Despite its blackness, tar is not wholly negative it can also symbolize repair and protection.

Target

Dreaming of a target indicates that we have a goal to aim for. To be shooting at a bull's-eye could be interpreted as a search for perfection whereas aiming at a person could suggest either hatred or sexual desire. If we were setting someone else a target in dreams, we would need to understand that the other person in the dream is a reflection of part of ourselves. Being set a target suggests goals are being imposed on us.

Tattoo

On one level, a tattoo will stand for an aspect of our individuality. A tattoo in dreams can also signify something that has left an indelible impression – this could be great hurt, but could also be a good memory. Sometimes, the image that is tattooed is worth interpreting if it can be seen clearly. On another level a tattoo can suggest a group identity, belonging to a group of like-minded people.

Tax

In dreams having to pay a tax suggests some kind of a penalty for living the lifestyle we have chosen for ourselves. Different taxes represent different symbolism. Thus, dreaming of car tax would indicate that greater effort is needed to move forward. To be paying income tax suggests that we may feel we owe a debt to society. To be paying council tax may suggest that we feel we have to pay for the 'space' in which we exist. Refusing to pay any taxes suggests an unwillingness to conform.

Tea

It will depend on whether the dream is about tea as a commodity, or a social occasion. On one level, tea represents a unit of exchange, whereas the social occasion suggests inter-communication. The Japanese tea ceremony suggests a unique way of caring for and nurturing someone, as does afternoon tea. Dreaming of tea cups in particular links with our need for divination – such as reading tea leaves.

Teacher

A teacher is an authority figure – often the first one we meet outside the family. It may be that we are looking for guidance, or an alternative guidance, as the teacher's views are often different from those we may get at home.

Tears

If we are crying in a dream, then it may be that in normal life we find it difficult to show our emotions. To dream of being in tears and then to wake up and discover that we are actually crying, suggests that some hurt or trauma has come sufficiently close to the surface to enable us to deal with it on a conscious level.

Teasing

To be teased in a dream indicates that our behaviour in everyday life may not be wholly appropriate. If we are teasing someone and pointing out their idiosyncrasies, we may actually be highlighting our own discrepancies. Teasing can also come about because of insecurity and an awareness of our own doubts and fears.

Teeth – See Body

Telegram

Receiving a telegram in a dream highlights communication in the most efficient way possible under the circumstances. It indicates that a part of ourselves is attempting to give us information in a way that is going to be remembered. If we send a telegram, then we want known something about ourselves that we cannot impart verbally. On another level, a telegram symbolizes the way we make knowledge tangible.

Telephone

The telephone in a dream connects us with contact and communication – either with another person or with a part of ourselves. Being contacted by telephone suggests there is information available to us that we do not already consciously know. If we recognize the number we are ringing, then obviously we may need to contact that person or establishment.

Telescope

A telescope enhances our view and makes it bigger and wider and using one in a dream suggests taking a closer look at something. We do need to make sure, however, that we are not taking a one-sided view of things. On another plane, a telescope can symbolize clairvoyance.

Temple – Also see Churches under Religious Imagery

A temple can often symbolize our own body – we need to treat it with care and respect, or suffer the consequences. There may be also be a sense of awe attached to the creative elements of a temple.

Temptation

Temptation is yielding to that which is easiest and not necessarily the best course of action – we need to be very careful. The idea of giving in to temptation suggests that it is bigger or more powerful than we are. Often dreams can show us the course of action we should be taking. On a more esoteric level, temptation is a barrier we must overcome. It is a conflict between ego and Self.

Tenant

To have a tenant signifies that we are prepared to have someone live in our space. If we are tenants, then we need to be taking more responsibility. On a more mundane level it may be an insight into how to handle a commercial transaction.

Tent

A tent in a dream would suggest that we feel we are on the move, and not able to settle down and put down roots. We perhaps need to get away from everyday responsibilities for a time. There is benefit to be gained by being self-sufficient and not dependent on anyone – we are not tied to any one place, but can be where we need to be at short notice.

Tests – Also see **Exams/being examined**

Dreaming of tests of any sort can indicate some form of self-assessment. Medical tests may be alerting us to the need to watch our health. A driving test would suggest a test of confidence or ability, whereas a written test would signify a test of knowledge. Testing something in a dream suggests that there has been some form of standard set, to which we feel we must adhere. This need not mean that we are setting ourselves against others, but simply that we have resolved to maintain a certain standard.

Text

For a text to appear in a dream would signify the need for encouragement and perhaps wisdom. Text from a book or a text of a play would indicate the need for the dreamer to carry out instructions in a particular way in order to achieve success. On another plane, a spiritual text is an encouraging message to enable us to progress through life.

Thaw

In dreams, to be aware of a thaw is to note a change in our own emotional responses. If we are aware of coldness within ourselves, on an emotional level we need to discover what the problem is or was, and why we have reacted as we did. In another way a thaw can suggest we have the ability to come to terms with old barriers and to become warm and loving.

Theatre – See **Stage**

Thermometer

A thermometer in a dream symbolizes how we judge warmth and feeling – we may be uncertain of how we come across to other people and need some kind of outside measurement. A clinical thermometer would portray our emotional warmth, whereas an external thermometer would suggest our intellectual abilities. Just as a thermometer measures temperature, so the way we handle situations around us will give indications of our health and ability.

Thief

Dreaming of a thief links with our fear of losing things, or of having them taken away. It may be love, it may be possessions. When a thief appears in dreams, we are aware of part of our personality which can waste our own time and energy on meaningless activity. A spiritual thief is that part of us which has no respect for our beliefs.

Thigh – See **Limbs** under **Body**

Thirst

We need to satisfy an inner need – it may be that we have been feeling low and need a boost. Also if we need to satisfy a thirst, then this translates to satisfying a desire. If we are thirsty in a dream, we need to look very carefully at either what we are being denied, or what we are denying ourselves, in waking life.

Thorn

To dream of being pierced by a thorn signifies that a minor difficulty has got through our defences. If the thorn draws blood, we need to look at what is happening in our lives that could make us vulnerable. In a woman's dream this could represent the sexual act, or rather, fear of intercourse. A thorn also represents suffering, particularly a physical suffering.

Thread

A thread symbolizes a line of thinking or an enquiry of some kind, probably regarding the way our lives are going. If we are threading a needle, besides the obvious sexual representation, we are perhaps our competency – after all, many of us know how difficult it is to thread a needle.

Threshold

Crossing the threshold in dreams indicates that new experiences and new responsibilities are on the horizon. Being lifted across a threshold formerly suggested marriage, or in this day and age, it is more likely to be a new relationship or experiences.

Throat – See **Body**

Throne
When we dream of sitting on a throne, we are acknowledging our right to take authority. When the throne is empty, we are not prepared to accept the responsibility for who we are. It may be that we are conscious of a lack of parenting. When someone else is on the throne, we may have passed over authority to that person or believe that they are somehow more 'worthy' than us. In dreams a throne can represent our ability to belong to groups, or to society. We often use word play or slang in interpretation, but in this case it is unlikely that the throne relates to the lavatory.

Thumb – See **Body**

Thunder/thunderbolts – Also see **Storm**
If we hear thunder in a dream, then it is a warning of some emotional storm to come. If the thunder is in the distance, then there is still time to compose ourselves and ride out any anger we may have. Thunder also has the potential to cleanse.

Tiara – See **Crown**

Tickling
The symbolism here revolves around approaching life with a degree of humour – after all, in everyday life tickling often helps break down barriers. However, it depends on whether we are a tactile person when awake as to the interpretation. If tactile, this would indicate there is perhaps a need for humour. If not, then any approach at intimacy should be made with humour.

Tide – Also see **Water** under **Environments**
We need to go with the ebb and flow of life and emotions a bit more. A high tide may symbolize high energy, whereas a low tide would suggest a drain on our abilities or energy.

Till

There is the old idea of tilling the ground – in dreams this translates as cultivating opportunities. A till, in the sense of a safe for money, can be taken to represent careful management of our resources.

We may also have the need to save and hopefully accumulate – it could be money, or it could be something less material, such as knowledge.

Timber – See **Wood**

Titans

Titans in dreams appear as huge, over-bearing god-like figures. In this context they represent the forces within us that allow things to manifest, or to happen. There are titanic forces that can arise in dreams: they are those parts of us that are untamed and untameable. When used properly, they represent the ability to create a world of our own.

Tobacco

If you are a smoker, then tobacco suggests a way of comforting yourself. If not, then the symbolism is more to do with being able to achieve a certain state of mind – possibly a mood lift or a more relaxed outlook.

Toilet

There has always been the inevitable association with sexuality. Nowadays, though, the symbolism is more to do with notions of privacy, and the ability to reach a state where we can release our feelings in private. If there is something wrong with the toilet in our dream, we are emotionally blocked. Going to an unfamiliar toilet suggests we are in a position where we do not know what the outcome to a situation will be. Cleaning a dirty toilet suggests we are losing our 'prudish' attitude.

Tomb

If we sense that we are a tomb raider, then we are entering the darker parts of our personality. If we are trapped in a tomb in a dream we may be trapped by fear, pain or old outdated attitudes in our waking life. If there are bodies in the tomb, these are usually parts of ourselves we have either not developed or have chosen to ignore i.e. killed off.

Tongue – See **Body**

Tools

Tools in dreams suggest the practical tools we have at our disposal for enhancing our lifestyle. Each tool will have its own significance; a drill suggests working through emotions and fears as well as attitudes that have become hardened, a hammer provides the energy to break down old patterns of behaviour and resistances, a saw suggests being able to cut through all the rubbish we have accumulated in order to make something new.

Top – See **Position**

Torch

In dreams, a torch can depict self-confidence and can also suggest the need to be able to move forward. It can be used not only for ourselves, but also for other people. Dreaming of a torch shows we can have the confidence to know that, because of our own knowledge, we have the ability to see the way forward. On another level we may feel that we need spiritual guidance, and this can sometimes be symbolized in dreams as a torch.

Tornado

A tornado denotes a violent and destructive energy, usually emotions or feelings against which we are powerless. A tornado sweeps all before it, but afterwards there is the potential for a new beginning.

Torpedo

The torpedo is often conventionally connected to aggressive male sexuality. A torpedo also suggests a way of directing energy – this may be a type of honesty in getting to the point that we can do with friends, or it may be a warning that such directness could be harmful, or at least distressing, to others.

Torture

When an image connected with torture appears in a dream, often we are trying to come to terms with a great hurt. This does not need to be on a physical level – it is more likely to be emotional or mental pain.

Totem/totem pole

A totem pole appearing in a dream links us with a very basic, primitive need for protection. A totem pole is also believed to have a strength and power of its own. When it appears in dreams we need to be looking at those parts of our lives that are based around our belief system, to find out if we are really living according to those beliefs.

Touch

Touch in dreams suggests making contact or transferring power in some way. We are linking up with other people, usually to our mutual advantage. We are perhaps becoming conscious of both our need for other people and of their need for us.

Within relationships touch can be an important act of appreciation. Often dreams will reveal our attitude to such concepts as touching and being touched.

Tourist

A tourist in a dream is someone who does not know his way around. If we are the tourist, then we need to look at how that aspect refers to our waking life. If someone else is the tourist, then we need to be aware of what help we can give other people. To play the tourist in a dream is to be aware of the fact that we have the necessary information to do what we want, but that we are choosing not to.

Town – See **Environments**

Track – See **Path** and also **Train** under **Journeys and Transport**

Train – See **Journeys and Transport**

Traitor

To dream of a traitor suggests that we are subconsciously aware of deviousness. This may be in someone else, or it could be a part of our personality that is letting us down. We may feel that our standards are not appreciated by others.

When we feel betrayed by others in a dream we become aware that an element of trust has been taken away and that a basic belief has been compromised. Someone may be actively conspiring to cause difficulty.

Transformation

Dreams where changes occur and things are transformed into something else suggest a shift in awareness and freedom of thought. A landscape may change from dark to light (negativity to positivity); a person may change from masculine to feminine; or one image may change into another. Once we understand the change is for the better, we are able to accomplish changes in our own life.

Transparent

If something appears transparent, then it may be that we are feeling vulnerable – though we may also be able to see things more clearly. On another level, transparency can indicate an honesty and openness within us.

Transvestism – See **Sex**

Trap/trapped

To be in a trap in a dream signifies that we feel we are trapped by outside circumstances. To be aware of trapping something or someone is attempting to hold on to them or what they represent. When we feel trapped in dreams, we are not usually able to break free of old patterns of thought and behaviour – we may need outside help. On a more spiritual level, it may suggest that we are holding ourselves back.

Travelling – See **Journeys and Transport**

Treasure

Treasure represents what we value – often something that we have achieved through hard work and effort. To find a box that has treasure in it is to have some understanding of the fact that we must break through limitations before we find what we are looking for.

Tree

The tree is symbolic in dreams of the basic structure of our inner lives. Different trees represent different things. For example, a tree with wide branches would suggest a warm loving personality, whereas a small close-leafed tree would suggest an uptight personality. As far as the roots of a tree are concerned, this is connected to how we relate to the earth. The trunk of a tree indicates how we may use all available energies to the best of our ability. In another sense a tree represents heaven, earth and water – the Tree of Life.

Trespassing
When we find ourselves trespassing in a dream, we are perhaps intruding on someone's personal space and vice versa. This may also suggest that there is a part of ourselves that is private and feels vulnerable. We should respect those boundaries. On a spiritual level we are perhaps approaching areas of knowledge where we cannot go without further prior exploration.

Triangle – See **Shapes**

Trophy
If we dream of a trophy, then we are recognizing that we have done something that deserves a reward. A cup suggests receptivity, whereas a shield indicates protection. A trophy may also signify that we need to, or about to, achieve a goal.

Trumpet
A trumpet suggests either a warning or a 'call to arms'. When we have conflict around us, for example, a trumpet is often the symbol that appears. A trumpet can also suggest the need to maximize our potential.

Trunk
A trunk used to represent a long journey; however today it is more likely to symbolize old ideas. A trunk also signifies that it is time to sort out any physical or mental 'rubbish' we may have stored up.

Tumble – See **Fall/falling**

Tunnel
A tunnel in a dream represents the need to explore our own unconscious, and those things we have left untouched. A tunnel can also symbolize the birth canal and therefore the process of birth. If there is a light at the end of the tunnel, it indicates we are reaching the final stages of our exploration. If something is blocking the tunnel, some past

fear or experience is stopping us from progressing. In another sense the image of a tunnel helps us to escape from the unconscious into the light, and also to go down into the depths.

Turf

To dream of being on 'sacred' turf – ground that is revered because of its association, such as Wembley, Lords etc. – is to wish for supreme success. Dreaming of our association with a particular piece of ground can activate memories and feelings connected with happy times. This may, by recollection, help to clarify a particular problem or situation.

Twins – Also see **People and Family**

In dreams twins may, if known to us, simply be themselves. If they are not known to us, then they may represent two sides of one idea. Often in everyday life, we come up against conflicts between two opposites. Twins in dreams can actually represent two sides of our personality acting in harmony. Duality must eventually reunite into unity. Twins illustrate the idea that while there is separation at the moment, unity can be achieved.

Typhoon – See **Storm** and **Wind**

U

Ulcer

An ulcer is a sore place where tissue has been eroded, and it is only cured with patience. In dreams we become aware of work that needs to be done to heal a great hurt. It will depend on where the ulcer is as to what needs healing. To dream of a stomach ulcer, for instance, would suggest an emotional difficulty, while a mouth ulcer would suggest some problem with speech or making ourselves understood to those around us. Spiritually it suggests some soreness of Spirit or spiritual dilemma. So a varicose ulcer might signify a fear of moving forward, or of finding our feet.

Umbilical

The Silver Cord is the spiritual connection seen psychically as the connection between body and soul. In dreams it is often experienced as the umbilical cord, signifying life-giving connections. Teenagers often dream of severing the umbilical cord as they grow into adulthood. When we have perhaps not yet learnt to take care of our own needs in a mature way and have an emotional dependency on others, the umbilical cord in dreams can signify that dependency.

Umbrella

As we mature we need to develop certain coping skills. In dreams these can be seen as a protective covering, often seen as the shelter and sanctuary of an umbrella. Often in a work situation we are under someone's supervision and this can be represented by the umbrella – again, it offers a degree of protection. Spiritual knowledge can also be shown in dreams as an umbrella.

Under/underneath – See Position in Dream Interpretation chapter

Underground

The subconscious or the unconscious is often perceived in dreams as a cave or place underground. Dreams give us opportunities to explore our own hidden depths. To dream of being underground will often allow us to come to terms with that side in a very easy way. To dream of being on an underground train or subway usually signifies the journeys taking towards understanding ourselves.

Undress
To be undressing in a dream suggests a need for spiritual openness and honesty, but can also suggest that we may be putting ourselves in touch with our own sexual feelings. When we find ourselves undressing in a dream we may also be needing to reveal our true feelings about a situation around us, and to have the freedom to be totally open about those feelings.

Unemployment
Dreaming of being unemployed suggests that we are not making the best use of our talents and resources, or that we feel they are not being properly recognized. It can also indicate that we feel inadequate, a fear many of us share.

Unicorn
When a unicorn appears in a dream we are linking with the innocent, pure part of ourselves. This is the instinctive, receptive feminine principle. There is a story that unicorns missed being taken into Noah's Ark because they were too busy playing. We need to be mindful of what is going on in the real world if we are to survive. The unicorn can also signify that rarest of qualities – unconditional love.

University
Dreaming of being in a university highlights our own individual potential and learning ability. Since a university is a place of 'higher' learning, we are being made aware of the breadth of experience and increase in knowledge available to us. We need to move away from the mundane and ordinary into specific areas of knowledge and awareness.

Up/upper – See Position in Dream Interpretation chapter

Urine – See **Body**

Urn – Also see **Vase**

For many people the tea urn is a symbol of community life. To dream of one suggests our ability to belong to a community and act for the greater good. Just as all receptacles signify the feminine principle, so does the urn, although in a more ornate form. In earlier times, a draped urn signified death. That symbolism is still carried on today in the urn used in crematoriums. Thus, to dream of an urn may alert us to our feelings about death and regeneration.

V

Valley

There are two meanings which can be given to a valley. The first is the fairly obvious one of the sheltering, more nurturing side of our personalities associated with the feminine: the second is the valley of death, a transition period between two states of being. There may be a need to explore the unconscious or lesser known parts of ourselves.

Vampire

Unpleasant or negative influences can be represented by the vampire in dreams. When heavy demands are made on us we are figuratively being 'sucked dry'. Often the fear of emotional and sexual relationships can be represented in dreams as a vampire. Ancient symbols that have represented such fear of the unknown can still appear in dreams; the succubus and incubus preying on young people's vital energy is often pictured as a vampire.

Van – See **Journeys and Transport**

Varnish

Varnish is a protective outer covering which is designed to enhance the appearance of an object. Dreaming of varnish can therefore signify either of these following meanings: either a layer of protection is required to preserve our creativity, or we are hiding imperfections.

Vase

As a holder of beautiful things, any receptacle – such as a vase, water pot, pitcher or urn – tends to represent the feminine within a dream, the accepting and receptive nature of the feminine, intuitive side. Such an object can also signify the Great Mother and hence, by association, creativity.

Vault

A vault represents the meeting place of the spiritual and physical.

Consequently, a vault also symbolizes death. While a vault *can* represent a tomb, it also represents the 'archives' or records to which we all have access. In dreams any dark, hidden place suggests sexual potency or the unconscious. It can also symbolize our store of personal resources, those things we learn as we grow and mature.

VD – See **Sex**

Vegetables – See **Food** and **Harvest**

Vegetation
Vegetation in a dream often symbolizes abundance and the capacity for growth on a spiritual level, though it can also suggest obstacles that we put in front of ourselves in order to grow – a patch of brambles might suggest irritating snags to our movement forwards, whereas nettles might represent people actually trying to prevent progress.

Veil
A veil in a dream suggests the Occult or some kind of secret which we are hiding from ourselves. It may be something of which consciously we are ignorant but which with a little delving can be revealed.

Velvet
There are two very distinct meanings which can be attributed to velvet; the ancient one which signifies discord, and the modern-day which suggests richness and sensuousness. It can also mean richness and giftedness.

Vermin – See **Animals and Birds**

Vertical – See Position in Dream Interpretation chapter

Vicar
When a vicar appears in a dream, we are usually aware of the more spiritual, knowledgeable side of ourselves. A vicar is a man of God, and we may need to acknowledge that there is much to learn on a physical as well as spiritual level. Less feared than the priest, in dreams he is often the authority figure to whom we have given control.

Vice

The side of ourselves which is rebellious and out of step with society may allow us to behave in dreams in ways which are not those we would normally try in waking life. We may in both cases need to make adjustments in our behaviour. Conversely, sloth, envy, apathy, etc. in one of our dream characters may enable us to handle that tendency within ourselves in waking life.

Dreaming of a vice in the sense of something which grips, suggests some kind of constraint in our lives.

Victim

If we are repressing our own ability to develop our spiritual potential, we will appear in a dream as a victim – a victim of our own making. The nature of the difficulty may reveal itself through the dream content. In dreams we are often aware of something happening to us over which we have no control, or some way in which we are creating a no-win situation.

Victory

The dream scenario may be a conflict between two aspects of ourselves, or require us to overcome some difficulty. This can often be recognized as a difficulty we have created for ourselves, and which by achieving victory gives us confidence in ourselves.

Violence

Any violence in dreams is a reflection of our own inner feeling, sometimes about ourselves, sometimes about the situations around us. Often the type of violence is worthy of notice if we are fully to understand ourselves. Violence in dreams can arise because we are unable to express our aggression appropriately in everyday life.

Viper – See **Serpent** and **Snake** under **Animals and Birds**

Virgin

Spiritually there is a kind of innocence and purity, which can often be dedicated to service. The virginal mind – that is, a mind that is free from deception and guile – is perhaps more important than physically being a virgin, and it is this aspect which often becomes evident in dreams. In a woman's dream such a figure suggests she is in touch with her own psyche.

Virgin Mother – See **Religious Imagery**

Visit

Our spiritual guide often first makes itself available by a visit in the dream state. To be visited by someone in a dream can suggest that there is information, warmth or love available to us. To be paying someone else a visit in a dream signifies that we may need to widen our horizons in some fashion.

Visions

The mind, once it is free of conscious restraint, appears to work on several different levels. Thus it is possible to be aware of three separate parts of the dream; the 'I' of the dream, the content, and finally – usually pictorially – information and knowledge. These are the visions of dreams. Many dreamers have suggested that this type of dream has a different 'feel' to it from other more mundane dreams. Manifestations of Spirit are accepted as visions.

Voice

A voice that speaks through, or to, us has two types of meaning. If we believe in the spirit realm, this is communication from a discarnate spirit. More psychologically, when we suppress certain parts of our personalities, they may surface in dreams as disembodied voices. It may also be that there is some information we need to remember.

Void – See **Abyss**

Volcano

An erupting volcano usually signifies that we are not in control of a situation or of our emotions – of which there may be a hurtful release. If the lava is more prominent, feelings will run very deep. If the lava has cooled there has been a deep passion which has now cooled off. If the explosiveness is more noticeable, anger may be more prominent. To dream of a volcano being extinct can indicate either that we have 'killed off' our passions, or that a difficult situation has come to an end.

Vomiting

Vomiting is a symbol of a discharge of unpleasantness. To dream of vomiting suggests a discharge of disagreeable feelings and emotions. It is a clearing of something within that makes us extremely uncomfortable. When we become overloaded, we may need to 'throw up' (or throw away) the distress it is causing us.

Vortex

A vortex in dreams usually suggests a centre of energy which either takes us down into the unconscious at some speed, or into a change of consciousness, which allows some kind of insight into ourselves. It usually suggests some way in which we feel we are out of control.

Vote

When we have given unconditional acceptance to something, we have placed our trust in it. To vote for something in dreams may suggest that we believe wholeheartedly in a particular cause, or are becoming conscious of our need to belong to a group of like-minded people.

Vow

A vow is a pact or agreement between two people or ourselves and God, or more correctly a spiritual promise made between us and our universe. To dream of making a vow is to be recognizing responsibility for our own life. It is more binding than a simple promise and the results are more far-reaching. It is an inner acknowledgement of the way we wish to be.

Wadding – Also see **Packing**

In dreams our need for security can become more noticeable than we allow it to be in ordinary, everyday life. We may need to take action to protect ourselves rather than defend ourselves. Wadding can also represent a fear of getting fat or becoming ungainly.

Wading

Spiritually, wading – particularly through water – suggests a cleansing process which ties in with baptism. It can often allow us to understand what our emotions can do to us, how they can stop us from moving forward, or how we can work with the flow. Moving through any other substance can suggest how we tend to impede our own progress – we can literally get 'bogged down'.

Wafer

The Body of Christ, the Bread of Life, is represented in Christian communion services by a wafer – a thin layer of matter which is usually very fragile. Thus in dreams a wafer represents something which is easily broken and which we need to treat with respect.

Wages

Spiritually, wages can represent payment for our actions, and the recompense we deserve coming our way. Often when we are doing something that we do not want to do – or which we do not enjoy – the only pay-off is in the 'wages' we receive. To receive a wage packet in a dream suggests that our value is tied up with other things such as loyalty and duty.

Wailing

Grieving and the making of sounds is used spiritually to banish bad spirits, or as in chanting to summon the spirits and to get in touch with a power that is greater than ourselves. Wailing is a prolonged way of releasing emotions. Through dreams we can often put ourselves in touch with emotions which we might not otherwise allow ourselves to access in ordinary life.

Waiting

To be waiting for somebody, or something, in a dream implies a need to recognize the importance of patience. We must wait for the passage of time. We may be looking to other people, or outside circumstances, to help us move forward or make decisions. If *we* are impatient, it may be that our expectations are too high.

Wake

A wake, in the sense of a funeral service, gives us an opportunity to grieve appropriately. If in dreams we find ourselves attending such an occasion, there may be some reason in our lives for us to go through a period of grieving, or we may need support to overcome a disappointment. We need to let go of some of those things which we hold dear.

Walking

In a dream, walking indicates the way in which we should be moving forward, a journey of exploration. To be walking purposefully suggests we know where we are going. To be wandering aimlessly suggests we need to create goals for ourselves. To take pleasure in the act of walking is to return to the innocence of the child, or to obtain relief from stress. To be using a walking stick is to recognize our need for support and assistance.

Wallet

In dreams, the wallet is a representation of how we look after our resources. These need not simply be financial resources, but can be of any kind. Many dreams can suggest our attitude to money, and to dream of a wallet is one of those dreams.

Interestingly, because the wallet can also take on the significance of a container, it suggests the feminine aspects of care and containment, and highlights our attitude to intuition and awareness.

Wallpaper

Wallpaper often symbolizes an outer facade of some kind. To be putting up wallpaper signifies covering up the old self (possibly superficially), particularly if the old wallpaper is not removed. To be stripping wallpaper in dreams suggests stripping away the old facade in order to create a new image. We may be wanting to make changes in our lives but need to experiment – and get a proper fit – first.

Waltz – See **Dance**

Wand

To dream of a wand can symbolize 'magical' powers which may influence us. We are aware of some force external to ourselves which needs harnessing. When we dream of using a wand we are aware of our influence over others. Conversely, if someone else uses a wand we are aware of the power of suggestion, either for negative or for positive within a situation in our lives.

Wanderer/wandering – See Tramp under Archetypes in the Enhancing your Dreams chapter

War

War is a way of dealing with distress and disorder. The outcome should be the re-establishment of order, although sometimes this can only happen through the passage of time. To dream of war, therefore, indicates that this natural process is taking place on an inner level. There is some kind of conflict, which may be going on inwardly, but may well have been deliberately engineered rather than spontaneous. We need to be more conscious of the effect our actions will have on others.

Wardrobe – Also see Furniture

A wardrobe, because it houses our clothes, also suggests how we deal with our self-image, or the various personalities we use within everyday life. Often because it is large, it can have the same significance as a passage, and therefore suggests a period of transition or rite of passage. This idea is well used in C.S. Lewis' *The Lion, the Witch and the Wardrobe*.

Warmth

A feeling of warmth in a dream can symbolize unconditional love. It touches our 'feel good' factor and enhances our sense of comfort and well-being. Psychologically, feelings of cheerfulness and hopefulness can create an awareness of warmth and can be interchangeable.

Warning

To be warning someone highlights our ability to be aware of difficulty and danger, either to others or to hidden parts of our personality. To receive a warning in a dream suggests that we are aware that either internally or externally something needs attention. We may be putting ourselves in danger. The environment within the dream may clarify this. To receive a written warning indicates we may be behaving badly.

Warrant

We may be seeking some kind of permission, and this can be symbolized by a warrant. It represents permission from a higher authority, either spiritual or physical. It will depend on the type of warrant as to what action needs to be taken. For instance, a search warrant suggests looking at our motives, whereas a warrant for arrest indicates we need to stop carrying out a particular action.

Warts

We are often distressed by anything which is out of the ordinary or wrong. Any blemish which comes to the attention in dreams can be accepted as evidence of there being a distortion in our view of ourselves or of the world. A great deal of folklore has grown up around warts and how to get rid of them. Dreaming of warts can connect with that part of ourselves which remains superstitious.

Washing – Also see **Water** under **Environments**

Since water is a symbol for emotion and the unconscious, washing stands for achieving a relationship with our emotional selves and dealing successfully with the results. Dreaming of washing either ourselves or, for instance, clothes, suggests getting rid of negative feelings – our attitude, either internally or externally, needs changing. Washing other people touches on our need to care for others. We may also need to maintain our spiritual integrity, and this can be represented by washing.

Waste

Waste in dreams signifies matter or information we no longer need. It can now be thrown away. Waste can also suggest a misuse of resources – we may, initially, be using too much energy on a particular project, and may need to reassess how we are running our lives.

Watch – See **Clock**

Wax

Wax is symbolic of the need for spiritual pliability, and the desire to move away from rigidity. Dreaming of wax is a great deal to do with the pliability that we are able to achieve in our lives. We should be prepared to give way, but also to be firm when necessary. More negatively, wax can also be taken to represent insincerity, with the ability to be affected by external events, and irrevocably changed.

Wealth – Also see **Money**

Wealth and status usually go naturally together, so when we are having problems in dealing with our own status in life we will frequently have dreams about wealth. It can also often indicate the resources that we have or of which we can make use.

Weather

Weather, as being part of the 'environment' of the dream, usually indicates our moods and emotions. We are aware of changing external situations and have to be careful to adjust our conduct in response to these. This would suggest that we need to recognize that we are part of a greater whole rather than just individuals in our own right.

Weather also can point to our internal responses to situations. If, for instance, there is a storm in our dream we are, perhaps, angry and aggressive. If we are watching a very blue, unclouded sky, it signifies fair weather and happier times ahead.

Weaving

Weaving is one of the strongest spiritual images there is. In most cultures there is an image of our fate being woven in a particular pattern. We are not supposed to be in control of that pattern, but must accept that God or the gods know what is best. However, it does suggest that we need to take responsibility for our own lives. To be doing any handicraft shows that we have situations in hand.

Weaving is also taken to signify life itself and often our attitude to the way we run our lives.

Web

When we dream of a web we are linking into one of the most basic of spiritual symbols. It is within the 'web of life' that the divine powers have interwoven fate and time in order to create a reality in which we can exist. We are the spiritual entrapped within the physical and not able to escape back to our own spiritual realm.

In everyday life, we may well be caught up in a situation that could trap us. We could be in a 'sticky' situation and not quite know which way to move. This can result in the symbol of a web appearing in the dream. We are 'caught in the middle' or we are trapped.

To dream of the web, as in the internet, shows we are still have much to learn from life, yet at the same time we have much to tell the world.

Wedding – See Marriage

Wedding ring – Also see Ring

Traditionally, the wedding ring was a symbol of total encircling love. To dream of this symbol is to link in with that basic concept of eternity. Within the human being there is the need to make vows, to give promises and above all to symbolize the making of those promises. To lose or be wearing the ring on any other finger than the third finger of the left hand in a dream suggests difficulties within the relationship.

Wedge

The triangle symbolizes the ability to manifest matter within the physical. The wedge esoterically indicates the passage of time which allows something to become real in our lives – for a dream to become reality. Dreaming of a wedge often indicates that we need to open up, perhaps carefully, to situations around us.

Weeds – Also see Plants

Weeds, plants which grow on waste ground, may indicate misplaced trust, misplaced energy or even misplaced attempts at success. To be digging up weeds would show that we are aware that it is important to free ourselves of the non-essential. Mental attitudes which clog us up and do not allow us to move forward, and old patterns of behaviour, can very often be shown in dreams as weeds. Plants growing wild do have healing properties, and our bodies can often give us information in dreams as to what we need.

Weeping – Also see **Mourning**
Weeping suggests uncontrollable emotion or grief, so to experience either ourselves or someone else weeping in dreams is to show that there needs to be a discharge of such emotion. We may be mourning some spiritual quality we have lost. Alternatively, we may simply be creating difficulty within ourselves and this enables us to express the feelings we have bottled up.

Something exuding moisture so that it seems to be weeping is often deemed to be miraculous, and this dream can appear quite often in stages of transition as we are moving from one state of awareness to another. The excess energy created at this time can be shown as a weeping plant, tree or some such image.

Weighing
To be weighing something in dreams is to be assessing its worth, deciding what is of value to us. Weighing something up is to be trying to make a decision in order to decide what the risks are in any situation. The old-fashioned image of the scales indicates that we are looking for justice and natural balance.

Weight
Weight in a dream indicates gravitas and seriousness and may well indicate the need to be practical and down to earth. Experiencing a weight in a dream is to be conscious of our responsibilities, or those things which are holding us down.

Well
Occasionally there is a degree of wordplay in the image of a well in a dream which suggests our ability to be 'well'. Through our intuitive, aware selves, we contact the depths of our very being and open up the potential for healing and success.

Wheel – Also see **Circle** under **Shapes**

When we need to make changes and move forward the wheel is an appropriate symbol. It represents the Wheel of Life, and the cycle of growth and decay. When we lose motivation, we may dream of losing a wheel.

Whip/lash

The whip or lash is an instrument of torture and suggests corrective punishment and self-flagellation. In trying to force things to happen, we may also be creating problems for ourselves, by trying to be either too controlled or controlling. The lash was often used by monks and nuns to mortify the flesh and bring the natural urges into subjection, and in dreams this image may still appear.

Whisky – See **Alcohol**

Whistle

A whistle blown in a dream can mark the end of a particular phase of time. It can also sound as a warning to make us aware of something such as a deviation or difficulty. As a method of controlling and training, there may be information in the way it is being blown. The whistle may also be seen as a phallic symbol.

Wig

A hairpiece or toupee highlights false ideas or an unnatural attitude. A judge's wig can suggest authority, wisdom and judgement.

Will

At a time when we need everything to be done properly and with a certain degree of precision, to dream of a will – our own or someone else's – is highlighting how our inner self can make us aware of what is right for us. To be making a will is to be stating our intent, and may also have to do with the way we need to look after those we love. To inherit from a will means that we need to look at the tendencies, idiosyncrasies and beliefs we have inherited from our families.

Because, for many, making a will is a very final action, in dreams such an act can signify a recognition that we are entering a new phase of life, and must clear up the old. There is the obvious play on words, where a will would indicate the will to do or to be – the determination to take action, for instance.

Wind

The power of the Spirit and the movement of Life are often perceived as wind, and in dreams we may recognize a powerful passionate part of ourselves through the symbol of wind. It also represents the intellect and the wisdom we have available to us.

Windmill

As a storehouse of fruitfulness and of conservation, in dreams a windmill can represent the feminine or the mother. The representation of a windmill in dreams also suggests the proper use of resources. Because wind often suggests intellect, it is therefore the use of intellectual assets.

Wine – Also see Alcohol

Wine suggests the potential for spiritual abundance and highlights our capability of using what we harvest to give fun and happiness. We are able to use the sum of our experiences to make something fine and new. A wine cellar thus signifies the totality of our past experiences. A wine bottle is sometimes taken to indicate the penis and masculinity, but also to suggest femininity and containment.

The wine glass is interesting in that it can have two meanings. Firstly, it stands for the happiness and joviality of celebration and secondly it can stand for pregnancy. A broken wine glass can depict sorrow, or in a woman's dream, miscarriage, or more accurately her fear of it.

Wings

Wings, connected with flight and freedom, can also be protective. An angel's wings depict the power to transcend our difficulties, often through the protection of greater knowledge. A broken wing indicates that a previous trauma is preventing us from 'taking off'.

Winter

Within the cycle of nature, winter suggest a time of lying fallow before rebirth; hence winter can also mean death or old age. In dreams, winter can represent a time in our lives which is unfruitful. When we are emotionally cold or lonely, images associated with winter can appear. In clairvoyance, the seasons can also indicate a time of year when something may happen.

Wireless – See **Radio**

Witch – See Archetypes in the Enhancing your Dreams chapter

Witness

In dreams to be a witness to, for instance, an accident, suggests that we need to observe some circumstance in our life very carefully. We may be being called to account for our actions or beliefs, or our way of looking at things. To be in a witness box suggests that we are accountable to a higher authority.

Wood – Also see **Forest** and **Tree**

Dreaming of wood, in the sense of timber, suggests our ability to appreciate the past and to build on what has gone before. If the wood is still standing and growing it is more likely to represent the feminine or fertility. If it is cut timber, then the purpose for which it is being used will be important. Wooden toys can indicate our need to be in control of our environment or of our lives. We all need some form of structure or shelter. When our behaviour becomes rigid or wooden, dreams will often attempt to make us aware of this and of the necessity to balance our feelings.

Wool

Wool has, from earliest times, represented warmth and protectiveness in dreams and is symbolic of spiritual protection. Nowadays it particularly represents gentleness and mothering. The best example of such a dream is that of Alice in *Through the Looking Glass*, when she is aware of the sheep in the boat knitting.

Worm

At its most basic interpretation, the worm can suggest the penis. The worm is not necessarily seen to be particularly clean, but is one of those images which can have several meanings. Depending on our attitude to sexuality and gender, there may be a sense of threat to our self-image, or a sense of ineffectiveness and insignificance.

Being given to the worms is a metaphor for death, so spiritual changes may shortly be taking place. If we are particularly conscious of a wormcast, that is, the earth the worm has passed through its body, then this is a transformation image and indicates we are capable of changing our lives into something more fertile.

Worship – Also see **Religious Imagery**
An act of worship is an acknowledgement of the power that belief has. Dreaming of being in a situation where we are worshipping an idea, a person, a concept or an object is to be opening ourselves up to its influence. If we are not particularly religious but find ourselves in the middle of such an act, we may be trying to decide how best to function in a group or team of people.

To be worshipping an object which is not a religious image may suggest that we are paying too much attention to whatever that object represents, and giving too much importance to a particular area of our lives. For instance, we may be too materialistic, be paying too much attention to sex and so on.

Wound
A wound symbolizes an experience – which was probably unpleasant – that we should take note of and learn from. The type of wound will be important in interpreting the dream; a large ugly wound will suggest more violence, whereas a small one may indicate that there has been a more focused attack.

Any wound or trauma in dreams will signify hurt feelings or emotions. If we are inflicting the wounds our own aggressive behaviour is being drawn to our attention; if the wounds are being inflicted on us we may be making ourselves into, or being, the victim.

Wreath
A wreath in dreams can have the same significance as any of the binding symbols such as harnesses and halters. It forms a bond which cannot be broken, or a sacrifice which must be accepted. So to receive a funeral wreath would suggest the ending, perhaps of a relationship, but also its continuation in a different form, perhaps as loving friends. A wreath in a dream in previous times could also suggest honour, though perhaps less so nowadays.

Wreck

A wreck of some kind symbolizes a failure, possibly through lack of control. We will have to rescue the situation and struggle through to reach his goal. Dreaming of a wreck, such as a car or shipwreck, suggests that our plans may be thwarted, whether we are at fault for the failure of our plans or someone else is.

Writing

Writing gives substance to our thoughts and allows us to communicate when spoken words are inadequate. In dreams we may learn how to communicate with ourselves in differing ways, and can often make things more tangible for ourselves. To dream of writing is an attempt to communicate information that one has. Sometimes the instrument we are writing with is important. For instance, a pencil would suggest that the information is less permanent than with a pen, whereas a typewriter or word processor would suggest a more technical approach.

X

If an X appears in a dream, we are usually 'marking the spot'. It can also represent an error or something that we particularly need to note.

If a cross appears in the shape of an X, this usually represents the idea of sacrifice or perhaps of torture. This symbol also signifies Man within the Cosmos.

Y

In Spiritual terms, the Y signifies duality becoming unity and represents the human form with outstretched arms. It is reaching towards spirituality.

Yacht – See **Boat** under **Journeys and Transport**

Yardstick
The yardstick represents the measurement of acceptable standards, often those that we have set ourselves. Symbolically it suggests correctness and rigidity and sometimes good judgement.

Yarn
A yarn – as in a tale or story – is most often to do with our sense of history, or of continuity. To be being told a yarn or story in dreams links with our need for heroes and heroines, and perhaps our need for a mentor. Yarn in the sense of knitting yarn or twine often signifies our ability to create order out of chaos. In olden times it also suggested spinning, an archetypal symbol for life, and often in dreams it is this image that is portrayed. We fashion our lives out of what we are given.

Yawn

In the animal kingdom a yawn is often a warning against aggression, and a yawn in dreams may be a way of controlling our own or another's abusive behaviour.

Yeast

Yeast is accepted as a substance which both lightens food and makes it palatable. At the same time it changes the substance and texture. In dreams it represents ideas or influences which can irrevocably change our lives or situations, often for the better.

Yew – Also see **Tree**

In former times the yew tree symbolized mourning and sadness, and the idea of eternal life. Such a symbol can surface as instinctive awareness in dreams.

There can be an aspect of word-play here, in that the 'yew' is in fact 'you' in the sense of someone other than the dreamer.

Yin-Yang

The yin-yang symbol signifies a state of dynamic potential. In dreams it indicates the balance between the instinctive, intuitive nature of the feminine and the active, rational nature of the masculine, and our need to establish a balance between the two.

Yoke

In ancient dream-lore a yoke was said to represent marriage.

Youth – See Archetypes in the Enhancing your Dreams chapter

Yule Log – Also see **Fire**

A Yule log represents a spiritual offering or sacrifice, particularly at the time of a spiritual or religious celebration. In dreams it will be seen as a symbol of light and new life, and frequently is a sign of prosperous times to come.

Z

Zigzag – Also see **Meander**

A zigzag can often suggest some kind of exploratory movement, or a passage through some difficulty which is not totally straightforward. It may also signify a discharge of energy such as a bolt of lightning.

Zip

Psychologically, we are capable of being either open or closed to our friends and family. Often a zip in a dream can highlight this. A stuck zip suggests a difficulty in keeping our dignity in an awkward situation.

Zodiac

Everyone has a fascination with horoscopes, without necessarily understanding the significance of the zodiac wheel. It is often only when we begin the journey of self-discovery that images and symbols from the zodiac will appear in dreams. Frequently, the animal or creature associated with our own star sign will appear, almost as a reminder of basic principles. The way we deal with that image will give us insight into how we really feel about ourselves.

The zodiac wheel is symbolic of our relationship with the universe. Sometimes the zodiac is used in dreams to demonstrate time or the passing of time and also suggest courses of action we might take. For instance, if we dream of a lion playing with a fish we might have to become brave (Leo) in dealing with sensitivity (Pisces). Each sign also rules a particular part of the body, and often a dream alerts us to a possible imbalance.

The spheres of influence are described below:–

    Aries The symbol is the Ram and it governs the head. The colour associated with the sign is red; its specific gemstones are amethyst and diamond.

    Taurus The symbol is the Bull and it governs the throat. The colours associated with the sign are blue and pink; its specific gemstones are moss agate and emerald.

Gemini The symbol is the Twins (often shown as masculine and feminine) and it governs the shoulders, arms and hands. The colour associated with the sign is yellow; its specific gemstones are agate and beryl.

Cancer The symbol is the Crab and it governs the stomach and higher organs of digestion. The colours associated with the sign are either violet or emerald green; its specific gemstones are moonstones and pearls.

Leo The symbol is the Lion and it governs the heart, lungs and liver. The colours associated with the sign are gold and orange; its specific gemstones are topaz and tourmaline.

Virgo The symbol is the Virgin and it governs the abdomen and intestines. The colours associated with the sign are grey and navy blue; its specific gemstones are pink jasper and jade.

Libra The symbol is the Scales and it governs the lumbar region, kidneys and skin. The colours associated with the sign are blue and violet; its specific gemstones are opal and lapis lazuli.

Scorpio The symbol is the Scorpion and it governs the genitals. The colours associated with the sign are deep red and purple; its specific gemstones are turquoise and ruby.

Sagittarius The symbol is the Archer and it governs the hips, thighs and nervous system. The colours associated with the sign are light blue and orange; its specific gemstones are carbuncle and amethyst.

Capricorn The symbol is the Goat and it governs the knees. The colours associated with the sign are violet and green; its specific gemstones are jet and black onyx.

Aquarius The symbol is the Water-Bearer and it governs the circulation and ankles. The colour associated with the sign is electric blue; its specific gemstones are garnet and zircon.

Pisces The symbol is the Fishes and it governs the feet and toes. The colour associated with the sign are sea-green and mauve; its specific gemstones are coral and chrysolite.

Zoo – Also see **Animals and Birds**

Dreaming of being in a zoo suggests the need to understand some of our natural urges and instincts. There may be an urge to return to simpler, more basic modes of behaviour. We perhaps need to be more objective in our appraisal than subjective.

LIVING
WITH CREATIVE
DREAMS

Before you reach the Tips and Techniques section, we thought it would be a good idea to briefly draw together all the various strands to help you to define what you mean by creative dreaming and what you expect from your newfound skill. It is also perhaps wise to lay down a partial schema for using the skill in everyday life.

Creative dreaming might be defined as dreaming with awareness. Simply to be aware that we are dreaming is only the first step and holds the door open between the conscious and the unconscious self. This allows a free flow of information and energy between the two states which can then be utilized to full effect.

Dreaming is often likened to entering a hidden room in an effort to find out what the room contains. Creative dreaming is much more akin to starting out from a small room (which we know) very well and exploring the rest of the house (which we do not know). As we enter each new room, there are new things to be appreciated, possessions we did not know we had to be discovered and also further old assets we have forgotten about. We do, however, need a plan of campaign to help us to accomplish our task, accompanied by a 'box of tricks' to make life easier. Hopefully this book will be your box of tricks and campaign map.

Your first assignment should be, purely for the sake of convenience, to set yourself some kind of time target for each task. In fact, it is almost a foregone conclusion that you will not stick to this; it is simply designed to give you a structure while you need it. You also should instigate some kind of discipline in your practice, so that you are using your sleeping time wisely and well.

You next need to learn to remember and record all your dreams, whether creative or not. For this you will need to train your memory and to keep a dream journal. Suggestions for doing these things are found both in the Managing Your Dreams chapter and Tips and Techniques.

Having learnt to record your dream, you should next train yourself to control your waking and dreaming. Creative dreaming develops best within the dozing periods after a time of proper sleep, and you will need to experiment with what suits you best. This will take time, so do not be too disappointed if you are not able to achieve creative dreaming very quickly. When it does happen, it will probably happen quite spontaneously and surprise you with its intensity.

Initially, you will probably find that creative dreaming does not happen very often. However, as you become more competent at recognizing that you are dreaming, you will be able to hold the state more often and for longer. This is when you can begin to use it to explore the hitherto hidden aspects of your personality and elements of universal knowledge which will help you to live your life more successfully. You should be able to access those things which have been available to the so-called primitive cultures through shamanistic and priestly knowledge – that which Jung called the Collective Unconscious.

If you subscribe to the belief that you are in charge of your own existence – that things happen because of you, not to you – creative dreaming can help you to adjust that existence. You can make things happen in such a way that you maximize your potential in life. Even if you believe that you are at the mercy of circumstances – that things happen despite you – you will be able to use creative dreaming both to help you understand what is happening to you and those around you.

As a game, learning how to fly, spin and shift space is great fun to do and can be a welcome relief from the problems and difficulties of waking life. This is the next stage of learning that you will experience. Creative dreaming and its techniques, however, should never be used purely to escape from the reality of the everyday world, but only to enhance it. The adjustments that you can make will intrigue and surprise you, but you should use this new skill wisely and well. It will depend on you and your personality whether you will be able to achieve results quickly or slowly or in small steps or large leaps.

As with all newly acquired skills, you will by now be developing your own versions of the various techniques suggested in this book. This is where you are becoming truly creative and hopefully will feel that you can experiment with your chosen path in the use of creative dreaming. Some will wish to use creative dreaming as a learning tool, some will wish to use it in the service of healing – both of themselves and others. If you wish to use creative dreaming to assist your spiritual progression, you will be able to do this, too. The choice is yours and the opportunities are endless. Finally as an encouragement we would like to offer one person's experience of the path to creative dreaming.

AN INSIDER'S VIEW

I have no idea what other people believe creative dreaming to be, or how much it differs from their normal dream state. What I can say is that I have been experiencing powerful dream sensations ever since I can remember.

My parents sometimes like to embarrass me (well, they always like to embarrass me actually, but that's another story) by telling dinner guests about how, when I was very young, they first realized that I was aware of dream sleep.

One evening when I was around three years old, I curtailed my usual playfighting with my dad, by saying I wanted to 'see the pictures in my pillow'. Even then I was aware that dreams have always affected my daytime mood and been part of my day-to-day life. I cannot remember a time when I have woken up and not been aware that I was in dream sleep before I awoke.

Although I have no proof – and have not made any sort of detailed study of this subject – I would suggest that during my dream cycle I dream far more than an average person and have therefore learnt to 'use' my dreams in a manner that is not necessarily 'the norm'. I am also one of those people who need at least eight hours' sleep per night and this need for sleep, coupled with my seemingly continual dream state whilst asleep, has no doubt meant that my experience of different types of dream sleep is also above average.

In the past year or so I have started having more dreams. Not only are they remarkably vivid – I presume that many, if not all, people have vivid dreams – but in them I have an element of control. This control is not just over my movements in my dream world but also over the dream world that surrounds me. In this state I am actually far more in control and conscious or aware than I ever am during my waking hours!

I imagine that many people reading this passage have had the feeling in a dream of suddenly become aware that – possibly due to the ridiculous nature of their surroundings – they are asleep. From what I have been told by friends, this usually means that they are just about to wake up. I have learnt to programme myself the night before, so that when I experience this feeling of knowing or suspecting I am in a dream, I can take control from that moment.

Firstly I concentrate on maintaining that dream feeling or state. I have found that unless you concentrate on some aspect of the dream – either a particular part of your surroundings or an aspect of yourself – you very quickly begin to wake up. It helps if you can let your fascination with the dreamscape hold your dream together.

When this was a relatively new experience to me, I used to spend what seemed like a long time checking on the level of detail that actually existed in my dreams. In many of these dreams, I would inspect a normally boring object with sheer fascination. I remember in one of these dreams approaching an average looking wall. I was almost challenging myself, in my dream, to have constructed a wall that under close scrutiny would bear close resemblance to the sort of wall that you would see on a daily basis in normal waking life.

Needless to say, it was as detailed as any wall I have ever seen whilst awake – with different shades of colour, scars from wear and tear and similarly rough to the touch. This sort of fascination with detailed inspection soon wears thin once you start to play with the possibilities in a completely creative dream. After I had convinced myself that my dream world environment was just as hard and 'real' as my daytime world, I began to think more deeply about the possibilities within this completely self-created universe. All the time I concentrated on keeping the dream feeling to inhibit my natural tendency to wake up.

During the waking hours, I had thought that anything was possible in a dream and that I could create completely different universes and completely alter the 'me' that was travelling within them. I am afraid that this is not necessarily true – or not true for me so far. It seems that there are certain rules even in the dream world. Yes, I can fly at will and am pretty much indestructible – although some dream events can still wake me – but I lapse in and out of control of my environment and cannot logically work through problems and challenges in the same way that I might during the day. I can also be moved much more quickly and on a far deeper level by emotion than during the waking hours; lust, fear, hatred and love are all felt but at heightened levels and can affect my rationality and destroy a consciously created dream 'story'.

In the past few months, I have been challenged on a couple of occasions by work colleagues to use these creative dreams for something tangible – in one particular instance to effectively 'remote view' some numbers left in an envelope on my boss's desk. The idea behind this was to establish whether what I was doing in my dreams had a practical and indeed financial angle – ultimately whether it could be used for profit.

For a few nights after this challenge was thrown down, I did not dream creatively. Of course, I dreamt, but not with the clarity or conscious level of awareness that has become normal. Then one night I realized that I was in a dream – I could see my hands in front of me and I looked at them, examining them. This is a technique that I use to gain control in my dreams and for some reason it helps.

I looked around myself in the dream and realized that I was in London – not very far away from my office. All I had to do was prevent myself from waking up and I would be in my office checking the numbers in a matter of seconds. I tend to get around by flying Superman-style – none of these big leaps or erratic uncontrollable flying situations for me! I realized very quickly that I was going to be at my offices within moments and the only real barrier to me was the River Thames. All I had to do was fly over the water, pass through the walls of the building – this can be quite uncomfortable but is not usually very difficult – and read the numbers.

Even in the dream I was very excited. I was slightly worried that time, in its many guises, is not the same in even the most contrived dream world and that I might be arriving at my office long before or long after the time when the envelope had been left for me to view.

Then the most annoying thing happened. As I crossed the river, and I caught sight of my office, I realized that I had crossed into the previous century. There were men and boys in flat-caps, wearing very brown and dull clothing. There were also horses pulling carts. I can remember thinking in my dream that I had been cheated – I had controlled all the other variables almost perfectly but had been outwitted by time.

This young man's account is truly fascinating, in that it contains all of the elements that most intrigue. There is no evidence to corroborate that creative dreamers are better at dreaming than anyone else, yet he testifies that he has always been a prolific dreamer. He highlights the element of control that he feels he has over his dreams and also the potential for the bizarre ('due to the ridiculous nature of their surroundings'). He also speaks of the necessary programming the night before and the need to concentrate on maintaining the dream feeling or state, lest he wake up.

He has used 'checking on the level of detail' as his way of reality checking and also later speaks of examining his dream hands – a technique he seems to have taught himself. We have already mentioned this elsewhere.

He speaks of his belief that 'anything can happen in a dream' but also notes that for him there appear to be certain rules that apply within his dream world. Logic does not operate and emotion is considerably heightened in the creative state, sometimes interfering with his rationality.

When challenged to use the ability for profit rather than pleasure, he temporarily loses the ability to dream creatively, and indeed loses clarity even in ordinary dreams. He flies 'Superman-style', which is presumably for him aerodynamically correct, but his control is disturbed by his own thoughts on the meaning of time. His perception is distorted to the point where there is a time slip, and though he has obviously remained aware, he can do little to succeed in his original task.

This young man has developed his own techniques over the years without the help of a manual for creative dreaming. He instinctively has used methods which have suited his own personality, but also has an almost 'textbook' approach in his development. People who have experimented with all sorts of altered states of consciousness are agreed that creative dreaming is but one of many states that requires a learning process of adaptation and adjustment.

Hopefully this book will act as a textbook for you and give you not only the basic methods but also the ability to adapt and adjust your dreaming and your whole lives. We wish you successful creativity and awareness.

TIPS AND TECHNIQUES

In this section, we gather together many of the exercises and the tried and tested techniques which enable you to develop the art of dreaming creatively. To have the courage to transcend the fears, doubts and barriers that we all have in becoming creative, we need to be in touch with our own inner being and the creative urge that is ours by right. We must move from feeling that we are prevented by circumstances from being the person we know we can be to taking control of our lives and being able to link to that stream of knowledge and awareness that enables us to create our future.

To do this we have to be intensely practical. To that end, this section contains the exercises, tips and techniques which will help you to develop creative dreaming. You may notice that some exercises have been repeated from earlier in the book. They have been repeated in this section so that they may be more easily photocopied. You may do this with the full permission of the publisher and author. Of course, you do not need to follow the order given, though this is the one that is probably the simplest, because it takes you from when you first remember and record your dreams to using them with full awareness.

Hopefully, you will be able to progress from the simpler ones to the more difficult, and to experiment with all of them before undertaking to develop your own personal action plan.

WORKPLAN

Dreamwork, for the purposes of this book, can be defined as any activity we choose to carry out once we have had a dream. It entails working initially only with the content of that particular dream. Later the dream can be investigated along with other dreams, to see whether it is part of a series or perhaps clarifies other previous dreams. The dream can be looked at in several different ways. You should be able to:

1. List all various components of the dream.

2. Explore the symbols of the dream with all their various meanings.

3. Widen the perspectives and components of the dream.

4. Work with the dream in as many different ways as possible to complete unfinished business.

5. Work with the spiritual significances within the dream.

6. Bring the message through to everyday life to make necessary choices and changes.

We will now look at these points in more detail.

1. The components

The components of a dream are all of the various parts of the dream: the scenario, the people, the action, the feelings and emotions. Each has its part to play in your interpretation and it is only when you consider the dream really carefully that you will be able to appreciate some of the more subtle meanings of the dream. In creative dreaming it is feasible to make changes to any or all of these things, though not necessarily all at once.

The more adept you become at recognizing your own individual way of creating your dreams, the easier your own interpretation will be. Making a simple list will help you to do this.

The following dream was submitted via the internet by a 19-year-old woman and illustrates perfectly the availability of dreamwork material.

Our italics show the important components of the dream.

> It was an *underwater* dream. I was in a very *large bubble* and there were *turtles* all around me.

> As far as I could see, *nothing but turtles*. They were all *different sizes*. I remember *steps leading down* into the water; it was kind of like a *swimming pool*.

> I could see the sides and I was very close to the steps. I remember looking around and seeing *all kinds of plants* and turtles and thinking, 'Why are there so many turtles in the pool?'

> I also remember that the only colours I saw were *blue and green* in varying shades. The underneaths of the *turtles* were a *pale yellow/green colour*. It was very *beautiful*.

> I can also remember *wanting* to get out of the *bubble* somehow, but I was *scared* that if I did, the *turtles would kill me*.

In this dream, the lady could have decided to become creative when she asked the question 'Why are there so many turtles in the pool?' Many dream researchers do not feel that creative dreams should be interpreted. If you remember, however, that dreams are always multi-level and may have different interpretations according to the needs of the dreamer, even creative dreams are capable of meaning.

Calvin Hall and Robert van de Castle, in an effort to be scientific, developed the method of quantitative coding which is still used nowadays in dream research. This led to the cognitive theory of dreams, which meant that dream content was divided into several categories. There were characters, emotions, interactions, misfortunes, objects and settings. By dividing dreams up in this way, they recognized that dreams expressed perceptions of family members, friends, social environment and self. Dreams reflected waking concerns, interests and emotional focus. Just as a matter of interest, when carrying out their research they discovered that there were strong similarities in dreams from people all over the world.

In your own work with dreams, you may like to record the number of times over a given period of, say, a month how many times – and it what form – these perceptions and concerns appear. For this you will, of course, have regularly remembered your dreams and taken care to record them, whether creative or otherwise, as fully as possible in your dream journal.

2. The symbols

When the mind has a message to impart, it will often present the information in symbolic form. It is important, therefore, for you to understand the symbolism of your dreams. You will, over time, develop your own symbolism: those things in dreams which have relevant meaning for you. The conventional symbolism of dreams is very rich in imagery. Though many exponents of creative dreaming do not attempt to interpret dreams in this way, it is always worthwhile taking a good look at your dreams, so that if they have symbols within them they can be properly interpreted. The dream dictionary contained within this book is an excellent source of reference. With any of your dreams, it is worthwhile making an alphabetical list of your dream content and then deciding whether it can be interpreted symbolically rather than literally.

3. The perspectives

Perhaps the most satisfactory work which can be done with dreams is to deliberately widen the perspective within the dream and to consciously push the dream further. Thus you might like to see what would happen next to one of the characters. For example:

What would happen if the action that was being carried out were continued?

How would the other characters react?

How would this change the dream?

If a particular character acted in a different manner would the whole dream change, or only parts of it?

How much would you want characters to support you or leave you alone?

You can see that these considerations are the beginning of you taking control within your dream, and you are therefore moving more authoritatively into dreaming with awareness. Another way in which you can change perspective is to look at your dream as if you were one of the characters. If this were so, would you 'direct' the dream differently? Would there be a different outcome? Working with your dream in this way enables you to become more aware of the effect on various parts of your personality (the characters in your dream).

4. Working with your dreams

You can use any method you are comfortable with to look at issues connected with your dreams. You might like to use either the Jungian or the Gestalt method of working which is shown below. The Gestalt method is a way of confronting or making friends with various parts of your personality, which tend to show themselves as characters or aspects of your dream.

You may like to look at some of the even earlier methods of interpretation. You might try to decide whether your dreams are messages from the unconscious (or from God) – which used to be called *oracula* – or are simply images known as 'visions'.

5. Working with the spiritual significances

From the idea that God, as seen in primitive societies, gives dreams, we would speak nowadays more of a recognition of spiritual influences. This is when your truly altruistic and selfless side recognizes that you must make adjustments to your everyday behaviour if you are to live your life as fully as possible. That part of you which 'knows best' attempts to inform you not only of the changes that need to be made, but also how to make them.

By and large, the spiritual significance of a dream has much to do with your sense of responsibility to the rest of your community or the world in which you live. Not everybody is able or willing to consider the greater good, but if a dream does allow itself to be interpreted in any other way, you may wish to look at it from this point of view. The three things to look for here are right thought, right speech and right action. The questions you might ask yourself are:

How does this dream help me to be a better person?

What information does it give me to help others?

What fresh understanding does this dream bring me?

6. Bringing the message through

Once you have explored the dream in every way possible, you will be able to apply the things that you have learnt in your everyday life. You will need to practise new patterns of behaviour, think in new ways, change some attitudes and create a new way of being. This is indeed where lucid dreaming can help you tremendously.

* * *

You will see various other techniques throughout this section for doing all of these things and will be able to practise your mode of behaviour carefully before actually making radical changes in your everyday life. Let us suppose, for instance, that you have concluded that you must become more proficient at handling difficult relationships. Using creative dreaming to assist you, you can both practise the new way of behaving and get a fair idea of what effect your behaviour will have on other people in your life. You will be able to judge whether that behaviour will be welcome or otherwise. When using creative dreaming in this way, try to be patient both with yourself and others.

GESTALT METHOD

The Dream

If all parts of the dream are reflections or aspects of me then the part I choose to communicate with is the person/thing in my dream represented by...?

(If you find it easier, place two chairs opposite one another and play each part in turn or use your own image in a mirror to signify the dream character.)
What I want to know is...

Result

QUESTIONING YOUR DREAM CHARACTERS

There are certain questions which can be asked during the course of a dream, even a creative one. The first is, 'Who or what are you?' In recognizing that you are dreaming, this question can do one of two things. It can confirm dreaming with awareness for you, in that you recognize that the being or entity that you are speaking to is in fact a dream image, or in becoming aware of the image you realize that you are dreaming and instinctively wake up. Identifying the image allows you to work with it, to make sense of it and to make use of it – thus laying the foundation for further elucidation.

The second question that can be asked from the creative state is, 'Why are you in my dream?' Such a question is probably more correct in dealing with bad dreams and nightmares, in that it initiates the process of confronting your negatives. Working from a positive viewpoint and remembering that your inner self is the one that produces the images, the question highlights the motive *behind* the image rather than what the image represents. This means accepting that you yourself have been responsible for the presence of the image, rather than that the image is attempting to tell you something. As time goes on you may find that with greater understanding the question becomes, 'Why is this in my dream?'

The next question to be asked is, 'What have you to tell me?' Some dreamers are able to set up a dialogue with their images. This is very similar to the Gestalt technique shown in this section. For those who prefer to adhere to a clearer focus, the question may be better phrased as, 'What information can I gain from you?' This requires a careful appraisal of all aspects of the image. This includes the way it is placed, how it holds itself, what part it plays in the overall scenario of the dream, what it does and so on. For those who are less practised at creative dreaming this question can be asked in the waking state after remembering the dream, but the more accomplished should be able to seek answers from a state of awareness.

A further way in which the dream image can be questioned is to ask, 'Why is this happening in this way?' or 'What is the purpose of this image's action or non-action?' In this way you will discover whether the image's purpose is solely to facilitate the other actions within the dream, or to impart further information. Thus, to be inside a large building might be to impress upon you its importance, the large empty space or its use as a public meeting place. If you wish to follow the Gestalt method of interpretation, you will be able to accept that each thing in the dream is an aspect of yourself. Therefore in the previous example you would question yourself as to which part of you is important, which part is empty space and which part is publicly on show.

'What do you want from me?' is a question which can take one in many different directions. The first thing to look at is what the dream itself requires. The dream as a complete entity contains a 'message' or information which often needs to be unravelled even if the dream is creative. Equally, as we have already seen, each part of the dream contains its own information. So it often helps in the waking state to make a list of what is relevant to a successful completion of the dream. As you become more competent at creative dreaming, you are capable of making lists in your head of what you have discovered. It is worthwhile remembering to record such findings as quickly as possible after the dream has ended.

Frequently, once you have woken up, you will need to find out how the dream relates to your waking life and the situations in which you find yourself. This often requires you to look at the content of the dream for clues in order to discover information which helps you to handle the main issue in your life. You can then review it for help in particular circumstances, perhaps at work or in your personal life. Be sure also to look for ways of expanding your ability to lucid dream by taking a specific aspect of the dream. Choosing to work creatively with the specific enables you to delve even deeper into the hidden aspects of your psyche. This is where working with the symbols of the dream on an individual basis can help you to become extremely creative.

DAILY AUDIT PLAN

If you are to use your dreams to help you to deal effectively with your everyday life, there are certain techniques that you must practise first in order to clear your mind successfully so that you can learn the art of creative dreaming. We show these, wherever practicable, on separate pages.

As part of your nightly routine to clear your mind ready for creative dreaming, it is wise to do what we call a daily audit. This consists of doing a review of your day and balancing the good with the bad. You might like to concentrate on your behaviour and decide whether you have acted appropriately or not, or simply to decide which parts and actions of the day have been productive and which not. Your audit will be of the issues which concern you most at that particular time. Your starting point should be the hour immediately preceding bedtime – you should then work backwards throughout the day until you reach your time of awakening.

1. Taking a sheet of paper, divide it into two columns. On one side list actions and types of behaviour you consider 'good' and on the other those you consider 'bad' or 'indifferent'.

2. Looking at the bad side first, review where your behaviour or action could be altered or improved and resolve to do better in the future. You may like to develop a ritual for yourself which represents your rejection of the disliked patterns of behaviour. This can be as simple as writing down the behaviour and discarding the paper on which it is written.

3. Now look at the good side and give yourself approval and encouragement for having done well. Resolve to have more of the good behaviour and, if you wish, form an affirmation which indicates this. You might take this affirmation into creative dreaming.

4. Where your behaviour has been indifferent, again resolve to do better and to give yourself more positive feedback for having made the effort.

5. Forgive yourself for not having achieved a best result and praise yourself for doing your best. This is the aspect of 'balancing your books'. Now let your day go, do not dwell on the negatives and go peacefully to sleep.

This exercise helps in the process of keeping you spiritually strong.

Incubating the Dream you Want

 (CARDS method)

The next action that you will wish to undertake is that of incubating the dream you want. This technique works well, as discussed earlier in the book, for incubating any dream but also as a preliminary to learning the art of creative dreaming itself. The stages are:

Clarify the issue under consideration and write it down.

Ask the question. State it as positively as possible and, to commit it to memory, write it down.

Repeat the question and then turn it into a statement (e.g. from 'What is...?' to 'I want to know about...'). If you wish, write it down in the form of a statement and place it under your pillow, since this seems to focus the mind.

Dream the dream and document it. Answers can take longer than just one night to appear. Keep a note of how long it takes.

Study the dream in detail and look for further clues. Decide if the dream has been helpful or whether more work is needed. Record your reaction to the dream.

REMEMBERING YOUR DREAMS

To be able to remember all your dreams you need to train yourself to do so. Good-quality sleep is the first prerequisite since, while you are learning, you may well be waking yourself up fairly frequently. Later you will remember creative dreams particularly, but first of all you must get into a particular routine.

1. Decide which sleep periods you are going to monitor. A good idea is to give yourself an approximate four-hour period to have a proper sleep, then to monitor everything after that in chunks of waking yourself up every hour or so.

2. If you have an illness or are taking medication, please check with your doctor or medical practitioner before undertaking this exercise.

3. Set your alarm or wake-up device – soft light or soothing music – for the time you wish to wake. Don't allow yourself to be 'shocked' into wakefulness, for example, by very loud music. It is counter-productive because it is most likely to chase away the dream.

4. When you have woken up, lie perfectly still. Do not move until you have recalled your dream with as much detail as you can remember.

5. Write down your dream and analyze it. If it was a creative dream record it as such. If not, then interpret it in your usual way.

6. It is here that your dream journal will come in useful, because in it you will also be able to record fragments of dreams which at the time may not seem to have relevance but, later on, may do so.

7. Dreams are remembered best from periods of REM sleep, so with practice, you should begin to discover when these periods are. Don't be too worried if at first your dream recall is deficient. You will get better with practice.

8. Try not to let the day get in the way when you first awake – begin to consider it when you have looked at your mind's night time activity.

Day's Residue

Use this space to analyze how the activities and experiences of your waking hours have influenced the content of your dreams.

Dream

I dreamt like this because in the last 48 hours I have

1. Seen:

2. Heard:

3. Recognized:

Keeping a Dream Journal

Here we repeat the instructions given earlier in the book on keeping a dream journal so that you develop good practice before you attempt creative dreaming.

1. *Any paper and writing implements can be used – whatever is most pleasing to you.*

2. *Always keep your recording implements at hand.*

3. *Write the account of the dream as soon as possible after waking.*

4. *Use as much detail as possible.*

5. *Note at which point in your dream you consider you 'went creative'.*

Be consistent in the way that you record your dreams. One simple scheme is given next.

Recording your Dream

This template gives an easy format for you to record your dream. Obviously the first three parts only need to be recorded if you intend to submit your dream to an external scrutiny. If you intend to keep your dream journal private, this method gives you the opportunity to look carefully at each of your dreams and return to them at a later date if necessary, perhaps to compare content, scenarios or other aspects. It can also allow you to quantify your own progress both in the process of developing creative dreaming and in that of self-development.

Name

Age

Gender

Date of dream

Where were you when you recalled the dream?

State the content of your dream.

Write down anything odd about the dream (e.g. animals, bizarre situations, dream signs, etc.).

What were your feelings in/about the dream?

HOW TO HAVE A CREATIVE DREAM

This technique is extremely simple and is used as a preparatory exercise to the MILD technique shown later.

1. Prepare yourself for sleep

As you prepare yourself for sleep give yourself the instruction that tonight you will have a creative dream. Form an affirmation of intent along the lines of a very simple statement such as, 'Tonight my dream will be a creative one.' Keep the statement that simple because you are simply learning to 'go lucid' initially. The content of the dream does not actually matter at this point.

2. Repeat your affirmation

Repeat your affirmation either out loud or to yourself as many times as you need to in order to fix it in your own mind. This in itself is helpful, since it is teaching you how to focus your mind on one thing at a time. An affirmation is a simple, positive statement encapsulating as succinctly as possible what you intend to happen.

3. Hold your intent in mind

Keep your mind on your intention, and then allow yourself to drift off into sleep.

4. Note the degree of awareness you have achieved

When you wake up, note the time and whether you remember having been creative. Also note how long you think you were in a state of awareness. Your estimation will probably not be very accurate to begin with, but this does not matter since you will become more proficient as time goes on.

REALITY CHECK

As the periods of awareness become longer, you will find that there is a need to check whether you are truly dreaming or not. Probably the best way of doing this is to look at the ground, or at your own hands and feet, to see if they are as they should be.

1. Ask yourself a question
The most sensible question to ask is, of course, 'Am I dreaming?' The simple asking of the question may initially be sufficient to chase away the dream, and you may well wake up. In time you will be able to apply other techniques to allow you to stay within the dream.

2. Look at your hands and feet
Checking your hands and feet for size and normality helps to stabilize the dream. If they seem larger or smaller than normal, then you are probably dreaming. In your dream, try to move them and watch what happens.

3. Carry out an action that you know is impossible in real life
This could be anything from jumping into the air for a huge distance, to rolling up a hill. The important thing is that it is an action which goes against the normal parameters of everyday life. If you perform the action, you are dreaming.

4. Look at the ground or the dream scenario
If there are bizarre elements in either of these, you are probably dreaming. If you do not believe that what you are perceiving is real, then you are probably dreaming. You might ask yourself the question, 'Is this real?'

5. Remind yourself that you are or have been dreaming
If you can, during the dream remind yourself that 'This is a dream'. Also when you wake up tell yourself, 'That was a dream.' Gradually you will come to recognize very quickly what is dream and what is not.

This reality check is also good to do even when you know you are awake, and helps to remind you that we live in a state of illusion anyway – that life itself is an illusion.

INCUBATING A SPECIFIC CREATIVE DREAM

When you have had some success with incubating the type of dream that you want, you can then progress to developing a specific lucid dream. We remind you to be patient with yourself, because you may not at first find that your incubation gives you the exact environment or content that you have requested. Gradually, however, you will find you are 'hitting target' more and more often.

1. Prepare the focus of your dream

Before you go to bed take the time to formulate a single idea or query which states clearly the subject of your dream. Write the phrase down and use a visual image, such as a picture or appropriate symbol, to fix the idea. Memorize the phrase and your representation of the scene. Create your dream scene or event verbally now. Remind yourself that when you dream of that particular event you will know that you are dreaming. Repeat to yourself at least three times, 'When I dream of [whatever you have decided], I will remember that I am dreaming.'

2. Go to bed

It is important not to let anything else intrude on your concentration. So, without further ado, go to bed and make yourself comfortable.

3. Keep the phrase or image in your mind

Concentrate on your phrase and aim to become creative. Imagine yourself dreaming about the issue and progressing into lucidity. If there is something you want to try in the dream, such as flying, concentrate on the idea of doing it once you are dreaming with awareness.

4. Meditate on the phrase

Keep your objective to become aware in focus until you fall asleep. If at all possible don't let any other thoughts come between thinking about your issue and falling asleep. If your thoughts wander, just revert to thinking about your phrase and becoming aware.

5. Follow your focus in the creative dream

When you feel have achieved awareness and are satisfied that you are considering your issue, carry out your aim (e.g. ask whatever question you wish to have answered, request ways to represent yourself, try your new responses or contemplate your position). Note your impressions and be aware of all contents of the dream.

6. Keep the dream active and sustain it if you can
To sustain the dream, learn to use the techniques in the exercise 'Prolonging a Creative Dream'. Initially, creativity will only occur in short flashes.

7. Come out of the creative state
When you acquire a good enough answer in the dream, come out of the creative state and make a point of rousing yourself into full consciousness. Before everything disappears, lie quite still thinking about what you have achieved.

8. Record the dream
Record the dream, deciding exactly how it has answered your question or intent.

THE MILD TECHNIQUE

Hopefully by now your own dreams will be beginning to intrigue you and you will be wishing to practise the technique of creative dreaming for yourself. To make it easy for you we repeat here the technique developed by other dream researchers.

1. Set up dream recall

Learn to wake up from dreams and to recall them. Initially you may need to use an alarm clock, soft music or diffused light. Eventually you will be able to wake up at will by giving yourself the instruction to do so. When you do wake from a dream, try to recall it as fully as possible and, if necessary, write it down.

2. Focus your intent

As you go back to sleep, concentrate intensely on the fact that you intend to recognize that you are dreaming. Use an expression to fix this idea in your mind, such as 'Next time I'm dreaming, I intend to remember I'm dreaming.' Keep focused on this idea alone and don't allow yourself to be distracted by stray thoughts.

3. See yourself become aware

Using your imagination, perceive that you are back in a dream you have had, whether it is the last one or another one that you clearly remember. Tell yourself you recognize it as a dream. Look for something odd or out of place that demonstrates plainly that it is a dream. Tell yourself 'I'm dreaming', and knowing what it feels like to be dreaming, continue to remember your chosen dream. Next, imagine what your next creative dream will feel like. See yourself carrying out your chosen plan. For example, note when you would 'realize' you are dreaming. See yourself carrying out a dream action, such as flying or spinning around.

4. Repeat until your intention is fixed

Repeat steps 2 and 3 until your intention is fixed; then drift off into sleep. Sometimes while falling asleep your mind may wander. If so, repeat the steps, so that the last thing in your mind before falling asleep is the thought that you will remember to appreciate the next time you are dreaming. Keep a record of how proficient you become.

PROLONGING A CREATIVE DREAM

All of these methods have been found to be useful in prolonging the creative dreaming state. More extensive explanations of the techniques and their relevance are given earlier in the book.

1. Spinning
As your original dream begins to fade, but before you become properly awake, try spinning on the spot. You should do this as rapidly as possible and begin from an upright position. You should find that you either re-enter your own dream or spin to a new scenario.

2. Continuing an activity
When you find yourself in the middle of a creative dream and it is beginning to fade, carry on with what you were doing in the dream but ignore the fact that the dream is losing clarity. As you continue with your activity, repeat over and over again to yourself, 'The next scene will be a dream.'

3. Rub your (dream) hands together
When you become aware that you are dreaming creatively and the dream begins to fade, try rubbing your hands together very hard – you should experience the movement and friction. Keep rubbing your hands together until you wake up or the dream scenario shifts. Keep repeating a phrase which ensures you stay with the dream such as, 'I am continuing to dream'.

4. Flying
Flying has much in common with spinning. You are inhibited only by your imagination. Experiment with flying in your own way, according to what you find most comfortable.

5. Sensory manipulation
Use the senses to help you to stay with the dream. Concentrate on each of the senses in turn and expand your awareness of each one. Listen, for instance, to your own breathing and then become aware of other inner sounds and voices. Try holding a conversation with one of your dream characters.

It is quite important that you develop your own way of prolonging your dreams. You will find that you are more comfortable with one particular way, but you could try experimenting with the others just to see what happens.

Note below how successful you were.

Analyzing your Dream

Whether your dream has been creative or not, you will want to get into the habit of analyzing its content more fully. It is suggested that you divide it into segments so that you can consider each part of the dream and whether that segment was perhaps either creative, or approaching creativity. You will also be able to pick up the theme of the dream by doing this.

The dream

The dream segments

The differences/similarities in the segments

The main theme of the dream

ADVANCED TECHNIQUES

Now having practised all of the basic techniques for creative dreaming, you are ready to move on to the more advanced methods of dreaming. Actually, before you do that, we suggest that you take time to consolidate what you have learnt. Think carefully about what you have been doing and consider whether you are satisfied with the results.

Is there anything that you could do to improve your methods?

Do you want to try anything else?

What do you now want to happen?

How do you want to use creative dreaming in the future?

Do you need to do further research into the subject?

Do you want to put yourself in touch with other people who are practising lucid dreaming?

The more advanced techniques help you to focus on your objectives, and to decide whether you are more interested in researching the actual technique or whether you want to be creative and help to make things happen.

It often helps to alter the way you express yourself to accommodate the creativity of dreams. If your day-to-day way of self-expression is through words, then experiment with colour or with form. If you enjoy music, try to find a particular piece which expresses the mood of your dream. If you are a sedentary sort of person, then express elements of the dream through movement such as dance or Eastern disciplines of *t'ai chi* or *qi gung*. The basic idea is that you can use your dreams to enhance your creativity in everyday life. They can act as starting points for projects or they can be used to explore other modes of self-expression.

Virtual reality for dreaming
As part of your advanced procedure for creative dreaming, you should be able to start building your own virtual dream reality. Start from a

waking state and focus your mind so that you will recall what you have done. A word of caution is needed here, however – not everyone can achieve the necessary measure of control to carry out the following exercise. It is an excellent exercise to practise in the development of creative dreaming but can seem too much like hard work.

As soon as you are aware that you are dreaming creatively, form a huge screen in front of you. This is your personal screen, of which you have total control, which you may think of as a television set, a cinema screen or a kind of projection created from the mind itself.

Onto this screen you will project your images and learn to command how this projection operates. You work with the colour, tone, brightness or anything else you may require. Initially you may wish to think of having control of the switches, though later you will probably find that you only need mind control – that is, to think of the changes and they will happen. This screen allows you to be objective about your attempts in the first place and to use it later to surround yourself with your creations. You may then find it easier to think of it like a night sky, on which to project your images. For some, this gives a greater sense of the connection with the cosmos.

One aspect of creative dreaming is that you can make use of all the senses in much the same way as you can in waking life. So try them all out, first attempting 'normal' changes, such as hearing a new sound or experiencing a different smell. Then, making use of the mind's ability in creative dreaming to invent the bizarre, create the wrong colour for something – perhaps a green cow, for instance.

Your rational mind will probably try to wake you up at this point. This is overcome by reminding yourself that you are dreaming. Take time and have fun, because you are learning how to remove the restrictions of perception that belong to the normal everyday world. You are also learning how to make your mind act as your servant rather than control you. Try to get a sense of what is happening within you as you make the changes, since it is this faculty that will eventually help you create your own reality in the everyday world.

REFINING THE SPINNING TECHNIQUE

We have already spoken of the spinning technique as a way of stabilizing dreams. We give a refined technique below. The steps to begin with are similar:

1. Take note of when the dream starts to fade and as soon as this happens begin to spin. At this point, you will still be conscious of your dream body; the action of spinning should be begun before you come too far into waking consciousness. It is important that you actually feel yourself spinning – you should try to use an image which enhances your reaction. So, if spinning like a ballet dancer feels inappropriate to you, it will not work. As you can see, some groundwork is essential in the conscious state so that you begin to switch automatically into whatever your 'control state' – that is, a state that you identify as dreaming – might be, even if you are dreaming. While awake, you can picture what spinning feels like, but in the dream state you must actually 'feel' the spinning.

2. Keep in mind whilst spinning that the next state you encounter will most likely be a dream. Taking each of the senses in turn, remind yourself that you will be dreaming. Whatever you see, hear, touch, feel or smell is more than likely to be a dream occurrence.

3. Always do a 'reality test' wherever you end up. When you come to stillness after spinning you may either still be dreaming or have woken up. If you are still dreaming, you may have transferred into a new dream state or you may have re-established your former dream scene, but it will be more vivid and stable. If you have woken up, then do test reality by observing the time or by recognizing the flawlessness of your bedroom – that is, that everything is as it should be in real life – there being no grotesque elements in your environment.

4. It is recommended that you constantly remind yourself that you are dreaming or are in the middle of a dream during any transformation which takes place while you are spinning. Hopefully, you will continue to be aware in the new dream, though you may make the

mistake of thinking that this new dream is real and actually happening.

5. It is now time to determine how you wish to proceed with your routine. You may simply wish to test the art of creative dreaming itself, in which case you will play with the act of becoming aware and leaving the creative state. You could, if you wish, practise altering the scenario of the dream or giving yourself orders which provide the means for you to astral travel, fashion new realities or complete different levels of being. If you believe in such things, you might also find yourself visiting other worlds; these techniques are shown elsewhere in this section.

CREATING A NEW DREAM SCENARIO

You might use this technique to produce a dream scenario, whether new or otherwise. The technique is very simple.

1. Select an objective

Before going to sleep decide on a person or place you would like to 'visit' in your creative dream. Choose initially something you are fairly confident of achieving – perhaps a visit to a close friend or relative. Often you may be able to check whether that person has been aware of you either in dreams or while awake. You could also choose a historical character or even an imaginary one. The choice is yours and the possibilities are endless. When you feel confident enough to do so, you could also choose a different time and place.

2. Develop a steadfast intention of achieving your objective

Having decided on your goal, write down your intent, using simple words to which you can relate, then strongly visualize yourself meeting your objective. State your firm intention to do so in your next dream.

3. Spin to your target in your creative dream

It is possible that, purely by chance, you find yourself in a non-creative dream with your target; in which case, do your best to become aware within the dream. You could also try it the other way round and become aware first, then visit. If you can, practise both ways and then decide which one – if either – you are more comfortable with. As soon as the dream begins to fade and you perceive you are about to wake up, put yourself into another spin. Repeat your chosen phrase until you find yourself in a new vivid dream scene – one hopes with a sense of achievement at having been successful in the task you set yourself.

DIRECTING YOUR DREAMS

This technique is a way of achieving changes of a mystical kind. It is different from the movement involved in spinning and flying and is more a matter of actually changing the environment in which your dream takes place. Remember that you can do anything you please in the dream state. You can either use the idea of the 'big screen' or of a stage production.

1. Decide that instead of moving yourself to a new location you will draw the location to you.

2. Start by changing something small in your dream surroundings and gradually work up to bigger changes.

3. Do everything at different speeds and play with what you are creating, much as you did in the virtual reality exercise.

4. You might then like to think of yourself as the director and producer of your own play. You can use any props you like and can experiment to achieve the right atmosphere.

5. Follow this up by creating a stage set for your next learning experience.

THE IFE TECHNIQUE

Life teaches us that we have to have restrictions. From an early age, we learn what is acceptable behaviour and what is not. We are taught that to be spontaneous is dangerous and that we must be 'sensible'. Within the framework of creative dreams, however, we have the freedom to be totally eccentric and to use patterns of behaviour which re-educate us in the art of personal freedom.

Most creative people have a very highly developed ability to create fantasies. If you dare to practise creative dreaming, you will find that you are capable of doing and being things that are not possible except in an altered state of consciousness. One yoga exercise that is practised to give a sense of the meaning of life is to try to discover what it is like to be a tree or flower or other sentient (aware) being. This exercise consists of three stages, which we will call the IFE technique.

- First ***Imagine*** what it would be like to be your chosen object.

- Then ***Feel*** how the object feels.

- Finally ***Experience*** being that object.

Because the rational aspects of everyday life are suspended during creative dreams, you should be able very quickly to reach a state of awareness where it is easy to do all of these things. You could practise being the opposite sex, being an animal – domestic or otherwise – or, if you are feeling brave, being something like a rock or the sea.

Initially, you will probably not be able to hold this state for very long, but with practice you will find that it becomes easier and that you can widen your perception to encompass other states of being as well. You might, for instance, try to experience what it would be like to be suspended in space or time, to belong to other worlds or to sense what you will be like in twenty years' time.

RELAXATION TECHNIQUE

There are many relaxation aids on the market, and it is perfectly right that you use the one which works best for you. Although this one appeared earlier in the book, we have included it here for ease of reference. It is a simple technique which can be practised with or without the help of relaxing music, according to preference. The technique is a good beginning to the exploration of meditative techniques and other altered states of consciousness.

1. Find a quiet spot where you will not be interrupted.

2. If you choose to lie down, ensure that you will not fall asleep. For the purposes of this exercise, you need to remain awake and aware.

3. Start with your feet and begin to tighten them as much as is possible, then relax them.

4. Then work progressively up your body, tightening and then relaxing each set of muscles in turn. Firstly, your calves, then your thighs, your buttocks and so on, until you reach your head.

5. Repeat this three times in all, in order to sense what relaxation is really like.

6. Finally, in one go, tighten all the muscles you have previously relaxed and let go.

You may choose now to use a deep breathing technique, a creative visualization or a meditation to help you in your process of creative dreaming. As a matter of interest, all of these methods are useful in dealing with the everyday stresses and strains of life.

CONTEMPLATION AND MEDITATION

When you are suitably relaxed, it is possible to use other techniques to help you in the art of creative dreaming.

1. A simple way of preparing for creative dreaming is to use contemplation. In this, as a precursor to meditation, you give yourself a visual image of the subject in hand.

2. You might, for instance, think of the words 'creative dreaming' as being carved out of a block of wood. Holding this image in your mind, let it develop in its own way and just watch what happens.

3. You might wish to consider the idea of a visit to Egypt or some other far-flung country, so again, you hold the idea in your mind and contemplate it.

4. When you have become proficient at contemplation, you can then attempt meditation, which is a further stage of allowing the image or thought to develop spontaneously of its own accord. You may then wish to take the results of your meditation into creative dreaming.

DEALING WITH NIGHTMARES

When in dreams you come up against a character or a situation which is threatening or has the quality of a nightmare, there are certain techniques that you can use in creative dreaming which help to remove the anxiety. One such exercise is shown below. It should be said that the more you are able to relax and use contemplation and meditation, the less likely you are to suffer from nightmares.

The RISC technique

A full explanation of the RISC technique is given in the Managing Your Dreams chapter. This is a very simple technique which was and is used therapeutically to help people to face bad dreams. It is, in many ways, the precursor of other lucid dreaming techniques.

1. **Recognition.** When you are having a dream which you feel is a bad one, recognize that you do not need the feelings that it leaves you with, whether that is anger, fear, guilt or any other negative feeling.

2. **Identification.** You need to be able to identify what it is about the dream that makes you feel bad. Look at the dream carefully and find out exactly what it is that disturbs you.

3. **Stopping a bad dream.** You must always remember that you are in charge. You do not have to let a bad dream continue. You can either wake up or, recognizing that you are dreaming, become aware.

4. **Changing.** Each negativity in your dream can be changed for the positive. Initially, you may have to wake yourself up to work out a better conclusion, but eventually, you will be able to do it while you are still asleep.

CONVERSATIONS WITH DREAM CHARACTERS

This technique is useful for dealing with dreams where you come up against a figure which frightens you or is one which you do not understand. It can also help in moving your understanding forward so that you can begin to integrate what you have already learned. When you have had an unpleasant dream, or perhaps when a creative dream has not gone as you expected it to, it is useful to work with it as soon as possible afterwards.

1. Taking the dream forward

You can do this by having imaginary conversations while you are awake. Get a pen and either your dream journal or a piece of paper, so that you can make notes of what happens. Visualize a dream character in front of you, one with which you have had some difficulty in a recent dream. Initiate a conversation with this character. You will probably have to suspend disbelief until you get used to the technique. You may feel a little foolish to begin with but please do persevere, since the benefits are tremendous. Decide that you will have a conversation with this character that will give you a resolution to your difficulty. Imagine yourself really talking to the dream character, remembering that it is better for you to begin the conversation. Sometimes it is easier to start with questions such as, 'What are you doing in my dream? Why are you pursuing me?' or other relevant questions. Spend some time to begin with working out what questions you wish to ask your dream character and write them down, but equally try to be as spontaneous as possible. It is more than possible that your questions may change as you become further involved with your character, but it is wise to give yourself a starting place. You may wish to choose a question from the list below or substitute questions which are relevant for you.

Why are you in my dream?

Who are you?

Why are you acting the way you are?

What are you trying to do?

What are you trying to tell me?

What do you want to know?

What do you want me to do?

What do you want me to be?

What part of me do you represent?

Why is this happening in this dream?

What do I need to know?

How can I help you?

How can you help me?

Write down your questions, and brief notes of the answers you get from the character. These may pop up and seem more like thoughts rather than speech, but record them all the same. You may well wonder if it is all your imagination but that is fine. Trust your own intuition and continue with the work because, as you become less critical of the process, you will find that it flows more easily. Don't try to evaluate what is happening while you are doing this – save that for later. Bring the conversation to an end when it seems to be running out of steam, going round in circles or has reached some kind of resolution.

Then evaluate what you have just done and ask yourself whether you are satisfied with the result or if there is something you would do differently next time. You are now well on the way to developing your own technique for dealing with nightmares and can try the same exercise on another dream.

2. Setting your dream purpose

Now that you have a technique for dealing with dream content and one for creative dreaming, you can combine the two. Tell yourself that the next time you have a difficult or frightening encounter with a dream character, you will become aware and have a conversation with them.

3. Conversing with dream figures

When you come across any character within a dream which is problematical, whether there is a conflict or not, try to establish if you are dreaming by asking yourself if you are. If you discover that you are in the middle of a dream, continue in the following way: turn and face the character and, using the technique above that you have practised, begin a dialogue using one of the questions from the list. Listen to the character's responses and try to get to the bottom of problems on its behalf – for instance, ascertain why it feels it has a right to harass you – as well as your own. Try to reach an agreement or resolution and, if at all possible, try to befriend the character. Continue with the dialogue until you reach a reasonable conclusion. Then, bring yourself back to full wakefulness and write the conversation down while you still remember it.

4. Evaluating the conversation

Try to decide if you have achieved the best possible result. If you are dissatisfied, think about how you might improve your results next time. For the time being, go back to step one and work consciously with the dream, using more of the questions to get a better result. You might also use the technique of Carrying the Dream Forward shown later in this section.

ADDRESSING RECURRENT NIGHTMARES

If you are subject to recurrent nightmares you can use an extension of the RISC technique to help resolve the problem.

1. Recalling and recording the nightmare

Recall the nightmare, including as much detail as possible, and write it down. Sometimes just writing it down is enough to take a great deal of the fear out of the situation. Examine the nightmare for various points where you might be able to influence the turn of events by doing something differently.

2. Choosing a point of influence and a new action

Choose a specific point in the dream where you felt that you were most in control, just before you now wish to change the dream. Choose a different course of action which you feel will alter the dream. By starting from a position of control, you will be more likely to be able to change things for the better.

3. Relaxing

Now you need to get into a frame of mind where you are completely relaxed and can work with your dream. Find a time and place where you can be uninterrupted for about half an hour. Close your eyes, and using your favourite relaxation method let go completely.

4. Re-running the nightmare

Beginning at the entry point you chose in Step 2, visualize yourself back in the dream. See it happening as it did before until it feels right to practise your new action and let the dream continue until you find out what happens and whether the action has the desired result.

5. Considering your reworked result

Return to normality when the imagined dream has ended. Treat the imagined dream as though it were a real one and document it. Be aware of your reaction to the new ending. If you still do not feel the ending is satisfactory, then feel free to rework it until you do. It is possible that working with the dream in this way is enough to stop it from recurring. It is as though the dream loses its power.

6. Dealing with the recurrent dream

If the dream occurs again, having taken yourself to lucidity follow the new plan of action. Having prepared your new mode of behaviour, carry it out to the best of your ability, and be clear as to the results you expect. Remember that the dream will never be able to harm you and that you choose to be in control.

CARRYING THE DREAM FORWARD

By the time you have experimented with your dreams sufficiently to be able to recognize lucidity and to wake yourself at will from a bad dream, you are in a position to manipulate your dreams even further. Almost inevitably we come up against the question of whether the technique about to be described is creative dreaming or not. To be frank, it really does not matter what name you choose to give it, but to save argument let us call it Focused Reverie. Here, the technique is to remember the dream up to the time you woke up, then choose to take the dream forward as a whole.

We have already suggested that you might work with characters and objects in your dream and ask yourself what happens next with each of them. Now that can be extended to include the whole dream. This is not the same as spinning yourself into a new environment, nor is it taking conscious control – it is simply to allow the dream to continue in its own way. The steps are quite simple:

1. Remembering the dream as it was, make contact with each part of the dream as though it was still happening to you.

2. Now put yourself in the position of observer and allow the dream to unfold around you.

3. Do not attempt to influence the dream at all. Just allow it to happen.

4. If the action or characters get stuck, then assume that that is the point at which you would have woken up.

5. Think about why the dream will not go any further. Resolve to deal with any issues that might arise.

6. You might choose the subject for your next creative dream from these issues.

RESOLVING YOUR DREAM

For the purposes of this exercise we suggest that you take one aspect of your dream, perhaps the main storyline, and become creative with it. As we have said previously, it does not matter what sort of quality you achieve in your creative projects: it is more important to recognize your own creativity. Here you are thinking about the dream itself and how to make it work for you. These are some questions you might ask yourself:

What will happen next to me as the main character?

What do I want to say?

What response do I need from the different parts of my dream?

What will happen next now that I am in control of my dream?

Do I want any of the characters, objects or aspects of the dream to act differently?

Who or what is acting out of character in my dream?

Does it help in the resolution of my dream to have them continue to act out of character? Should I impose some kind of further control?

By working with your dream in this way you are learning not only to gain some control over the dream itself but also to work towards a resolution of the dream – that is, to work out what the dream is trying to put across. You are able to decide whether there is more or less control needed in your life. This means that you can either choose to be totally spontaneous or to focus more clearly on your aims and objectives.

TOOLS FOR CREATIVE DREAMING

Crystals

Many people believe that working with crystals can enhance dreaming, both creative and otherwise, and help one to ground the wisdom that is available for each of us through these natural objects. It is as though the subtle energies act as both receivers and transmitters and give the ability to tune into those aspects of knowledge both of ourselves and of the world in which we live. On pages 34-35 we have given some suggestions for crystals you may wish to use.

Programming a crystal

It is a simple matter to programme your crystals in order to help you in your dreamwork whilst remembering their inherent qualities.

1. You should choose your crystal or crystals for working with dreams very carefully. If you wish, you may also have a small bag, made of any material which appeals to you personally, in which to keep them safe – this way, they could be hung at the head of the bed or placed under your pillow while you sleep. Choose the best you can afford, and the nicest example you can find. Don't worry too much about minor imperfections, just let your intuition guide you to the right stones for you. Often as you choose your crystal, you will feel a slight tingling in your hand or fingers as you do. This tells you which stone is the one for you. You can use each crystal for a specific purpose or programme the crystals as a group to enhance your dreaming. For creative dreaming, you might try red jasper or rhonite. Clear quartz is also a good crystal to use for clarity. It does not matter whether the stone is polished or rough-cut: it is your preference.

2. Thoroughly cleanse and clear your crystal. You can do this by standing it in the sunshine for as long as possible, by leaving it outside on a bright moonlit night, or leaving it in salt (preferably sea salt) water for a period of 24 hours. This will remove any previous programming and adverse or negative influences.

3. It is better to use and programme these particular crystals only for

working with dreams. Let us suppose that you wish to programme the crystals to help you with creative dreams. Programme each crystal for at least a period of three nights and a maximum of ten. (Three nights cover all aspects of the physical, mental and spiritual and ten is numerologically a representation of all knowledge.) Programme your crystal every night before you go to sleep by using an affirmation or question of intent as follows: 'My dreams will be creative and reveal inner knowledge' or 'What knowledge do I need to understand lucid dreaming in relation to myself?'

Remember that at this stage not only are you programming your crystals, but you are also learning to focus your mind. You can do this before you give yourself the instruction to remember your dreams. This specific programme will help you lay your foundation for working with dreams. Understanding yourself will ultimately help you to achieve creative dreams. Obviously if there is no true desire or need either to understand yourself or to achieve lucid dreaming behind the statements, your results (or non-results) will reflect your lack of commitment. All of your programming should be what you really desire, or want to know.

4. Do remember that whatever your mind can conceive can be incorporated into a programme for your time of dreaming, not just creative dreaming. Your programming should be very clear and as creative as you wish to make it. Holding your crystal, either in both hands or in the hand that you feel to be more powerful, gather your full attention, then begin to formulate your thoughts clearly and simply. If it feels right, then you might like to write them down, so that you can commit them properly to memory. Then sit quietly with your crystal until you sense the rightness of it.

This method works to bring concepts into reality, both on a physical and spiritual level. By programming the crystal, you are allowing the use of very subtle but powerful energies to be channelled into existence and perception.

5. Concentrate on your crystal and allow your energy and intent to flow into it. Repeat this at least three times. Try not to let your attention wander during this period. If it does, just start again. The more you do it, the easier it becomes. Repeat this action for each crystal.

6. Programme your crystal shortly before going to bed and put it in your chosen place. Bring your desires or wants to the forefront of your mind, thinking of them as already fulfilled. (In the case of creative dreaming, you would try to sense what it would be like to have had a creative dream.) Now completely let your mind go free and then relax. Do this three times and then go straight to sleep. Your last thought should be your programming of the crystal and the feeling of your wish already having been fulfilled.

Programming your crystal is just one way of having you concentrate fully on making your dreams work for you. For too long it has been thought that the dreaming self is entirely separate from the conscious self. We are now finding that we can build pathways between the two; this crystal gateway is one that can be used by both believers and non-believers alike. At the very least, the crystal acts like worry beads and helps us to focus our intent, while at best the subtle energies open up new vistas of awareness which give us access to the rich sources of knowledge of ourselves and mankind.

Archetypal Images

When we talk of archetypal images here, we are not referring to the Archetypes covered in depth in the Enhancing Your Dreams chapter but 'archetypal' in the sense of 'a typical representation'. They act as excellent triggers for creative dreams.

In the case of the Tarot, you use the cards as a mental and visual starting point to help you to make sense of them and the feelings they evoke in you. There are eight steps to this process:

1. Sit quietly where you will not be interrupted.

2. Holding the card you have chosen from your own pack, look at it in detail. What comes to mind as you do so?

3. Think about your own life at this moment and how the card you have chosen applies to you. How can you apply your knowledge of the meanings of the card in the situations in which you find yourself?

4. Contemplate the card and allow yourself to internalize its power.

5. Now close your eyes and try to visualize yourself as part of the action of the card. How does it feel to be the main character? How do you interact with the other aspects of the card?

6. Decide to have a dream about this card and choose whether it will be creative or not.

7. Note in your dream journal which card you have chosen and go to sleep with it in mind.

8. When you wake up, follow the usual routine for recording your dreams.

Myths, Astrological Planets, Numbers, etc.
Remembering we gave extensive information on these in Enhancing Your Dreams, these should be treated in the same way:

1. Choose a particular trigger – a myth, planet or number, and think about how the story or the qualities might apply to your life at this moment.

2. Contemplate the story and feel how powerful it is.

3. Put yourself in the position you wish to be in, that is, as a character in the myth, on a planet or expressing its qualities. Imagine what it would be like to be part of that scenario. If working with numbers, think of the qualities of the number you have chosen and sense them within you.

4. In the case of sacred geometry, think of the shape – a square, a pentagram and so on – and try to get a sense of what it feels like to be in that shape. Gradually you should be able to become aware of the qualities of each figure and can progress to a more solid shape.

5. Try testing the boundaries of that shape and move the figure to be larger or smaller. Play with the shape in any way you like. Make it into a solid object and try to find out what it would be like to be inside such an object.

6. Allow yourself to go to sleep, and remember that in creative dreaming, you can do anything you choose to. It is simply a matter of telling yourself you can. Have fun but at the same time remember that you are training yourself to control your environment.

MEETING WITH SPIRIT

When you feel ready to meet your own concept of your Higher Self, your Spirit Guide or any other aspect of Spirit such as your personal representation of healing energy – perhaps the caduceus – you might like to try the following:

1. Decide what will be the focus of this particular meeting and form a statement of intent such as 'I wish to meet my personal totem animal' or 'I wish to meet my Spirit Guide'.

2. Think very carefully about how your life might be changed by this meeting, but try not to have too many expectations.

3. Visualize a scenario where it would be possible for you to meet the entity you have chosen. The path you visualized for your personal journey as suggested in 'Developing Your Spiritual Self' in the Creating your Own Reality chapter might be suitable. Imagine how you would feel were you able to have such a meeting.

4. Allow yourself to drift gently off into sleep, knowing that in due course, whether it be this night or another, that meeting will take place.

CREATIVE PROJECTS

Dreaming with awareness is a rich source of information for creative projects that you might like to try. Such projects help to ground the energy developed in dreaming and mean that you have a tangible result.

1. Choose a dream which is best suited to the project in hand. This project could be a story, play or dance. Make a note of it in your dream journal.

2. Write down the titles of pieces of music which appeal and fit the theme, words you might use or shapes that interest you. Spend some time thinking about your project and enjoy the research entailed.

3. Make as many notes as you like and see whether any other of your recorded dreams can be made use of in developing the project. You will often find that you go through a particularly productive period, though sometimes you may feel very stuck.

4. Make a note of any problems and negativities that arise in creating the project. These can be resolved through lucid dreaming.

5. It is worthwhile carrying a notebook or tape recorder with you at all times, so that you can note down any inspirations which occur. This may also give you further material for creative dreaming.

6. You may find you run out of enough energy to complete the project. This is another way in which creative dreaming could be used to help to give you the impetus to finish off what you have started.

You will note that there are several instances where dreaming with awareness can help in the process of creativity. This is perhaps one of the best outcomes of the art of creative dreaming: to realize that you have within you a huge store of previously untapped energy which is now accessible.

DREAM JOURNAL

The following pages are for you to write down your own personal dream interpretations.

Refer back to pages 93–8 if you need to refresh your memory about how to keep a journal.

Dream Journal

Date:

Dream Content:

Striking Images:

Themes:

Interpretation:

Dream Journal

Date:

Dream Content:

Striking Images:

Themes:

Interpretation: